EXPLORING THE UTOPIAN IMPULSE

Ralahine Utopian Studies

Series editors:
Raffaella Baccolini (University of Bologna, at Forlì)
Joachim Fischer (University of Limerick)
Tom Moylan (University of Limerick)

Managing editor:
Michael J. Griffin (University of Limerick)

Volume 2

PETER LANG
Oxford · Bern · Berlin · Bruxelles · Frankfurt am Main · New York · Wien

Edited by Michael J. Griffin and Tom Moylan

EXPLORING THE UTOPIAN IMPULSE

ESSAYS ON UTOPIAN THOUGHT AND PRACTICE

PETER LANG
Oxford· Bern· Berlin· Bruxelles· Frankfurt am Main· New York· Wien

Bibliographic information published by Die Deutsche Bibliothek
Die Deutsche Bibliothek lists this publication in the Deutsche
Nationalbibliografie; detailed bibliographic data is available on the
Internet at ‹http://dnb.ddb.de›.

British Library and Library of Congress Cataloguing-in-Publication Data:
A catalogue record for this book is available from *The British Library*,
Great Britain, and from *The Library of Congress*, USA

ISSN 1661-5875
ISBN 978-3-03910-913-5

© Peter Lang AG, International Academic Publishers, Bern 2007
Hochfeldstrasse 32, Postfach 746, CH-3000 Bern 9, Switzerland
info@peterlang.com, www.peterlang.com, www.peterlang.net

All rights reserved.
All parts of this publication are protected by copyright.
Any utilisation outside the strict limits of the copyright law, without
the permission of the publisher, is forbidden and liable to prosecution.
This applies in particular to reproductions, translations, microfilming,
and storage and processing in electronic retrieval systems.

Printed in Germany

Contents

Acknowledgements 9

MICHAEL J. GRIFFIN AND TOM MOYLAN
Introduction: Exploring Utopia 11

Utopian Thought

RUTH LEVITAS
The Archive of the Feet: Memory, Place, and Utopia 19

EUGENE O'BRIEN
"Towards Justice to Come": Derrida and Utopian Justice 43

SUSAN MCMANUS
Truth, Temporality, and Theorizing Resistance 57

CHRISTOPHER YORKE
Three Archetypes for the Clarification of Utopian Theorizing 83

VINCENT GEOGHEGAN
Utopia and the Memory of Religion 101

Utopian Texts

ANTONIS BALASOPOLOUS
The Fractured Image: Plato, the Greeks, and the Figure of the
    Ideal City 117

GERALDINE SHERIDAN
Technological Utopia/Dystopia in the Plates of the
    Encyclopédie 139

MATTHEW BEAUMONT
The Party of Utopia: Utopian Fiction and the Politics of Readership, 1880-1900   163

DAN SMITH
H.G. Wells's First Utopia: Materiality and Portent   183

MICHAEL G. KELLY
Immanence and the Utopian Impulse: On Philippe Jaccottet's Readings of Æ and Robert Musil   207

PHILIP SCHWEIGHAUSER
Who's Afraid of Dystopia? William Gibson's *Neuromancer* and Fredric Jameson's Writing on Utopia and Science Fiction   225

PAULA MURPHY
Paradise Lost: The Destruction of Utopia in *The Beach*   243

MICHAEL J. GRIFFIN AND DARA WALDRON
Across Time and Space: The Utopian Impulses of Andrei Tarkovsky's *Stalker*   257

CAITRÍONA NÍ DHÚILL
"One loves the girl for what she is, and the boy for what he promises to be": Gender Discourse in Ernst Bloch's *Das Prinzip Hoffnung*   273

AIDAN O'MALLEY
Rhyming Hope and History in the "Fifth Province"   293

Utopian Polities

TIMOTHY KEANE
The Chartist Land Plan: An English Dream, an Irish Nightmare   313

LUCIAN M. ASHWORTH
The League of Nations as a Utopian Project: The Labour Party Advisory Committee on International Questions and the Search for a New World Order 335

JENNY ANDERSSON
Beyond Utopia? The Knowledge Society and the Third Way 357

ANDREW J. BROWN
Witchcrafting Selves: Remaking Person and Community in a Neo-Pagan Utopian Scene 375

BARRIE WHARTON
From Shukri Mustafa to the *Ashwaiyat*: Utopianism in Egyptian Islamism 397

Notes on Contributors 417

Index 423

Acknowledgments

Above all, we want to thank our contributors, not only for their essays but also for their initial presentations at the first international conference of the Ralahine Centre for Utopian Studies, "Exploring the Utopian Impulse," held 10 to 12 March 2005 at the University of Limerick.

We also thank all those who helped to organize and produce the conference, especially Carmen Kuhling, David Lilburn, Marie Kirwan, Claire Ryan. And we are grateful to our funding sources: the Irish Research Council for the Humanities and Social Sciences; the Research Office, College of Humanities (COH), and Departments of Languages and Cultural Studies and of Sociology at the University of Limerick (UL); the Queens University, Belfast, Institute for Irish Studies; and Loretta Brennan Glucksman and the late Lewis Glucksman.

For their ongoing support, we thank our colleagues at UL: especially, Vice President for Research, Vincent Cunnane; College of Humanities Dean, Pat O'Connor; former COH Dean of Research, Eugene O'Brien; former Department of Languages and Cultural Studies Head, Martin Chappell, and his successor, Jean Conacher; our Ralahine Centre fellow travelers (Joachim Fischer, Associate Director; Luke Ashworth; Liam Bannon; Bríona nic Dhiarmada; Michael Kelly; Carmen Kuhling; Patricia Lynch; Serge Rivière; Tina O'Toole; Geraldine Sheridan; Mícheál Ó Súilleabháin); and our co-workers in the Department of Languages and Cultural Studies.

We are particularly grateful to the people who worked with us in producing this volume – the second in the Ralahine Utopian Studies book series: our Peter Lang editor, Alexis Kirschbaum; our cover designer, David Lilburn; our copy-editor, Maureen O'Connor; our production editor, Letizia Cirillo, and our managing editor, Raffaella Baccolini. We thank Barrie Wharton for allowing us to use his photograph on the front cover.

Michael particularly thanks Luke Gibbons who initiated him in the history of Ralahine and in the utopian possibilities in Irish Studies while working at the University of Notre Dame, and his colleagues in the Department of Languages and Cultural Studies at the University of Limerick. He also thanks his family for their ongoing support and indulgence.

Tom thanks Lyman Tower Sargent, Vince Geoghegan, Ruth Levitas, and Tadhg Foley for their continuing support. Finally, and again, he is deeply grateful for the ongoing inspiration given to him by his daughters, Katie Moylan and Sarah Moylan, and his partner, Susan McManus.

Permissions

Every effort was made to reach the copyright holders of the documents included herein. Any additional arrangements or oversights will be corrected in subsequent editions.

MICHAEL J. GRIFFIN AND TOM MOYLAN

Introduction: Exploring Utopia

In the current global political and cultural climate, it has been argued that utopian alternatives or anticipations of any sort are to be rejected as either useless dreaming or as blueprints for societies susceptible to authoritarian control. However, given the understanding of Utopia put forth by Ernst Bloch, Fredric Jameson, and others, these dark times of closure, exploitation, privilege, and violence call out more than ever for Utopia's transformative energy as a necessary stimulus to sociopolitical transformation.

The Ralahine Centre for Utopian Studies was established at the University of Limerick in 2003 to pursue research on utopianism. The Centre's research agenda is based on the premise that sociopolitical values, policies, and practices can be creatively and productively understood through the intervention of a utopian problematic – or set of analytical categories – that can trace those critical yet hopeful impulses that seek to bring about a better world (however diverse, debated, conflicted, or contested such tendencies may be in the cultures out of which they arise). These utopian impulses can be identified and studied in their dual move of a negation of the present moment and a figuration of a better reality that can be articulated through a variety of texts and social practices. Such anticipatory expressions and experiences can be most usefully read as modes of future-bearing production that generate a pedagogical and political sense of possibilities. Utopianism, consequently, is best understood as a process of social dreaming that unleashes and informs efforts to make the world a better place, not to the letter of a plan but to the spirit of an open-ended process. The research of the Centre therefore aims to identify and study utopian tendencies as and when they are articulated through theories, texts (literary, both eutopian *and* dystopian; legal; political; theological; filmic; visual; musical; architectural; and others), and social practices (such as religious and secular intentional communities, political movements, and cultural practices). While the Centre encourages research in all aspects of utopianism, it has a particular commitment to examining and extending the scope of utopian theory itself; and, given its location and social base, it has an additional commitment to the study of utopianism in Irish culture.

In March of 2005, the Ralahine Centre held its first international conference. Along with keynote presentations by Fredric Jameson and Luke Gibbons, forty-five presentations by scholars from ten countries were given over three days. The papers addressed many areas of utopian studies: literary, cultural, historical, sociological, political, theoretical, and philosophical; and papers on Irish dimensions in utopian studies constituted one stream of the conference. In this volume, we are publishing essays derived from this conference. Rather than a conference proceedings, *Exploring the Utopian Impulse* represents our refereed selection of works that uniquely address the question of the nature and expression of Utopia, and do so by way of their investigations of utopian theory and textual and sociopolitical practice. Some of the essays are written by scholars who have long worked within the paradigm and debates of the now international field of utopian studies; others are pieces by scholars who have taken up the utopian problematic in order to cast new light on their own objects of study. All the contributors take seriously the reality and potential of the utopian vocation. Even as some insightfully critique Utopia, others extend its reach beyond the limits of the modern western tradition within which utopianism has traditionally or most recognizably been received. The explorations offered herein will take readers back over familiar ground in new ways as well as carry them into new territories of hope and engagement.

Exploring the Utopian Impulse is divided into three sections: Utopian Thought, Utopian Texts, and Utopian Polities. In Part One, Utopian Thought, theoretical and philosophical perspectives are brought to bear on the nature and problematic of utopianism. "Art desires what has not yet been," wrote Theodor Adorno in *Aesthetic Theory*, "though everything that art is has already been. It cannot escape the shadow of the past." Literary and philosophical utopian design, although future-oriented ("what has not yet been"), originates in a temporal scene. The past imbues the present and the present the future. Syllogistically, the past imbues the future; and Ruth Levitas begins this collection by opening up the utopian possibilities of memory, too readily conceived in its retrospective impetus as antithetical to Utopia. In a meditation on the utopian resonance of collective and individual memory, she stresses the importance of place, and memory of place, in utopian writing. Even though utopias describe places that are not, they are articulated in real time and real space by social actors who are ineluctably influenced by the spatial environments which produced them. Levitas's essay is a historical, geographical, textual, theoretical, and ultimately personal exploration of Utopia. As such, it is a salutary overture to the essays which follow.

Eugene O'Brien provides an introductory guide to the history of utopian thought as a precursor to his investigation of the future-bearing, utopian implications of Jacques Derrida's concept of justice. A more open-ended conception of justice, as offered by Derrida's deconstructive processes, counters the ossifying dangers that have befallen utopias in the past and thus makes Utopia, and its theorization, more dynamic and radical in its promises and its risks. Next, Susan McManus explores the utopian possibilities that inhere in temporality. Temporality can, she suggests, be theorized as an affective-epistemological form, with implications for the critical understanding of political agency: theorizing temporality's affectivity consequently opens up political possibilities of utopian desire and freedom. Christopher Yorke also engages with the issue of utopian temporality, offering three archetypes with which he proposes to clarify some of the vaguer claims made for Utopia as an identifiable genre. He argues that the archetypes of utopian historicism, utopian presentism, and utopian futurism can allow for greater discretion, less essentialism, and a more categorical temporalizing mode in utopian discourse. In the last of the theoretical essays, Vincent Geoghegan augments Levitas's study of memory as he connects Utopia to religion and to memory. He explores the problematic relationship between and among the three phenomena and theorizes towards a "post-secular" dimension in utopian philosophy. Thus, a refunctioned sense of religion returns as a resource and a space for the generation of utopian hope, while memory can consolidate the progressive potential of religious traditions and their sense of community.

In Part Two, Utopian Texts, the possibilities that inhere in utopias, as represented in print and visual culture, are investigated, as are the incongruities and faults which fissure them. Antonis Balasopolous complicates the too-singular identification of the classical Greek utopian *polis*. Reading "against the grain of an inert Platonism" allows him to appreciate the aporetic tension which sustains the utopian impulse throughout the Greek tradition. Moving from the classical ground of Utopia to the French Enlightenment, Geraldine Sheridan demonstrates that a free market utopia is depicted in the *Encyclopédie*'s technological plates. However, she also analyzes the dystopic elements of alienation and exploitation that corrupt the images of work and progress presented. In so doing, she suggestively identifies a dialectic of Utopia within the dialectic of Enlightenment.

Matthew Beaumont takes the study of utopian texts into late nineteenth-century England and identifies a "Party of Utopia" in the utopian readerships of "the last epoch to have been defined by a utopian rather than dystopian impulse." As Beaumont has it, utopian fiction – particularly in Edward Bellamy's *Looking Backward* and William Morris's *New from Nowhere* – implicitly addresses itself to "a community of readers that it hopes is capable of implementing its ideals in practice." Dan Smith then reassesses the utopian vision of H.G. Wells, seeking to rescue it from the negative ramifications of the author's more unsavory adventures in eugenicism. He reads Wells's utopian thought as complex and contradictory; however, the contradictory nature of that expression is seen as self-reflexively "characteristic of the contested and unstable nature of utopian thought itself." Accordingly, Smith identifies a "critical utopian" quality in Wells, especially evident in his first novel, *The Time Machine*.

Michael G. Kelly proposes an "intertextual, intercultural, and transgeneric" study of the lived and the possible, as he argues for a more nuanced understanding of the relationship of personal poetic practice to utopianism. His subjects are two early essays by French-language poet Philippe Jaccottet: one on the Irish literary revivalist Æ; the other on Robert Musil, of whose writings Jaccottet is the principal French translator. These essays "support and counterbalance" one another in theorizing the extent of utopian possibility in poetry. Shifting genres, Philipp Schweighauser conjoins William Gibson's *Neuromancer* with Fredric Jameson's writing on Utopia and science fiction. *Contra* celebrants of the critical potential of postmodernism who have co-opted the work of Jameson, Schweighauser re-invigorates Jameson as a detractor of political postmodernism. Schweighauser's reading of Gibson's cyberpunk, accordingly, draws on Jameson and relates his adversarial stance to the cultural and political critique which, he proposes, infuses *Neuromancer*.

Utopia, viewed through a Lacanian filter, is about desire for the unattainable; and Paula Murphy relates this desire to the prevalence of utopian ideals in popular culture. In particular, she reads the film version of Alex Garland's novel *The Beach* as symptomatic of a materialistic western world bereft of the sort of moral prohibition that might intensify a more authentic form of desire. In a similar thematic, Michael J. Griffin and Dara Waldron's essay argues that Andrei Tarkovsky's *Stalker* is a meditation on the problem of utopian attainment. In *Stalker*, Utopia is linked to the extra-linguistic realms of music and a mysterious room. The attainment of the elusive utopia for which music and the room are metaphors is seen as potentially corrupting; as such it is the communal impulse towards Utopia, rather than its arrival, that is compellingly allegorized.

John Donne's "Elegy 19: To his Mistress Going to Bed" (in)famously genders new world utopias as spaces of heterosexual conquest, and in this trope Caitríona Ní Dhúill traces a link between early modern discourses and twentieth-century utopian thought. Ní Dhúill takes as her subject Bloch's *Das Prinzip Hoffnung* and problematizes its utopian discourse. The tenor of Bloch's text is heteronormative, she argues, and in it utopian space is feminized in a gendered language of exploration and conquest. Ní Dhúill analyses "the extent to which the polarities of gender discourse can be inscribed in utopian thinking," drawing on the poetry of Seamus Heaney to demonstrate the persistence of masculinist political geographies. The same poet is then linked to a principle of hope in an Irish context. Heaney's *The Cure at Troy*, an adaptation of Sophocles *Philoctetes*, voices through its chorus the utopian anticipation that "hope and history" might rhyme. Aidan O'Malley reads this possibility into the utopian motif of the "Fifth Province" in Irish political and cultural criticism. He theorizes the ongoing, necessarily incomplete, process of trying to construct this space. All versions of the Fifth Province, he argues, generate possibilities for an Ireland whose four provinces have experienced a hitherto dissonant relationship with hope.

Finally, in Part Three, Utopian Polities – broadly understood as intentional communities or political initiatives – are documented and assessed. Timothy Keane studies the utopian credentials of the Chartist movement, focusing on the Irish associations of its leadership. This Irish dimension within Chartism provides him with a productive context within which to view the Ralahine Owenite experiment in County Clare in 1830; equally, he contextualizes the failure of the Irish body politic in the following decades of famine and ruin as a nightmarish and cautionary tale that informed the development of the Chartist land plan in England. While this example of Irish concerns uncovers an urgency in English political utopianism, a similar urgency imbued the global utopianism of the League of Nations over half a century later. Lucian Ashworth documents the work of a group of international experts associated with the British Labour Party who contributed, in many and various ways, to the development of the League as a global utopia. "The League," writes Ashworth, "was always a work in progress, and was never held up, even by its most enthusiastic supporters, as a complete and finished work." Relatedly, Jenny Andersson interrogates the sustainability of utopian constructs in our era of accelerated knowledge technologies. She thus assesses the tension in the partially utopian discourse of Third Way social democracy as one running between the desire for a better future and the pragmatic requirements of modernization and adaptability.

The last two essays in this volume examine utopian polities that are resistant to concepts of secular modernization, although resistant in markedly different modes. Andrew Brown describes a spatially dispersed but energetic utopian initiative in the city of Eugene, Oregon: one characterized by "witchcraft, politicized neo-paganism, goddess worship, and ecofeminism." Participants in this enclave seek to transcend the administered identities of mainstream American culture, but not in the strict confines of an intentional community or strictly delineated or separated urban space; rather, they operate in what Brown terms a utopian "scene," a "set of social networks that is not well defined or well boundaried." Neither well-defined nor well-boundaried, the phenomenon of political Islam is arguably the most important locus of political discourse in today's international context. Appropriately closing the volume, Barrie Wharton's essay offers a timely study of the relationship of utopianism to Islamism. He complicates what could be perceived as an occidental hegemony in the field of utopian studies and suggests that a distinct utopianism underpins alternative Islamic societies. He examines this confluence in the specific context of contemporary Egyptian society and focuses in particular on the utopian resonances in figures and phenomena such as Shukri Mustafa and the *ashwaiyat*, or urban slums of Cairo and Alexandria.

Across its three sections, the collection engages critically and creatively with Utopia in theory and practice. As collected, they constitute the second forum for some of the many and varied voices being encouraged by the Ralahine Centre for Utopian Studies. The first such forum was Volume One in the Ralahine book series, *Utopia-Method-Vision: On the Use Value of Social Dreaming*. This second volume signals the ongoing, engaged commitment of the Ralahine Centre to exploring the utopian problematic in all its dimensions and manifestations.

Michael J. Griffin and Tom Moylan
Limerick and Belfast, December 2006

Ruth Levitas

The Archive of the Feet: Memory, Place, and Utopia

Utopia and Memory

The relationship between memory and Utopia is a complex one. At first glance they are antithetical: memory refers to the past, Utopia to the future; memory is what has been, Utopia is what is to come, the novum, the Not Yet. Yet reflection reveals this apparent antithesis as illusory.[1]

First, Utopia is not always located in the future. Images of lost paradises and golden ages are placed in the past, accompanied by versions of the Fall. Usually these are beyond the memory of any living individual, inscribed in the collective memory as myth or history, as something that must not be forgotten. The more recent past may be the repository of utopian longing as well, perhaps especially

---

1   Vita Fortunati convened a conference in Lisbon in January 2005 on "Memory and Utopia," where an early version of this essay was presented; and this essay is based on that paper and a subsequent one given at the "Exploring the Utopian Impulse" conference at the Ralahine Centre for Utopian Studies at the University of Limerick in March 2005. My thanks to the organizers of and participants in both conferences. I am also extremely grateful to Mervyn Miller for unearthing confirmation of Warwick Draper's involvement with the Garden Cities and Town Planning Association and with Letchworth. All photographs by the author, but Robert Hunter provided much-needed technical help with them. The illustration of Hampshire House is taken from a reproduction of a watercolour by Warwick Draper in the annual report of the Hampshire House club. I am grateful to the Hammersmith and Fulham Archives and Local History Centre for permission to reproduce the image of Hampshire House, and for general advice and assistance in researching the history of Hammersmith.

following cataclysmic disasters such as wars and tsunamis: expect the phrases "before the war" or "before the tsunami" to be recurrent in individual life histories and social scripts, as versions of "before the Fall." At a more banal level, successive generations persistently locate a golden age when crime was minimal and "you didn't have to lock your door" approximately thirty years earlier.

Second, a remembered utopia is always a reconstruction of the past. But if the Not Yet has the otherness of the novum, representations of future utopias are always simultaneously dependent on existing cultural resources. Indeed, the intelligibility of all cultural production rests on shared memory, since languages and systems of signs are learned. This endorses Fredric Jameson's long-standing insistence that Utopia is literally inconceivable, as well as terrifying in its implication of the annihilation of our selves as we know them.

Third, utopian representations of the future – claims that the future may be qualitatively different from the present – involve a process of transcending the past. This is never a simple forgetting. It always involves *managing* the past, both individually and collectively. Thus, memory and forgetting, and their management, are necessary component parts of the utopian project. Forgetting may be more typically associated with dystopias. George Orwell, of course, addresses the erasure of collective memory in *Nineteen Eighty-Four*. In Doris Lessing's *Shikasta*, a crucial element in the dystopic process is forgetting, especially forgetting what we might be (individually) and what we are here for (collectively).

Memory, Embodiment, and Place

Commentators from different disciplines have pointed out that there are different kinds of memory. Ernst Bloch works with a distinction between *anamnesis* and *anagnorisis* (see *Principle*). *Anamnesis* is "simple" recall, perceived by Bloch as intrinsically conservative.

Anagnorisis is a process of recognition, where the gap between past and present is not collapsed. As Vincent Geoghegan puts it:

> In *anagnorisis* memory traces are reactivated in the present, but there is never simple correspondence between the past and the present, because of all the intervening novelty. The power of the past resides in its complicated relationship of similarity/dissimilarity to the present. The tension thus created helps shape the new. The experience therefore is creatively shocking (22).

If *anagnorisis* is more evidently critical than *anamnesis*, neither should be assimilated to nostalgia. Indeed, the whole concept of nostalgia is problematic, implying as it does an outsider's critical assessment of longing for the past. The definition of memory and desire as nostalgic is almost always a political and delegitimizing act, similar to the rejection of radical alterity as "pejoratively" utopian.

An orthogonal distinction can be made between *individual* and *collective* memory. In her book on war photography, *Regarding the Pain of Others*, Susan Sontag argues that

> strictly speaking, there is no such thing as collective memory. [...] All memory is individual, unreproducible – it dies with each person. What we call collective memory is not a remembering but a stipulating: that *this* is important, and this is the story about how it happened, with the pictures that lock the story in our minds (76).

This appears to contradict the arguments of anthropologists and sociologists: most notably Maurice Halbwachs, who insists that all memory is social. Individuals, he says, remember as members of groups, and it is their membership of these groups – and the legitimation given by the groups to their memories – that gives them structure, coherence, and a sense of validity. In contrast, dreams for Halbwachs are fragmentary and disorganized: "dreams show unstable fragments and images that cannot provide the group support that makes waking life and memory cohesive and structured" (23). The contradiction between Sontag and Halbwachs is, however, less acute than it seems. For the implication of Halbwachs's position is not that the distinction between individual and collective memory is false, but that both are social. Both are dependent on, and reproductive of, individual belonging to social groups, and to social cohesion and solidarity in a Durkheimian sense – quite literally, they involve the remembering of the group.

The frameworks which groups provide are not merely abstract belief systems. As Paul Connerton explains Halbwachs, the mental spaces within which memories are mapped always refer back to the material spaces that groups occupy. Halbwachs draws on Auguste Comte's claim that our mental equilibrium depends on the consistency of our physical environment, and argues that collective memory depends on a socially specific spatial framework. Thus, Connerton notes that

> our images of social spaces, because of their relative stability, give us the illusion of not changing and of rediscovering the past in the present. We conserve our recollections by referring them to the material milieu that surrounds us. It is to our social spaces – those which we occupy, which we frequently retrace with our steps, where we always have access, which at each moment we are capable of mentally reconstructing – that we must turn our attention, if our memories are to reappear (37).

Connerton introduces another crucial element here, that of embodiment. He argues that despite the merits of Halbwach's argument, there is too much emphasis on the cognitive – one might say too much emphasis on the extent to which memory involves recognition. If "we preserve versions of the past by representing it to ourselves in words and image," or by its *inscription*, memory also operates through *incorporation* and *performance* (72). The collective aspect of this process involves commemorative ceremonies. At the individual level, memory is embedded in practical habit, in daily social practice, in specific physical places. Habit involves the capacity to reproduce actions, the kind of "muscle-memory" involved in riding a bicycle or playing a musical instrument. This is procedural memory. For Connerton, then, "habit is a knowledge and remembering in the hands and in the body; and in the cultivation of habit it is our body which 'understands'" (95). Thus, in habitual memory, "the past is […] sedimented in the body" (72). Habit might thus seem closer to *anamnesis* than to *anagnorisis*. Connerton also argues, however, that all habits are affective dispositions, embodying desire as well as capacity. This characteristic is, he says, more apparent in "bad" habits such as smoking. More accurately, perhaps, it is apparent in habits we are trying to break, or whose performance is otherwise frustrated by a social or spatial context.

If Sontag emphasizes the visual aspects of memory, and its stipulatory character, Connerton emphasizes its spatial and embodied character. It is, as David Harvey says, in the nature of capitalism to constantly tear down and rebuild the physical infrastructure of our lives. Earthquakes and tsunamis can, of course, have the same effect; but, whereas ecological catastrophes are recognized as traumatic, the deliberate razing and reconstruction of the physical environment is not. Cities in particular are subject to repeated reconstruction. Georges Eugène Haussmann's Paris involved driving boulevards through medieval quarters, bringing the imposition of order on (apparent) disorder. Nineteenth-century London was dissected by rivers and canals, later by railways including the underground (largely built by cut and cover methods), and later – especially in the twentieth century – by roads and motorways. Victorian London was marked by the scaffolding that Charles Baudelaire saw as characteristic of modernity. The war-time destruction of Berlin that led W.S. Sebald to suggest ruins to be the natural condition of all bigger cities gave way to simultaneous demolition and rebuilding, i.e. demolition to clear the path of the Wall, rebuilding as a divided city. Since 1989, the Wall itself has been torn down, and 1990s Berlin is evoked by images of cranes (see Figure 1).

These spatial changes cut across the temporal span of individual lifetimes. The city we experience is not just the city that is there, but the one we remember, and also, perhaps, the one we hope for. Thus as Andreas Huyssen puts it,

> an urban imaginary in its temporal reach may well put different things in the place: memories of what was there before, imagined alternatives to what there is. The strong marks of present space merge in the imaginary with traces of the past, erasures, losses and heterotopias (7).

Figure 1. Rebuilding Berlin, 1998

Or, as Italo Calvino says, "real and imaginary spaces commingle in the mind to shape our notions of specific cities" (quoted in Huyssen 49). Yet, changes to the landscape are disturbing. The marks of present space are indeed strong. When a building is demolished and the site redeveloped, it is extraordinary how quickly it becomes difficult to remember what was there before. It is perhaps partly for this reason that the architect Daniel Libeskind proposed leaving the site of Potsdamer Platz as an urban void. Libeskind used architectural voids in his design for the Jewish Museum in Berlin to represent the irreplaceable absence of annihilated German Jewry. Potsdamer Platz, once at the centre of the life of Berlin, was effectively erased by the Wall. As Libeskind argued:

> Take the open area at the Potsdamer Platz. I suggest a wilderness, one kilometre long, within which everything can stay as it is. The street simply ends in bushes. Wonderful. After all, this area is the result of today's divine natural law: nobody wanted it, nobody planned it, and yet it is firmly implanted in our

minds. And there in our minds, this image of the Potsdamer Platz void will remain for decades (quoted in Huyssen 56).

This is not, of course, what happened to Potsdamer Platz: for it was redeveloped by multinational companies such as Sony and Mercedes-Benz in a way that obliterates rather than echoes its pasts.

In a different key, the proliferation of books of old photographs of localities may be nostalgic; but it also involves, as Sontag suggests, a stipulation that it is important to remember. The effectiveness of such photographs, however, depends very much on being able to identify the street layout, the precise location. This is a matter of embodied memory as well as visual recognition. Thus, Walter Benjamin's *flâneur* moved memorably through the city. Simon Schama has remarked that our embodied sense of physical place, the way in which our body knows where to go, which way to turn, is laid down very early. When street layouts, rather than specific buildings, change, what is generated is a dream-like sense of dislocation and an *embodied* sense that something is wrong. If the social spaces wherein we retrace our steps are not simply occupied by different buildings but are effectively obliterated so that we cannot walk that way, they are literally no longer *recognizable*. William Morris said, in *News from Nowhere*: "I thought I knew the Broadway from the lie of the roads that still met there" (24). Physical obliteration also represses, or at least compounds, the forgetting of the social performances previously enacted in them. It creates an absence in what Schama calls "the archive of the feet" (24).

Questions of memory and place are, as Schama avers, significant in the visual and fictional representation of place – and thus in the representation of no-place, or Utopia. Utopian texts are only a fraction of the possible cultural manifestations of utopianism; but, in regard to texts, the questions of individual and collective memory can be explored in three different registers: author, text, and audience. Texts, as Paul Ricoeur argues, have the distinctive character of a portability that transcends the social conditions of their production and reception, opening them to a "potentially unlimited series of socially-situated readings" (quoted in Connerton 96). Within a text, it is possible to explore the treatment of both individual and collective memory, and their embodied and spatialized character. These questions are, however, not independent of the working of individual and collective memory in the authorship of the text, and in the place of its composition. And, third, the resonance of memory depends on the audience. As Kenneth Roemer argues, if we suppose the meaning of a text to lie in audience responses to it, then we have to consider the entry and re-entry of the text into the cultural matrices of different times and places, and altered geographies.

Remembering Hammersmith, Tracing Utopia

These issues are illustrated by, and illuminate, some aspects of memory and place in the authorship and reception of London's Hammersmith utopias: the most famous of which is, of course, expressed in Morris's *News from Nowhere*.[2] It is ironic that it is called *News from Nowhere*, as it is more clearly located in a specific place than many other utopias. The changes to place that are registered in the text – which are considerable – assert nevertheless that it is the same place at a different time, and not on some similar yet parallel planet of which we, the readers, know little (as in H.G. Wells's *A Modern Utopia*, or Lessing's *Shikasta*). Thus, Morris's changes – estranged as they are from the still familiar Hammersmith – contribute substantially to its dreamlike quality.

The specific spatial referents of Morris's utopia are (in reverse order) Kelmscott, the village on the Upper Thames where Morris rented his holiday retreat, Kelmscott Manor, the Thames Valley, London, and Hammersmith. *News from Nowhere* was written in 1890. From 1878 until his death in 1896, Morris lived in this (then) western

---

2 Geoghegan has explored the use of history and memory in Morris's text in contrast with Bellamy's *Looking Backward* (see "The Utopian Past"). I am concerned with the contexts of the production and reception of Morris's text, particularly their spatial aspects.

suburb of London, on the north side of the Thames, in a house with panoramic views of the river which he called Kelmscott House. For five years before this, he lived a mile or so north-west, in Horrington House which no longer exists. The importance of Kelmscott Manor in Morris's utopianism is often stressed – not least because the Kelmscott edition of *News from Nowhere* is prefaced by an illustration of Kelmscott Manor that has been repeatedly reproduced: the picture that locks the story in our minds (see Figures 2 and 3). Moreover, the archive of the feet can take you to the very spot where that image places the viewer: the camera captures the same image in the twenty-first century.

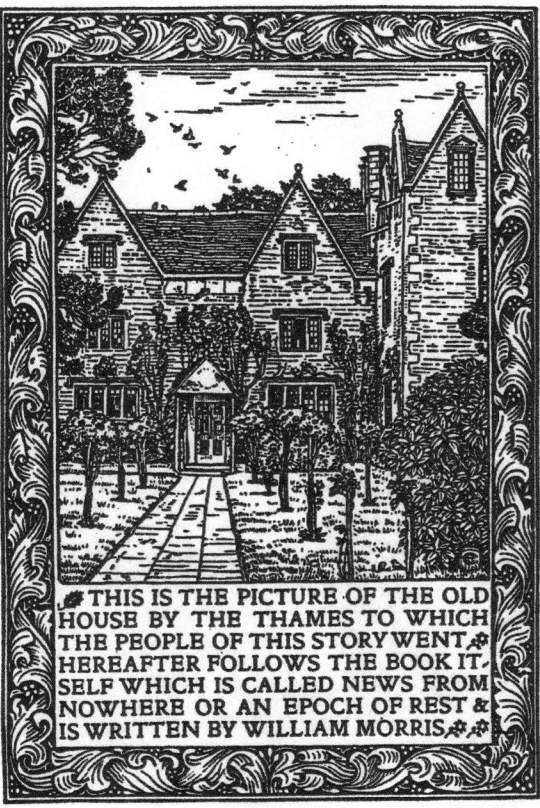

Figure 2. Frontispiece, *News from Nowhere,* Kelmscott Press Edition

Figure 3. Kelmscott Manor, 2002

In the first section of *News from Nowhere*, Morris reconstructs London. He tears it down, and replaces it with his "medieval" utopia. A decentralized network of villages, with their own markets (although nothing is bought or sold), theatres, and parliaments. Hammersmith is the prototype, and the description of Hammersmith transformed percolates through the first four chapters. The usual interpretation of this is that Morris is reconstructing London to correspond to an idealized medieval topography, and there are phrases that appear to bear this out. The vernacular architecture is described as "so like medieval houses of the same materials that I fairly felt as if I were alive in the fourteenth century"; while the positive comparisons of the public architecture are to Gothic, Byzantine, and Florentine styles (24). What seems, then, to be operating here is a particular form of collective memory, and an idealized history of the middle ages. Of course, as always in Morris, this is a look back to look forward. To represent Morris as a medievalist is to radically misunderstand him. But to read the image of a transformed Hammersmith as essentially "medieval" also depends on forgetting – specifically, forgetting the history of Hammersmith; for the look back in *News from Nowhere* is also to the recent past, within Morris's own memory and certainly the living memory of his audiences. Comparing maps in 1870 and 1894 – from just before Morris moved to the area to just after *News from Nowhere* was written – it is evident that this was precisely the period during which most of Hammersmith was built. The Metropolitan Line (now the Hammersmith and City Line of the London Underground) was extended to Hammersmith in 1864, and the District Line followed in 1870. Rail and housing developments covered land that had previously been farms, market gardens, plant nurseries, or private gardens. Most of the major public and civic buildings were rebuilt during this period. The "ugly" bridge which Morris replaces was built in 1887; indeed, Nikolaus Pevsner also detested it (see Pevsner 178). One very evocative account of this transformation comes from William Richmond, another Hammersmith resident and family friend of the Morrises, who designed the mosaics in St Paul's Cathedral (see Stirling). The loss of rural Hammersmith was recent, and Morris was writing against the recent changes, as his contemporary audience would have recognized. The text thus appeals to individual memory both in its construction and its initial reception, most clearly a memory that is embedded in a specific place.[3]

The recovery of this context is enabled by the resources of collective memory. By this I mean that I spent a long time in the local Hammersmith history archive, looking at old maps and photographs, and reading the wonderful edition of Morris's letters edited by Norman Kelvin. But my research was itself initiated by, and layered over, individual memory – and loss. I had first read *News from Nowhere* when I was seventeen – in Hammersmith. Kelmscott House lies on the route of my childhood riverside walks – and it is now the premises of the William Morris Society, of which I am a member (see Figure 4).

Figure 4. Kelmscott House, 2002

3 For a fuller discussion of the changing history of Hammersmith and its impact on *News from Nowhere*, see Levitas, *Morris, Hammersmith and Utopia*.

The coach house that Morris used for weaving carpets, which became the meeting hall for the Hammersmith Socialists, is still in use for public lectures (see Figure 5). Speaking there among the ghosts of Morris, George Bernard Shaw, and Charlotte Perkins Gilman, is a strange and awesome experience. Over the coach house door is an inscription quoting the text Morris placed in the guesthouse in *News from Nowhere*: "Guests and neighbours, on the site of this Guest-hall once stood the lecture room of the Hammersmith Socialists. Drink a glass to the memory! May 1962" (15). Thus, present space merges in the imaginary with the past, recalling in loops and layers the Hammersmith Socialists, but also the founders of the William Morris Society itself, and the implication that the inscription was indeed installed in "1962": in Morris's future, their present, our past.

Tracing another layer of memory: Morris refers to the Creek, a little tributary of the Thames. When I was a child, my mother would lift us up to peer over the wall to where this stream, culverted in 1936, emerged from the flood defenses. The creek is central to Hammersmith's collective memory: murals in the town hall, painted as late as the 1950s, show it as the tumbling stream of Morris's utopia. In Morris's time, and until the 1930s, it was a smelly working dock. Yet it was only after my mother's death, as I explored the archive, that I realized she was drawing on personal memory, for she had lived by the river before 1936. Apart from one area redeveloped in the 1920s, and the related disappearance of the Creek, the 1894 maps show a street layout that was familiar in my 1950s childhood. It was then possible, to a substantial extent, to identify the routes Morris would have walked. And to a substantial extent, it still is possible to do so, and so to defer to the archive of the feet.

Figure 5. The Coach House, Kelmscott House

However, in the late 1950s, a six-lane dual carriage way was built through the heart of Hammersmith. It links the M4 into central London. Kelmscott House as it now stands has a substantial garden by

London standards; but in Morris's time the garden stretched back 600 feet (see Elletson).

An earlier occupant of the house, Francis Ronalds, had used the length of the garden in experiments resulting in his invention of the electric telegraph. Most of the garden was subject to compulsory purchase (for £2000) by the London County Council in the early 1950s. The land taken was so extensive that it accommodates not only the full width of the road but a block of flats on the other side. This was also the first road in Britain where traffic took precedence over pedestrians. Hence, this road, like the land cleared for the Berlin Wall, creates a void. There are echoes of the former road layout: the roads that ran from King Street to the river – built during Morris's time, and themselves seen as a destruction of the landscape – are now truncated into two attenuated halves, north and south of the new road. In some, but not all, cases, there are pedestrian subways. But there has been significant loss, both of buildings and of the sense of space. The archive of the feet is here thrown into disarray, and part of it has been stolen. This spatial void has created a void in memory, contributing to the loss of "imagined alternatives to what is," the loss of Hammersmith's utopian potentialities.

Morris's utopia is the best-known utopia nurtured in Hammersmith. But there were others, partly as an echo and legacy of Morris and *News from Nowhere*. Indeed, Hammersmith can be seen as a cradle of utopias. Eric Gill and Douglas (Hilary) Pepler met there, eventually forming the arts and crafts colony at Ditchling, in Sussex – still accessible, with its own museum. As well, Edward Thomas Craig, old Owenite and steward of the Owenite community at the Ralahine estate in Ireland, was, with Morris, among the founder members of the Hammersmith branch of the Social Democratic Federation. Craig died in Hammersmith; and, though his grave is now unmarked, his house is still standing. Craig called 10 Andover Street, now 62 Perrers Road, "Ralahine Cottage" (see Figure 6).

Figure 6: 62 Perrers Road, E.T. Craig's last home

Willie Yeats not only went to the Hammersmith Socialists (and stormed out in high dudgeon); he also lived for a time in that piece of utopian urban planning of which Morris deeply disapproved, the garden suburb of Bedford Park, and then described as in Hammersmith (see Figure 7). Yeats's sisters, Lily and Lolly, learned the embroidery skills they were to take to Ireland from May Morris.

And Yeats himself first encountered the Order of the Golden Dawn, which was to contribute to the development of Irish utopianism, in Bedford Park. All of these are remembered, and the utopian aspects of their work, acknowledged, in different areas of scholarship: Gill and Pepler in histories of the Arts and Crafts Movement and its key players; Craig in the history of Owenism and of Irish utopianism; Yeats in the extensive scholarship sometimes alluded to as "the Yeats industry."

One person whose projects are far less well documented is Warwick Draper (1873–1926). Draper lived at 13 Hammersmith Terrace from 1901, five doors down from May Morris at number 8. In 1910, he moved to Kelmscott House, where he stayed until 1915. After Draper left, moving eventually to Bedford House on Upper Mall, Kelmscott House had a series of occupants and then stood empty for some time until Helena Stephenson bought it to save it from demolition. Draper was engaged in a series of utopian or quasi-utopian projects; and, although strongly influenced by Morris, he also found other sources feeding his wish to make the world otherwise. Educated at Rugby and Oxford, Draper was a resident at Toynbee Hall in 1897; and before being called to the Bar in 1898, he studied with Ralph Neville, president of the Garden City Association (GCA).

Draper had a successful legal career, but alongside this was involved in a series of projects for social reform, as well as writing a scarcely known utopian text. Those projects included participation in the Toynbee Hall settlement in the East End of London. Draper himself became chair of the GCA, playing an active part in the foundation of Letchworth in 1905, and an executive member of the Council of the later Garden Cities and Town Planning Association (see Culpin; and Garden City Association). Together with his neighbors, Pepler and Fred Rowntree, Draper set up a social club called Hampshire House in the poorest area of Hammersmith in 1905, substantially modeled on Toynbee Hall. In 1909, he wrote his first utopian sketch, a projection of how he would like Hampshire House to be in 1955.

Figure 7: 3 Blenheim Road, home of the Yeats family

Draper's skills as a barrister were put to good effect in 1912, when the first serious proposals were made to build a new road through Hammersmith, cutting across the garden of Kelmscott House, where Draper was living, and through the site of Hampshire House itself. The plan was at least temporarily defeated. The process seems to have intensified Draper's interest in local history, for a year later he published *Hammersmith: A Study in Town History*. In 1918, he published a second, more extensive utopia, *The Tower*, under the pseudonym Watchman, republished in 1919 as *The New Britain*. (The dedication to his wife, Grace Devett, in the 1919 edition makes reference to an earlier unpublished sketch written before the First World War). In the aftermath of the war, he again used his advocacy skills to protect the local landscape, this time to prevent the construction of a gas works on a large open section of Chiswick's riverside. Draper favored a plan to build a small garden suburb on part of the land, as well as preserving much of it as open space. Local action was again followed by local history: he went on to write *Chiswick*, a more substantial history than the Hammersmith volume, and published it in 1923. Draper was also a staunch supporter of the League of Nations.[4]

The only elements of Draper's career that are at all well known, even at the local level, are the histories of Hammersmith and Chiswick. I have never seen copies of his guild socialist utopia (which, like the history of Hammersmith, makes recurrent reference to Morris) outside the British Library. The disappearance of texts from collective memory is one thing, especially as *The New Britain* is a text very much of its time, and is not of overwhelming literary merit; and Draper's contribution to the physical infrastructure of the boroughs was important at the time, helping to delay building the road for a good forty years, and preserving open space and playing fields in Chiswick to this day. But it is hardly surprising that these campaigns are not generally remembered eighty and ninety years on. However, the lack of historical reference to Hampshire House is more surprising. It is even misrepresented on occasion as having been in

---

[4] On the League of Nations as a utopian project, see Ashworth in this volume.

Hampshire.[5] It plays no part in histories of the settlement movement, because technically speaking it was not a settlement, but a social and educational establishment. Draper aspired to "proper" settlement character, but whereas settlements generally involved providing residential accommodation to bring university students and other social workers into deprived areas, Hampshire House drew on the proximity of middle-class reformers in the riverside enclave where Draper and others lived. However, the foundation and the fate of Hampshire House are suggestive in terms of the effects of spatial obliteration, urban voids, and social memory.

Hampshire House and grounds adjoined the garden of Kelmscott House. From 1905 until the outbreak of war in 1914 it provided space for a range of social and educational activities for adults and children, intended principally to improve the lives of those who lived in the poorest area of Hammersmith, near the river and the creek. Like Toynbee Hall, it accommodated the delivery of free legal advice through "the poor man's lawyer" (almost certainly Draper), organized art exhibitions, theatrical performances, and a mock Parliament. During the war, it provided support to Belgian refugees, including work in the Hampshire House workshops. A new hall was built within five years of its opening, and the garden was partly used for allotments. One of its most successful offshoots, the pioneering photographic club, was called on to provide photographic records of old Hammersmith as part of the campaign against the road. Like the rest of the settlement movement, some aspects of the provision at Hampshire House declined in importance in the 1920s, with increased municipal provision. Nevertheless, it remained in use until the 1950s, eventually being bought by the photographic society itself.

Toynbee Hall still exists. Hampshire House, like the garden of Kelmscott House, was compulsorily purchased and demolished to make way for the new road (see Figure 8). Whereas you can still walk

---

5 See Matt Hulse's video on Hilary Bourne and Ditchling, with references to the Hampshire House workshops, which Pepler was involved in, as in Hampshire.

to Toynbee Hall, and can still, despite the road, walk to Kelmscott House, you cannot walk to the site of Hampshire House. Indeed, it is difficult to identify on the ground where, exactly, it was. You cannot stand on it: you can only pass over it fleetingly. Benjamin's *flâneur* had time to read urban objects; but it is difficult to read an object that isn't there, and you can't stroll on a dual carriageway. Huyssen points out that the *flâneur*, "though always something of an outsider in his city, was still figured as a dweller rather than a traveler on the move" (50). The objections to the road, from the start, were that it benefited people who simply wanted to move through a place, rather than those who dwelt on it. But further, the road creates a void, an erasure of place. Here though, rather than the void creating a space in which absence calls up loss of what was and what might have been, it conjures nothing but itself.

Figure 8: Hampshire House, from a watercolor by Warwick Draper (permission of Hammersmith and Fulham Archives and Local History Centre)

The disappearance of Hampshire House and its history can be seen quite simply as the work of planners (see Figure 9). It was demolished to make way for the road. The wider forgetting of its history is, I think, directly linked to its total physical erasure. It might not have disappeared so utterly from view if the house had been put to other use or if the roads that led to it were still extant. But not only was Hampshire House destroyed; the place where it stood was expunged by the road. It has been physically obliterated, and thus forgotten, *oublié*. You cannot walk that way again.

Figure 9: Annihilating place: the Great West Road.

Thus, individual and collective memory, in both inscribed and embodied forms, operate not only within the text. They affect, in ways we may forget, the generation of the text itself. They affect how we read particular texts. And our embodied and spatially embedded memories govern which utopias survive and which disappear, apparently without trace from memory, as they are lost from the archive of the feet.

Works Cited

Bloch, Ernst. *The Principle of Hope.* Trans. Neville Plaice, Stephen Plaice, and Paul Knight. 3 Vols. Oxford: Blackwell, 1986.
Connerton, Paul. *How Societies Remember.* Cambridge: Cambridge University Press, 1989.
Culpin, Ewart G. *The Garden City Movement up to Date.* London: Garden Cities and Town Planning Assoc., 1914.
Draper, Warwick Herbert. *1955: Or the Hampshire House Jubilee.* Hammersmith: Hampshire House Club, 1909.
Draper, Warwick Herbert. *Hammersmith: A Study in Town History.* London: James Chamberlain, 1913.
____*The New Britain.* London: Headley Brothers, 1919.
____*Chiswick.* London: Philip Allan, 1923.
Elletson, Helen. "A History of Kelmscott House." *William Morris Society Newsletter* (July 2005): 11–12.
Garden City Association. *Town Planning in Theory and Practice: A Report of a Conference Arranged by the Garden City Association, Held at the Guildhall, London, on October 25th 1907, under the Presidency of the Lord Mayor of London.* London: Garden City Association, 1907.
Geoghegan, Vincent. "Remembering the Future." *Not Yet: Reconsidering Ernst Bloch.* Ed. Jamie Owen Daniel and Tom Moylan. London: Verso, 1997. 15–32.
____"The Utopian Past: Memory and History in Edward Bellamy's *Looking Backward* and William Morris's *News from Nowhere.*" *Utopian Studies* 3.2 (1992): 75–90.
Jameson, Fredric. *Archaeologies of the Future: The Desire Called Utopia and Other Science Fictions.* London: Verso, 2005.
Halbwachs, Maurice. *On Collective Memory.* Chicago: University of Chicago Press, 2005.
Harvey, David. *Spaces of Hope.* Edinburgh: Edinburgh University Press, 2002.
Hulse, Matt. *Hilary Bourne's Ditchling.* Ditchling: Ditchling Museum, 1997.

Huyssen, Andreas. *Present Pasts: Urban Palimpsests and the Politics of Memory*. Stanford: Stanford University Press, 2003.

Kelvin, Norman (ed.). *The Collected Letters of William Morris*. 4 Vols. Princeton: Princeton University Press, 1984–1996.

Lessing, Doris. *Shikasta: Re, Colonised Planet 5: Personal, Psychological, Historical Documents Relating to the Visit by Johor (George Sherban), Emissary (Grade 9) 87th of the Period of the Last Days*. London: Cape, 1979.

Levitas, Ruth. *William Morris, Hammersmith, and Utopia*. London: William Morris Society, 2005.

Morris, William. *News from Nowhere*. London: Longmans Green and Company, 1891.

Orwell, George. *Nineteen Eighty–Four*. Harmondsworth: Penguin, 1949.

Pevsner, Nikolaus. *The Buildings of England: London*. Vol. 2. Harmondsworth: Penguin, 1952.

Roemer, Kenneth. *Utopian Audiences: How Readers Locate Nowhere*. Amherst: University of Massachusetts Press, 2004.

Schama, Simon. *Landscape and Memory*. London: Harper Collins, 1995.

Sebald, W.S. *On the Natural History of Destruction*. London: Hamish Hamilton, 2003.

Sontag, Susan. *Regarding the Pain of Others*. London: Hamish Hamilton, 2003.

Stirling, A.M.W. *The Richmond Papers*. London: William Heinemann, 1926.

Wells, H.G. *A Modern Utopia*. London: Chapman and Hall, 1905.

Eugene O' Brien

"Towards Justice to Come": Derrida and Utopian Justice

The name "utopia" is often applied retroactively to various ideal states described before Thomas More's work, most notably to that of Plato's *Republic* and Augustine's *City of God* (which in the fifth century enunciated the theocratic ideal that dominated visionary thinking in the middle ages). With the Renaissance, the idea of Utopia became worldlier, but the religious element in utopian thinking lingered, as in the politico-religious ideals of seventeenth-century English social philosophers and political experimenters. Among the famous pre-nineteenth-century utopian writings are François Rabelais's description of the Abbey of Thélème in *Gargantua* (1532), Tommaso Campanella's *The City of the Sun* (1623), Francis Bacon's *The New Atlantis* (1627), and James Harrington's *Oceana* (1656).

In the eighteenth-century Enlightenment, Jean-Jacques Rousseau and others gave impetus to the belief that an ideal society – a Golden Age – had existed in the primitive days of European society before the development of civilization corrupted it. This faith in natural order and the innate goodness of humanity had a strong influence on the growth of visionary or utopian socialism. The end in view of these thinkers was usually an idealistic communism based on economic self-sufficiency or on the interaction of ideal communities. Henri de Saint-Simon, Étienne Cabet, Charles Fourier, and Pierre Joseph Proudhon in France and Robert Owen in England are typical examples. Actual experiments in utopian social living were tried in Europe and the United States, but for the most part the efforts were neither long-lived nor more than partially successful, even though their histories remained influential.

The humanitarian socialists were largely displaced after the middle of the nineteenth century by political and economic theorists, such as Karl Marx and Friedrich Engels, who advocated the achievement of the ideal state through political and revolutionary action. The utopian romance, however, became an extremely popular literary form. These novels depicted the glowing, and sometimes frightening, prospects of the new industrialism and social change. One of the most important of these works was Edward Bellamy's *Looking Backward* (1888), which had a profound influence on economic idealism in America. In England, Samuel Butler's *Erewhon* (1872), William Morris's *News from Nowhere* (1891), and H.G. Wells's *A Modern Utopia* (1905) were notable examples of the genre. The twentieth century saw a veritable flood of literary utopias, most of them "scientific utopias" in which humans enjoy a blissful leisure while all or most of the work is done for them by docile machines.

However, the actual signifier "utopia" first occurred in More's *Utopia*, published in 1516. More's title was compounded from the Greek words for "no" (*ou*) and "place" (*topos*) and thus meant "nowhere." During his embassy service to Flanders in 1515, More wrote Book II of *Utopia*, describing a pagan and communist city-state in which the institutions and policies were entirely governed by reason. The dignified order of such a state was intended to provide a challenging contrast with the unreasonable polity of England, and all of Christian Europe, divided by self-interest and greed for power and riches, which More then described in Book I, written in England in 1516. The description of the several utopias in More's text is put in the mouth of a mysterious traveler, Raphael Hythloday, in support of his argument that communism is the only cure against egoism in private and public life. The fact that Hytholday is a traveler is of note; for the connection between the utopian vision with its sense of the placeless, or with an enabling concept of space, and the movement toward, or discovery of, that no-place is an ongoing trope in this discourse. The fact that the idea of Utopia is enunciated in literature is also significant, as this is the genre which can allow for the unrealized to be given voice. Jacques Derrida has made this point:

> "What is writing in general?" and, in the space of writing in general, to this other question which is more and other than a simple particular case: "What is literature?"; literature as historical institution with its conventions, rules etc.,

but also this institution of fiction which gives *in principle* the power to say everything, to break free of the rules, to displace them, and thereby to institute, to invent and even to suspect the traditional difference between nature and institution, nature and conventional law, nature and history. Here we should ask juridical and political questions. The institution of literature in the West, in its relatively modern form, is linked to an authorization to say everything, and doubtless too to the coming about of the modern idea of democracy (*Acts of Literature* 37).

In Maurice Blanchot's terms, such a structure is paradigmatic of what he terms the "space of literature" in that different poles of oppositions are placed in a structure which sees them "quitting themselves and detaining each other together outside themselves in the restless unity of their common belonging" (*Space of Literature* 200). In such a space, "when everything seems put into question," the true function of writing can become operative. In this sense, the nullity of the space of literature deracinates the predesignations of ideology, culture, and history and instead provides a space wherein contradictions can possibly be recontextualized in a more productive encounter (*Gaze of Orpheus* 38). Derrida has also made the point that literature is, in a real sense, connected to "a juridical institution, to acquired rights," and, in the context of his discussion of Roman civilization, to the concept of *civitas* (*Demeure* 24). For him, "foundational to *litteratura* is the freedom to say, accept, receive, suffer and simulate anything" (Rapaport 33). This is precisely why the relationship between literature and the expression of utopian ideas is so crucial.

Here we inhabit Blanchot's space of literature, as different traditions are placed in a structure which sees them "quitting themselves and detaining each other together outside themselves in the restless unity of their common belonging" (200). The idea of literature as clearing a space allows for the positing of ideas which hitherto do not have an experiential reality. It allows for negotiation between the actuality of place and existing social structures, and ideas which could ameliorate that place and those structures. So Utopia is a "no-where," a "placeless-place" which exists in the human imagination. It is an impossibility that drives us to create new worlds of the imagination that are better, fairer, and generally more just than those which actually exist. Susan McManus makes a similar connection with the work of Jean-Jacques Rousseau, in the context of law-making. She notes that for Rousseau, "the Legislator can be shown to operate via a creative epistemology of the possible, rather than an epistemology of the given that can only reify, and reproduce relations of power" (50).

Is there an adequation between this idea and deconstruction? In an interview with the online journal *Culture Machine*, Derrida was asked about political thought and deconstruction; the conversation turned towards the issue of Utopia:

> Q: Since the self-criticism of the Left, there is no utopian thought anymore. Conservative cultural criticism has finished it off. Your philosophy, it seems to us, is not willing to renounce Utopia entirely, yet without naming it. Should one see in the event or in the *'tout autre'* a new name for Utopia?
> JD: Although there is a critical potential in Utopia which one should no doubt never completely renounce, above all when one can turn it into a motif of resistance against all alibis and all "realist" and "pragmatist" resignations, I still mistrust the word. In certain contexts, Utopia, the word in any case, is all too easily associated with the dream, with demobilisation, with an impossibility that urges renouncement instead of action. The "impossible" of which I often speak is not the utopian, on the contrary it lends its own motion to desire, to action and to decision, it is the very figure of the real. It has duration, proximity, urgency ("Intellectual Courage").

Despite what would seem to be an overt renunciation by Derrida of Utopia as a worthwhile concept, I would argue that such an adequation between Derridean deconstruction and utopian studies is there for the making, and that the catalyst that will bring this about is a meditation on the notion of justice. What Derrida seems to mistrust is the corralling of the utopian into the realm of the imaginary, the literary, the non-political. However, underwriting most notions of Utopia is a quest for justice, a desire for a culture or community which will be more just, fair, and equitable than those which have existed heretofore. Indeed in More's *Utopia*, there is a section dealing with "lawes not made according to equitie," where the author makes the point that unless social ills that cause crime are removed, society just creates criminals and then punishes them. This desire for fairness and justice is, I would argue, a core aspect of the utopian imperative at both theoretical and practical levels. As More put it:

> Caste oute these pernicyous abhominations, make a lawe, that they, whiche plucked downe fermes and townes of husbandrie, shal reedifie them, or els yelde and uprender the possession therof to suche as wil go to the cost of buylding them anewe. Suffer not these riche men to bie up al, to ingrosse and forstalle, and with their monopolie to kepe the market alone as please them. Let not so many be brought up in idelnes, let husbandry and tillage be restored, let clotheworkinge be renewed, that ther may be honest labours for this idell sort to pass their tyme in profitablye, whiche hitherto either povertie hath caused to be theves, or elles nowe be either vagabondes, or idel serving men, and shortelye wilbe theves (13–14).

It is interesting in the context of More's demand for justice, a demand couched in the future tense, that we will see a similar cast of mind in the work of Derrida. Writing in "The Force of Law," Derrida speaks of the necessity of "a desedimentation of the superstructures of law that both hide and reflect the economic and political interests of the dominant forces of society" (13). It is here that I see a central articulation between deconstruction and utopian studies. In terms of the so-called ethical turn in deconstruction, wherein issues of politics, law, and society have become increasingly central to Derrida's writings, if one were to look for an overarching structure within which to fit these musings, then that structure would have to be a utopian one. As Lyman Tower Sargent cogently points out, utopianism is "social dreaming" (5). Indeed, Derrida, in describing deconstruction's relationship to philosophy, uses a term redolent of the etymological meaning of Utopia. Speaking to Richard Kearney about philosophy, Derrida says that "my central question is from what site or non-site (*non-lieu*) can philosophy as such appear to itself as other than itself, so that it can interrogate and reflect upon itself in an original manner" (*Interviews* 159).

This very use of the term *non-lieu* situates the Derridean imperative, an imperative that is unfailingly critical and interrogative of the givens of any discourse, as utopian. It is from a "non-place," a *non-lieu,* a "no-where," that ameliorative ideas must be drawn, and towards which they must be directed. Such a space – of literature and, by an ethical extension, of the literature of law – is both a *terminus ad quem* and a *terminus a quo*: both a destination and a point of origin, or more correctly the oscillation between them. It is also parallel to Rousseau's creative epistemology (McManus 53). And, given the imperative towards justice which underwrites most utopian texts, be these writerly, political, or societal, the connections with deconstruction are all the stronger.

If we consider Derrida's recent intervention into the legacies of Marx, another utopian writer, in terms of justice, we find him looking:

> not for calculable and distributive justice. Not for law, the calculation of restitution, the economy of vengeance or punishment, [...] not for calculable equality therefore, not for the symmetrizing and synchronic accountability or imputability of subjects or objects, not for a rendering of justice that would be limited to sanctioning or restituting, and to doing right, but for justice as incalculability of the gift and singularity of the an-economic ex-position to others (*Specters of Marx* 22–3).

In other words, there is a singular difference between the law and justice: one enforcing, through an originary violence, the dictats of hegemonic power within a culture; the other stemming from a *non-lieu*, from a utopian desire to deconstruct such a position in favor of an attitude dominated by a respect for the other. As Willy Maley puts it: "In defining law in contradistinction to justice, Derrida is marking the distance between a calculation and a call, between a verdict and a vision, between a sentence and a summons" (54). For Derrida:

> Law (*droit*) is not justice. Law is the element of calculation, and it is just that there be law, but justice is incalculable, it requires us to calculate with the incalculable; and aporetic experiences are the experiences, as improbable as they are necessary, of justice, that is to say of moments in which the decision between just and unjust is never insured by a rule ("Force of Law" 16).

Justice is not rule bound, or bound in any way whatsoever. It has no boundaries. Derrida speaks of "a difficult and unstable distinction between justice and *droit*, between justice (infinite, incalculable, rebellious to rule and foreign to symmetry, heterogeneous and heterotropic) and the exercise of justice as law or right, legitimacy or legality, stabilizable and statutory, calculable, a system of regulated and coded prescriptions" ("Force of Law" 22).

To me, this is a utopian concept. For Derrida, notions like justice, democracy, and literature are utopian in that they are addressed to the *non-lieu*, the place of becoming, the "no-where"; and they are both non-spatial and atemporal. By this I mean that just as Utopia is not a given place, so justice is something that has no definite fixed existence. In this sense, Derrida speaks about the achronicity between past, present, and future. In *Specters of Marx*, he says that "an inheritance is never a given, it is always a task," meaning that the past must always be interpreted (54). In the case of the concepts of both justice and democracy, he chooses to do so in terms of an unspecified future as opposed to looking for guardrails from the past – he speaks of this as an "experience of the emancipatory promise" (59).

In each case, a judge straddles the aporetic relationship between the law and justice. Three people, accused of the same crime, can garner three totally different sentences – as the system of codifications and rules is manipulated according to the hovering concept of justice. The relationship between the two is probably best summed up by Derrida's notion of hauntology, a pun on the French pronunciation of ontology. In *Specters of Marx*, he sees ghostly hauntings as traces of possible alternative meanings. Derrida's spectrality involves acknowledging the other that haunts the self; it involves acknowledging the possibility that the "h" in *hauntology* is a hovering presence over the certainties of ontology; and, above all, it is predicated on the future. Speaking both of the ghost in *Hamlet*, and the ghost that haunts Marx and Engels's *Communist Manifesto* (where the first noun is "specter"), he makes the point that, at bottom, "the specter is the future, it is always to come, it presents itself only as that which could come or come back" (39). This orientation towards the future is part of the connection between the utopian and justice, and I would suggest that hauntology is its mode of operation. As McManus notes, hauntology is "the between, possibly the beyond, the opposition of material and utopian" (98). Hovering behind, beyond, in a non-place from the carefully codified statutes of judicial codes and codices, is the utopian notion that regulates these in spirit if not in fact: namely, justice. Each instance of the application, of the trial, of legal ideas, is driven by this desire to achieve justice. As Derrida notes, deconstruction is already engaged by the infinite demand of justice, for justice. His invocation of a utopian idea of justice, of the possibility of true recognition of the other, represents the radical potential for dissident thought within the debate. The possibility of a socialist ethics thus erupts through the discreet boundaries of bourgeois disciplinary and cognitive categories such as the political, the economic, the ethical.

To think Utopia in this way, without simple idealism, however, requires a messianic attitude; and this, I suggest, opens us to the other legacy of Marxism: namely the messianic redemption narrative. This belief in revolution – in revolution as a process and a future, only visible as the radical potential within capitalist society, identifiable as the struggle of the workers for control of their lives, yet at the same time absolutely radically, different – permits, however tenuously, the thought of difference. As Ernst Bloch puts it:

> a sense of justice in itself, even one that is democratic, only has value as a signal and nothing more. Even as a pure and direct sentiment, it is too vague, too easily reworked, too susceptible to cliché; it needs a shrewd ally. Even if good sense is given a good ear for listening, it must always be an ear that is capable of self-critique and assessment (*Natural Law* 5).

Such a form of critique is also to be found in Derrida's notion of the relationship between present and past in terms of tradition. On being asked about the role of deconstruction within the academy, Derrida says that the life of any institution implies that "we are able to criticize, to transform, to open the institution to its own future" ("Villanova" 6). He goes on to talk about the paradox of the moment of inauguration of any institution, which, while starting something new, is at the same time true to a memory of the past, and to things received from the culture, adding that such a moment must "break with the past, keep the memory of the past, while inaugurating something absolutely new" ("Villanova" 6). Derrida, looking at the notion of inauguration, notes that there are no guarantees and that "we have to invent the rules" ("Villanova" 6). He goes on, in this context, to make a keynote statement about the operative mode of deconstruction, something which, as is clear from his "Letter to a Japanese Friend," he has often been at pains to avoid. Speaking about the moment of inauguration, he suggests that there "is no responsibility, no decision, without this inauguration, this absolute break. That is what deconstruction is made of: not the mixture but the tension between memory, fidelity, the preservation of something that has been given to us, and, at the same time, heterogeneity, something absolutely new, and a break" ("Villanova" 6). This tension is a trope that carries through in all of his answers.

On discussing Greek philosophy, Derrida notes that what he looks for is the heterogeneity in the texts – how the *khôra*, for example, is incompatible with the Platonic system – before going on to speak more broadly about how a specifically Greek philosophy had within it an "opening, a potential force which was ready to cross the borders of Greek language, Greek culture" ("Villanova" 9). From this discussion, he progresses to the concept of democracy, a further thread in the ethical theme of these answers, making the point that while the concept of democracy is a Greek heritage, it is a heritage that "self-deconstructs [...] so as to uproot, to become independent of its own grounds" ("Villanova" 10). Here is a reprise of the Blochian notion of self-critique in action; and, once again, the utopian trace through Derrida's writing seems overt.

The same resonance can be found in Derrida's discussion of community, itself a very utopian trope. Take, for example, his discussion of identity, which arises on his being asked about the notion of community, as suggested by the American motto, *E pluribus unum*. Derrida sets out to connect his position with the broadest sense of community: international law, which, while *de jure* is a valuable structure, *de facto* is in the hands of "a number of powerful, rich states," a situation that he feels "has to change" ("Villanova" 12). It is in the name of such a necessary change that he offers a "new concept of citizenship, of hospitality, a new concept of the state, of democracy" ("Villanova" 12). Pursuing this line, and referring again to the epistemology of deconstruction, he argues that he has always focused on "the heterogeneity, the difference, the dissociation, which is absolutely necessary for the relation to the other"; and here again we see the strong ethical drive that powers so much of his later work. Taking Martin Heidegger's notion of *Versammlung* (gathering) as a starting point, Derrida proceeds to tease out the status of the limit points of such totalizing drives in terms of identity. He suggests that the identity of a culture is "a way of being different from itself" and, when this is taken into account,

> you pay attention to the other and you understand that fighting for your own identity is not exclusive of another identity, is open to another identity. And this prevents totalitarianism, nationalism, egocentrism and so on [...] in the case of culture, person, nation, language, identity is a self-differentiating identity, an identity different from itself, having an opening or gap within itself ("Villanova" 13–14).

Tracing Derrida's deconstructive notions of community in *Points* (wherein "there is doubtless this irrepressible desire for a "community" to form but also for it to know its limit – and for its limit to be its opening") and in *On the Name* (wherein he speaks about his dislike of the connotations attached to the term "community" such as "fusion" and "identification"), John Caputo focuses on Derrida's deconstructive notion of cultural identity (355, 46). Caputo stresses that this does not mean a leveling of identity, but rather an "opening it up to difference. He thus wants to distinguish an airtight, impermeable, homogenous, self-identical identity from a porous and heterogeneous identity that differs with itself" (114). Derrida himself – a French-speaking Algerian Jew, whose family originated in Spain – embodies such deconstructive notions of identity, calling himself an "over-acculturated, over-colonized European hybrid" (*Other Heading* 7). Thus, in terms of community, he is oriented towards future changes caused by altered circumstances – he is looking at a community that will be ethically and legally open to the future as opposed to one which is constructed on the narrow tramlines of the past. Such self-critique, as well as residing in the hauntological relationship between law and justice, and specifically the idea of such justice as residing in the future, as a demand or promise, can be found in Derrida's notion, borrowed from Walter Benjamin, of messianism.

For Derrida, speaking at Villanova University in 1994, the messianic structure is "a universal structure" that is defined by waiting for the future, by addressing the other as other, and, hence, by refusing to base notions of the present and future on a lineal descent from a particular version of the past ("Villanova" 22). He goes on to note that the messianic structure is predicated on a promise, on an expectation that whatever is coming in the future "has to do with justice" (23). What he terms messianism, on the other hand, is culturally and temporally limited and constrained to the "determinate figures" of "Jewish, Christian, or Islamic messianism" (23). He goes on: "As soon as you reduce the messianic structure to messianism then you are reducing the universality and this has important political consequences. Then you are accrediting one tradition among others, and a notion of an elected people, of a given literal language, a given fundamentalism" (23).

According to Derrida, the term "messianism" refers predominantly to the religions of the messiahs – i.e., the Muslim, Judaic, and Christian religions. These religions proffer a messiah of known characteristics, and often one who is expected to arrive at a particular time or place. The messiah is inscribed in their respective religious texts and in oral traditions that dictate that only if the other conforms to a particular description is that person actually the messiah. Temporally and spatially, this orientation is towards the past, towards a fixed point in time, a *terminus a quo*, from which all dogma can be traced and which regulates any future development: it is a classic logocentric space, whereas in Derrida's messianism without religion, such thinking about the "idea of justice" can take place, and can be oriented towards present and future as opposed to the past (*Specters of Marx* 59). This is the crux of the utopian imperative: how can an ideal become integrated into the real without becoming reified into another dogma, another doxa, another dystopia.

I would suggest that the answer is also to be found in Derrida. Of course, to conclude, in a classic deconstructive move, the connection between the imaginary utopian dream and real-world political action is always problematic. There is an almost programmatic process at work in lived utopian communities: namely, of a utopian dream inspiring a community to live by its creed, followed by the advent of the second generation, followed by the replacement of dream by dogma and the gradual reification of the utopia into a possible dystopia. Deconstruction, with its constant focus in iterability and singularity – with the notion that much of what we do is iterative in that aspects are repeated over and over, but that each single instance is, in its way, unique – would appear to offer the possibility of a semi-permanent state of interrogative and immanent critique that would guard against the twin dangers of Utopia: on the one hand, of the dream remaining just that, a regulative idea with no place in the real world; on the other, of the dream becoming ossified in reality and drained of its radical potential. Because, of course, if we look at the plurality of the signifier "utopia," no-where can also, if we take into account a different spacing of the letters, become "now-here." It is in that spacing shift that I would situate a deconstructive articulation with utopian studies, because it is in that space that utopian ideas for greater social justice can become reality, but retain their radical edge.

Such tensions are also to be found in Derrida's notion of justice. A judge, says Derrida, "if he wants to be just, cannot content himself with applying the law. He has to reinvent the law each time" ("Villanova" 17). Hence, the tension between the law and justice is a deconstructive one, and we return to one of the initial defining remarks about deconstruction being, among other things, the tension between a sense of memory and a sense of the new ("Villanova" 6). For Caputo, the politico-ethical consequences of Derrida's sense of European identity and community consists in "opening itself without being able any longer to gather itself" to the heading of the other; and Derrida's expression of this in *The Other Heading* is an important enunciation of such a perspective (Caputo 122). It is, therefore, in the nature of the undecidable, of the iterability of the law and the singularity of justice, that the utopian imperative of deconstruction comes into being. Each utopian instance of justice is singular, but never repeatable. The paradigms underlying it may be similar, but each instance is different. Hence, each instance must be thought through individually, and must be constantly subjected to critique. This, I would suggest, is the interstitial connection between justice to come and the utopian imperative of deconstruction.

Works Cited

Augustine. *City of God*. Ed. G.R. Evans. Trans. Henry Bettenson. Harmondsworth: Penguin, 2004.
Bacon, Francis. *The New Atlantis*. London: Lightning Source, 2004.
Bellamy, Edward. *Looking Backwards: 2000–1887*. London: Broadview, 1996.
Blanchot, Maurice. *The Gaze of Orpheus*. Ed. P. Adams Sitney. Trans. Lydia Davis. New York: Station Hill, 1981.
____*The Space of Literature*. Trans. Ann Smock. Lincoln: University of Nebraska Press, 1982.
Bloch, Ernst. *Natural Law and Human Dignity*. Trans. Dennis .J. Schmidt. Cambridge, Massachusetts: MIT Press, 1996.
Butler, Samuel. *Erewohn*. London: Prometheus, 1998.
Campanella, Tomasso. *City of the Sun: A Poetical Dialogue*. Trans. A.M. Elliot and R. Millner. London: Pluto, 1981.
Caputo, John (ed.). *Deconstruction in a Nutshell: A Conversation with Jacques Derrida*. New York: Fordham University Press, 1997.
Derrida, Jacques. *Acts of Literature*. Ed. Derek Attridge. London: Routledge, 1992.
____"Deconstruction and the Other: Dialogue with Derrida." *Dialogue with Contemporary Continental Thinkers: The Phenomenological Heritage*. Ed. Richard Kearney. Manchester: Manchester University Press, 1984. 145–62.
____*Demeure: Fiction and Testimony*. Trans. Elizabeth Rottenberg. Stanford: Stanford University Press, 2000.
____"Force of Law: The Mystical Foundation of Authority." *Deconstruction and the Possibility of Justice*. Ed. Drucilla Cornell, Michel Rosenfeld, and David Gray Carlson. Trans. Mary Quantance. New York and London: Routledge, 1992.
____"Intellectual Courage: An Interview with Jacques Derrida: Interview with Thomas Assheuer." 5 March 1998 <http://culturemachine.tees.ac.uk/Cmach/Backissues/j002/Articles/art_derr.htm>.
____"A Letter to a Japanese Friend." *A Derrida Reader: Between the Blinds*. Ed. Peggy Kamuf. Hemel Hempsted: Harvester Wheatsheaf, 1991. 269–76.
____*On the Name*. Ed. Thomas Dutoit. Stanford: Stanford University Press, 1993.

_____*The Other Heading: Reflections on Today's Europe*. Trans. Pascale-Anne Brault and Michael Naas. Bloomington: Indiana University Press, 1992.

_____*Points ... Interviews, 1974–1994*. Ed. Elizabeth Weber. Trans. Peggy Kamuf. Stanford: Stanford University Press, 1995.

_____*Specters of Marx: The State of the Debt, the Work of Mourning & the New International*. Trans. Peggy Kamuf. London: Routledge, 1994.

_____"The Villanova Round Table: A Conversation with Jacques Derrida." *Deconstruction in a Nutshell*. Ed. John Caputo. New York: Fordham University Press, 1997. 4–28.

Harrington, James *The "Commonwealth of Oceana" and "A System of Politics"* Ed. J. G. A. Pocock. Cambridge: Cambridge University Press, 1992.

Maley Willy. "Beyond the Law? The Justice of Deconstruction." *Law and Critique* 10 (1999): 49–69.

McManus, Susan. *Fictive Theories: Toward a Deconstructive and Utopian Political Imagination*. London: Palgrave Macmillan, 2005.

More, Thomas. *Utopia*. Ed. and trans. Robert M. Adams. London: Norton, 1997.

Morris, William. *News from Nowhere*. Harmondsworth: Penguin, 1993.

Rabelais, François. *Gargantua and Pantagruel*. Trans. Peter Anthony Motteux. London: Wordsworth, 1999.

Rapaport, Herman. *Later Derrida: Reading the Recent Work*. London: Routledge, 2003.

Sargent, Lyman Tower. "The Three Faces of Utopianism Revisited." *Utopian Studies* 5.1 (1994): 1–37.

Wells, H.G. *A Modern Utopia*. Harmondsworth: Penguin, 2005.

SUSAN MCMANUS

Truth, Temporality, and Theorizing Resistance

> A spectral moment, a moment that no longer belongs to time, if one understands by this word the linking of modalized presents [...] Furtive and untimely, the specter does not belong to that time.
> Jacques Derrida, *Specters of Marx*

> And you should know that the zapatista dead are very restless and talkative. They still speak, despite being dead, and they're shouting history. They're shouting it so that it can't go to sleep, so that memory won't die, so that our dead will live, shouting.
> Subcommandante Marcos, *Our Word Is Our Weapon*

Truth

The complicated problem of truth forms a reinvigorated horizon in contemporary radical, critical, and utopian political theory. This horizon is shaped by four aspects: first, the reclaiming and refunctioning of "truth" as a cognitive form that is at once situated and perspectival, as well as anticipatory, "fictive," or imaginative; second, the possibility that such truths can be deployed to cultivate "combative lucidity" or transformative knowledges of, and orientations within, the world; third, the ways in which the "affective register" of the subject can enhance ethical energies and political agency; and fourth, the possibilities that inhere in temporality itself.[1] These aspects of the horizon of truth overlap. For theorists such as Jacques Derrida, Alain Badiou, and Antonio Negri, for example, figures of truth are theorized via the disordering effects of spectrality, the radical interruption of the Event, or the imaginative refusal invoked by the experience of *cairos*. Such truths are active at once on the temporal and affective register of subjectivity, first, as complication or interruption of temporal linearity, the disorderly experience of time's "untimeliness," and, second, as creative and imaginative qualities of the affective-cognitive capacities of the subject.

As well, the contemporary critical attention focused on the affective register of subjectivity can supplement the mapping of this horizon. Drawing inspiration from the modern altercanon (Benedict Spinoza, Friedrich Nietzsche, Michel Foucault, Gilles Deleuze), work by theorists such as William Connolly and Jane Bennett explore the affective as it inflects, and is inflected by, the epistemological, in order to cultivate ways of knowing and orienting the subject in the world that are potentially socially transformative. This endeavor draws sustenance from an implicitly utopian ethics grounded in an affirmative attachment to the potential that inheres within the world. The significance of such explorations in theorizing a politics of resistance is marked; for the vital maneuvers of radical, critical, and utopian theory seek to figure truth as a *dislocation* from the dominant knowledges of the times, and to do so in such a way that makes agency possible.

In this essay, I propose that an exploration of the fourth aspect of the problematic of truth, the possibilities that inhere in temporality itself, is crucial. Temporality (the experience of time/untimeliness) can, I suggest, be theorized precisely as an affective-epistemological

---

1   On truth, fictions, and politics in poststructuralist theory, see Haraway's "cyborg" as a world-changing fiction within social reality; Braidotti, as in "political fictions may be more effective, here and now, than theoretical systems" (7); Foucault, as in "I have never written anything but fictions" (193); and Badiou (discussed below). On the "affective register," see Connolly; Bennett.

form, and doing so has implications for the theorization of both agency and truth. Mapping temporality's affectivity reveals potentially dissident ways of moving from hope to desire, thus delineating new possibilities for agency, and creating new (post-representational) figures of truth.

The most sustained meditations and explicit reflections upon the questions of time, truth, and resistance emerge from debates within utopian studies. Utopianism – as impulse, process, or problematic – is at once a dissident orientation within, and a refractory theoretical perspective upon, the world. Utopianism denotes those cultural practices, theoretical perspectives, and lived political experiences that locate possibilities of freedom on the horizon of the complex of current regimes or configurations of power/knowledge.[2] While in this way future-oriented, the temporality of the utopian impulse is nevertheless recondite and nonlinear, mapping instead time's layered excess as the overlap of future into both present and past, and of past into present and future. The utopian Not Yet, the alterity on the horizon that utopian impulses anticipate and articulate, *inflects* the lived present; the alterity of the horizon seeks to *alter*, to exert a transformative force within – and against – the hegemonic and instrumental logic of the present. Similarly, the past is not closed, for echoes and resonances remain to be activated in the present and future. Utopianism thus marks both lived and theoretical gestures of refusal that dislocate the dominant logic of the times, and it is this *dislocation* that generates (fragmentary, *in potentia*) figures of truth and agency. The utopian challenge, then, is to elicit, make palpable, different strata of possibilities within the contested political present, so as to render vivid ways of knowing the world that venture beyond the existent, that are not captured and contained by the exigencies of the present ordering of things.

Consider Ernst Bloch's evocation of the time of struggle, the time of a self-transforming present, wherein "unbecome future

---

2   It is the formal quality of Utopia to be resolutely oppositional. The rejection of the blueprint paradigm is now firmly established in utopian studies: the critical maneuvers of Utopia are formal and temporal (see Jameson).

becomes visible in the past, avenged and inherited, mediated and fulfilled past in the future. A past that is grasped in isolation and clung to in this way is a mere commodity category – that is, a reified *Factum*, without consciousness of its *Fieri* [to be done] and of its continuing process" (9). That is to say, the time of the present is composed of *multiple* temporalities, and so the horizon of possibilities of the present remains always open and contested (to be fought for). A key maneuver of Power is to commodify or otherwise reify that past as complete, so as to consolidate and sustain hegemony in the present and to mark the future as nothing other than the reproduction and repetition of that hegemony.[3] On the contrary, for the radical, the past is not closed, over, or finished; for echoes remain to disturb the finality of any victory of the powerful. Walter Benjamin, too, was compellingly alert to the potential that inheres in the untimeliness of the present moment: "the past carries a temporal index by which it is referred to redemption. There is a secret agreement between past generations and the present one. [...] Like every generation that preceded us, we have been endowed with a *weak* messianic power, a power to which the past has a claim" (ii). That *other* time, the untimely or out-of-time, is the time of potential disruption that *inhabits* "homogenous, empty time" as the *possibility* of critical interruption, redirection, resistance. Its untimeliness is a form of (motivating, directing) temporal disjuncture that reveals the possibility of the different and other, as well as rendering alertness to forms of temporal (as well as spatial) solidarity in the processes of struggle.

Benjamin and Bloch are exemplary in their depiction of the ways in which temporality as a dissident affective form shapes both truth and agency in politically counter-hegemonic ways. For the utopian, tracing temporality's affective force shows possible ways of moving from desire to hope. This utopian project, then, plays a part in the "education of desire," as Ruth Levitas, drawing on Morris, has argued

---

3   Radical theory draws a distinction between *potesta* (already constituted Power) and *potentia* (constituent Power), privileging the disruptive creativity of the latter. This distinction is not available in the English language.

(*Concept* 6; see also "Educated Hope").[4] So, tracing temporality is also a way of mapping the movement of hope within historical processes, of mapping threads that hook up *le temps*, *histoire*, and *le monde*, and it is just such a movement that Fredric Jameson has argued the utopian novel achieves (*Archaeologies* 7).

There are political inflections, then, inherent in the ways that subjects experience and represent time, and in the multitude of ways in which time is lived. Temporality thus conceived is a potent force, shaping memory as well as desire, in-forming imagination and possibility.[5] To be sure, affective subjectivity is always-already shaped, disciplined, invested; that this is so indicates a psychic social economy wherein the constitution of time and the constitution of subjectivity are significantly interlinked. Thus, it is of further importance to explore the ways in which the subject is a *product* of time or, put otherwise, to trace the ways in which subjectivity itself is ineluctably constituted by temporal dynamics that are also profoundly political. I propose this as a formal claim: that is, while recognizing the multiplicity of cultural-temporal formations, subjectivity is inextricably formally entwined with temporality *as such*. "My

---

4   Levitas argues, drawing on Morris, that utopian "desire" needs to be educated in order to translate into a politically active hope. I agree; and to that end I propose, in the larger project of which this essay is a part, a series of utopian techniques of the self, drawn from a cartography of affective forms, as a way of shaping the affective energies that can sustain such a utopian politics (see *Concept*).

5   Braidotti argues that politics is "as much to do with the constitution and organization of affectivity, memory and desire as it has with consciousness and resistance," but the time of resistance itself is intrinsically connected with affectivity, memory, and desire: the world out there (ontology) is not detached from the ways we know and experience it (epistemology and affect) (20). Bloch was aware of the "temporal emotions," of which hope was the most vital as only hope could attain the status of a "directing act of a cognitive kind" (12). Radical or utopian time is not linear, composed of moments that succeed one another; rather, time is layered, composed of multiple possibilities. Figuring (as writing, or feeling, voicing) the untimeliness of time reveals possibilities for agency even as we accept that we subjects are ineluctably, thoroughly constituted.

subjectivity," David Wood provocatively remarks, "comes from a time that is not my own" (12). That there is a non-coincidence of the subject with her times declares that there are spaces of possibility as well as, darkly, possibility's disappearance. "The time is out of joint" resonates throughout Derrida's *Specters of Marx*, evoking the disjuncture of time in two possible directions: potential critical interruption, or, bleakly, the impossibility of setting the times straight. Theorizing or figuring temporality in terms of a potentially affective untimeliness, then, reveals "possibilities [...] for intervention, for resistance, for creativity, for production, for transformation, for intervention in the world," as untimely figurations stage a "kind of *dramatic* opening up of our capacity to think both our relation to that which has framed us, and also our capacity to imagine how we might transform what comes after us" (Wood 12). Put otherwise: figuring untimeliness may reveal many utopian "elsewheres" here and now.

Time

> I began then to think of time as having a shape, something you could see, like a series of liquid transparencies, one laid on top of another. You don't look back along time, but down through it, like water. [...] Nothing goes away.
> Margaret Atwood, *Cat's Eyes*

What, then, *is* time? Or, what temporal modalities do "we" (late modern? western?) subjects encounter? Do we "encounter" time, or are we "temporal" beings? And what are the affective, epistemological, and ethical implications of the ways that we figure or represent time? Such questions belie easy responses; for time, too, is something complicated. The constitutive force of temporality engenders, literally, different worlds, as, in a Deleuzian vein, Claire Colebrook suggestively proposes: "the world is not something in which time takes place; there are flows of time from which worlds are perceived" (41). Radically different flows of time inflect radically different temporal-cultural formations and vice versa. One need only consider the many and varied *grammatical* tenses to note that the multitude of ways in which time is experienced are culturally specific.[6] It is, nevertheless, possible to very briefly delineate on a formal level *some* of the ways in which time has been apprehended.

Two key axes can be identified. The first axis opposes time as primarily conceptual to time as primarily constitutive. The second axis opposes those conceptions of time that are primarily chronological, linear, forward-moving, to those conceptualizations that mark time differently, as otherly ontic, layered, folded. While Deleuze or Negri, for example, theorize time in all its constitutive complexity, for modern philosophers such as Immanuel Kant, time "in-itself" could not be grasped. For Kant, time functioned as a regulative idea, a fiction, a way of apprehending objects in space rather than a property of those objects. (Kant's maneuver here strikes me as a peculiarly disciplinary confinement of the experience of temporality to the conceptual apparatus of the subject.) Exploring the latter axis through the lens of the experiential, the relentless forward movement of chronological time – undeniable, commonsensical – is again belied by the subject's equally undeniable experience of time as layered, folding: indeed, the experience of *déjà vu* speaks to such a temporal-experiential folding. Time's arrow is intangible, ethereal, otherly (time does not yield itself up to the grasp of the subject). That "time" in itself cannot be approached univocally or directly suggests, as Elizabeth Grosz has argued, that "time is neither fully 'present,' a thing in itself, nor a pure abstraction […] It is a kind of evanescence that appears only at those moments when our expectations are

---

6   Time can be approached through music (the metronome, keeping time) or through configurations of secular time vis-à-vis sacred time (e.g., as marked by monasticism). Interesting is the possibility of theorizing temporality via its disciplinary or other formations; such projects nevertheless are beyond the boundaries of this essay. I thank the participants in the Ralahine Workshop, 3 March 2006, Ralahine Centre for Utopian Studies, University of Limerick, for their suggestions.

(positively or negatively) surprised" (5). Time, and temporal modalities, register significance on many and varied levels. However, those registers, Grosz suggests, manifest themselves (if at all) to the subject affectively, through the "surprise" of the temporal. (I do not want to suggest that the concept of time that concerns me as a political theorist is primarily "subjective" or experiential or social, as *opposed to* natural, or ontological conceptions of time. Instead, I would rather propose that those ontic conceptualizations resonate within the political imaginary.) For now, I aim to delineate some of the keynotes of the modern experience of time, through a dual exploration of the quotidian and the theoretical.

Time, Grosz avers, manifests itself to the subject in the experience of the affective form of surprise. Some keynotes of surprise would certainly have to include Marcel Proust and the recall of the past in the present invoked by the scent and taste of a madeleine cake. Henri Bergson's figuring of duration that encompasses both the sedimentation of the past within the present and the unpredictability of the inventiveness of the present as it extends into the future sounds another vital temporal rhythm.[7] As well, utopists have sought to unpack the utopian potential that inheres in mixed temporalities; consider Vincent Geoghegan's work on memory in Bloch, and his assertion of the import of the distinction between *anagnorisis* as recognition and *anamnesis* as recollection (wherein, productivity and possibility resides in the work of the former, while the latter delivers only repetition).[8] And, as a final cultural keynote, Samuel Beckett's dramatic staging of the vast expanses of cosmic and existential time evokes, perhaps, the sheer complexity of "homogenous, empty time" itself.

---

[7] The skeptical Bloch comments of Bergson that "there is absolutely no genuine Novum in Bergson; he has only in fact developed his concept from sheer excess into capitalistic fashion-novelty and thus stabilized it. [...] The social reason for Bergson's pseudo-Novum lies in the late bourgeoisie, which has within it nothing new in terms of content. [...] The mighty realm of possibility thus becomes for him an illusion of—retrospection" (202).

[8] "The power of the past resides in its complicated relationship of similarity/dissimilarity to the present" (Geoghegan 22).

However, in terms of quotidian experiences of time, surely the exemplary manifestation of the subject's experience of, and relation to, time in modernity is the utterly *un*surprising presence of the timepiece, the clock, the watch. As Raoul Vanegeim notes, "ours is the time of the watch-maker," denoting at once ontological, ideological, and experiential formations of the temporal in modernity (226). Vanegeim diagnosed a modern malaise of "survival sickness" whose most telling and disconsolate symptom is that time is no longer lived; *time itself* is "dead" or felt only and wretchedly as "time-that-slips-away": "people are *bewitched* into believing that time slips away, and this belief is the basis of time actually slipping away" (151). The modern time of progress and linearity, for Vanegeim and theorists like him, signifies not the disenchantment of the world but rather its *double* enchantment, wherein the surprise of temporality is perhaps irredeemably lost in a newly mythical temporal formation: the cyclical time of capital's reproduction. Conceivably, this is the gloomy paradox of the modern experience: as time is inscribed upon our very bodies down to the merest millisecond – only then, desultory, instrumental, quantifiable time supersedes the time of, and time *as*, epiphany, Event, *cairos*. To be sure, delineating the contours of the affective dimensions of temporality must necessarily consider the historically specific modes and flows of time within which historically specific subjectivities are produced. I shall return to this point in the next section, as I delineate some of the mechanisms whereby such temporal experiences are produced. For now, I ask, what is the sickness (what are the affects) that clock-time signifies?

Survival sickness destroys the layered qualities of temporal experience. The epiphany – as with Margaret Atwood's Elaine in *Cat's Eyes*, as much as Marcel (that "nothing goes away") – is thus replaced by utter loss: "no matter that lived space is a universe of dreams, desires, and prodigious creative impulses: in terms of duration, it is merely one point following another, and its emergence is governed by one principle only, that of its own annihilation" (226–7). Or: "linear time – objective time, time-which-slips-away – invades the space that has fallen to daily life in the shape of negative time, dead time, the expression of the temporality of destruction" (226–7). The affective impact of clocktime is indeed a dangerous sickness, one that threatens an annihilation of the quotidian itself. The utterly unsurprising, the watch, thus leaps from the quotidian to become one of the more fascinating, perplexing, cosmological riddles of modern philosophy: for what else are Nietzsche's various formulations of eternal recurrence counterpoised to, if not to the forms of revenge that humanity takes against time-that-slips-away?[9] Eternal recurrence confronts "time, and its 'it was.'" For Nietzsche, the melancholy of "time and its 'it was'" produces *ressentiment* (that is, reactive formations of desire) because linear conceptualizations of temporality herald a loss of the past and (perhaps paradoxically) inculcate a sense of the future as mere repetition; and so, change is structurally ruled out. In one formulation from *The Gay Science*, a demon who may be malignant, or may be a great god, asks: "How well disposed would you have to become to yourself and to life to *crave nothing more fervently* than this ultimate eternal confirmation and seal?" (341). Nietzsche thus proposes that the processes of thinking this thought of eternal recurrence acts as a kind of "technique of the self" whereby the perceived necessity of linear time (and its mythical repetition – power as Power) becomes loosened in a psychic unlocking or unfreezing of time's "flow."

Part of the significance of Nietzsche's reflections on untimely temporalities is simply this: in his speculations, he allows ontological or cosmological configurations of time to play and work within social, historical, and experiential formulations; he refuses a forced or false analytical distinction between these temporal levels, revealing instead their interplay. That is to say, the quotidian is revealed as an aspect of the cosmological. Second, he marks a critical distinction between modes of time that generate senses of irretrievable loss (and thus reactive modes of subject-formation) and modes of temporal experience that seek to inculcate a sense of agency *within* temporality.

---

9   Expressions of eternal recurrence include "The Greatest Stress" in *The Gay Science* and *Thus Spake Zarathustra* ("The Vision and the Riddle," "The Convalescent"). Nietzsche counterposes the despair, *ressentiment*, revenge against life that characterize "time and it's 'it was'" with eternal recurrence as a way or sublating ressentiment.

That Nietzsche formulates his "most abyssal thought" at the high point of modernity is not innocent or coincidental; time as an *affective* form is, of course, deeply interwoven with historically specific modes and flows of time within which historically specific subjectivities are constituted. Utopian, radical, and critical theorists (e.g., Benjamin, Deleuze and Félix Guattari, Foucault, Negri, Badiou) all mark some kind of distinction between empty or dead temporal modes (time as measure, the time of reproduction, repetition) and that *other* time, the untimely time (radical or revolutionary temporalities: time to come, messianic time, the Event). How are these temporalities produced? And how can empty forms of time be disrupted in politically dissident ways? How can re-figuring the temporal reveal agency, and create truth? If in western modernity the surprise of the temporal is captured by linearity, chronology, and quantification, then attention to critical maneuvers that cut through modernity's production of dead time might be politically, ethically, and epistemologically important. To that end, in the following sections, I explore some mechanisms whereby survival sickness is produced, some critical interruptions that re-figure temporality, and some of the ways in which such interruptions reconceptualize the problematic of truth itself.

Modern Time

> Time is the work of attrition to that adaptation to which people must resign themselves so long as they fail to change the world. Age is a role, an acceleration of "lived" time in the plane of appearances, an attachment to *things*.
> Raoul Vanegeim, *Revolution*

In this section, I explore an important way in which the "surprise" of the temporal has been deadened in western modernity, and I consider the ethical-epistemological implications of this move. For "time-that-slips-away," empty or dead time, is a naturalized rather than natural (or indeed, ontological) temporal mode. Both Guy Debord and Vanegeim focus on the historically specific *mechanisms* whereby dead time is *produced*. I have chosen to focus my current discussion on the deadening of time in late-modernity on these thinkers partially because both are relatively neglected in political theory; but, more importantly, because both (as situationists) evince the entwinement of theory and practice. Both *imaginatively* inhabit the "homogenous, empty time" that is the object of their critique; and so, both stage the confrontation of resistance to capital and capital's recuperative dynamic. Their analyses thus help shape a necessary theorization of time, truth, and resistance, as they trace the form of modern experience of our shared, complicated, layered present moment. Both also draw theoretical sustenance from an altercanon that certainly includes renegades such as Spinoza, Nietzsche, Max Stirner, as well as some of Karl Marx's modes. This range of work is, then, important in informing a transformative subjectivity *sans ressentiment* (see *Fictive Theories*, ch. 4, and Conclusion).

The temporality of modernity works, as both Debord and Vanegeim argue in a Marxist vein, through the specific flows of capital. Time, quite literally, became money, deployed to measure wage-labor. A common temporal unit came to measure labor-power (the worker's capacity for labor) and also became a means of reducing various concrete forms of labor to simple units of abstract labor. *Capital* is, in a very specific sense, living labor that has been reified, congealed in its object, and thus become that which can be exchanged; hence, surplus value can be extracted from living labor. Temporal processes of human productivity consequently become *frozen* into things that can be exchanged (and exploitation is thus significantly temporal).[10] The temporality of capital, then, is bound up with a time that is known only through measure and commodity. This has implications that resonate through ontological conceptualizations of time, to how the world can be known, and to the subject's experience

---

10 See work on the Italian/*autonomista* tradition for similar analyses, Negri in particular.

of that world. Citing the Marx of *The Poverty of Philosophy*, Debord argues that in time-as-measure, time itself becomes thing-like, quantifiable, and thus exchangeable, to the detriment of living time: "It is under the rule of time-as-commodity that 'time is everything, man is nothing; he is at most *time's carcass*'" (147, emphasis added). This loss of time heralds a death, as human subjects become literally emptied out. Vanegeim concurs, arguing that these mechanisms are precisely the means by which "dead time" (and so "survival sickness") are produced, as "the bourgeois order [...] increases the dead time in daily life (imposing the need to produce, consume, calculate)" (159).

I have already gestured, via Nietzsche's critical interruption, toward the paradox whereby the time of measure (quantitative, linear) generates its other. Debord calls this "pseudo-cyclical time"; but he proposes that "pseudo-cyclical time is in fact merely the *consumable disguise* of time-as-commodity of the production system, and it exhibits the essential traits of that time: homogenous and exchangeable units, and the suppression of any qualitative dimension" (149). Debord thus augments Nietzsche's existential analysis with an analysis of the moves made by capital to produce such a malaise and temporal confusion. Linear time becomes the time of repetition and also the time of pseudo-novelty, as the commodity form produces ever new manifestations: "The ruling class, made up of specialists in the ownership of things who for that very reason are themselves owned by things, is obliged to tie its fate to the maintenance of a reified history and to the preservation of a new historical mobility" (143). At once cyclical and linear, exchangeable and marked by increasing novelty, the time of capital is indeed the time of a peculiar metaphysics.

With such a peculiarity marked by the chronological, the linear, the instrumental, and the quantitative, Vanegeim discerns in capitalism's peculiar metaphysics the "confused geometry of Power": "The quantitative and the linear are indissociable. A linear, measured time and a linear, measured life establish the co-ordinates of survival: a succession of interchangeable instants" (88). As the time of capital encompasses space, other times (precisely as differing quotidians *and* differing cosmologies) come to signify, in our times, other possibilities.[11] That is to say, there are multiple dynamics at work: if we accept Debord's analysis, then "the development of capitalism meant the unification of irreversible time on a world scale [...]. What appears the world over as *the same day* is merely the time of economic production – time cut up into equal abstract fragments. Unified universal time still belongs to the world market – and, by extension, to the world spectacle" (145). While the utopian horizon can no longer be theorized as the "outside" of capital's colonization of time/the times, critical interruptions remain "that straddle [...] a border zone of temporality, something that conforms to the temporal code within which 'capital' comes into being while violating that code at the same time, something we are able to see only because we can think/theorize capital, but something that also reminds us that other temporalities, other forms of *worldling*, coexist and are possible" (Chakrabarty 57).

Thus, alter-temporalities, shaping alternative worlds that interrupt the dominant temporalization and its modes of world-creation, still exist. The political task at hand, then, is that of evoking those times. In his analysis of Benjamin's theorization of time, Giorgio Agamben points out that

> messianic time is not chronologically distinct from historical time [...] another world and another time must make themselves present in this world and time. This means that historical time cannot simply be cancelled and that messianic time, moreover, cannot be perfectly homogenous with history; these two times must instead accompany one another according to modalities that cannot be reduced to a dual logic (this world/other world) (168).

That time is not reducible to its historical production, and that time is even non-synchronous with itself, speaks to subversive possibilities. From Benjamin, to the "black time" of Malcolm X, to "women's time" of the radical feminist movement, to the zapatistas, who evoke

---

11   See Smith's discussion of Johannes Fabian's exploration of the colonial construction of the other through temporal axes of "underdevelopment" (12–13).

"another calendar: that of resistance," the demand to live time as a "time that is filled with the presence of the Now" in all its complexity and reconditeness (Benjamin xiv). This move is necessary for any politics of resistance.

In this section, I have argued that the temporality of modernity is produced largely through the mechanisms of capital. These mechanisms affect the ontological imaginary as much as the political, epistemological, and affective registers. The forms of agency and ways of knowing that dominate this temporal moment thus seek to flatten time's complexity and layered qualities. The subject is produced as calculable, quantifiable, ordered; knowledge is cumulative, commodified, again quantifiable. As modern capital more fully operates, and colonizes, on a global scale, the dead time of western modernity becomes (productively) infested with other temporal modalities that interrupt its rhythms from within. Thus, attention to other temporal rhythms can be a critical practice of interrupting the naturalization of capital's temporality. Also vital is the interpretative work of paying attention to the possibilities to which the disjuncture or critical tension between hegemonic time and *other* forms of temporality give rise. In the next section, I turn my attention to the ways in which such a critical disjuncture can be *cultivated*.

That "Other" Time

> What do I want? Not a succession of moments, but one huge instant. A totality that is lived, and without the experience of "time passing." The feeling of "time passing" is simply the feeling of growing old. And yet, since one must survive in order to live, virtual moments, virtual possibilities, are necessarily rooted in that time. When we try to federate moments, to bring out the pleasure in them, to release their promise of life, we are already learning how to construct "situations."
> Raoul Vanegeim, *Revolution*

In what follows, I focus critical attention on maneuvers that sever modernity's production of dead time in potentially dissident ways. Through what means can a revolutionary temporality be grasped? Can temporality, figured in untimely ways, link desire to hope, to history? Some possibilities lie in the constellations, ghosts, specters produced as critical ruptures within modernity, ruptures that can be deployed to figure new ways of critically re-orienting subjects in their worlds. Receptivity to the voices of specters and ghosts as ciphers of possibility might just inculcate an agency that is receptive to a transformative inflection of the Not Yet.

For both Vanegeim and Benjamin, this receptivity can be generated through historiographical critique that aligns itself with (past and present) cultures of resistance, and thus with voices that have been subjugated, neglected, forgotten, or suppressed in accordance with truths or priorities informed by dominant ways of producing knowledge. Methodologically as well as politically, Vanegeim sounds a warning against a future that is nothing other than "historians repeating themselves" (232). As he and Bloch both know, the future that is mere reproduction or repetition of the prevailing order is the *unreal* future; and so Vanegeim points to the ways in which political subjects can unwork the seemingly insurmountable, apparently ontological and natural barriers between those who have struggled in earlier times and in their own times: "past revolts take on a new dimension in my present, the dimension of an immanent reality crying out to be brought into being" (233). He addresses those who would *practice* resistance as well as, methodologically, those who would *study* resistance in shaping a sensibility that is attuned to the absent presence of the past as it "ris[es] from the dead and run[s] through the streets of our daily lives" (231).[12] And so, as, for example, the zapatistas (or, indeed, Evo Morales or Hugo Chavez) hear the motivating absent-presence of five hundred years of struggle (not

---

12   Levitas made these maneuvers palpable in her presentation at the "Exploring the Utopian Impulse" conference at the Ralahine Centre for Utopian Studies, University of Limerick, on 10 March 2005.

defeat), they gesture toward a utopian invocation of the new wherein immanent possibility, memory, and the Not Yet future generate agency and counter-hegemonic truth in the present moment of struggle. As such, their political practices can be read via an unruly, nonlinear temporality that generates another world, "another form of worlding" (Chakrabarty 57).

Grosz puts it thus: "The task is to make elements of this past live again, to be re-energized through their untimely or anachronistic recall in the present. The past is what gives us that *difference*, that tension with the present which can move us to a future in which the present can no longer recognize itself" (117). The vital moment in disrupting linearity has its *counter*-analogy precisely in the commodity form and the energy, the life, congealed therein: that is, how can the thingification of time and energy be made to speak? What would it say here-and-now? And so, the critical interest is not in the past as it reflects, prefigures, and naturalizes the hegemonic order of the present (or as it shows its "Scotland Yard Badge," as Bloch seriously jokes to Benjamin); rather, as Grosz suggests, it lies "in that which in the past still retains its dynamic potential" (114). Thus, "the meaning of such moments lies not in their inaugural force within a preordained narrative, but in the possibilities opened by their recovery" (Lowe and Lloyd 5). In the remainder of this section, I explore the post-representational configurations of knowledge/agency in Benjamin and Derrida, as Benjamin's "messianic temporality" and Derrida's "spectrality" help to delineate the "fictive" forms of agency and truth that are vital to a transformative politics.

Benjamin cultivates a form of critical receptivity to the Not Yet by means of a historiographical critique that undercuts the conventional historian's claims to coherence and undermines progressivist interpretations of history. His theoretical intervention is at once epistemologically and politically radical: his theoretical practices are concerned to re-value temporal experience in a way that demands action and that elicits agency. This is a necessarily layered endeavor. Attentive to the silencing of suffering in those modes of historical analysis that reiterate the story of the victors, Benjamin elicits the silenced, the unvoiced, those who have labored to produce histories that denied them. This is an ethical project, for sure. In accord with Theodor Adorno, for example, Benjamin's theoretical praxis is attuned to the ways in which the production of history and historical knowledge can become complicit with suffering, either in its refusal to recognize or give voice, or in attempting to justify its necessity. However, this is not simply an ethical endeavor, but an epistemological one – and a significantly temporal operation.

Benjamin deploys these unvoiced voices in order to critically interrupt the smooth surfaces of the hegemony of the present order. His critical historical praxis endeavors to "grasp [...] the constellation which his own era has formed with a definite earlier one" (xviii). Establishing a critical interruption, he "recognizes the sign of a messianic cessation of happening, or, put differently, a revolutionary chance to fight for an oppressed past" (xvii). Benjamin thus fashions a counter-hegemonic sensibility in his encounters with what is past. More so, he figures the past precisely as active within the present configuration. Constellations become "readable" in "moments of danger"; that is to say, the presence of the past does not always have the same force (ghosts only speak in times of crisis). Benjamin's figuring of the past within the present, then, is post-representational when it speaks to the possibility of fashioning a future that breaks with the hegemonic tendencies of the present.

Benjamin's re-visioning of the chronological in favor of "cairological" or "qualitative" time "suggests multiple and singular temporalities that discursively unite past and present moments" with epistemological and political implications (Curthoys online). Transformative political agency is always "untimely" (see also Chambers 27). Breaking with the time of measure, the time of commodities, Benjamin evokes a "tiger's leap" over "empty" world historical time in favor of evoking the transformative force of those other times that refuse to be consigned to the dustbin of history (xiv). Thus severed from the linear order of succession, and marking the non-synchronicity of the present with itself, those other temporalities enable a critical engagement with the problem of agency and truth.

In Derrida, I find a no less radical form of praxis. Derrida engages Marx by means of an exploration of the ways in which the simple invocation of Marx's name unsettles the contemporary moment. (*Specters* was written in the context of a triumphant neoliberal hegemony given its most succinct articulation in Francis Fukuyama's injudicious claims of the "end of history.") The specter, Derrida argues, marks the presence of the unresolved and active past within the force field of possibilities in the present. The specter is out of time (out of its temporal chronology): "A spectral moment, a moment that no longer belongs to time, if one understands by this word the linking of modalized presents [...] Furtive and untimely, the specter does not belong to that time" (ix). As such, the specter speaks a different kind of truth to the dominant knowledges of the present.

As Wendy Brown has argued, these post-representational constellations of past, present, and future moments of struggle act as critical *interruptions*, as a "political and intellectual gesture of disinterring repressed emancipatory hopes and experiences" (157). Seizing hold of a "memory as it flashes up in a moment of danger," or engaging the still unsettling presence of the past in order to affect and redirect the flow of the present, makes possible the recovery and invention of possibilities that otherwise become precluded (Benjamin vi). It is in this context that Brown reads Derrida's engagement with Marx (or Marx's specters) as finally an engagement with the work of a transformative agency: "learning to live with haunts or specters – with things that shape the present, rendering it as always permeated by an *elsewhere* but in a fashion that is inconstant, ephemeral, and hence not fully mappable" (145). She provocatively suggests that agency can be rewritten as a form of conjuration: "what lives on [...] what is conjured [...] how past generations and events occupy the *force-field* of the present, how they claim us, and how they haunt, plague, and inspirit our imaginations and visions for the future" (150). The specter, then, is perhaps one of the most crucial "crags and jags" that render the world malleable to intervention, and agency is circumscribed *and* enabled because of its force.

The affective-ethical-epistemological work of utopian impulses therefore speaks to an active rendering of the world and to the weaving of past into future by political subjects. Attention to temporal dynamics is vital to utopian figurations as they seek to delineate the complexity of relations that compose the present moment, and yet they also seek to make that totality *glimmer* with potentiality. "History" does indeed "already think [...] the thinking subject and is inscribed in the forms through which it must think" (Jameson, *Late Marxism* 24); but within that history, and the futures it contains, there reside fissures and glimpses of potentiality to be elicited and activated. In terms of agency, then, part of what emerges in the utopian subject, when desire turns into hope as a "directing act of a cognitive kind" is the return of a past that has been silenced or *repressed* (Bloch 12). This return thus creates a new space wherein one can "choose" to be constituted by a different past: one can recognize herself as *constituted*, for sure, but also as a *constituent* part of a world and a history that remains in process.[13] A vital dynamic of messianic time and spectrality/hauntology, then, is a dramatic and felt *switch* from a serial constitution in "homogenous empty time" to a homologous constitution across moments that are disconnected in the linear-temporal movement. The maneuvers that Vanegeim, Benjamin, and Derrida theorize here make such a switch palpable and possible at the affective-cognitive (and historical) level.

The Untimely

> Philosophy is an experience of thinking about the breach in time.
> Alain Badiou, *Manifesto for Philosophy*

It is in this context that I aim to analyze recent theoretical work wherein figures of truth are mapped precisely in terms of a disruptive untimeliness. Since agency can be given an energizing direction from the potential of the past and the future as they inhere in the present, the time of truth in contemporary theory is similarly untimely.

---

13   And thus, in Adornian mode, potentiality can be elicited from the "damaged life."

Critical, radical, and utopian modes of political theory have sidestepped or undercut the epistemological or metaphysical privilege claimed by "truth" (in any a-temporal formulation) as a ruse of Power. Critical modes of theory, then, seek instead to confront, and so to counter, power (and power/knowledge regimes) in their entwined and overlapping material and discursive forms. Such a confrontation with the powerful lies of the present is undertaken, not in the name of truth, but in the name of possibility. Like utopianism's double gesture, these critical maneuvers are characterized by a double move of (genealogical) critique – directed within and against the hegemonic and hegemonizing forces in the complex of tendencies that compose the present – and (utopian) anticipation – wherein newly fashioned, but immanently grounded, figurations seek to make that totality *glimmer* with potentiality. This dual move undercuts the cohesion and closure of the present as always-already a powerful form of falsity and imaginatively fabricates new possibilities.

One of the most significant dynamics of contemporary theory is, however, the project of reclaiming and refunctioning discourses of truth. I have suggested that this project has two registers: the refunctioning of "truth" as a cognitive form that is at once situated and perspectival, on the one hand; and as anticipatory, "fictive," or imaginative, on the other. Mapping this configuration in the context of the ethical, political, affective, and epistemological implications of the theorization of untimely temporalities might help to explain why Badiou, even as he is a vital theorist of truth, can pose the problem thus: "the vital political question of our times is not truth, but fiction" ("Truth Process" online). Contemporary radical theory thus evokes dissident *fictions* as disruptive, untimely, transformative *truths*.

Badiou's articulation of the structure of a truth is exemplary. He proposes: "as long as nothing happens, aside from that which conforms to the rules of a state of things, there can admittedly be cognition, correct statements, accumulated knowledge; there cannot be truth" (*Manifesto* 36). On the contrary, he characterizes truth as "first of all something new" ("Truth Process" online). Badiou thus distinguishes between knowledge as the order of cognition and truth. The former is characterized by science, "techne," and is "always a continuation, an application, a repetition" that is "only concerned with what already is" ("Truth Process" online). The latter is an interruption to the order of cognition itself: "A truth appears in its newness because an eventful supplement interrupts repetition" ("Truth Process" online). Crucially, truth takes the form of the Event itself: that which occurs in time, but after which one is literally looking at a new world. For Badiou, Events can occur in four realms: of politics (e.g., French Revolution), science (e.g., Galileo and physics), art, and love. Events are thus truthful openings that create radically other possible ways of living, being, and acting, and radically challenge or reject the conceptual discipline of the order from which they erupt. As James Ingram puts it, truth for Badiou is "something between a principle and an epiphany, as when we speak of the truth of an artwork or a love. Truths are both world-disclosing and practical: they cast the world in a new light and demand that we do something" ("Can Universalism Still Be Radical?" 565–6). Consequently, the distinction between knowledge as cognition and truth as Event is made on the basis of the different temporal orders to which each belongs: this maps to the temporal framework with which I have been concerned, wherein knowledge can be theorized as belonging to the time of measure, chronology, and quantification, while truth belongs to "eventual time" itself.

The most important political question of our times might, then, not be one of truths but fictions, because, in their formal structure of a critical rejection of that which merely is, fictions contain the possibility of the Event – the possibility of a radical and thoroughgoing challenge to the present hegemonic order in the name of a counter-hegemonic interruption that could generate new truths as not only new orientations within the world, but, quite literally, new worlds themselves. Truth, then, belongs to the order of the messianic and those other structures that question and anticipate the other, different, and better lives that might be possible. So too, Negri explicitly draws together the critical connections between temporal modes, imaginative and critical truths, and counter-hegemonic forms of political agency. For the moment, then, I give him the closing words:

Time is the concrete reality of my life in so far as it is the substance of my collective, productive and constitutive-of-the-new being. Outside of a materialist, dynamic and collective conception of time it is impossible to think the revolution. Time is [...] a horizon [...]. Revolution is born from the pathways of a constitutive phenomenology of temporality [...]. [Thus, I] repropose the project of the imagination to Power, or better, against Power. As the classics teach us, the imagination is the most concrete of temporal powers (21).

Works Cited

Agamben, Giorgio. *Potentialities: Collected Essays in Philosophy*. Ed and trans. Daniel Heller-Roazen. Stanford: Stanford University Press, 1999.

Atwood, Margaret. *Cat's Eyes*. London: Virago, 1990.

Badiou, Alain. *Manifesto for Philosophy*. Ed. and trans. Norman Madarasz. Albany: State University of New York Press, 1992.

———. "On the Truth Process: An Open Lecture by Alain Badiou.". European Graduate School, EGS, Saas-Fee, Switzerland, August 2002. 30 October 2005 <http://www.egs.edu/faculty/badiou/badiou-truth-process-2002.html>.

Benjamin, Walter. "Theses on the Philosophy of History." *Illuminations*. Ed. Hannah Arendt. Trans. Harry Zohn. London: Fontana, 1992.

Bennett, Jane. *The Enchantment of Modern Life: Attachments, Crossing, and Ethics*. Princeton: Princeton University Press, 2001.

Bloch, Ernst. *The Principle of Hope*. Trans. Neville Plaice, Stephen Plaice, and Paul Knight. 3 Vols. Oxford: Basil Blackwell, 1986.

Braidotti, Rosi. *Metamorphoses: Toward a Materialist Theory of Becoming*. Cambridge: Polity, 2002.

Brown, Wendy. *Politics Out of History*. Princeton: Princeton University Press, 2001.

Chakrabarty, Dipesh. "The Time of History and the Times of the Gods." *The Politics of Culture in the Shadow of Capital*. Ed. Lisa Lowe and David Lloyd. Durham: Duke University Press, 1997. 35–60.

Colebrook, Claire. *Gilles Deleuze*. London: Routledge, 2002.

Connolly, William E. *Why I Am Not A Secularist*. Minneapolis: University of Minnesota Press, 1999.

Curthoys, Edward. "Benjamin's Imaginary." *Theory and Event* 3.2 (1999). 25 August 2005 <http://muse.jhu.edu/journals/theory_and_event/v003/3.2r_curthoys.html>.

Debord, Guy. *The Society of the Spectacle*. Trans. Donald Nicolson Smith. New York: Zone, 1994.

Derrida, Jacques. *Specters of Marx: The State of the Debt, the Work of Mourning, and the New International*. Trans. Peggy Kamuf. New York: Routledge, 1994.

Foucault, Michel. *Power/Knowledge: Selected Interviews and Other Writings 1972–1977*. Trans. Colin Gordon. London: Longman, 1986.

Geoghegan, Vincent. "Remembering the Future." *Not Yet: Reconsidering Ernst Bloch*. Ed. Jamie Owen Daniel and Tom Moylan. London: Verso, 1997. 15–33.

Grosz, Elizabeth. *The Nick of Time: Politics, Evolution, and the Untimely*. Durham: Duke University Press, 2004.

Haraway, Donna. "A Cyborg Manifesto: Science, Technology, and Socialist Feminism in the Late Twentieth Century." *Simians, Cyborg, and Women: The Reinvention of Nature*. 23 July 2005 <http://www.stanford.edu/dept/HPS/Haraway/CyborgManifesto.html>.

Hobbes, Thomas. *Leviathan*. Ed. C.B. Macpherson. London: Penguin, 1968.

Ingram, James D. "Can Universalism Still Be Radical? Alain Badiou's Politics of Truth." *Constellations* 12.4 (December 2005): 561–73.

Jameson, Fredric. *Archaeologies of the Future: The Desire Called Utopia and Other Science Fictions*. London: Verso, 2005.

———. *Late Marxism: Adorno, Or, The Persistence of the Dialectic*. London: Verso, 1990.

Levitas, Ruth. *The Concept of Utopia*. Syracuse: Syracuse University Press, 1990.

———. "Educated Hope: Ernst Bloch on Abstract and Concrete Utopia." *Not Yet: Reconsidering Ernst Bloch*. Ed. Jamie Owen Daniel and Tom Moylan. London: Verso, 1997. 65–79.

Lowe, Lisa and David Lloyd. "Introduction." *The Politics of Culture in the Shadow of Capital*. 1–34.

Marcos, Subcomandante Insurgente. *Our Word Is Our Weapon: Selected Writings*. Ed. Juana Ponce de León. New York: Seven Stories, 2002.

McManus, Susan. *Fictive Theories: Toward A Deconstructive and Utopian Political Imagination*. New York: Palgrave, 2005.

Negri, Antonio. *Time for Revolution*. Trans. Matteo Mandarini. New York: Continuum, 2003.

Nietzsche, Friedrich. *The Gay Science*. Trans. Walter Kauffman. London: Penguin, 1974.

―― *Thus Spoke Zarathustra. The Portable Nietzsche*. Trans. Walter Kauffman. London: Penguin, 1976.

Smith, Paul. *Millennial Dreams: Contemporary Culture and Capital in the North*. London: Verso, 1997.

Vanegeim, Raoul. *The Revolution of Everyday Life*. Trans. Donald Nicolson Smith. London: Rebel, 1983.

Wood, David. "The Art of Time: An Interview with David Wood." *Contretemps* 3 (July 2002). 24 June 2005 <http://www.usyd.edu.au/contretemps/3July2002/time-wood.pdf>.

CHRISTOPHER YORKE

Three Archetypes for the Clarification of Utopian Theorizing

Clarifications

My aim in this essay is to offer a strategy for translating universal statements about Utopia into particular statements.[1] I do this by drawing out the implicit, temporally embedded points of reference in such statements. Universal statements that I find troublesome are those of the form "utopia is x," where "x" can be anything from "the receding horizon" to "the nation of the virtuous." To such statements, I want to put the following questions: which utopias; in what sense; and when was that, is that, or will that be, the case for utopias? Through an exploration of these lines of questioning, I arrive at three archetypes for the clarification of utopian theorizing which can serve to provide the answers: namely, utopian historicism, utopian presentism, and utopian futurism.[2] I argue that the employment of

---

[1] I would like to thank Dudley Knowles, Tony Milligan, and Masaki Ichinose for their input on earlier drafts of this essay.

[2] It is important to note that I herein use the terms "historicism", "presentism", and "futurism" in novel ways, in that they are divorced from their usual contexts of use. The term "historicism" is culled from its philosophical context in which history is considered to be reality's sole defining factor. Similarly, I separate "presentism" from the metaphysical doctrine that what exists in the present is all that exists. For the purposes of this essay, I commit myself to nothing so extreme. My utopian historicism and presentism simply demarcate, respectively, that the past or the present is the chosen temporal frame of reference for a particular statement about Utopia. "Futurism," likewise, is severed from its most famous context as a modernist artistic movement.

these archetypes temporally grounds statements about Utopia in the past, present, or future, and thus forces discussion of discrete particulars instead of abstract universals with no meaningful referents.

Given the imprecise manner in which the term "utopia" is often employed in discourse – whether academic or non-academic – confusion frequently, and rightly, ensues. There are various possible sources for this confusion. The first of these is the sheer volume and wide variety of sociopolitical schemes that have been regarded as utopian by utopian theorists, historians, or authors of fiction. Bibliographers of utopian literature (such as Lyman Tower Sargent) face the challenging task of sorting out those visions of other worlds that belong in the utopian canon from those that do not. However, utopian bibliographies generally err on the side of inclusiveness, and a sufficient range and number of utopias remain in the realm of discourse to make the practice of distinguishing a utopia from a non-utopia (or even a dystopia) challenging at best and baffling at worst. For example, should Dante's *Paradiso* be considered a utopian work or not? There is no easy answer to this question, and thus there is ample room for dispute on this subject between active or prospective utopian bibliographers.

Another cause of imprecision and concern in utopian theory is definitional in nature. Ruth Levitas has pointed out the fact that most dictionaries give at least two competing definitions of "utopia," such as the following from *Chambers Twentieth Century Dictionary*: (1) "any imaginary state of ideal perfection," and (2) "an impossibly ideal scheme, especially for social improvement" (quoted in Levitas 3). Thus, in the minds of many careless language-users, the "best imaginable" and "impossible" states are conflated, by definition, in the term "utopia." The ultimate implication of such a conflation is that Utopia is impossible because the ideal is unachievable.

Utopian futurism, as I here construe it, is concerned with the form, content, and function of eventual manifestations or visions of Utopia.

Defining Utopia instead as an expression of desire for the betterment of sociopolitical conditions, as Levitas does, steers us clear of the basic definitional conflation discussed above, but still leaves us with no expectations regarding the content, form, or function of utopian articulations (8). Levitas takes this open-endedness to be a virtue, as it serves to explain the wide variety of past and extant utopias, as well as utopias to come (181). However, her definition of Utopia as an expression of desire does not resolve the problematic ambiguity of how "utopia" as a term is generally employed in discourse, which does not typically accord with her definition. I believe that the ambiguity that concerns us here turns on implicit assumptions regarding, as Levitas puts it, the content, form, and function of utopias – in other words, the speaker's views on the permissible scope of utopian visions, the manner in which these can be acceptably communicated to others, and the observable power these wield or lack in the sociopolitical sphere (Levitas 4–6). Such premises will shift over time, of course; but the appropriate way to address these changes is to take note of the discrete temporal frame to which each statement refers, rather than appeal to a universal and timeless human quality (such as desire) that accounts for diversity in the field but gives little explanatory ground for perceived consistency within it.

The Universal Voice in Utopian Theory

Due at least in part to their desire to resolve the ambiguity that dogs utopian discourse, theorists in the field of utopian studies often lapse into making universal statements about what they consider to be the essential features of utopias. For one theorist, utopias might be only those ideal societies that have as their focus laws and institutions; for another, utopias might be only those ideal societies that focus on individual freedom and self-realization. Unfortunately, the accumulation of opposing universal statements within the canon of utopian studies gives the appearance that subjectivism is the dominant theoretical framework in the field. J.C. Davis has commented on this seemingly muddled state of affairs in utopian theory, and has identified what he considers to be the main problem:

The difficulty that we are laboring under at the moment is that the adjective "utopian" is being used as a catch-all label for all forms of ideal society. Two problems can and do arise from this. The first is that contradictory statements are made about Utopia by authors who are examining different forms of ideal society. Thus we may be told that utopianism is an expression of great optimism, or of profound pessimism; that Utopia enables men to live naturally, or that it is designed to subdue and discipline human nature; that in utopia the state withers away, or that it becomes more complex and comprehensive, even that state and society become coincident; that utopia begins with ideal men, perfect human beings, or that it assumes that unrighteous and recalcitrant people will be its raw material (*Utopia and the Ideal Society* 17–18).

Subjectivism in utopian theory and contradictory statements about Utopia arising from conceptual confusion are the problems that Davis attempts to mitigate via the introduction of five distinct types of ideal society (see Table 1): Cockaygne, Arcadia, the Perfect Moral Commonwealth, the Millennium, and Utopia ("History of Utopia" 8–10). Utopia, for Davis, is simply that variety of ideal society that takes humanity and nature as flawed, and that possesses a perfected set of laws and institutions that optimally respond to those flaws, such that progress from that state is not possible (given that "progress" from a state of perfection is more accurately described as regression). Davis's definition of Utopia is precision-cut, due to his understanding that "if there are rules to the game [...] the vaguer or more elastic one makes one's operative definitions, the more carefully one has to justify exclusions" ("History of Utopia" 6).

Ideal Society	Nature	Institutions	Human Nature	Progress
Cockaygne	Surreally bounteous	Eliminated completely	Insatiable	Not possible
Arcadia	Consistent, not excessive	None, except family	Consistent, not excessive	Not possible
Perfect Moral Commonwealth	As is	Those agreed upon	Perfected	Institutional reform
Millennium	Dependant on deity	Incidental	Fundamentally flawed	Dependant on deity
Utopia	As is	Perfected	As is	Not possible

Table 1. Davis's Five Types of Ideal Society.

By breaking up the broad and undifferentiated concept of Utopia into five subtypes of ideal society, of which Utopia properly defined reappears as only one of these subtypes, Davis has narrowed the scope for potential contradiction, but not completely eliminated it. Theorists are still free to make temporally ungrounded universal statements about Utopia under Davis's schema, such as the claim that "utopia is a nursery for tyrants" (read: for now and forever). It is just that the number of candidate utopias referred to by this type of universal statement is fewer, and thus the chance of the universal statement having a plausible but contradictory theoretical competitor is significantly reduced.

What is ultimately missing from Davis's analysis, however, is a convention for reducing or eliminating the application of universal statements that evoke the concept of Utopia in a deceivingly atemporal manner. Utopia in the general sense really refers to nothing in particular, not even a quality shared by all the discrete utopias that together make up its frame of reference. To make a Wittgensteinian point: we cannot expect more precision from the generic concept Utopia than from the generic concept "game"; although there are meaningful generalizations that can be made within the scope of a *particular* game, such as "in the game of chess, all chess pieces start off in a set arrangement on the chessboard." There are no corresponding universals (metalanguage) to capture the generic "game" concept; not even "all games are leisure activities" (because, as it happens, some games are played professionally). To quote Ludwig Wittgenstein: "the concept 'game' is a concept with blurred edges" (Wittgenstein §71). Thus, there is no individual cord that runs the entire length of the conceptual rope; nothing we can grip onto that is essential to "games," any more than there is anything we can speak of that is essentially "utopian."

What can be done to address this manifest conceptual opacity, I suggest, is to reform linguistic practice. We can limit our scope of reference to particulars, eschewing any "meta-utopian" universal statements in our discourses. I suggest that employing a temporal frame of reference when making statements about Utopia is a possible solution to this quandary. If one can determine what era, or what exact moment in time (if this is possible), a theorist is implicitly referencing in her or his statements, then more often than not a seemingly universal statement about utopias can be broken down into particular statements about this or that utopian vision, social movement, or publication.

My methodological recommendation is not meant to detract from Davis's classificatory schema, for his distinctions and his analyses are in fact most helpful. I am not offering a competing theory, but rather a supplementary tool for theoretical disambiguation. Whereas Davis focuses on certain salient features of various visions of ideal societies – such as their relation to nature, their approach to social institutions, their implicit assumptions about human nature, their attitudes toward perfection, and the means (if any) they employ to bring about progress – my approach targets the universal statement itself as the culprit of conceptual confusion. Decoding a universal statement about Utopia into a particular statement, via identifying its implicit temporal frame of reference, narrows the scope of the statement until the author can be understood, in all probability, to mean only one thing. This can dramatically aid us in evaluating apparently universal statements about utopias, and in checking their consistency with other statements made on the subject. Now it falls to me to say more about such universal statements and their implicit, temporally particular frames of reference.

Decoding Universals into Temporal Particulars

David Plath's dramatic first line from his book, *Aware of Utopia*, is a statement that implicitly utilizes the universal form. Provocatively, he proclaims that "utopia is a bore" (ix). Plath's statement, however, does not express any clear fact. To say that "utopias are boring" is meaningful only insofar as "unicorns are charming" is: which is to say, it is a statement that lacks the usual criteria we might employ in verifying its truth or falsity. We might interpret Plath to be here passing judgment on the worth of utopian schemes *tout court*. Cases could be made for or against such a judgment, but what evidence would our arguments rest upon? We cannot access the testimony of utopians, either actual or fictional, without first determining Plath's temporal frame of reference – his scope, as stated, is too broad to effectively attack or defend. We need therefore to analyze whether Plath's statement refers to the utopias of the past, present, or future; and this in turn will reveal further underlying assumptions that he is making about that specific set of utopias.

Initially, we might reword Plath's universal statement as "all utopias are boring" or "life in any utopia would be boring." At the first level of objection, we should note that reasonable disagreement is possible. I could say that "utopia is exciting" (or "all utopias are exciting" or "life in any utopia would be exciting"); and this seems at least as plausible as Plath's statement. Without reference to particular cases, there is no way to break this deadlock between the two conflicting universal statements. It seems that in order to make any headway, we have to infer an intended temporal target for Plath, which we can attempt by decoding it within the greater context of his article, or by using other background information at our disposal. Although this is usually not a serious problem with most authors, a great deal of interpretive legwork will nevertheless be required to properly contextualize the statement; and in that process opportunities for misunderstanding will necessarily present themselves. Eventually, we may surmise that Plath is commenting on the sociopolitical stagnancy of ancient depictions of perfectionist utopias; or perhaps we may take him to be claiming that the utopian writers of a certain era generally made poor novelists. At a certain point, we, as readers, will have to choose one of these paths for our take on Plath.

Even if we can agree on one of these interpretations of Plath, and make sense of his statement within the context of his own work, we may still have difficulty evaluating his point when it is contrasted with the work of other utopian theorists. For example, we may read in George Kateb that "the form of a modern utopia need not bear much resemblance to any of the utopias devised in the past by idealist or perfectionist thinkers" (15). Given this broader context, it becomes more important for us to be able to decisively determine which kind of utopias – modern or ancient – Plath regards as "boring." If we interpret Plath as referring, even partially, to modern utopias, we need to formulate for him his most likely response to H.G. Wells's assurance that "the Modern Utopia must be not static but kinetic, must shape not as a permanent state but as a hopeful stage, leading to a long ascent of stages" (4). If we take the statement "utopia is boring" to refer to modern utopias, then defenders of Plath will need to come up with an answer to the question, "how can a kinetic utopia consisting of an ascent of stages be boring?"

In light of these objections, we might charitably interpret Plath's statement such that it reads: "the utopias of *antiquity* are a bore." But that is still too broad. Many utopias, even ancient ones, remain distinct enough from political reality to capture the popular imagination: Plato's work, most notably, remains fresh and vital material to modern readers. Let us, then, refashion Plath's statement so that it is even more particular: "I, David Plath, presently believe that the utopias of antiquity, especially utopias x, y, and z, would have been boring to live in, for reasons *i*, *ii*, and *iii*". Although such statements of opinion have but a weak role to play in utopian theorizing, we are still in a better position than had we rested with the initial statement "utopia is a bore."

Here, I want to recall that my central concern is the great potential for misunderstanding and vacuity that unnecessarily universal statements generate: thus, I chose Plath's opening line not as the worst offender in this regard but simply as a token of a problematic universal statement. To be fair, I admitted that Utopia is a paradoxical concept at the best of times, even when analyzed within a clearly delimited scope (as in Davis's schema). By "paradoxical" I mean, for instance, that we are routinely asked by critics – in the tradition of Karl Popper – to accept that humankind's best efforts to produce a state wherein perpetual peace could attain would inevitably result in the bloodiest of conflicts. This is precisely the kind of sharp ironic contrast that dominates much of utopian theory, and which tends to leave students of utopianism conceptually confused: how can attempts to create the best form of sociopolitical organization result in some of the worst? Of course, as we look back on the events of the twentieth century with a cringe, we may feel inclined to concede that, indeed, the violence required to bring about a utopia of peace creates only a surface paradox, caused by the lack of similitude between peaceful utopian ends and aggressive utopian means. However, we need to remember that the twentieth century is just one era among many, and that it may not have always been, and may not always be, necessarily the case that striving for perfection causes widespread suffering.

There are other contested sites within utopian theory, wherein paradoxes arise that are seemingly insoluble, or at least more deeply troublesome: namely, those wherein we have two antinomic universal statements, both intelligible, and both of which are part of the canon of utopian theory: i.e., "utopia is necessarily authoritarian" and "utopia is necessarily individualistic." Of course, it is acceptable if two theorists happen to disagree on some theoretical point or another – this is typically the manner in which academic disciplines make progress. However, as it happens, utopian theory is thoroughly dominated by such disagreements, to the point that the idea of a coherent body of utopian theory seems to be a hopeless proposition unless we are willing to abandon the Law of Non-Contradiction. From Paul Turner's introduction to his translation of Thomas More's *Utopia*, I take the following Walt Whitman lines:

> Do I contradict myself?
> Very well then ...I contradict myself;
> I am large ... I contain multitudes (12).

It is my position that we cannot afford to be quite so beatific about contradictions in the canon of utopian theory. Whereas from a literary standpoint, it is not crippling to have contradictions spring up within a given utopia, or between two or more utopias, from a theoretical standpoint consistency is a highly desirable quality.

Temporal Particulars: Three Archetypes for the Clarification of Utopian Theorizing

To iterate: what I am objecting to is the proliferation of unwarranted universal statements about the essential features of Utopia, a proliferation that serves to confuse the real issues at stake in discourses about Utopia. But how can we make ourselves theoretically clear? I argue that by employing three theoretical archetypes that operate specifically in terms of temporal particulars rather than universals, we can end up with fewer antinomic premises and conclusions in the body of utopian theory. The three archetypes I propose are: 1) utopian historicism, which asks the questions: what was the form of presentation used for utopias in the past; what was the substantial content of past utopias; and what socio-political function did utopian visions have in the past; 2) utopian presentism, which asks the questions: what is the form of presentation used for utopias in the present, what is the substantial content of current utopias, and what sociopolitical function do utopian visions presently fulfill; and 3) utopian futurism, which asks the questions: what will the form of presentation for utopias likely be in the future, what will the substantial content of future utopias likely be, and what sociopolitical function will utopian visions likely have in the future?[1] Thus – with reference to Levitas – the form, content, and function of utopias are taken as central in this schema; although they are here divided in a manner according to their implicit or explicit temporal frames of reference.

These theoretical archetypes – utopian historicism, presentism, and futurism – can, I suggest, provide useful tools for analyzing and evaluating statements about utopian theory. When they are ignored, utopian theory as a whole can appear to be a mass of paradoxical or antinomic statements. For example, we may hear that "utopia is aspatial and atemporal" and also that "utopia is a spatiotemporal concept"; and that while it is often maintained that "utopia is unrealizable by definition," it is also heard that "progress is the realization of utopias." By employing these theoretical archetypes, I hope to show that many of these puzzles and seeming inconsistencies within utopian theory can be fruitfully resolved.

Allow me, then, to demonstrate a possible application for the archetypes, via the juxtaposition of some sample quotations, below (see Tables 2.0, 2.1, 2.2). Despite their obvious differences, what links these quotations is that they all employ a certain voice: namely, a universal or overly general tone, which I believe leads to conceptual confusion. Many of these generalizations can be broken down into temporal particulars and made more intelligible. Of course, it is hard to part with the universal voice: grand, sweeping aphorisms take better hold of the human imagination than the recitation of dry facts; and utopian theorists – to indulge in a relatively benign generalization of my own – no doubt often want to express themselves in a memorable fashion. However, I think that we must try to reign in the universal voice so that antinomies of the kind exhibited below arise less frequently in the discourse of utopian theory:

Judith Shklar:	Oscar Wilde:
Utopia is nowhere, not only geographically, but historically as well. It exists neither in the past or in the future. Indeed, its esthetic and intellectual tension arises precisely from the melancholy contrast between what is and what will be (164).	A map of the world that does not include Utopia is not worth even glancing at, for it leaves out the one country at which Humanity is always landing. And when humanity lands there, it looks out, and, seeing a better country, sets sail. Progress is the realisation of utopias (1089).

Table 2.0. Shklar vs. Wilde.

Here, we appear to have two competing metaphysical claims: Judith Shklar holds that Utopia does not exist anytime or anywhere; while Oscar Wilde holds that history is a series of spatio-temporally concrete manifestations of Utopia (in the only part of his passage I would identify as historicist). Although these passages contradict each other, both of the claims appear to have some sense to them, and we seemingly have little cause to favor one over the other. However, it is by noting the presentist voice employed by Shklar as she describes what motivates utopian longing in the here and now, disavowing any concerns with the past and future, that we can see that she is chiefly concerned with Utopia's function in fomenting sociopolitical tensions in the present. And by noting the historicist voice used by Wilde as he describes the function utopias of the past have played in motivating sociopolitical development, we can begin to see that Wilde and Shklar are each just stating differing loci of interests rather than contesting each other's metaphysical doctrines. Wilde's presentist comment, in the first sentence of the passage, is actually in accord with Shklar's remarks about the intellectual importance of Utopia.

Francis and Barbara Golffing:	Ralf Dahrendorf:
Each generation entertains its own image of the future, and that image is eminently historic. Even as the world has not stood still since Campanella, or Bacon, or William Morris wrote, so neither has that counterworld – no-world, no-place (*Utopos*) – stood still which forms its inevitable complement. [...] The office of any utopia is to *orient* mankind: that is to say, turn men's faces toward the sun. But the only sun that matters, as every true utopist knows, is the rising sun (39).	Utopias have but a nebulous past and no future; they are suddenly there, and there to stay, suspended in mid-time [...]. It is hard to link, by rational argument or empirical analysis, the wide river of history – flowing more rapidly at some points, more slowly at others, but always moving – and the tranquil village pond of Utopia (104).

Table 2.1. Golffing and Golffing vs. Dahrendorf.

The contradiction in this case is a more subtle one about the function of Utopia: Francis and Barbara Golffing seem to be claiming that the role of Utopia is to orient humanity to the future; while Ralf Dahrendorf holds that there is really no temporal link by which humankind *could* orient itself to a utopian future, as Utopia exists only outside of time, in "mid-time." Again, on the surface both claims appear to be plausible, and there seems to be no way to break the deadlock between them. Yet, looking more closely, we can see that the Golffings remarks range across each archetype identified thus far. Their first sentence is an irreducible universal statement, the second a historicist comment, the third a presentist interpretation, and the fourth a futurist gloss. Dahrendorf, on the other hand, can be read mainly as a historicist, albeit a frustrated one, as he finds difficulty in connecting visions of Utopia to concrete historical events (it should be noted here that many other utopian historicists do not make this complaint). But failing to recognize the sociopolitical function of past utopias does not preclude such functions from obtaining with present utopias; having a "nebulous past and no future" is no conceptual obstacle to existing as an influence in the present, a point Dahrendorf might concede to the Golffings, despite the unfocused nature of their attack. There remains, however, an indissoluble antinomy between these utopian theorists – but then again, this is a symptom of a healthy academic climate. Centrally to my point here, it is important to note that utilizing the archetypes led us to the specific site of theoretical dissension: the Golffings second sentence which refers to the ever-changing unitary counter-world of Utopia, developing with (and perhaps against) the history of the world that informs it; versus Dahrendorf's vision of multiple static utopias that remain unrelated to history. Let us move to a consideration of one final case:

Chad Walsh:	George Kateb:
Utopia is not very bacchanalian. Life is real and earnest; one must do his appointed task. Too much individualistic self-expression, sexually or otherwise, may elicit frowns or worse. There is, however, adequate opportunity for socially-approved channels of self-expression, such as begetting and conceiving eugenic children, inventing useful procedures, and composing odes to strengthen the social solidarity of the utopians (59).	There are rationalist utopias, hedonist utopias, ascetic-spiritual utopias, paradisal utopias, agrarian utopias, mechanized utopias, utopias of virtue, or craft, or play. More summarily, utopian theorists have ranged themselves on both sides in their answers to these basic questions: Shall Utopia be a place of abundance or austerity? Shall utopian politics be aristocratic or democratic? Is work or leisure the right mode of existence? Is the good life one in which public involvements or private pursuits absorb the main energies of the individual? (5).

Table 2.2. Walsh vs. Kateb.

Here, Chad Walsh seems to be arguing for some universal stipulations on the content of Utopia: namely, that utopias must be those visions of an ideal society that exhibit chastity and industriousness. These stipulations disregard the fact that the Marquis de Sade's *Philosophie dans le Boudoir* is often considered to describe a utopia of sorts – as is, less problematically, Henry Neville's *Island of Pines* – and in both of these works sexual promiscuity and self-indulgence feature heavily. Kateb, on the other hand, accepts the *de facto* plurality of utopias in the past and proceeds to catalogue some of the many types of utopian visions that he has encountered previously, among which are counted some that can be described as hedonistic. We can diffuse the apparent tension between these two utopian theorists by noting that Walsh is implicitly employing a historicist voice and dealing with the issue of utopian content in a partially normative, rather than wholly descriptive, manner; while Kateb is chiefly utilizing a historicist voice to discuss a wider scope of past utopias, and describing their contents in a purely descriptive way. Perhaps Walsh, by refraining from employing a universal tone, might have been more specific about the time in which the chaste utopias he is discussing dominated the utopian landscape; at which point, Kateb could question his claim to the upright characters of those utopias with more precision. It is unnecessary vagueness brought on by employing the universal that grinds this debate to an apparent deadlock.

Distinctions

While I am confident that the three archetypes I propose for the clarification of utopian theorizing might easily be applied to deflating a broader set of seeming antinomies, I am aware that they are neither exhaustive nor as ideally exact as could be hoped for. One could easily tease out mixed archetypes, or invent new archetypes altogether unconsidered here. The universal voice, so derided by myself, might even be employed to collect statements one considers to neatly capture the necessary and timeless features of Utopia. Of course, I would discourage the application of this latter theoretical filter whenever possible, because as I have stated previously I believe that this is where utopian theory goes wrong: when we imagine that there is a Platonic Form of Utopia somewhere in the heavens that exemplifies all the necessary features of utopias, to which we can then hold up each particular instance of Utopia for the purposes of comparison. I argue instead that the theoretical situation, as it stands, looks rather more like Wittgenstein's family resemblance story. To recast the point: just as there is very little that is essential to the concept "game," there is very little that is essential about the concept of Utopia. And, just as we can say that *some* games involve throwing dice, but not *all*, so too must we avoid making similar sweeping statements about utopias, and thus mistakenly overstepping our epistemic bounds:

> It is as if someone were to say: "A game consists in moving objects about on a surface according to certain rules..."
> and we replied: You seem to be thinking of board games, but there are others. You can make your definition correct by expressly restricting it to those games (Wittgenstein §3).

Works Cited

Alexander, Peter, and Roger Gill (eds.). *Utopias*. London: Gerald Duckworth, 1984.
Dahrendorf, Ralf. "Out of Utopia: Toward a Reorientation of Sociological Analysis." *Utopia*. Ed. Kateb. 103–26.
Davis, J. C. "The History of Utopia: the Chronology of Nowhere." *Utopias*. Ed. Alexander and Gill. 1–17.
____ *Utopia and the Ideal Society*. Cambridge: Cambridge University Press, 2003.
Golffing, Francis, and Barbara Golffing. "An Essay on Utopian Possibility." *Utopia*. Ed. George Kateb. 29–39.
Kateb, George. *Utopia and Its Enemies*. New York: Schocken, 1976.
Kateb, George (ed.). *Utopia*. New York: Atherton, 1971.

Levitas, Ruth. *The Concept of Utopia*. London: Phillip Allan, 1990.
More, Thomas. *Utopia*. Intro. and trans. Paul Turner. London: Penguin, 1988.
Plath, David. "Foreword." *Aware of Utopia*. Ed. David Plath. Champaign: University of Illinois Press, 1971. ix–xvi.
Sargent, Lyman Tower. *British and American Utopian Literature, 1516–1985: An Annotated, Chronological Bibliography*. New York: Garland, 1988.
Shklar, Judith. *Political Thought and Political Thinkers*. Chicago: University of Chicago Press, 1998.
Walsh, Chad. *From Utopia to Nightmare*. London: Geoffrey Bles, 1962.
Wells, H.G. *A Modern Utopia*. London: W. Collins Sons, 1926.
Wilde, Oscar. "The Soul of Man under Socialism." *Complete Works of Oscar Wilde*. Ed. J.B. Foreman. London: Collins, 1973. 1079–104.
Wittgenstein, Ludwig. *Philosophical Investigations*. Trans. G.E.M. Anscombe. Upper Saddle River: Prentice Hall, 1958.

Vincent Geoghegan

Utopia and the Memory of Religion

Certainly since the work of Ernst Bloch there has been keen interest in the relationship between religion and Utopia.[1] This has focused on two main aspects: 1) religion as a *resource* of utopian material; and 2) religion as a *space* in which utopian material can be generated. In this context, the relevance of memory should be clear in terms of 1) the nature of religious *traditions*, and 2) religions as *communities of memory*. While there are fascinating possibilities in exploring the relationship between the three categories of Utopia, memory, and religion, there are some major problems, and in this essay I want to address elements of both.

Let me begin with religion, and somewhat elliptically with etymology. The gods are absent in the etymology of the word "religion" (see Glare; Lewis and Short; Ahmed; McCarson). The predominant interpretation grounds the word in the Latin root *lig* which denotes "binds" and "binding" (as in "ligature"). The archaic Indo-European source of this root is suggested by the Urdu-Hindu word *lag* which means "join," as contrasted with the term *alag*, meaning "separate." That this root lent itself to conceptions of social binding is indicated by the fact that *lig* is the basis of the Latin word *lex* (law). The prefix "re" suggests the possibility that bounds might come undone and thus need to be re-established; hence, the Latin word *religare* (to bind again) is considered by most modern authorities to be at the base of the word "religion." The need to *re-*

---

[1] Earlier versions of this essay were given as papers at two ACUME Conferences on Cultural Memory – held in Lisbon, Portugal (January 2005) and Menaggio, Italy (April 2005) – and at the Ralahine Centre, University of Limerick, Ireland (March 2005): my thanks to Vita Fortunati for organizing the first, and to Tom Moylan, Michael Griffin and Carmen Kuhling for organizing the second.

bind introduces a temporal dimension; and this has led some commentators, including Jung, to interpret *religare* as "linking back"; but there is clearly the possibility of the forward glance also: thus, re-binding as renewal.

A temporal reading is also present in Cicero's entirely different etymology of "religion," arguing for a source in the word *relegere*, "to re-read" (Cicero 152–3). In the pagan Roman world, as S.N. Balagangadhara has argued, it was a commonplace for religious sceptics (like Cotta in Cicero's *The Nature of the Gods*) to take philosophical issue with the existence of gods, and yet at the same time advocate the necessity for devout religious observation, and the participation in such devotions. This was not, as Enlightenment thinkers argued, because they cynically distinguished elite from popular belief, but because the cultic practices were handed down from ancestral times and thereby embodied the living being of an historical community. As Cicero wrote: "It is wise and reasonable for us to preserve the institutions of our fore-fathers by retaining their rites and ceremonies" (quoted in Balagangadhara 42). The Romans, indeed, perceived the emergence of Christianity as a malign form of what I term a disruption of tradition. Balagangadhara suggests that to the Romans the Christians had no tradition, and therefore, in a real sense no *religio*: hence, their ascription of "atheism" to the new cult. This, in turn, propelled the Christians in the direction of asserting the antiquity and universality of their theistic *beliefs*, and thus to the creation of the modern western notion of a "religion" (see Balagangadhara 31–64). Certainly to the Emperor Julian, who sought to restore paganism in the fourth century CE, the Christians, or "Galilaeans" as he contemptuously termed them, had impiously broken with the venerable traditions of their age, having "turned aside from the gods to corpses and relics" (Julian 135). The Christians returned the compliment, dubbing Julian, "the Apostate."

As Richard King has argued, the differing etymologies of the word "religion" can be traced to historical struggles over control of meaning: as the earlier Ciceronian understanding of religion as re-reading was challenged by Christianity (notably the writer Lactantius) in the third century CE, when Christians proposed "re-binding" to promote a notion of orthodox belief in a true God (i.e., humans "bound" to God) against the earlier "pagan" and more pluralistic notion of varying traditions (36). This focus on the etymology thus provides a critical distance from the dominant modern conceptions of religion, or more accurately "religions" as belief systems centered on a family of transcendent concepts: the sacred, the holy, the divine, and so forth. This interpretation, then, foregrounds the human context in which these belief systems emerged, without necessarily engaging in a reductive maneuver that seeks to disparage or deny the transcendent elements. It, therefore, follows in the footsteps of Ludwig Feuerbach – who, although committed to an atheist perspective (with its reductive dangers), sought in his analysis of "the true or anthropological essence of religion" to understand what type of human conversation was contained in religious traditions (33; and see Geoghegan, "Religion and Communism").

We do however have to be careful when speaking about "religion" that we do not succumb to an untenable universalism. Certainly, Bloch speaks as if religion is an unproblematic historical given, once one understands its linkage to a ubiquitous utopian impulse: "where hope is, religion is" (1193). From this perspective, while religious traditions might be complex and varied, the underlying phenomenon of "religion" is a *historical* universal. Religious discourse, however, including the concept of "religious" discourse itself, has to be rooted in the historically shifting modalities of human conversation, and one cannot assume that "religion" is a human *cultural* universal.

The etymology of religion, as we have seen, also suggests possible connections with the phenomenon of memory. Some initial remarks on the vocabulary of memory are therefore in order. There is a wide range of memory words, many used synonymously. I would like to concentrate on the active side of memory, and, somewhat hesitantly, suggest the following distinctions:

Recalling. This activity lies on the furthest frontier of memory. It is the point where consciousness acknowledges material that seems to have emerged on its own volition: namely, those memory traces that seem to have pushed themselves forward – in Augustine's words, the things that "come spilling from the memory, thrusting themselves upon us" (214).

Recollection. This is a more active and conscious searching for memories, and the initial assemblage of these traces into more complex unities. Recalling can occur in the midst of recollection. Indeed, Augustine's reference to memories spilling out occurs in his analysis of a process of recollection: thus, these memories arise "when what we want is something quite different, as much as to say 'Perhaps we are what you want to remember?'" (214).

Remembering. This appears to involve a strong epistemological claim: "I remember" is a statement that affirms these traces as authentic representations of something pre-existing. This ambition to establish temporal truth is at the heart of Paul Ricoeur's study, *Memory, History, Forgetting*. Although Ricoeur deploys his own taxonomy (or phenomenology) of memory, his central conviction is that "we have nothing better than memory to guarantee that something has taken place before we call to mind a memory of it" (7).

Recognition. This involves the active working through of memories, reflecting on their significance, finding resonances. This seems to be the point where utopian work is likely to be done: namely, as a re-cognition, the creation of something new out of the old. This is the activity that Bloch is drawn to in his, not entirely helpful, distinction between the potentially utopian *anagnorisis* (recognition) and the epistemologically conservative *anamnesis* (recollection) (see Landmann 178–9).

Neurobiology has distinguished "procedural memory" (the memory of how to do things) from "declarative memory" (the memory of named things); and within "declarative memory" we find the further distinction between "episodic memory" (personal memories) and "semantic memory" (general memories of the world) (Rose 137–8). Religious memory clearly owes a good deal of its material to semantic memory. In the historical transfer from oral to written culture, there were fears that this shift would seriously impair memory, as writing legitimated a widespread forgetting of specifics. Plato, for example, has Socrates cite the remarks of a King of Egypt on the dangers of writing: "Those who acquire it will cease to exercise their memory and become forgetful" (96; and see Weinrich 20). However, as Steven Rose argues, writing can be construed as a form of "artificial memory" that is "profoundly liberatory, transforming both what we need to and what we are able to remember" (387–8). The religious texts of the world are thus an incredibly rich source of material available for collective appropriation, interpretation, and development; and, as shown by the example of Bloch, they can be powerful repositories of utopian material (see 1183–311).

Shared memories are an important form of social binding, and religious memory has been a particularly potent form of social memory. Re-ligion is therefore intimately related to fundamental memory concepts. Many religious memories are of moments when memory is disrupted, when the old, at least partially, begins to be forgotten as something new is ushered in. Frequently, the narration in religious memory focuses on the innovative religious figure who reveals a truth previously unknown or unrecognized which revolutionizes human perceptions of reality and its potential. The memory of these deeply subversive acts, concepts, and imagery linger on in the dogma of conservative creeds that seek to de-temporalize and de-utopianize this material into eternal truths. The tradition of the disrupted tradition thus lives on – as a gold-bearing seam of Utopia, to use Bloch's metaphor. Furthermore, in the memory of the subversive religious act lies the exemplar not merely of the selective appropriation of earlier traditions but also of the introduction of genuine novelty, the utopian space of genuine creation.

The process of secularization, however, needs to be considered when delving into these matters. The privatization of religion has undoubtedly led to an attenuation of a sense of the social in religion, and an attendant under-theorization of the role of memory in religion. William James's *The Varieties of Religious Experience* is often seen as an example of an individualist treatment of religion. In fact, it would be more accurate to say that James is uninterested in the social dimension in religion rather than in denying its existence. James defined religion as "the feelings, acts and experiences of individual men in their solitude, so far as they apprehend themselves to stand in relation to whatever they may consider the divine" (31). Charles Taylor locates James's analysis in a Protestant tradition, and he contrasts it with an alternative collective conception of religion that points to the social dimension in the individual response. He illustrates this with his experience of sitting at home watching the local hockey team triumph on television: "the sense of my joy here is framed by my understanding that thousands of fans all over the city, some gathered at the rinkside, others also in their living rooms, are sharing in this moment of exultation" (*Varieties* 28). In effect, Taylor echoes Émile Durkheim's claim that "religion must be something eminently collective" (Durkheim 46). What he does not explore is the vital element of shared memory in this collective response: the triumph of the local team is located in, and derives emotional intensity from, the memory of earlier defeats and victories, and of the pains and pleasures associated with supporting the team over time.

Avishai Margalit's concept of "shared memory" is appropriate here (see 50–2). The various supporters of Taylor's hockey team have experienced the performances of their team in differing locations and times; and through inter-communication they have built up certain shared notions of the past of their team. Margalit distinguishes this activity from "common memory," which is "a simple aggregate" of individual memories, lacking the vital mediating factor of communication (51). The term "shared" perhaps also suggests a voluntaristic, non-coercive form of integration, distinguishable from oppressive forms of integration from above – a distinction of particular salience in any analysis of the emergence of religious traditions. Furthermore, this type of concept of collective memory therefore need not involve the dissolution of the memorizing individual. Ricoeur is surely right in distinguishing between the highly defensible thesis that "no one ever remembers alone" and the indefensible thesis that "we are not an authentic subject of the attribution of memories" (122). This latter thesis is theoretically confused and, at least potentially, politically pernicious.

Both James and Durkheim agree in locating part of the definition of religion in terms of the object religion addresses: for James it is the "divine," and for Durkheim the "sacred." This reflects a differentiation that is neither temporally nor spatially ubiquitous. Furthermore, over-restrictive western models of the "religious" have produced fundamental misreadings of non-western phenomena; the modern pattern of discrete creeds and faiths (the so-called "world religions") represents but one possible development in the human conversation (see King). The phenomenon of religion, therefore, is not an unproblematic universal, but rather a category heavily marked by the project of one tradition – the western Christian – that has set the definition of what a religion is and, aided for different reasons by non-western indigenous forces, has created out of a mass of local traditions a set of faiths based, like the Christian, on texts, priests, etc. Indeed, one might note in passing Bloch's privileging of the Judaeo-Christian tradition as the cutting edge of religious development – with Christianity named as the very apex of the history of religion (1193). In short, anyone using religion as a resource or a space for the utopian needs to be aware that not merely "religions" carry deep ideological baggage, but also the very category of "religion" itself.

Karl Marx recognized this condition in his early work on religion and politics. In *On the Jewish Question*, he argues, seemingly paradoxically, that it is not the religious state which represents the triumph of Christianity, but the modern secular state. This is because the division between civil society and the state in liberal democracy is an expression of the egoistic individualism dominant in civil society, and this egoistic individualism is at the heart of modern Christianity. Liberal democracy is thus profoundly Christian. For Marx, the fact that in liberal democracy individuals acknowledge themselves via the intermediary of the state means not that they are merely doing something *analogous* to religious behavior but that this activity is itself religious:

> The members of the political state are religious owing to the dualism between individual life and species-life between the life of civil society and political life. They are religious because men treat the political life of the state, an area beyond their real individuality, as if it were their true life. They are religious insofar as religion here is the spirit of civil society, expressing the separation and remoteness of man from man (*On the Jewish Question* 159).

One should also note the assault of rationalism on memory that began to gather pace in the seventeenth century. As Harald Weinrich has argued, rationalist and Enlightenment philosophers saw the ancient and medieval veneration of memory as indicative of a defense of thoughtless prejudice, but now memory had to be put firmly in its place under the sovereignty of reason: "In the works of many

Enlightenment authors [...] one can speak of a genuine war between reason and memory that will be clearly decided in favor of reason and to the disadvantage of memory" (73). This, in turn, has implications for utopianism; for as in earlier periods, the utopian was clearly marked by the ideological and intellectual struggles of the time. Thus, rationalist themes in utopias began to emerge (Bacon's *New Atlantis* comes to mind); and against them the critique of "abstract speculation," which looked to the resources of tradition and memory as a bulwark (as in Edmund Burke's critique of the French Revolution), generated its own utopian visions in the process.

In reality, all points of the ideological spectrum have had recourse to the resources of historical memory.[2] For example, liberal constitutionalism, in both France and America, drew on the classicism of antiquity in their attempts to reshape political institutions. Maurice Halbwachs, in one of his explorations of "collective memory," analyzed the way in which the new bourgeois functionaries in the French *ancien régime* had to acquire noble titles to associate themselves with the legitimating traditions of the old nobility; although their ultimate goal was the overcoming of this order: "In this way the new structure was elaborated in the shadow of the old [...]. It is upon a foundation of remembrances that contemporary institutions were constructed" (125). It was this bourgeois reliance on the symbols and imagery of the past that exercised Marx in *The Eighteenth Brumaire of Louis Bonaparte*: Luther's adoption of the mask of Saint Paul, the Roundhead's use of the Old Testament in the English Civil War, the French Revolution's deployment of ancient Rome, and the 1848 revolutionaries' appropriation of the French Revolution, all were seen as attempting to present a "new scene of world history in this time-honored disguise and this borrowed language" (*Eighteenth Brumaire* 104). Significantly, Marx uses the language of memory when he draws the analogy between the bourgeois rifling of the past and the acquisition of a new language, claiming that someone only acquires fluency in a new language when they cease to translate the

---

2   Claeys brings out the immense complexity of themes and influences in British utopias of the eighteenth century; see also Becker.

new language back into their old tongue, when, therefore, this person "forgets his native tongue" (*Eighteenth Brumaire* 104). Thus, the proletariat in their coming revolution cannot follow the lead of the bourgeoisie in this respect, for "the social revolution of the nineteenth century cannot draw its poetry from the past, but only from the future" (*Eighteenth Brumaire* 106).

Religious memory has, of course, provided a particularly powerful source of utopian vision. A notable example is the impact of John Foxe's *Acts and Monuments*, published in 1563. The heart of this historical and apocalyptic work, which gained the popular title of "Foxe's Book of Martyrs," gave graphic accounts of the torments and agonizing deaths of English and Scottish Protestants, particularly during the reign of the Catholic Queen Mary – accounts augmented by harrowing woodcut drawings of these events, which greatly added to its popular appeal. This work, frequently re-published (often in cheap installments) over the subsequent centuries, became deeply embedded in the Protestant imagination, not only in England where it made a powerful contribution to a sense of English identity, but, following the accession of the Scottish King James to the English throne in 1603, to a broader audience who claimed a British identity, as defined in contradistinction to European Catholicism (see MacCulloch 285; Colley 25–8). Arthur Williamson has even argued that "virtually all English utopian thought prior to 1660, and even much utopian thought prior to 1800, found its bedrock in John Foxe"; and he notes, for example, that the only non-scriptural citation in the work of the radical Digger, Winstanley, is Foxe (Williamson online). There is a certain irony here in that, according to the Oxford English Dictionary, the earliest pejorative use of the word "utopia" in English appears in Foxe's "Book of Martyrs" (*OED* 370)![3]

---

[3] "I do not [...] thinke, that [...] there is any such fourth place of Purgatory at all (unless it be in M. Mores *Utopia*)" (*OED* 370). I am grateful to an unpublished paper by Toby Widdicombe for this reference.

Some valuable thoughts on the relationship between memory, religion, and Utopia can be found in Danièl Hervieu-Léger's 1993 work, *La Religion pour Mémoire* (published in English as *Religion as a Chain of Memory*). Hervieu-Léger's sensitivity to the complex historical and spatial patterns of religious belief and behavior makes her unwilling to try and find some universal concept of transcendental belief, such as the sacred, to unite such diversity. Nor is she willing simply to fall back on a simple description of this plethora of material. Instead, she focuses on the process of religious belief, the way people believe, and in particular on the basis of legitimation of those beliefs. The fundamental legitimating factor for Hervieu-Léger is a memory-based tradition. This understanding of religion connects back to ancient conceptions of *religio*. She posits a "chain of belief" that she sees as a form of collective memory linking generations of believers into a self-conscious community (123). This need not become a conservative backward-looking process, however; for religious innovation can be achieved through developing a utopianism grounded in, but not subordinated to, the dynamic historic traditions of a religion:

> Utopia serves to create in a renewed way an alternative imagined continuity: a continuity reaching back further than the one that suits the social conventions of the present, a continuity which reaches more nearly the foundation that feeds the consciousness of the chain, a continuity with a past that is blessed and beneficent, and which stands in opposition to the misfortunes, the dangers and the uncertainties of the present (Hervieu-Léger 144–5).

The problem for Hervieu-Léger is that long-term economic, technological, social, and cultural changes have undermined "societies of memory" and therefore threaten the very oxygen of chains of belief (123). Her hope lies in "attempts […] to remobilize and recreate memory" in the utopian space still available in modern societies (143).

Historically, there has always been a plurality of memory communities. This has been both a strength and a weakness. The collective memory of groups enabled people to transcend particularity in the name of particularity – *individuals* were integrated by "*our*" memory. Nation-building rested on this capacity. The obvious dangers in this process can be seen by returning to my earlier John Foxe example. The shared memory of Protestant martyrdom played well in predominantly Protestant England, Scotland, and Wales; but with the coerced integration of overwhelmingly Catholic Ireland into the United Kingdom, the integrated Protestant memory of the larger island not only found little resonance in the smaller locale, but was especially experienced there as deeply oppressive. The results are well known: centuries of conflict and, given the partial success of the Reformation in the north of the island, the partition of Ireland and ongoing conflict in Northern Ireland. There is also an important ethical question here: do the ethical claims of members of one's own community override those of non-members? Contemporary defenders of liberal nationalism, such as David Miller, answer this question in the affirmative; thus, when one has to choose between helping members and non-members, members have a priority.

However, in *The Ethics of Memory*, Margalit tackles this problem in a more productive manner. He distinguishes thick relations between individuals from thin relations, and he grounds this distinction in the presence or absence of collective memory. Thus, thick relations are between group members, and "memory is the cement that holds thick relations together" (8). Thin relations on the other hand are between less immediately related individuals – those who do not have a genuinely shared memory. On this basis, Margalit determines that thick relations are the realm of ethics and thin relations the realm of morality: "morality is long on geography and short on memory. Ethics is typically short on geography and long on memory" (8). This is a useful distinction in that it recognizes the different types of obligation involved in dealing with differing relationships, but it does not *necessarily* imply a hierarchy of obligations, with the ethical trumping the moral in hard cases. I stress *necessarily* because Margalit himself, in deploying this distinction, does end up with a position not dissimilar to Miller's, in that he argues that when confronted with two people drowning, one of which is one's wife, one's "obligation [...] is not to be impartial," but rather to save one's wife (8). He is, however, clearly aware of problems with this stance, since he adds: "picking between the two, rather than choosing his wife, might be justified"; but he continues, "it would be ethically cursed," which doesn't sound like a contest of equals (8).

For Margalit, morality is couched in principles, but ethics "depends on comparisons to paradigmatic cases" (38). Significantly, he turns to the Biblical parable of the Good Samaritan as a paradigmatic story of an ethically reprehensible absence of care for neighbors, and of a moral act from a stranger. In this respect, Margalit signals an undoubted trend in modern social and political thought—a trend I have discussed elsewhere under the term "post-secularism" (see "Religious Narrative, Postsecularism and Utopia"): that is, the wish to reconfigure the relationship between the religious and the secular which, while defending the achievements of the secular, wishes to develop a more nuanced approach to the religious.

The theme of forgetting has a relevance to these issues. The secular privatization of religion has, to say the least, made religion somewhat of a public embarrassment. Richard Rorty's defense of Jeffersonian secularism gives a sense of the climate of pressure surrounding religion in the west. Public discussion of religion, he argues, violates the liberal deal between the Enlightenment and religion, and threatens to contaminate the inclusive conversations of a liberal society: "The main reason religion needs to be privatized is that [...] it is a conversation-stopper" (171). To provide what he considers an analogous example, he cites the hypothetical case of a person in a gathering of professionals who suddenly says: "Reading pornography is about the only pleasure I get out of life these days"; "the ensuing silence," Rorty comments, "masks the group's inclination to say, 'So what? We weren't discussing your private life; we were discussing public policy. Don't bother us with matters that are not our concern'" (171). In this context, it is perhaps not surprising that religion becomes marginalized to the point of invisibility in the public realm. An interesting example is provided by Taylor in "A Catholic Modernity." In the preamble to this piece, Taylor, a long-standing Roman Catholic, says that he is going to discuss "some issues that have been at the center of my concern for decades," but, he continues, "they have been reflected in my philosophical work, but not in the same form as I raise them this afternoon, because of the nature of philosophical discourse (as I see it, anyway), which has to try to persuade honest thinkers of any and all metaphysical or theological commitments" (13). In other words, philosophical discussion in the public realm has had to strip itself of any religious particularity to count as proper discourse. It is as if there has been a form of repressive forgetting of religion in the public realm, with perhaps the post-secular turn as a return of the repressed?

Works Cited

Ahmed, Khaled. "WORD FOR WORD: Zulqarnain – Alexander or Cyrus." 14 November 2004 <http://www.dailytimes.com.pk/default.asp?page=story_14-11-2004_pg3_4>.
Augustine. *Confessions*. Harmondsworth: Penguin, 1961.
Balagangadhara, S. N. *"The Heathen in His Blindness": Asia, the West and the Dynamic of Religion*. 2nd edn. New Delhi: Manohar, 2005.
Becker, Carl L. *The Heavenly City of the Eighteenth-Century Philosophers*. New Haven and London: Yale University Press, 2003.
Bloch, Ernst. *The Principle of Hope*. Trans. Neville Plaice, Stephen Plaice, and Paul Knight. 3 Vols. Oxford: Blackwell, 1986.
Cicero. *The Nature of the Gods*. London: Penguin, 1972.
Claeys, Gregory. *Utopias of the British Enlightenment*. Cambridge: Cambridge University Press, 1994.
Colley, Linda. *Britons: Forging the Nation 1707–1837*. New Haven and London: Yale University Press, 1992.
Durkheim, Émile. *The Elementary Forms of Religious Life*. Oxford: Oxford University Press, 2001.
Feuerbach, Ludwig. *The Essence of Christianity*. Trans. George Eliot. New York, Evanston and London: Harper & Row, 1957.
Geoghegan, Vincent. "Religion and Communism: Feuerbach, Marx and Bloch." *European Legacy* 9.5 (2004): 585–95.
―― "Religious Narrative, Postsecularism and Utopia." *The Philosophy of Utopia*. Ed. Barbara Goodwin. London: Frank Cass, 2001. 205–24.
Glare, P.G.W. (ed.). *Oxford Latin Dictionary*. Oxford: Clarendon, 1982.
Halbwachs, Maurice. *On Collective Memory*. Chicago and London: University of Chicago Press, 1992.

Hervieu-Léger, Danièl. *Religion as a Chain of Memory*. Cambridge: Polity, 2000.
James, William. *The Varieties of Religious Experience*. Harmondsworth: Penguin, 1985.
Julian. *The Works of the Emperor Julian*. Vol. 3. Cambridge, Massachusetts: Harvard University Press, 1998.
King, Richard. *Orientalism and Religion: Postcolonial Theory, India and "the Mystic East."* London and New York: Routledge, 1999.
Landmann, Michael. "Talking with Ernst Bloch: Korcula, 1968." *Telos* 25 (1975): 165–85.
Lewis, Charlton T. and Charles Short (eds). *A Latin Dictionary*. Oxford: Clarendon, 1966.
McCarson, Bonnie. "What is Religion?" 6 June 2004 <http://www.suite101.com/article.cfm/jungian_psychology/95713>.
MacCulloch, Diarmaid. *Reformation: Europe's House Divided 1490–1700*. London: Penguin, 2004.
Margalit, Avishai. *The Ethics of Memory*. Cambridge, Massachusetts: Harvard University Press, 2004.
Marx, Karl. "The Eighteenth Brumaire of Louis Bonaparte." *Collected Works*- Vol. 11. London: Lawrence & Wishart, 1979. 99–197.
___ "On the Jewish Question." *Collected Works*. Vol. 3. London: Lawrence & Wishart, 1975. 146–74.
Miller, David. *On Nationality*. Oxford: Clarendon, 1997.
Oxford English Dictionary. 2nd edn. Vol. 29. Oxford: Clarendon, 1989.
Plato. *Phaedrus and the Seventh and Eighth Letters*. Harmondsworth: Penguin, 1981.
Ricoeur, Paul. *Memory, History, Forgetting*. Chicago: University of Chicago Press, 2004.
Rorty, Richard. *Philosophy and Social Hope*. London: Penguin 1999.
Rose, Steven. *The Making of Memory: From Molecules to Mind*. London: Vintage, 2003.
Taylor, Charles. "A Catholic Modernity?" *A Catholic Modernity?* Ed. James L. Heft. New York and Oxford: Oxford University Press, 1999. 13–37.
___ *Varieties of Religion Today: William James Revisited*. Cambridge, Massachusetts: Harvard University Press, 2002.
Weinrich, Harald. *Lethe: The Art and Critique of Forgetting*. Ithaca and London: Cornell University Press, 2004.

Williamson, Arthur. "Review of Robert Applebaum." *Literature and Utopian Politics in Seventeenth-Century England*. H-Ideas, H-Net Reviews. 24 October 2003 <http://www.h-net.org/reviews/showrev.cgi?path=215951070961366>.

ANTONIS BALASOPOULOS

The Fractured Image: Plato, the Greeks, and the Figure of the Ideal City

The Duplicities of Oneness

Since the subject of the ideal city in Greek political and philosophical thought inescapably involves the question of beginnings, we might do well to begin where the Greeks themselves found it proper to begin.[1] "It is necessary to begin from *archē*" – "*ἀρκτέον ἀπ' ἀρχῆς*": Plato's Timaeus suggests, in a phrase that augurs more than the tautology-generating translation of *archē* as "beginning" would allow (48b3).[2] "It is necessary to begin from *archē*": Greek oratory and historical narrative, Nicole Loraux tells us, consistently privilege *archē* over the technically more appropriate *kratos* when they wish to speak of the origin of institutional power in the city. In so doing, they tactfully skirt around the connotative suggestion that such power is an effect of the successful domination (*kratein*) of one individual or party over another (*Divided City* 69). Evading such associative reference to

---

[1] Research for this essay was made possible by a grant from the Hellenic Studies Program at Princeton University. My thanks to Dimitri Gondicas, Peter Brown, Alexander Nehamas, and Stathis Gourgouris for their valuable guidance and insight.

[2] In Greek, *archē is* "the spatial or temporal point from which someone or something begins; the ultimate cause; a foundational principle; authority and the persons who exercise it" (*Major Greek Dictionary*). It is important to note that Timaeus's words introduce the displacement, in the midst of the cosmogony, of the causal *archē* of the benevolent Creator by that of the errant principle of *anagkē* (necessity) (Kalfas 46–7). This is why a translation like "it is necessary to begin at the beginning" would be a misleading translation indeed.

a temporally prior process of conflict (*agon*) and strife (*neikos*), the discourse of *archē* evokes the indivisible conceptual unity of foundation and authority. It designates, as Jacques Derrida would put it, both natural/historical "commencement" and legal "commandment" at once (*Archive Fever* 1). *Archē* thus also redoubles as the sign of a *telos*, both in the sense that its referential circularity puts an end to the disaggregating operations of further analytical retrospect and in the sense that such invulnerability to analytical (*lūo* = unbind, undo) division is the ultimate goal of all authority that would lay a claim to legitimacy in the classical world.

It has been one of the crucial goals of poststructuralist theory and contemporary cultural anthropology both to highlight and query the ideological stakes and epistemological implications of Greek *archē*. Poststructuralism has done so by drawing attention to the forms of difference, excess, and indeterminacy that Greek *logos* stumbles upon in its very attempt to formulate itself as an autonomous, self-authorizing foundation of knowledge. Anthropology and anthropologically informed cultural history, on the other hand, have worked to foreground the epistemological and ethical challenges posed by "the other Greeks" – the Greeks of ritual and myth as well as the "others of Greeks" – women, metics, slaves, "barbarians." It is a consequence of such interventions that the articulation of the terms that loom large in the politico-philosophical nostalgia for the integral totality of Greek *archē* – politics, philosophy, and the *polis* – has opened itself up to interrogation. For to envision the *polis* as the historical origin both of the interrogation of the foundations of civic authority (in short, politics) and of inquiry into the authorizing principles of knowledge, virtue, and truth (in short, philosophy) is to raise the profoundly Greek question of whether such a *polis*, even if it is empirically single, is really One. It is to ask, in other words, whether *polis* or its historically privileged synonym – democratic Athens – designates the utopic *locus* of a consubstantiation of philosophical reflection and political action or, on the contrary, the origin of a disjuncture and even enmity between the two: the *polis* of the philosophical concept as opposed to the *polis* of political history, even if both are born of the same city.

The way both the Greeks and their exegetes have positioned

themselves towards this question is fatally overdetermined by the centrality, in both the philosophical and political thought of the former, of the problems of unity and division, harmony and conflict, singularity and multiplicity. There is little doubt that Greek thought in the classical period tends to exaggerate the dependence of civic stability and functionality on the absolute self-identity of the One. Being at odds with the ubiquity of dissent, division, and *stasis* in the historical experience and mythological imaginary of the Greeks themselves, such theologico-political faith in the indivisibility of *archē* could ironically be maintained only at the cost of generating a series of second-order divisions between different, and largely incompatible, discourses of the city.[3] Hence, as Pierre Vidal-Naquet observes, the historian of ideas discovers that the disjuncture between the historical and the philosophical approach to the city is already entrenched in the Greek world; so that a thinker as versatile as Aristotle could treat the history of philosophical ideas in the *Metaphysics* in perfect isolation from that of the institutions of the Athenian *polis* in his *Constitution of Athens* (*Politics Ancient and Modern* 28). The art historian, as François Lissarrague and Alain Schnapp have noted in a different context, discovers the workings of another curious division of representational labor, since Greek visual art seems subject to a law of "censorship of the political" which prevents it from depicting images of assembly, debate, or non-mythological warfare (see Lissarague and Schnapp; Loraux, *Divided City* 48–9, 272–3; and Vidal-Naquet, *Politics* 71). The political historian, finally, confronts the existence of a strange non-coincidence between a democratic practice demonstrably based on majority rule, the rotation of civic duties, and public debate, and a theoretical discourse that was never reconciled to what it understood as the fatally dissensual and divisive nature of the democratic process.

Indeed, as both Loraux and Vidal-Naquet have suggested, the

---

[3] On the persistence of *stasis* in the anxieties of the Greek political imaginary, see Cohen 25–33, esp. For an historical account that highlights the near permanence of political instability in Athens, see Aristotle's *Constitution of Athens*.

Greeks do not appear to have thought highly of the "invention" of politics, especially of politics in the democratic sense (see Loraux, *Divided City* 70, 101; Vidal-Naquet, *Politics* 69; and Rancière, "Ten Theses" par. 12 online). Democrats themselves, in fact, were not only averse to the word "democracy" and its allusion to the coercive preponderance of a *demos* of *hoi polloi*, but also prone to appropriate the symbolic vocabulary of aristocratic privilege by extolling the *polites's eugeneia* (noble birth) and *aretē* (excellence) (see Loraux, *Born of the Earth* 21). Such was the power of the spell cast by the ideal of the undivided and unanimous city that one of the basic tenets of modern liberal democracy – that of the citizen's right to choose from among the publicly stated agendas of antagonistic parties – was well-nigh unthinkable, even for those aligned to the "democratic" cause (Vidal-Naquet, *Politics* 70). Even if one were skeptical about seeing such a poverty of democratic theory in light of Claude Lefort's position that democracy "cannot be apprehended in its political form," one would still have to concede that the practice of the Greek democratic city remains fatally non-contemporaneous with a consciousness that would emerge from such practice. Far from constituting a value-instituting norm, democracy remains, even in the understanding of its own practitioners, something akin to a "scandal" – or at least a "provisional accident," a "state of exception" from the norms of oligarchic domination.[4]

Modern attempts to contain or repress the import of such asymmetries and disjunctures – between philosophy and history, between theory and practice, between consciousness and experience – have done little more than to repeat the original quandary of the Greeks; for in the very effort to "assign the direct apprehension of 'the truth of political things'" to the supposedly singular location of the classical democratic *polis* (McClure par. 27 online), they have effectively worked to reproduce the specter of that *polis's* divisions within the theater of critical discourse itself. Witness, for instance, the paradox that manifests itself in Cornelius Castoriadis's "The Greek

---

[4] I quote from Rancière: see "Ten Theses" pars. 10–17 online. See also Rancière's elaboration in "Comment and Responses" pars.11–12 online.

Polis and the Creation of Democracy." What distinguishes the democratic *polis* for Castoriadis is its conception of the political as a fundamentally self-instituting formation that produces collective life without access to any externalized and essentially metaphysical principles of law, justice, or virtue. Seen as a subject that denounces submission to heteronomy, the Greek citizen ostensibly realizes the power to transform "*this* world" on the strength of collective thought and action (Castoriadis 273). It is this vision, Castoriadis concludes, that makes philosophy and politics consubstantial; for neither can come into existence until the questions of truth in the first case and justice in the second become genuinely "open," which is to say only provisionally and vulnerably answerable (272). Although he insists that it was the destruction of the theological nature of faith in the unified order of the *cosmos* that made Athenian democracy possible, Castoriadis paradoxically re-imports into the account of the specificity of that democracy the ideal of a perfectly integrated unity – the triadic consubstantiation of *polis*, politics, and philosophy. In the democratic *polis*, he asserts in the final page of his text, beauty, wisdom, and the care for the common good are inextricable from each other and constitute the true content of political experience. The Athenian citizen "exists and lives in and though the unity of these three" (288).

As with the Greeks themselves, however, the attainment of unity turns out to demand the generation of a series of second-order disjunctures and divisions. It is not long before one notices the absence of "that archenemy of democracy, Plato" in Castoriadis's account of the trajectory of philosophy in the Athenian *polis* (277). Arriving far too late to affect or be affected by democracy's revolutionary moment, Platonic philosophy is dismissed as a throwback to a world before democracy, an appeal to "a total order which includes us, our wishes, and our strivings as its organic and central components" (Castoriadis 273). Yet, even if one were to leave aside the fact that it is difficult to understand the nature of this peculiar beast that is Athenian political philosophy without the "philosophical monstrosity" of Plato, one can hardly avoid noticing the paradox of a discourse that celebrates the total world-view of the Greek democratic "miracle," while excoriating the "theological" nature of Platonic totalization (Castoriadis 273). It is likewise impossible to ignore the ironic correspondence between Castoriadis's exclusion of Plato from the properly democratic and philosophical city and the expulsion of the poets from Plato's own philosophical *polis* in *The Republic*. In both cases, the construction of a fully integrated and operative political community necessitates the excision from its body (proleptic in Plato, retroactive in Castoriadis) of a discourse (poetry in Plato, Platonic philosophy in Castoriadis) that is figured as alien to the true nature and goals of the *polis*. The utopian image of organic totality is thus in both cases the aftereffect of a prior division and expulsion – of the charlatans of mimesis in the first case, of the bogeyman of totalization in the second.

From Philosophy without a City to the City without Philosophy

I have begun by reflecting on the vicissitudes of *archē* and the duplicities of Oneness only to end up with Plato. Such an end has been almost inevitable; for it is Plato who marks the origin of the suspicion that there may be, in one and the same city, two antagonistic and mutually hostile visions of the city affiliated with *doxa* and *epistēmē*, the "opinions" of politics and the "knowledge" of philosophy respectively.[5] The suspicion is both familiar and influential. What Hannah Arendt calls "the historical occasion which gave rise to the conflict between the *polis* and the philosopher" has often been seen as something that engenders the desire for a cognition of the eternal that claims its autonomy from the worldly concerns of politics (16). With Plato, philosophy attains its vocational dignity through an act of defection from the realm of the political – the realm where, according to Arendt, philosophy itself had located the

---

5   On the distinction between *doxa* (belief) and *epistēmē* (knowledge) and its implications for the philosopher's superior qualifications for political leadership, see Plato, *Rep.* 476d–480a.

possibility of freedom from the compulsions that constitute the domain of "the social" (30–1). As Jacques Rancière acerbically points out, however, the opposition between "the political" and the "social" on which such an argument rests "is a matter defined entirely within the realm of political philosophy," where the latter ironically amounts to a "philosophical repression of politics" itself ("Ten Theses" par. 31 online). Positing the consensually accepted existence of "a way of life that is proper to politics," the Arendtian critique of Plato takes as the foundation or *archē* of the political what a democratic politics worth the name is by definition compelled to dispute or bring into question ("Ten Theses" par. 3; and see par. 32 online): the division of those properly "equipped" for politics from those "who have no specificity in common apart from their having no qualification for governing" ("Ten Theses" par. 12 online).

It would be tempting to leave the matter rest by observing that, once again, "Platonism" has been caught insinuating itself in the very language its critics use to denounce it. But that should not obscure the significance of asking which "Plato" "Platonism" actually designates, especially when "Platonism" becomes identified with a devaluation of the political in the name of philosophy. Interestingly, Arendt's critique of "Plato's misrecognition or disavowal of politics" seems exclusively premised on a reading of *The Republic*, "where the whole utopian reorganization of *polis* life is not only directed by the superior insight of the philosopher but has no other aim than to make possible the philosopher's way of life" (Lefort 51; Arendt 14). This, however, is far from an accurate depiction of the relationship between *polis* and philosophy in Plato's later dialogues.

The preamble to the *Timaeus* already suggests that the identification of Plato with the subordination of the "active life" of politics to the "static contemplation" of philosophy is problematically one-dimensional. Socrates, for one, is less than content with the picture of the Republic-like *ideal polis* he is reported to have described on the previous day: "My feelings are rather like those of a man who has seen some splendid animals, either in a picture or really alive but motionless, and wants to see them moving and engaging in some of the activities for which they appear to be formed" (*Tim.* 19b4–b9). Attributing to himself what he designates as the inability of the poets to properly do justice to the *polis* and its men, Socrates suggests that only men who are both "*philosophoi*" and "*politikoi*" can achieve the task at hand. The task, addressed to Socrates's interlocutors, is to replace the deathly stillness and inaction of a "merely" philosophical contemplation of the ideal city with the active life that characterizes the city in the process of political becoming (*Tim.* 19d1–e8).

To the controversial possibilities such a proposition already appears to contain, let me add this: in the political imaginary of fifth and fourth century Greece, the "movement" that Socrates wishes to see instilled in the city is semantically linked not merely to (internal as well as external) turmoil and conflict but also to the figure of the alien against whom autochthony pits the ideal of a city of "the motionless same."[6] To the extent that his words are to be taken earnestly, they constitute a serious "internal" critique of the *Republic,* suggesting that "the deficiency of the ideal State" lies precisely in "its 'stately' perfection" (Stankiewicz 58). But is this not placing too much trust in the earnestness of a philosopher sometimes prone to being duplicitous? Is it not possible that the direction of Socrates's irony is not toward his own shortcomings, but toward those of his interlocutors? The answer is simple: it is impossible to determine Socrates's intentions toward Timaeus and Critias, since he never subjects their accounts to any scrutiny.

There is in fact "no questioning, no request for clarification, no criticism, no reformulation of any of the points made by the speakers" in the *Timaeus-Critias* (Johansen 182). Socrates the philosopher practically disappears from the discussion of a *polis* he has proclaimed himself unable to do justice to (*Tim.* 19d1–d2). But he will not absent himself before he has also erased the very question of philosophy's contribution to the exercise of rule in the virtuous city; for his recollection of the "previous discussion" of the ideal *polis* in the preamble of the *Timaeus* surreptitiously drops any reference to the philosopher-ruler – the man who grasps the "eternal and immutable"

---

[6] Loraux, *Born of the Earth* 59. On the connection between *kinesis* and conflict (including war) see Clay 54; and Loraux, *Divided City* 59–61.

and is therefore the only one equipped to guide the *polis* along the track of virtue and truth (*Rep.* 484b5; and see *Rep.* 473d–e; see Dawson 86, Schofield 31–3). The preamble thus reflexively anticipates the structural anomaly that sets the *Timaeus-Critias* apart from the main body of the Platonic *oeuvre*: they can only catachrestically be called "Socratic dialogues," since they are marked both by the virtual absence of philosophical dialogue and by the effective disappearance of the figurehead of Platonic philosophy itself.

Political philosophy minus Socrates. This, indeed, seems to be one of the features shared by the main part of *Timaeus*, the vast majority of *Critias*, and the entirety of *The Laws*.[7] But are these explorations of the possibility of civic virtue in the frail and ephemeral world of "becoming" any longer to be designated as philosophy at all, especially when by "philosophy" we mean Platonic idealism? *Timaeus*, as Derrida has shown, presents philosophical reasoning with a *stricto sensu* unthinkable concept – *khōra* – that can be apprehended only through "bastard reasoning," as if in "a kind of dream" (*Tim.* 52b2–b3; see Derrida, "Khōra" esp. 90–1, 96, 103–4, 124–7; and Sallis, "Daydream."). That the narrative of the *Critias* possesses a philosophical core, on the other hand, has been difficult to demonstrate for a number of Platonists, given that no work has been more sharply detached from the corpus of Platonic philosophy than the *Critias*.[8] This should not suggest that these works can be grasped in terms of mere absence or lack, however. If the philosopher, and perhaps philosophy too, are missing, what emerges in their place, and what imbues these texts with their substantive content, is the increasingly prominent reality of the place of the city itself. The task

---

[7] Socrates's speaking presence is restricted to the preamble of the first, reduced to a single and strictly procedural interjection in the preamble of the second, and completely eliminated in the last of these texts – the last, too, of Plato's written works according to general consensus on the chronology of Plato's compositions.

[8] Dombrowski remarks that there has been "a poverty of philosophical interest" regarding Critias's narrative (117). Taylor's monumental book on Plato confirms the verdict in practice, dedicating a mere two paragraphs to a work that "calls for no special consideration," as he puts it (461).

of the late dialogues, as Jean-François Pradeau has demonstrated, is to explore the place of the world and of its political organization and to draw on the double role of place as both the product and the material precondition of thought (see Pradeau, *Le Monde* 238–77 and *Plato* 114–66.

The cognitive novelty of this development becomes starker when one compares the vibrantly topological imagery of the late dialogues with the abstract nature of what Doyne Dawson has called the "high utopianism" of *The Republic* (77–81). In the earlier text, where Socrates's presence was dominant, the philosopher's words had yielded a *polis* without the least pretension to materiality, one that in the words of the young Glaukon would remain "*ἐν λόγοις κειμένη, ἐπεί γῆς γε οὐδαμοῦ* " ("situated in words and nowhere on earth") (*Rep.* 592a11, translation mine). Glaukon's disenchanted appraisal resonates in a very specific way with Socrates's own ambivalence towards the role of the philosopher. If he is likely to rule little more than a city of words, it is because the democratic *polis* has deprived him of the space that should properly be his own. In it, he feels like "a foreign seed in alien soil," not unlike, Socrates encourages us to think, the errant sophists of the *Timaeus*.[9] His vocation, on the other hand, has become "a piece of territory" occupied by a "whole crowd of squatters" who rush into philosophy like a "crowd of criminals taking refuge in a temple" (*Rep.* 495b, 497d). Yet, it would also need to be acknowledged, and Socrates is not averse to admitting it, that philosophy has deprived *itself* of a place (see Rep. 495b–c, 496b–497a). Since taking sides and engaging in political *agon* is a fundamental demand of civic belonging, a philosophical discourse that valorizes its insulation from the antagonistic and volatile domain of political life is inevitably one that ironically condemns itself to civic marginality and irrelevance.[10] *The*

---

[9] On the ironic similarities the preamble to the *Timaeus* establishes between Socrates and his sophist opponents, see Derrida, "Khōra" 107–8.

[10] The civic ethos of active participation in the affairs of the city, even when such affairs were dominated by conflict and division, is illustrated by the Solonian law "enacting that any who, in a time of civil factions, did not take up arms

Republic's "high" utopianism could also therefore be reinterpreted in terms of a vision of the *polis* that is divorced from *topos* in a double sense: lacking itself a place in the *polis* that exists in the real, it will also lack any concrete reference to the spatial and material organization of the *polis* in its ideal form.

In contradistinction, the later texts will provide topophilic visions of the virtue and health of the body politic. If *The Republic* was a work in which the overvaluation of philosophical autonomy had been accompanied by an undervaluation of *topos*, the trilogy of *Timaeus-Critias-The Laws* will grasp the "subject matter of politics" through a series of discourses – topography, *chorography*, *astūgraphy* – that predicate political technique on the optimal organization of the space of the *polis* (see Pradeau, *Plato* 121–2). The city will henceforth "no longer be examined by substitution or by default, but will finally become the object of political doctrine," Pradeau remarks (*Monde* 314, translation mine). Yet Pradeau's work – perhaps the most extensive and perceptive extant discussion of the spatial logic of late Platonic utopias – is significantly limited by its organizing, and incipiently "Platonizing," assumption of a fully coherent and unwaveringly philosophical Platonic corpus. From the *Menexenus* to the *Statesman* and from *The Republic* to the *Timaeus-Critias* and the *Laws*, Pradeau traces the same advocacy of philosophy as the *technē* of engendering "the unity of the city" (*Plato and the City* 5–6). Subsequently, no conflict is ever diagnosed between the figural energies released by late Plato's "spatial turn" and the production of a knowledge that is understood as "philosophical," because it is "total," "systematic," and "coherent" (*Monde* 15). In the remainder of this essay, however, I will venture that a careful look at the well-known description of Athens and Atlantis is likely to shed considerable doubt on the assumption that late Plato's civic cartography unproblematically submits to the demands of a politico-philosophical doctrine premised on "unity," "totality," "systematicity," and "coherence."

---

with either party, should lose his rights as a citizen and cease to have any part in the state" (Aristotle, *Constitution* 8.5).

A Tale of Two Cities

The *Critias* exhibits a certain curious asymmetry: the city that Plato describes concretely and in a manner that genuinely moves beyond the ou-topic abstraction of *The Republic* is not antediluvian Athens. Rendered through a description as sparse as the city's asceticism would seem to dictate (Attica, after all, has not changed dramatically enough to require extensive descriptive reconnoitering), *Critias*'s primitive Athens seems to have been produced through an imaginative exercise in what Fredric Jameson would call "world reduction" (*Archaeologies* 271). Notwithstanding its natural fertility, the Athens that Critias's fable projects is a utopia of the bare minimum: a stripped-down *Republic* from which the metaphysical and philosophical core has been excised, a polity without poets or philosophers, without an agora, without writing, with "no navy, no harbor, no marketplace, no mines, and no elaborate temple architecture" (Gill 295). Ironically, as a result, the *Critias* will be virtually always remembered for what is understood as its *parergon*, the description of a society it is supposed to condemn: "to the general reader, if Plato's account is a description of an ideal state, it is Atlantis, with its fabulous natural and material civilization, that seems to be the ideal and not the austere Attica" (Gill 296–7).[11] Lackluster, one is tempted to say Spartan, as an encomium to Athens, the "Atlantic" (as the *Critias* will also be known) has based its most durable claims to posterity as the utopic portrayal of a city that is Athens's ostensible antitype and foil.

Is the *Critias* an "ambiguous" utopia, one that precociously anticipates the representational problematic of Ursula K. Le Guin's *The Dispossessed*? I will content myself with suggesting that it presents its reader with an unsettling disjuncture between the *polis* that is virtuous and the one that is concretely imagined. This gap radically challenges, *inter alia*, Pradeau's assumption that in his late

---

[11] On Atlantis's durable utopian appeal, see Vidal-Naquet, *Black Hunter* 264–7 and *Politics* 38–65.

work Plato manages to reconcile the idealism of *The Republic* with a "systematic philosophy of the city" premised on a grasp of the materiality of its object (*Plato* 166). In fact, it is arguable that antediluvian Athens can embody the utopia of the absolutely stable and unified city to the extent that its description *is still* based on "substitution" (it "miraculously" resembles the republic of Kallipolis) and "default" (it is a stripped down variant of an already familiar city placed in the same geographical area as its modern equivalent).

But let me leave Athens for the moment and turn to what Louis Marin would call the "discursive spatial figures" of the Atlantic description (9). Critias refers to Atlantis as an island (*nēson*) that is so vast as to be also a continent "larger than Libya and Asia together" (*Crit.* 108e6–e7), but in practice he will describe only the center of its capital city – a circular island but fifteen stades in diameter. Atlantis is hence both a formless, vast territory that is in excess of the bounded and limited character of the virtuous *polis* and a concretely delineated site. Within the section focusing on the capital city's description (from 113c on), this disjunction between limited/ordered and unlimited/disorderly space will replicate itself again – this time through the description of the capital's ancient center. As Critias tells it, the capital city was created when Poseidon, after having intercourse with Cleito, the mortal daughter of earth-born Evenor, surrounded the mound on which she lived with a concentrically formed series of land and sea rings that served as protective barriers around Cleito's divinely impregnated body:

> becoming desirous of [Cleito], Poseidon had intercourse with her, and fortified the hill where she had her abode by a fence of alternate rings of sea and land, smaller and greater, one within another. He fashioned two such round wheels, as we may call them, of earth, and three of sea from the very center of the island, at uniform distances, thus making the spot inaccessible to man, for there were as yet no ships and no seafaring (*Crit.* 113d4–e2).

At the moment of its divine inception by Poseidon, the as yet undeveloped city is still innocent of the thalassocratic and commercial nature Platonic commentary has sometimes attributed to it *tout court*. Rather than functioning as symbolically antithetical elements, land

and sea emerge here as mutually reinforcing means of containment, circular boundaries that serially contain each other. In this configuration, sea water is not a passageway but a moat that prevents access to a womb-like center: "the place where the race of the first ten princes had been conceived and begotten" as the text later puts it (*Crit.* 116c6–c7).

It will not be long, however, before we read that the capital's harbor and canal have become "constantly crowded by merchant vessels and their passengers, whose vast numbers occasioned incessant shouting, clamor, and general uproar day and night" (*Crit.* 117e5–e8). The advent of maritime and commercial disorder – a shorthand for the fall into history itself – seems rather abrupt; but it has been carefully prefigured in the description of a second stage of urban development. Attempting to develop Poseidon's fortified islet into a functional city, the god's princely descendants are forced to undertake the task of further planning and construction. Pragmatically inevitable though it is, the project of city-building ends up disturbing the initial equilibrium the god had secured between the elements of land and sea:

> They first *bridged the rings of sea* round their original home, thus making themselves a road from and to their palace [...]. They began on the seaside by *cutting a canal to the outermost ring.* [...] the "ring" could now be *entered from the sea by this canal like a port,* as the *opening* they had made would admit the largest of vessels. [...] *at these bridges they made openings in the rings of land which separated those of water,* just sufficient to admit the passage of a single trireme (*Crit.* 115c4–e3, emphasis added).

Attempting to create a city by moving beyond the clearly insufficient confines of Poseidon's small island, the princes inadvertently end up exposing "their original home" to the vicissitudes of movement and change. Once functioning as mutually reinforcing boundaries, land and water are now reconfigured as bridges and canals, means of overcoming the resistance of both the "stable" and the "unstable" element to unrestricted movement. The prophylactic function of Poseidon's original plan is thus effectively reversed, and the city exposes itself to its "outside" in direct proportion to the extent of its development. Sensing the risks involved in such a civic configuration, the princes embark on a frantic effort to overcompensate for the rupture of the original boundaries, surrounding each of the rings, the Poseidon and Cleito sanctuary, and finally, the entire city with enclosures (*Crit.* 116a1–a6, 116c3–c7, 117d8–e8). All this does, however, is to move the developing city ever further from the divine harmony of the original settlement. The Atlanteans' divine *phūsis* or *moira* is increasingly adulterated, and decline inevitably follows the ever-widening dispersion of the community from the cohering kernel of the god's seed (*Crit.* 120e1, 121a9).

Pradeau, among others, has read the Atlantean description as a figurative translation of a politico-philosophical doctrine that showcases the vital importance of regulating and controlling the movement of the city's elements.[12] Atlantis is hence cast as an unhealthy body politic whose increasing disaggregation and incoherence serves as a foil to the stability that characterizes an ideal Athens. But such a reading remains curiously unsatisfactory. Although Poseidon's plan certainly resonates with the *Timaeus's* focus on boundary-setting as a means of preventing the "pollution" of the divine "seed" by an inferior element, the spatial configuration of Atlantis also questions the reliability of superimposing "politics" onto "physics" (*Tim.* 73c–73d, 69c–69e). In the *Critias*, the sea that will eventually "pollute" the quasi-divine center with commercial disharmony and finally flood the continent is the same element that has earlier served to protect that center from profanation and pollution.

At the same time, Pradeau's reading eclipses the workings of a second, and far more primary, analogical operation: that between Atlantic city-building and the process of figuration itself. To understand the logic of this second analogy and to appraise its significance for utopian genre criticism, I must take a brief detour through Jameson's remarks on the impact of narrative figuration on wish-fulfillment:

---

[12] See Pradeau, *Plato* 121, 126–31, and "Physiologie Politique "; see also Vidal-Naquet, *Black Hunter* 264, 270–4.

daydreaming and wish-fulfilling fantasy are by no means a simple operation, available at any time or place for the taking of a thought. Rather, they involve mechanisms whose inspection may have something further to tell us about the otherwise inconceivable link between wish-fulfillment and realism, between desire and history. [...] the fully realized fantasy [is] one which is not to be satisfied by the easy solutions of an unrealistic omnipotence or the immediacy of a gratification that then needs no narrative trajectory in the first place, but which on the contrary seeks to endow itself with the utmost representable difficulties and obstacles. [...] It then sometimes happens that the objections are irrefutable, and that the wish-fulfilling imagination does its preparatory work so well that the wish, and desire itself, are confounded by the unanswerable resistance of the Real (*Political Unconscious* 182–3).

Viewed through this prism, the plight of the Atlantean city-planners reads symptomatically like the quandary facing Plato himself. If Poseidon's descendants end up unraveling the coherence of the city in the very process of attempting to endow it with plausible existence, the philosopher who would submit the "concept" of the ideal polity to "ludico-mythological drift" would also surrender it to the destabilizing play of the figure: the more descriptively concrete and hence verisimilar the projected city becomes, the greater the fissure that divides the initial premise from its semiotic realization in fictive discourse (Derrida, "Khōra" 101).[13] The price of the movement from the philosophical to the literary utopia that *Critias* incompletely attempts is thus precisely the "incoherence" the latter demonstrably reveals within the "ideological axiomatic" of the former (Jameson, *Political Unconscious* 183). What it takes to keep Athens, the projected image of the ideal same, protected from such incoherence, conversely, is the no less unsatisfactory renunciation of parts of the original wish. The elimination of the "philosopher-ruler" and the

---

[13] I draw upon Derrida's emphasis on the "dynamic tension" between the "thetic effect" of the politico-philosophical "concept" and the "textual drift" of its mythological form in the *Timaeus* ("Khōra" 102, 123). I am also advocating the utility, for a comprehension of the *Critias* as utopian text, of Marin's discussion of the non-conceptual nature of utopic figuration (8).

marginalization of an apolitical Socrates anticipate the stringency of this process, which culminates in an imaginary censorship of the possibly unstable elements of the city so relentless as to leave us with what is no longer a city at all. In the words of Aristotle's trenchant critique of *The Republic*: "It is however obvious, that the more the city develops into One, the more it ceases to be a city [...] for the city is by nature the multitude [*plēthos* ...] even if it were possible to unify the city, it should not be done; for that would instead undo the city" (*Politics* II 1261a17–a24, translation mine).

It is now possible fully to appraise the significance of the relation of the *Critias* to the enigmatic request Socrates makes in the preamble of the *Timaeus*. For the *Critias* "realizes" Socrates's wish to see a city that is verisimilar yet incorruptible, "moving" with the life imparted by the spatial play of the figure yet fixed in the immobilizing perfection of the concept in a manner that, as Jameson would have it, ends up fleshing out the antinomies already dormant within the wish itself. Far from resolving the problem of the ideal city's realizability posed in the *Republic,* the dialectically related figures of both Atlantis (the city that is no longer One) and Athens (the One that is no longer a city) reveal the workings of an antinomy Greek political philosophy could neither resolve nor pretend to ignore. What the *Critias* leaves us with, then, is not a didactic lesson on the opposition between virtuous and imperfect cities but a figurative exploration of the political community's enigmatic difference to itself. Not yet and no longer "philosophy," it is an attempt to fashion a myth that does what all myths are supposed to do: relate "the original problem" (of a conflict within Greek thought on the *polis*) to the "derivative" one (of a conflict between two irreconcilable cities) (Lévi-Strauss 814). If we are still orbiting within the magnetic field of the Same – for antediluvian Athens and Atlantis are *recto* and *verso* of the same city – this Same is, mythically and against all properly "philosophical" reason, not One. As Jean-Pierre Vernant says:

> was there not, in the Greeks' very conception of the *politeia*, an ambiguity sufficient to mark, to varying degrees, the entire body of their political thought? [...] Since the term *politeia* refers both to the social group as a whole (society), and also to the state in the strictest sense, it is difficult to construct an altogether

coherent theory about it, for, depending on one's point of view, the *politeia sometimes appears multiple and heterogeneous* (with all its diversity of social functions) and *sometimes as a unified entity* (with its equal and common prerogatives that define the citizen as such) (227, emphasis added).

I may now at last properly return to where I started, namely to the question of *archē*: or rather, to *archē* itself as a question (born from one or born from two?), the site of a mythic uncertainty that would cancel out any naïve hopes of a salvaging "return." What is vitally at stake in advocating a "turn" to the Greeks is not the hope of uncovering, in all its monumental fixity, an "ancient origin." It is rather, as Kirstie McClure would put it, the installation "of what might be called paradoxical contemporaneity" (par. 29 online). Unlike the *archeophilic* attempt to "resolve" the question of the political in the present by returning our thought to its Greek *archē* – to "all those ancient issues of constitution and citizenship, of civil society and parliamentary representation, of responsibility and civic virtue" – the exploration of such contemporaneity is founded upon what Etienne Balibar would characterize as an active labor of incompletion (Jameson, *Singular Modernity* 2; Balibar, "Contradiction" 146). The Greeks are our contemporaries to the extent that they incomplete themselves, to the extent, too, that they open the thought that would "return" to them to its own incompletion – its own inability, if you want, to fill the "empty place" "of the historical resolution of a contradiction" upon which the Greeks were both "primitive" and "modern" enough to stumble (Marin xiii). Reading Plato against the grain of an inert Platonism is hence the precondition for an understanding of our relation to Greek thought, not in terms of "continuity, simple progress, even less deduction" but of a "connection" predicated on the persistence of an *aporia* that "political philosophy" has not been able to neutralize (Balibar, *Masses* 59). Hence, the necessity of coming to terms with Plato's membership in "the unacknowledged party of utopia" (Jameson, *Postmodernism* 180), a membership bestowed on all those who persist with the work of "a political and social imagination" that has not yet "found its concept" (Marin 163).

Works Cited

"Archē." *Major Greek Dictionary*. 2nd edn. Athens: Tegopoulos-Fytrakis, 1999.
Arendt, Hannah. *The Human Condition*. Chicago: University of Chicago Press, 1958.
Aristotle. *The Constitution of Athens*. Trans. Frederic G. Kenyon. *Readings in Western Civilization I: The Greek Polis*. Ed. Arthur W.H Adkins and Peter White. Chicago: University of Chicago Press, 1986. 229–78.
____ *Politika*. Vol. I. Athens: Kaktos, 1993.
Balibar, Etienne. "The Infinite Contradiction." *Yale French Studies* 88 (1995): 142–64.
____ *Masses, Classes, Ideas: Studies on Politics and Philosophy Before and After Marx*. London: Routledge, 1994.
Castoriadis, Cornelius. "The Greek Polis and the Creation of Democracy." *The Castoriadis Reader*. Ed. and trans. David Ames Davis. London: Blackwell, 1997. 267–89.
Clay, Diskin. "The Plan of Plato's Critias." *Interpreting the Timaeus-Critias: Proceedings of the IV Symposium Platonicum*. Ed. Tomás Calvo and Luc Brisson. Sankt Augustin: Academia Verlag, 1997. 49–54.
Cohen, David. *Law, Violence and Community in Classical Athens*. Cambridge: Cambridge University Press, 1993.
Dawson, Doyne. *Cities of the Gods: Communist Utopias in Greek Thought*. New York: Oxford University Press, 1992.
Derrida, Jacques. *Archive Fever: A Freudian Impression*. Trans. Eric Prenowitz. Chicago: University of Chicago Press, 1996.
____ "Khōra." Trans. Ian McLeod. *On the Name*. Ed. Thomas Dutoit. Stanford: Stanford University Press, 1995. 89–127.
____ *Writing and Difference*. Trans. Alan Bass. Chicago: University of Chicago Press, 1978.
Dombrowski, Daniel A. "Atlantis and Plato's Philosophy." *Apeiron* 15 (1981): 117–28.
Gill, Christopher. "The Genre of the Atlantis Story." *Classical Philology* 72.4 (1977): 287–304.
Jameson, Fredric. *The Political Unconscious: Narrative as a Socially Symbolic Act*. Ithaca: Cornell University Press, 1981.
____ *Postmodernism, Or The Cultural Logic of Late Capitalism*. Durham: Duke University Press, 1991.

___ *A Singular Modernity: Essay on the Ontology of the Present.* London: Verso, 2002.

___ "World Reduction in Le Guin." *Archaeologies of the Future: The Desire Called Utopia and Other Science Fictions.* London: Verso, 2005. 267–80.

Johansen, Thomas Kjeller. *Plato's Natural Philosophy: A Study of the Timaeus-Critias.* Cambridge: Cambridge University Press, 2004.

Lefort, Claude. *Democracy and Political Theory.* Trans. David Macey. Minneapolis: University of Minnesota Press, 1988.

Le Guin, Ursula K. *The Dispossessed.* New York: Harper, 1974.

Lévi-Strauss, Claude. "The Structural Study of Myth." *Critical Theory since 1965.* Ed. Hazard Adams and Leroy Searle. Tallahassee: University Press of Florida, 1986. 809–22.

Lissarrague, François and Alain Schnapp. "Imagerie des Grecs ou Grèce des imagiers?" *Le Temps de la Réflexion* 2. Paris: Gallimard, 1981. 275–97.

Loraux, Nicole. *The Divided City: Memory and Forgetting in Ancient Athens.* Trans. Corinne Pache and Jeff Fort. New York: Zone Books, 2002.

___ *Born of the Earth: Myth and Politics in Athens.* Trans. Selina Stewart. Ithaca: Cornell University Press, 2000.

Marin, Louis. *Utopics: Spatial Play.* Trans. Robert A. Vollrath. New Jersey: Humanities Press, 1984.

McClure, Kirstie M. "Disconnections, Connections, and Questions: Reflections on Jacques Rancière's 'Ten Theses on Politics.'" *Theory and Event* 6.4 (2003): 33 pars. 10 May 2005 <http://muse.jhu.edu/journals/theory_and_event/v006/6.4 mcclure.html>.

Plato. *Critias.* Ed. Yiannis Kordatos. Athens: I. Zaharopoulos, n.d.

___ *Politeia.* 2 Vols. Athens: I. Zaharopoulos, n.d.

___ *The Republic.* Trans. Desmond Lee. London: Penguin, 2003.

___ *Timaeus.* Ed. Vassilis Kalfas. Athens: Polis, 1995.

___ *Timaeus* and *Critias.* Trans. Desmond Lee. Harmondsworth: Penguin, 1977.

Pradeau, Jean François. *Le Monde de la Politique: Sur le Récit Atlande de Platon, Timée (17–27) et Critias.* Sankt Augustin: Academia Verlag, 1997.

___ *Plato and the City: A New Introduction to Plato's Political Thought.* Trans. Janet Lloyd. Exeter: Exeter University Press, 2002.

___ "La Physiologie Politique du *Critias* de Platon." *Phronesis* XLIII. 3 (1997): 317–23.

Rancière, Jacques. "Comment and Responses." *Theory and Event* 6.4 (2003):

28 pars. 10 May 2005 <http://muse.jhu.edu/journals/theory_and_event/v006/6.4ranciere.html>.

———. "Ten Theses on Politics." Trans. Rachel Bowlby and Davide Panagia. *Theory and Event* 5.3 (2001): 33 pars. 10 May 2005 <http://muse.jhu.edu/journals/theory_and_event/v005/5.3ranciere.html>.

Sallis, John. "Daydream." *Revue International de Philosophie* 205 (1998): 397–410.

Schofield, Malcolm. *Saving the City: Philosopher-Kings and Other Classical Paradigms*. London: Routledge, 1999.

Stankiewicz, Max. "Chora and Character: Mimesis and Difference in Plato's *Timaeus*." *Extreme Beauty: Aesthetics, Politics, Death*. Ed. James E. Swearingen and Joanne Cutting-Gray. London: Continuum, 2002. 56–66.

Taylor, A.E. *Plato: The Man and His Work*. London: Methuen, 1960.

Vernant, Jean Pierre. *Myth and Thought among the Greeks*. London: Routledge and Kegan Paul, 1983.

Vidal-Naquet, Pierre. *The Black Hunter: Forms of Thought and Forms of Society in the Greek World*. Trans. Andrew Szegedy-Maszac. Baltimore: Johns Hopkins University Press, 1986.

———. *Politics Ancient and Modern*. Trans. Janet Lloyd. Cambridge: Polity Press, 1995.

GERALDINE SHERIDAN

Technological Utopia/Dystopia in the Plates of the *Encyclopédie*

The utopian vision and tone of the text of Denis Diderot's *Encyclopédie* (1751–1765) undoubtedly fit with Lyman Tower Sargent's category of "utopian social theory" (21): the *philosophes* had little doubt that social progress would go hand in hand with scientific progress, and would be brought about by the kind of rational intervention in history best exemplified by the Encyclopedic undertaking itself. This included, I will contend, a free-market utopianism, contrary to Sargent's assertion that "the explicit position of those advocating a free market is anti-utopian" (21). Here I am particularly concerned with the *Encyclopédie*'s collection of some 2,800 plates which constitute, along with the *Descriptions des arts et métiers* by the Royal Academy of Sciences on which they were modeled, the most important visual record of the world of the worker in Old Regime Europe (*Recueil de planches*).[1]

Diderot's conviction that his work would help to bring about a new era of peace, happiness, and prosperity was based, to a significant degree, on the attention lavished on the trades and crafts. Why the Encyclopedists's lofty aspirations crystallized around the creation of objects, and what we now refer to as the field of technology, is an interesting question; and in particular we may ask how their concerns were transposed (and, at the same time, transfigured) in the visual medium of the copper-plate engraving.

---

1 See Schwab for a catalogue of the plates. For a history of the *Encyclopédie* (*Ency.*), see Proust, and Lough. On the *Descriptions des arts et métiers*, see Cole and Watts.

The word "technology" came into use in the period which concerns us here, in the early-to-mid-eighteenth century. Its first appearance in the modern sense is in Edward Phillips's *Dictionary* of 1706.² However, it is Christian Wolff who uses the word to sum up the technical aspirations of the seventeenth century, including the Cartesian application of the science of mathematics to an understanding of the mechanical.³ He, and more importantly his mentor Gottfried Leibniz, had long urged that the great scientific minds of Europe (including their friends in the Royal Academy of Sciences in Paris) should turn their attention to the study of the humble objects of everyday life, and the "mysteries" of their manufacture.⁴ Their concerns dovetailed with the economic aspirations of Jean-Baptiste Colbert, Louis XIV's powerful minister; and the challenge was finally taken up by the influential Abbé Jean-Paul Bignon, nephew of the Chancellor Pontchartrain, who drew around him a small group of gifted mathematicians with an interest in "the mechanical."⁵ It was this group who, as early as 1692, set out an

2   Definition: "Technology a Description of Arts, especially the Mechanical" (quoted in Guillerme and Sebestik 85, and see 28ff. for an excellent analysis of the evolution of the term).

3   In *Philosophia rationalis sive logica* in 1728 (Preliminary Discourse, Chapter "De Partibus Philosophiæ") (quoted in Guillerme and Sebestik 28–9). Guillerme and Sebestik cite Wolff's assertions with regard to the technique of splitting wood: "Les forces du coin et l'attaque qui le pousse peuvent être démontrées mathématiquement. Il y a donc une connaissance philosophique et mathématique de cet art servile, d'où la philosophique puise toute sorte de certitude" (*Philosophia* §39). See also Guillerme and Sebestik's remark that it is only in 1777 with Beckmann that "Technologie" acquires the status of an academic discipline (38).

4   See three letters from Leibniz to Filleau des Billettes, to which attention was drawn by Salomon-Bayet (232n). And see the letter from Réaumur to Formey which refers to correspondence between Wolff and Réaumur (Huard 38).

5   Jean-Paul Bignon was appointed President of the Académie Royale des Sciences in 1691; he was to become a member of all four royal Académies, as well as Director of the Book-trade and of the *Journal des Savants*; and from 1718 to 1741 he presided over the royal collections as Bibliothécaire du Roi. Thus, he controlled and directed a large part of French intellectual life. On Bignon and the Académie Royale des Sciences, see Bléchet, and Sturdy 226.

agenda which involved raising "that which is the most useful," the artifacts of contemporary civilization, to a new level of intellectual esteem. The crafts and trades had been undervalued, Jacques Jaugeon, one of the group, suggested: first, because they were associated with their materials of origin; and second, because they were the product of the work of the hands, and "sont des effets en apparence d'un ordre si bas et si borné qu'on croit ne devoir pas les élever au dessus de ce qu'ils sont ni donner à ceux qui les exercent une plus heureuse estime" (2). Over half a century later, Diderot, himself the son of a master cutler, famously took up this theme in the *Encyclopédie* and professed his desire to confer a new value and esteem on trades and artisans, eulogizing the philosophic, scientific, and mathematical skill and knowledge of tradespeople in the article "Art":

> Dans quel système de Physique ou de Métaphysique remarque-t-on plus d'intelligence, de sagacité, de conséquence, que dans les machines à filer l'or, faire des bas, & dans les métiers de Passementiers, de Gaziers, de Drapiers ou d'ouvriers en soie? Quelle démonstration de Mathématique est plus compliquée que le mécanisme de certaines horloges, ou que les différentes opérations par lesquelles on fait passer ou l'écorce du chanvre, ou la coque du ver, avant que d'en obtenir un fil qu'on puisse employer à l'ouvrage ? Quelle projection plus belle, plus délicate & plus singulière que celle d'un dessin sur les cordes d'un sample, & des cordes du sample sur les fils d'une chaîne ? qu'a-t-on imaginé en quelque genre que ce soit, qui montre plus de subtilité que le chiné des velours?

Along with the agenda of the earlier group, Diderot also adopted the specific concept and layout of the copper plate in two parts which they had developed.[6] It is hardly surprising that Roland Barthes, astute interpreter of cultural phenomena, was one of the first scholars to highlight – in an essay written to accompany a collection of the plates – the density of these images, which encompass what he calls a "philosophy of the object" (11). If we look at a typical plate, we see the *vignette* or work scene in the top third, and the tools, equipment,

---

6 Diderot's extensive plagiarism of the Academy's plates is well established: see, for example, Huard, 35–46, Proust, 49–51 and 68–70, Seguin 26–33, and Pinault.

and machine components in the bottom section (see Plate 1). This image represents a pinmaker's workshop: the copper wire is being drawn, then cut by the boys sitting on the floor, who were expected to cut 4,200 pins an hour; they were pointed by the grinders on the left. Barthes remarked how the *vignette*s reintroduce the disemboweled machines represented in the bottom portion of the majority of the plates into a human environment, as the plates – unlike written texts – can be read in both directions, bottom to top as well as top to bottom, with an interesting circularity that offers a resistance to meaning ("Image" 13). The machines or tools, taking up much more space than the pictorial representation of the workers' functions, offer an interesting inversion of the relationship between human person and machine at a particularly critical moment in the history of manufacture. In the representation of the tools, for example, we often see a disembodied hand, which has become an appendage of the tool, rather than vice versa, as in a detail from the plate on needle-making.

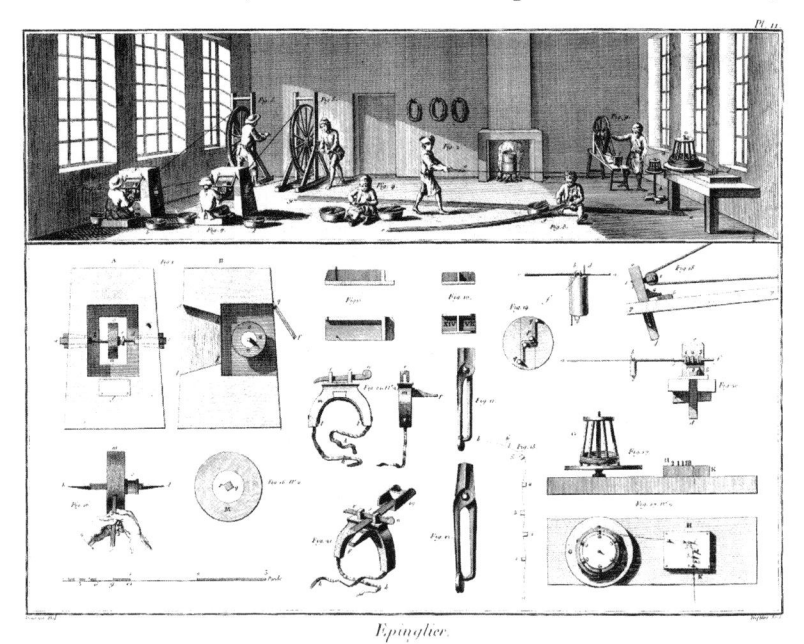

Plate 1. *Recueil de Planches*, 'Epinglier, pl.II'. Courtesy Archives des Sciences, Paris.

Technological Utopia/Dystopia in the Plates of the Encyclopédie   143

On the one hand, as Vincent Milliot pointed out, in this assimilation of the artisan and the mechanical we can find echoes of a new dignity which associates the knowledge and skill of the worker with a new scientific mode of functioning; but on the other hand, "cette visée rationaliste [...] constitue une véritable utopie, qui, sous couvert de réhabilitation du travail manuel, déplace sans l'abolir vraiment la condescendence des élites vis-à-vis des classes laborieuses" (26).

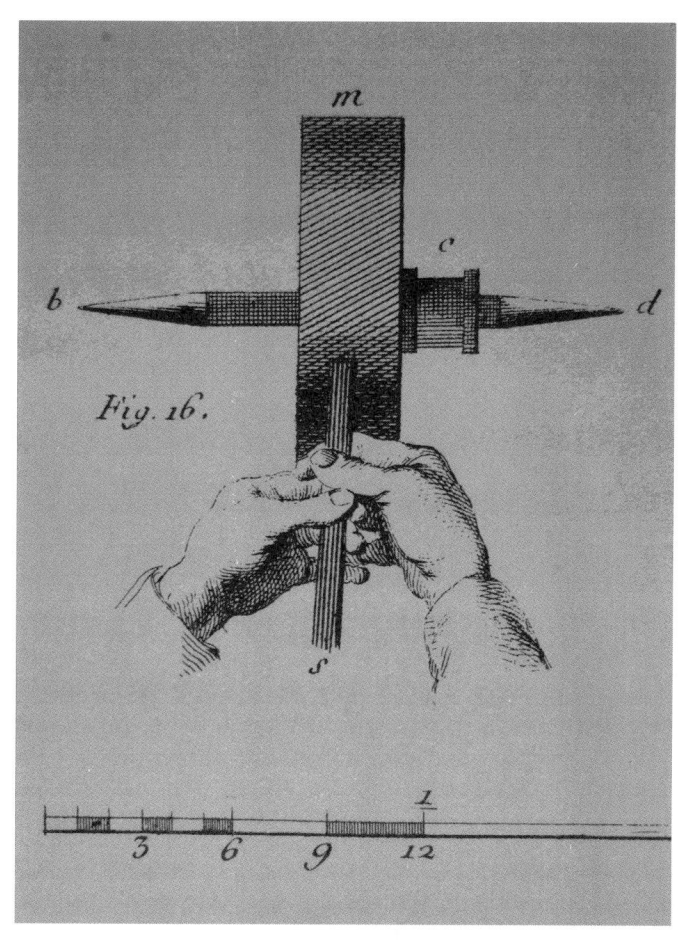

Plate 1. Detail. *Recueil de Planches,* 'Epinglier, pl.II'. Courtesy Archives des Sciences, Paris.

Part of the alienation which the modern reader experiences when faced with these images is a direct result of the innovative methodology which evolved in the course of their creation. The complex history of the work carried out by Bignon's small talented group of *méchaniciens* (philosopher-technologists) in the early 1690s, prior to their admission to the Académie des Sciences, cannot be recounted in detail here. Suffice it to say that the group struggled to apply a rationalist, mathematical paradigm to the description of technological processes: their engraver was asked to *réduire* (to reduce: a geometric term applied to the division of a figure into different parts) the original "landscape"-type drawings, made by an artist in an actual artisan's workshop, in order to better represent a rational ordering of discrete steps in production.[7] This ordering was to correspond to the logical description presented in the parallel text. Interestingly, in his discussion of the *Encyclopédie* plates, Barthes, who would not have known this earlier material, was to use the language of structural linguistics to describe this function of division as a *declension,* with the bottom section of the plate, which breaks down the components, having a paradigmatic, and the *vignette* a syntagmatic function ("Image" 13). As Jacques Guillerme and Jan Sebestik have underlined, the whole question of a "technological" language, both at the level of terminology and syntax, was of crucial importance to the Académie des Sciences and the *Encyclopédistes.*[8]

7   See Archives de l'Académie des Sciences, Paris: set of documents foliated consecutively from f.149 to f.160 and inserted at the back of vol.13 of the Procès-verbaux of the Académie Royale des Sciences, with the title "Description des Arts et Métiers. Des Seances de l'annèe 1695 jusqu'en 1696. Addition, jointe a ce volume de registres." Parts of this document are reproduced by Salomon-Bayet 245–50.

8   "Tout comme les structures corporatistes et le secret des fabrications, l'irrégularité terminologique fait obstacle au développement des manufactures. Instrument de divulgation, l'*Encyclopédie* aspire à réaliser la communicabilité universelle des arts, en constituant un vocabulaire homogène, réglé comme celui de la géométrie, toute attribution étant normalisée. Cette constitution de la *terminologie technique unitaire* achève et unifie le monde des arts et métiers, en permettant de la considérer comme un réseau complexe mais unique d'opérations transformatrices, rationnellement décrites [...]. Cette unification

For the latter, the unification of the network of transforming operations, hitherto carried out by multiple artisans belonging to rival communities, was seen as the basic condition of technical progress; and this utopian rationalization was to be constituted in the multiple languages – graphic and iconic – of the *Encyclopédie*. However, this movement was also, as Barthes again noted, one of appropriation, of possession, paradoxically achieved through fragmentation:

> L'Encyclopédisme du XVIIIe siècle, [est] fondé, lui, sur un savoir d'appropriation. Formellement (ceci est bien sensible dans les planches), la propriété dépend essentiellement d'un certain morcellement des choses: s'approprier, c'est fragmenter le monde, le diviser en objets finis, assujettis à l'homme à proportion même de leur discontinu: car on ne peut séparer sans finalement nommer et classer, et dès lors, la propriété est née. Mythiquement, la possession du monde n'a pas commencé à la Genèse, mais au Déluge, lorsque l'homme a été contraint de nommer chaque espèce d'animaux et de la loger ("Image" 12).

In what follows, I will show how the attempt to fragment and "appropriate" the human dimension of work in the plates yields some disconcerting results.

Before looking in detail at the functioning of the utopian impulse in the plates of the *Encyclopédie*, it is important to raise the question of intentionality: Sargent underlines that the intention of the author is a significant element in determining whether any work belongs in the corpus of utopian artifacts (6). This consideration is all the more crucial in categorizing visual images as utopian, given that they are even less amenable than the written word to being contained within the boundaries of their originator's overt intentions. My contention is that Diderot set out to present a utopian vision consonant with the definition sketched by Crane Brinton: "Things [...] are bad; [...] things must become better [...] here on earth and soon; things will not

---

ne concerne pas seulement la normalisation du vocabulaire. Elle va jusqu'à la syntaxe du langage des arts, à la détermination des rapports logiques dans une fabrication ou dans une machine donnée" (Guillerme and Sebestik 34–5).

improve to this degree by themselves, by a 'natural' growth or development of things-as-they-are; a plan must be developed and put into execution" (quoted in Sargent 4). We know that Diderot did not run around Paris studying the artisans in their workshops, with his artist reproducing a kind of photographic reality, as was once believed: the plates of the *Encyclopédie* are less a reflection of contemporary practices, than a restructuring of reality to fit a program for improvement.[9] The plates had a specifically didactic purpose, and as such belonged to a different genre than most other representations of work in this period (see Sewell, "Visions" 268). By the nature of the medium, however, there is a constant tension between the dream and the reality: on the one hand, we see some of the key configurations of the nineteenth-century industrial world slip into place in Diderot's brave new world, while on the other we are simultaneously allowed glimpses of the underbelly of pre- and proto-industrial society. The world as it is represented here would have been both familiar and alien to contemporaries, hovering between a specific moment of history and a curious timeless zone.

I am, of course, reading these images with the benefit of hindsight, with a very different set of ideological receptors from those of the first audience: but, as Barthes asserted, "L'information n'est pas close avec ce que l'image pouvait dire au lecteur de son époque: le lecteur moderne reçoit lui aussi de cette image ancienne des informations que l'encyclopédiste ne pouvait prévoir" ("Image" 14). Sargent has also pointed out that it is perfectly possible for a work the author intended as a positive utopia to be, from another perspective, a dystopia, in part because of the basic ambiguity which, he argues, lies at the heart of all utopian expression (12, 26).

We can, however, identify a number of elements in these plates which were specifically intended to function as utopian: the first being the abolition, or at least reduction, of the distinction between workers crucial to the guild system. One of Diderot's main objectives was to smash the power of the trade guilds that dominated most aspects of production under the Old Regime, particularly (though not solely) in

---

[9] See Proust 191ff. for an account and refutation of these myths.

France, and that jealously guarded the rights of masters to regulate access to their trade, the conditions of production, and the market. The weight of tradition, in this as in other aspects of life, was identified by the *philosophes* as irrational and regressive. The abolition of the guilds in favor of a free and individualized market for workers and goods was presented as the rational alternative, promoting universal good over the self-interest of particular groups: there are, Diderot thundered in the *Encyclopédie*, "des têtes étroites, des âmes mal nées, indifférentes sur le sort du genre humain, et tellement concentrées dans leur petite société, qu'elles ne voient rien au-delà de son intérêt." Diderot's own approach is to disregard the guilds' ancient regulations and distinctions, since he identifies them as the main culprits in maintaining a closed shop and protectionist ethos, and to focus instead on economic imperatives and profit. As Cynthia Koepp has highlighted, the *Encyclopédistes* consistently disparage what she calls the "popular culture of work," but they fail to offer any compensating advantages to a social group destined, by the new ideology of the social division of labor, to remain at the bottom of the scale, with little access to literacy: for all the pious assertions of the "usefulness" of the workers, there was a prevailing view that the general good would be best served by their being restricted to only the most rudimentary primary education (241–2).

Plate 2. *Recueil de Planches*, 'Papeterie, pl. Ière'. Courtesy Archives des Sciences, Paris.

Let me now look at one of Diderot's triumphant examples of progress: the manufacturing of paper (see Plate 2). This was an activity where labor was mostly concentrated within one large institution. A contextualizing image sets the scene: this is the great paper manufactory of L'Anglée, situated about sixty miles south of Paris, near Montargis. Built in 1738 with the support of the Duke of Orléans, in its proportion and balance it represents the high point of classical eighteenth-century architecture; the canal systems, which furnished the water essential for power, and also for the paper itself, are highlighted. The buildings on both wings provided housing for the workers and their children: this was a paternalistic establishment, with all aspects of the lives of the hundreds of workers contained within this "ideal city." The curious thing is that all trace of the workers has been eliminated from the image: even the windows are blank, with no view to the inside. The "humanizing" element is external in every sense, separated from the building by the water. Who are the people in the horse-drawn canal boat? Eighteenth-century tourists from Paris? Or people involved in some aspect of the paper trade? Whoever they are, the pointing hand tells us this building is worthy of our admiration: in its scale and rational occupation of the space, it represents a new order imposed on the chaotic world of manufacture.

Plate 3. *Recueil de Planches*, 'Papeterie, pl. IX'. Courtesy Archives des Sciences, Paris.

Technological Utopia/Dystopia in the Plates of the Encyclopédie   149

Plate 4. *Recueil de Planches*, 'Papeterie, pl. XIII'. Courtesy Trinity College Library, Dublin

In other images belonging to the same series, however, the missing workers become visible. The most valued activities – the making of the paper moulds, the filling and emptying of the moulds with fiber – are undertaken by men whom we can assume to be apprentices or qualified journeymen (see Plate 3). The frockcoats they wear are a good indication of relatively high status within the culture of a trade (see *Recueil de planches*: "Papetterie" pl. X). In many of the plates, however, the tasks are performed by women and children, people whose very existence as workers was typically ignored or contested in written registers and records. The women we see in the images, whether cutting up the rags, or removing imperfections from sheets which they separate and count, represent in all probability young women drawn in from the surrounding villages, who might work for ten to twelve years to assemble the most basic dowry to marry (see *Recueil de planches*: "Papetterie" pl. I bis). Theirs was the cheap labor on which the enterprise thrived (see Plate 4). Likewise, the ubiquitous children: in Plate 5, we can see how the rancid, fermented rags are cut up once again before being thrown into the mill (see Plate 5). This is done by little boys who hack the rags against a large blade set into the workbench. In the image we see the blocks made available so that even the smallest – and youngest – child can reach the bench (as the text helpfully explains): as they were living in the complex shown in Plate 2, they could be brought in to work as young as seven or eight years of age. The distinctions crucial to the guild system are eroded here in favor of an undifferentiated workforce: this is achieved by the equal size and juxtaposition of the images, as much as by the text which, in general, highlights difference only in terms of the labor costs – clearly much less in the case of the women and children. The privileges of guild membership, with its hierarchies and traditions, is reversed in favor of a new value system: the cheaper and more numerous the labor, the better the economic outcome.

Plate 5. *Recueil de Planches*, 'Papeterie, pl. III'. Courtesy Archives des Sciences, Paris.

The second aspect of these plates that we can highlight is the rational ordering and breakdown of tasks, based on an analytical model. In the *Encyclopédie*, we can see how this operated in a typical series, the plates devoted to Fan-making, one of the great luxury trades for which Paris was famous. In the *vignette* of the first plate, a woman seated at the table ("Fig. 1" in Plate 6) glues two sheets of paper together, using the small sponge and bowl of glue. The woman seated to the front ("Fig. 2") peels off the now double sheets from the pile supplied to her and, wetting the sides, she spreads them on the hoops or frames of the appropriate size. The worker standing behind them ("Fig. 3") has the sole function of taking the hoop and hanging it up to dry. "Fig 4" removes the dry paper from each hoop, and passes the pile to the woman ("Fig. 5") who rounds off two of the corners with a scissors. The second plate in the series (not reproduced here) represents a room where the fans are painted, probably with gouache, and where, we are told, two workers could operate, although we see only one young woman in the image: she is copying the picture which will decorate one side of the fan from the model in a frame in front of her. With the third image (Plate 7) we are back in a workshop, where the relatively skilled work of assembling the fan is carried out: one worker marks out the lines along which she will then fold the leaf, before the second worker inserts the sticks of the fan between the two sides of the paper alongside each fold.

Plate 6. *Recueil de Planches*, 'Eventailliste, pl.I'. Private Collection.

152   *Geraldine Sheridan*

Plate 7. *Recueil de Planches*, 'Eventailliste, pl.III'. Private Collection

The clear fragmentation of tasks in this labor-intensive activity is presented in a manner that resembles the classic division of labor as advocated by Adam Smith. Indeed, it is very likely that Smith based his example of pin-making, in Book I of *The Wealth of Nations* (8 and n4), on the corresponding article in the *Encyclopédie* ("Epingle") where Alexis Delaire (who did actually visit Parisian workshops) comments that one pin undergoes eighteen operations before being sold to the consumer.[10] The flat presentation of the workers in a row, and the lack of communication between them, are striking, and evoke the layout of an assembly line. The unrelentingly analytical approach, having broken down the process of production as a whole into discrete

---

10   In fact, Réaumur had remarked on the same phenomenon some fifty years earlier, in a draft preface for the *Descriptions,* never actually published: "Une épingle que nous ne regardons pas, passe, comme nous le disons, par plus de 20 mains différentes, et chaque main lui donne une façon" (ms. Houghton, 432.1 (1), f.2).

steps, assumes that the process consists of the simple adding up of these discrete steps. Clearly, one worker must pass the paper or hoop to the next person, but no such contact is indicated. The nature of the still image is such that movement cannot be directly depicted, but it can be signified by gestures, which are completely absent here. In this, as in the vast majority of plates there is no eye contact between the workers – each is an isolated figure in the accomplishment of their own task: there is no community. As William Sewell has shown, this contrasts starkly with earlier prints which emphasized the unity of a trade, and suggested a common purpose of which our plates are devoid: he gives the example of a sixteenth-century print depicting sugar-making, by Hans van der Straat, in which all the stages of the process are shown together in one image, from the harvesting of the cane to the stacking of the sugar loaves ("Visions" 268). The workers lean or look towards each other, all contributing to the finished product exhibited on the table, and the whole suggests a common purpose of which our plates are devoid.

Another noteworthy "utopian" element is the portrayal of sanitized, classically proportioned, and extremely unrealistic workshops, where great windows offer plenty of natural light. These are far from the realities we know to have prevailed in the crowded, unsanitary conditions of eighteenth-century Paris, where apprentices, journeymen, and female servants were often poorly accommodated in the vicinity of the workshops themselves. Some flavor of this life, with its counter-community of workers versus paternalistic masters, can be gleaned from Robert Darnton's "The Great Cat Massacre," where the apprentices decided to take revenge for the ill treatment they suffered (including poor quality food) by killing the mistress's cats (75–104). The classical room featured in Plate 7, with its perfectly balanced cupboards and four huge windows, is utterly devoid of signs of social life: only the person as producer is of interest in this world. There are no personal items or clothing belonging to the worker(s), no food or pet animals, no discarded materials lying on the floor. The degree to which this is a dehumanized space reflects the dark side of Diderot's opposition to the corporations: if the guilds represented technical conservatism, and a closed shop mentality, they also ensured solidarity and exchange between workers, as depicted in other *genres* of engravings.¹¹ This image contrasts with a nineteenth-century plate of an artisan's workshop, reproduced and analyzed by Sewell, this time depicting shoemakers who were noted for their radicalism ("Visions" 283). Tools, objects, bits of cut-off leather clutter the surfaces of their workshop; there is a picture of Napoleon – obviously their hero – on the wall, and a little songbird in a cage, signifying cheeriness and life, along with wine flagons, the staple drink of the working man. The only window is the shopfront where their wares are displayed. There is strong individualization of the workers, through their features and varied head-gear, and a relaxed companionability is implied, with one smoking his pipe. These are characters, we can imagine, who would not be so easily controlled as the contained, unobtrusive workers of Diderot's ideal working world.

This leads me to another element in this utopia: the figures are almost always lacking any individuality of features or dress, other than as an indicator of status. They are also ageless, eternally in the prime of life, and at their most productive. They show no evidence of the deformation of the human body subjected to an average twelve to fourteen hours of work each day, much of it heavy physical effort which bent and broke the human form by the age of thirty. As Barthes remarked, the vision proffered by these plates is of a "monde sans peur," a world without fear, in keeping with the rationalistic positivism of the *philosophes*: these young, machine-like workers are impervious to pain and illness ("Image" 12). And yet, there are many signs of the unhealthy conditions rampant in the work environment, but they are incidental, and go unremarked in the text. Everywhere we see stoves with noxious materials boiling all day within the workshops (see the pin-makers' workshop in Plate 1), including glue for fan-making, lead for type-casting, salts, and chemicals for all sorts of

---

11   See Koepp's conclusion: "To the extent that workers were perceived as marginal and disruptive, their private languages, their corporate groups, their rites and rituals served to insulate them somewhat from the dominant official culture, to render them culturally self-sufficient, and to provide some small defence against the kinds of economic movements transforming industry in the eighteenth century – in other words, to allow them a source of autonomous power" (257).

treatments and finishes; but we are left to imagine the fumes and their effects on the workers. The *Encyclopédistes* cannot have been totally unaware of the increasing volume of writing describing work-related illnesses in this period, as recorded by Arlette Farge; it was well established, for example, that convulsive trembling was caused by the handling of mercury, and the fumes from mercurial substances in workshops (997). "Ne sommes-nous pas forcés de convenir que plusieurs arts sont une source de maux pour ceux qui les exercent?," remarked Bernardino Ramazzini in the Preface to his *Essai sur les maladies des artisan,* first published in Latin in Modena in 1700 (quoted in Farge 995). Yet Diderot chose to deny the noxious effects of the fumes of regulus, well known to tradesmen, in his *Encyclopédie* article "Caractères d'imprimerie." His attitude towards the health of the foundry workers appears cavalier, and betrays his own prejudice against guild solidarities and "secrets":

> On recommande aux ouvriers occupés à ce fourneau [...] de se garantir avec soin de la vapeur du régule, qu'on regarde comme un poison dangereux : mais c'est un préjugé; l'usage du régule n'expose les Fondeurs à aucune maladie qui leur soit particulière, sa vapeur n'est funeste tout au plus que pour les chats : les premières fois qu'ils y sont exposés, ils sont attaqués de vertiges d'une nature si singulière, qu'après s'être tourmentés pendant quelque tems dans la chambre où ils sont forcés de la respirer, ils s'élancent par les fenêtres: j'en ai vu deux fois l'expérience dans un même jour.

In this instance, the traditional wisdom of the workers was based on valuable experience and observation concerning the deleterious effects on their health, evidence rejected by Diderot with a curious disregard for the implications of his own anecdote concerning the effects of these same fumes on animals.

However, even in those treatises expressly devoted to occupational illnesses, including several manuscript *Mémoires* from 1787–1788 by Pajot des Charmes, Farge notes a serene, anodyne tone which only rarely betrays indignation, but which, like the plates examined here, has a contrary effect on the modern reader: "Discrétion, bon aloi, linéarité des descriptions s'appuyant sur des connaissances de type scientifique ont paradoxalement une façon étrange de faire ressortir le malheur. Ainsi contenu, il prend, par endroits, sa totale dimension tragique" (995). We are shocked by many of the images in the *Encyclopédie* precisely because their detached, didactic presentation jars so unexpectedly with the information encoded incidentally by the artist. We might take as an example one image from the silk industry of Lyon, where there was a notoriously high mortality rate among the young girls (see Plate 8; and see Garden 53 and 143, Hufton 92ff., and Davis 167–97). In this charming, bucolic image, the seated woman is taking up the single filament from each silk cocoon in a pan in front of her, in which water is kept near boiling by a little furnace beneath it. The bowl on the ground beside her is filled with cold water so that she can cool her hand occasionally. Two threads, each made up of separate filaments from a number of cocoons, are being reeled onto the machine operated by a hand-crank; developed in Northern Italy, this type of machine was used right into the next century. We are told in the plate-legend that this work is done outdoors in June and July, when it is warm enough not to need an inside workshop, but the fact that the work was also frequently done inside at other times of the year, in a steamy atmosphere where tuberculosis thrived, is blithely passed over, as is the fact that the skin on the girls' hands was gradually destroyed by contact with the boiling water.[12] These little figures carry out their tasks with the efficiency, joylessness, and lack of feeling of machines, good automatons (see Koepp 243; Sewell, *Work* 68–9).

---

12   See Farge on the studies of illness in craft workers in the latter part of the century: "le vocabulaire relativement serein, toujours précis, employé pour parvenir à décrire des conditions d'emploi par moments insupportables, qui tirent le corps humain au-delà de ce qu'il peut subir et désagrègent à la fois sa santé et sa dignité, témoigne de la façon dont des notables 'peuvent' parler du peuple" (995). On the detail of the processes of silk production, see Hills.

Plate 8. *Recueil de Planches*, 'Soierie, pl. I'. Courtesy Trinity College Library, Dublin

It is only a very rare image in this collection that allows any vulnerability in the worker, as does one image from crown glassmaking; we can almost feel the terrible heat from which the leather-clad workers are poorly protected as they lift the burning hot pots of molten material out of the huge furnaces (see Plate 9). They have to turn their backs to withstand the blast of heat. Interestingly, Farge notes just one example in the work of Pajot des Charmes where the author expresses revulsion at the conditions of work, and it is precisely in relation to such a glass-making workshop: "Il n'est point d'étranger qui ne se trouve révolté de l'odeur fade et méphitique qui règne dans les ateliers" (995). In this chokingly hot atmosphere little boys were employed: in the detail of Plate 10 we see one carrying away the molten impurities from the poured liquid in his ladle (see Plate 10). Such images spill out meaning beyond the containing rationalism of their didactic function, and bring us up short in the face of information not deemed important enough to merit explanation or exclusion.

Robert Mauzi suggests that these plates represent a privileged moment in the history of western society, between the two tragic eras represented, on the one hand, by the theological interpretation of work as God's punishment on mankind (which, incidentally, Sargent identifies as the source and origin of anti-utopianism) and, on the other, by the era of industrialization and the alienation of the machine (21–2). The *Encyclopédie*, Mauzi declares, had the good fortune to be born at a moment in history when the relationship between humans and work could appear to be happy (22); perhaps, however, Mauzi did not look closely enough, for there were many signs of industrial alienation already inscribed in the *Encyclopédie*'s visions of a new labor. The drive towards rationalism, geometric order, and the primacy of process was ultimately disrupted in the plates by the very nature of the visual medium. Barthes's comments about journalistic photographs and their accompanying texts may be applied here to these much earlier attempts at recording reality: "Il est cependant impossible [...] que la parole 'double' l'image; car dans le passage d'une structure à l'autre s'élaborent fatalement des signifiés seconds" (945).

Thus we have seen how representations of stoves spewing out noxious fumes are captured within images which purport to represent modern, pristine workspaces; how the boiling cauldron for dissolving the sericin of silk cocoons betrays the unspoken/ unspeakable pain suffered by the young silk-winder. And how could the ubiquitous presence of child labor be anything other than a signifier of human suffering and exploitation to the modern observer, subverting the *philosophes*' vision of "progress"? Despite Diderot's clearly utopian intentions, elements of a dystopian world where the person is reduced to the level of instrument, where human needs are ignored or exploited, assert their presence. We may call to mind the quip by Max Beerbohm:

> So this is Utopia
> > Is it? Well–
> I beg your pardon;
> > I thought it was Hell (quoted in Sargent 1).

Plate 9. *Recueil de Planches*, 'Verrerie en bois, ou grande verrerie, pl. XVII'. Courtesy Archives des Sciences, Paris.

Plate 10. *Recueil de Planches*, 'Manufacture des glaces. Glaces coulées, pl. XIX'.

Works Cited

Barthes, Roland. "Image, Raison, Déraison." *L'Univers de l'Encyclopédie*. Paris: Les Libraires Associés, 1964. 11–16.
―――. "Le Message photographique." *Œuvres complètes de Barthes*. Ed. Eric Marty. Paris: Seuil, 1993. I: 937–49.
Bléchet, Françoise. "L'abbé Bignon, président de l'Académie royale des sciences: un demi–siècle de direction scientifique."
Règlement, usages et science dans la France de l'absolutisme. Ed. Christiane Demeulenaere and Eric Brian. Paris: Lavoisier, 2002. 51–70.
Cole, Arthur H., and George B. Watts. *The Handicrafts of France as Recorded in the* Descriptions des arts et métiers (1761–1788). Boston: Baker Library, 1952.

Darnton, Robert. *The Great Cat Massacre and other Episodes in French Cultural History.* New York: Vintage, 1985.

Davis, Natalie Zemon. "Women in the Crafts in Sixteenth-century Lyons." *Women and Work in Preindustrial Europe.* Ed. Barbara A. Hanawalt. Bloomington: Indiana University Press, 1986. 167– 97.

Descriptions des arts et métiers, faites et approuvées par Messieurs de l'Académie royale des sciences avec figure. 76 vols. Paris, 1761–1789.

Encyclopédie, ou dictionnaire raisonné des sciences, des arts et des métiers, par une société de gens de lettres. Ed. Denis Diderot and Jean Le Rond d'Alembert. 17 vols. Paris: Libraires Associés, 1751–1765.

Farge, Arlette. "Les Artisans malade de leur travail." *Annales E.S.C.* 5 (1977): 993–1006.

Garden, Maurice. *Lyon et les Lyonnais au XVIIIe siècle.* Paris: Flammarion, 1970.

Guillerme, Jacques, and Jan Sebestik. *Les commencements de la technologie.* Paris: Thalès, 1968.

Hills, Richard L. "From Cocoon to Cloth. The Technology of Silk Production". *La seta in Europa secx. XII–XX: Atti della 24esima Settimana di Studi, Istituto Internazionale di Storia Economica "F. Datin (4–9 May 1992)."* Ed. Simonetta Cavaciocchi. Florence: Le Monnier, 1993. 59–90.

Huard, Georges. "Les Planches de l'Encyclopédie et celles de la *Description des arts et Métiers* de l'Académie des Sciences." *L'Encyclopédie et le progrès des sciences et des techniques.* Ed. Suzanne Delorme and René Taton. Paris: Presses Universitaires de France, 1952. 35–46.

Hufton, Olwen. *The Prospect before Her: A History of Women in Western Europe.* London, Harper Collins, 1995.

Jaugeon, Jacques. "Description et perfection des arts et mestiers. Des arts de construire les caracteres, de graver les poinçons de lettres, de fondre les lettres. d'imprimer les lettres, et de relier les livres. Tome premier. Par Monsieur Jaugeon de L'Academie Royale des Sciences. M. VCCIII." MS. 2741: Bibliothèque de l'Institut, Paris f.2. Unpublished.

Koepp, Cynthia J. "The Alphabetical Order in Diderot's *Encyclopédie*." *Work in France: Representations, Meaning, Organization, and Practice.* Ed. Steven L. Kaplan and Cynthia J. Koepp. Ithaca : Cornell University Press, 1986. 229–57.

Lough, John. *L'Encyclopédie.* London: Longman, 1971.

Mauzi, Robert. "Une Souveraineté Éphémère." *L'Univers de l'Encyclopédie.* Paris: Les Libraires Associés, 1964. 17–22.

Milliot, Vincent. "Le travail sans le geste. Les représentations iconographiques des petits métiers Parisiens, XVIe–XVIIIe siècle." *Revue d'Histoire Moderne et Contemporaine* 41.1 (January–March 1994): 5–28.

Phillips, Edward (compiler). *The New World of Words or Universal English Dictionary. The Sixth Edition, Revised, Corrected and Improved.* London: Kersey, 1706.

Pinault, Madeleine. *Aux Sources de l'Encyclopédie: la Description des arts et métiers.* 4 vols. École Pratique des Hautes Études, Ive Section, Histoire du Livre, Mémoire, 1984. Typescript.

Proust, Jacques. *Diderot et l'Encyclopédie.* Paris: Colin, 1962.

Ramazzini, Bernardino. *De morbis artificum diatrib.* Modena: Capponi, 1700.

Recueil de planches sur les sciences, les arts libéraux et les arts mécaniques, avec leurs explications. 11 vols. Paris: Les Libraires Associés, 1762–1772.

Salomon–Bayet, Claire. "Un Préambule théorique à une Académie des Arts." *Revue d'Histoire des Sciences et de leurs Applications* 23 (1970): 229–50.

Sargent, Lyman Tower. "The Three Faces of Utopianism Revisited." *Utopian Studies* 5.1 (1994): 1–37.

Schwab, Richard N. *Inventory of Diderot's Encyclopédie.* Vol. VII: *Inventory of the Plates.* Oxford: Voltaire Foundation, 1984.

Seguin, Jean-Pierre. "Courte histoire des planches de l'Encyclopédie". *L'Univers de l'Encyclopédie.* Paris: Les Libraires Associés, 1964. 26–33.

Sewell, William Hamilton. *Work and Revolution in France: the Language of Labour from the Old Regime to 1848.* Cambridge and New York: Cambridge University Press, 1980.

―――. "Visions of Labor: Illustrations of the Mechanical Arts before, in, and after Diderot's *Encyclopédie*." *Work in France: Representations, Meaning, Organization, and Practice.* Ed. Steven Laurence Kaplan and Cynthia J. Koepp. Ithaca: Cornell University Press, 1986. 258–86.

Smith, Adam. *The Wealth of Nations.* Ed. Edwin Cannan. New York: Random House, 1937.

Sturdy, David. *Science and Social Status. The Members of the Académie des Sciences, 1666–1750.* Woodbridge: Boydell, 1995.

MATTHEW BEAUMONT

The Party of Utopia: Utopian Fiction and the Politics of Readership 1880–1900

In the concluding paragraph of "Utopianism after the End of Utopia" in *Postmodernism, or, The Cultural Logic of Late Capitalism*, an account of an exhibition of contemporary conceptual art, Fredric Jameson makes a tantalizing reference to what he calls the "Party of Utopia":

> Yet in our time, where the claims of the officially political seem extraordinarily enfeebled and where the taking of older kinds of political positions seems to inspire widespread embarrassment, it should also be noted that one finds everywhere today – not least among artists and writers – something like an unacknowledged "party of Utopia": an underground party whose numbers are difficult to determine, whose program remains unannounced and perhaps even unformulated, whose existence is unknown to the citizenry at large and to the authorities, but whose numbers seem to recognize one another by means of secret Masonic signals (180).

"One even has the feeling," he concludes with a mischievous wink, "that some of the present exhibitors may be among its adherents" (180).

I have the feeling that a substantial number of academics associated with the constantly expanding field of utopian studies are not merely adherents to, or fellow travelers of, the Party of Utopia, so much as paid-up members, if not committed full-timers. Jameson himself explicitly dedicates *Archaeologies of the Future* to a handful of comrades in the Party – scholars and writers Peter Fitting, Darko Suvin, Susan Willis, and Kim Stanley Robinson – who collectively constitute what might be called its central committee; and it is consequently difficult to resist the suspicion that he is therefore its unofficial general secretary. Certainly, it is tempting to identify the Party of Utopia as a means whereby unaffiliated leftist intellectuals can maintain some belief in an alternative to capitalism after the collapse of actually existing communism. In this respect, it can be speculated that it is related to the spectral association that, two or three years after Jameson's invocation of the notion, Jacques Derrida called the "New International":

> a link of affinity, suffering, and hope, a still discreet, almost secret link, as it was around 1848, but more and more visible, we have more than one sign of it. It is an untimely link, without status, without title, and without name, barely public even if it is not clandestine, without contract, "out of joint," without coordination, without party, without country, without national community, [...] without co-citizenship, without common belonging to a class (85–6).

Derrida's is an International fit not so much for the proletariat in the epoch of globalization as for a virtual community of intellectuals and academics that feels exiled in the prevailing climate of postmodernism and postmodernity. "Many of us will feel deep sympathy with [Derrida's] conception of a new International," Jameson subsequently commented, "as far as radical intellectuals are concerned" (29). The understated qualification with which Jameson concludes this sentence seems appropriate to the attempt to appraise the Party of Utopia too. I feel deep sympathy for Jameson's conception, as far as radical intellectuals are concerned.

It is not my intention in this essay, however, even if it were possible, to compose a detailed portrait of the Party of Utopia as it is presently constituted (or as it currently can be imagined). To do so is probably an important task, one that has become more urgent over the last ten or fifteen years, in the interval between the first and second Gulf Wars, as the officially political has become even more extraordinarily enfeebled, and as the older kinds of political position, at least those adopted or reinvented by the anti-capitalist movement, appear, conversely, to inspire slightly less widespread embarrassment than they did at the time of the implosion of the Soviet Union. Instead, it is my intention in this essay to appropriate the concept of the Party of Utopia as a metaphorical representation of utopian readerships, specifically those of the late nineteenth century, the last epoch to have been defined by a utopian rather than dystopian impulse (in the capitalist west if not elsewhere). It is my contention that utopian fiction in this period implicitly posits a Party of Utopia, a community of readers that it hopes is capable of implementing its ideals in practice.

The Party of Utopia posited by utopian fiction is founded on the readership that it "interpellates" or hails. I take the notion of interpellation from Louis Althusser, whose theses on "Ideology and Ideological State Apparatuses," it will be recalled, explained that, in its general mechanism, ideology is the operation whereby the individual is "always already" constituted as a subject: that is, as a structurally ambiguous social entity, comprising both "a free subjectivity, a centre of initiatives" and "a subjected being, who submits to a higher authority" (182). "*All ideology hails or interpellates concrete individuals as concrete subjects*," Althusser insisted; "it 'recruits' subjects among the individuals (it recruits them all), or 'transforms' the individuals into subjects (it transforms them all)" (173–4). Utopian interpellation operates analogously, I would argue; although it does not conform strictly to this theoretical model, in that the utopian text hails or interpellates its individual, concrete readers as the constituents of a collective, abstract subject. Its conviction is that this readership can either implement the utopian program or create the ideological conditions in which it could be implemented. Utopian fiction thus seeks to recruit its readers to a notional party of potential activists, to a Party of Utopia. Consequently, it posits as homogeneous and unified a readership that is in fact heterogeneous and conflicted.

This type of interpellation appears to be a common characteristic of utopian fiction, at least in its most explicitly political manifestations (it is not, of course, a universal characteristic of the utopian novel, which in its satirical or deconstructive rather than constructive forms evidently does not invest its readership with an equivalent political responsibility to the future that it depicts). Indeed, the tendency to identify its readership as a singular historical subject rather than a disparate agglomeration of individuals is arguably its deepest utopian impulse, underlying the attempt to portray a community of perfectly happy people. It is a meta-utopian impulse. My essay, then, is intended to supplement, and not to critique, Kenneth Roemer's fascinating account of the utopian audiences that characterized the reception of Utopia in the United States at the end of the nineteenth century (see Roemer) – and not only because its main focus is Britain. I therefore approach readership itself as a utopian fiction rather than a historical fact; and, instead of plotting the sociological coordinates of utopian readership, I sketch its ideological construction, the politics of readership.

At the end of the nineteenth century a self-consciously utopian political discourse proliferated with unprecedented rapidity across Europe, North America, and Japan. In England, the country on which my essay largely concentrates, and in the United States, hundreds of fantastic novels, periodical essays, and polemical pamphlets – each one prophesying a future society from whose perspective the present state of affairs seemed manifestly unsatisfactory – were printed during the period between 1870 and 1900. "At the present day," confirmed the Secularist G.W. Foote in 1886, "social dreams are once more rife" (190). Foote's pronouncement was at the time typical of reformist political commentators, who identified the expansion of what might be called utopian consciousness as a perfectly natural effect of the mephitic social climate that characterized Europe at the *fin de siècle*. In 1884, one particularly messianic contributor to the publication edited by Foote had gone so far as to prophesy that Utopia "is the great spiritual motive power of the world, and is rapidly rising to high-pressure" (121).

My conception of utopian consciousness corresponds to what Raymond Williams described as a "social experience in solution"; that is, the "structure of feeling" symptomatic of an "emergent social formation" 133–4). At certain times, he wrote, "the emergence of a new structure of feeling is best related to [...] contradiction, fracture, or mutation within a class (England in 1780–1830 or 1890–1930), when a formation appears to break away from its class norms, though it retains its substantial affiliation, and the tension is at once lived and articulated in radically new semantic figures" (134–5). A noticeable realignment of the middle classes occurred in England from the early 1870s, in reaction to the adaptations of British capital on the one hand and the uneven development of the labor movement on the other. This ideological drama was in part played out in the political and intellectual impact of socialism on middle-class consciousness. Socialism appealed to intellectuals of the middle class to the extent that it opened up the possibility of ameliorating the capitalist system; but it appalled them, many of them at least, to the extent that it threatened to overthrow it altogether. The generalized expression of this tension was the utopian structure of feeling typical of the late-Victorian epoch. At the *fin de siècle*, the future itself functioned as a new semantic figure in which this tension was articulated.

The multiplication of literary utopias in the late nineteenth century can broadly be explained therefore by the peculiar socioeconomic conditions in which they were produced. The early 1870s heralded an epoch of economic uncertainty and political instability. The so-called "Great Depression," from the mid-1870s to the mid-1890s, exposing the decline of Britain's industrial supremacy, fissured the confidence of the middle class in the capitalist system. The apparition of the specter of communism, the most ominous of the utopian futures on offer at the time in Europe, reinforced this effect. The Parisian Communards' experiment with proletarian democracy in 1871 momentarily dramatized the possibility of an historical alternative to capitalism. And during the riots and industrial unrest of the later 1880s, when the "New Unionism" and the nascent socialist movement were in their ascendancy, memories of the Commune rematerialized. In this climate, there was a widespread sense, across the political spectrum, that some sort of systematic social transformation, either dystopian or utopian, was imminent.

Of course, this was not ultimately the case. History did not deliver a new civilization. Instead, as the dramatic events that culminated in 1914 seemed to demonstrate, it merely aborted the old one. The period from roughly 1870 to 1900 was suspended between two worlds, one apparently dying and the other powerless to be born. This delicately balanced state of historical postponement provided the optimum conditions of possibility for utopian publications. Jameson has argued that it is necessary "to posit a peculiar suspension of the political in order to describe the utopian moment" ("Politics" 45). No doubt this is an overstatement, as Perry Anderson has indicated (69). However, Jameson offers a convincing evocation of the political ambivalence that characterizes times of explosive utopian activity (he gives among others the example of "the great utopian production of the populist and progressive era in the U.S. at the end of the nineteenth century," a conjuncture that is of obvious relevance to the argument that I am developing):

> These are all periods of great social ferment but seemingly rudderless, without any agency or direction: reality seems malleable, but not the system; and it is that very distance of the unchangeable system from the turbulent restlessness of the real world that seems to open up a moment of ideational and utopian-creative free play in the mind itself or in the political imagination (45–6).

Utopian fiction functioned at the *fin de siècle* as a means of understanding such uncertain political conditions, those of a social experience in solution, and as a means of shaping the hopes and fears that it raised, fears and hopes that finally remained unfulfilled. It is in this overarching historical context that a Party of Utopia secretly took shape, in the spaces of affiliation between the writers and readers of utopian fiction, during the fractured decades of the 1880s and 1890s. This is not a real but an imaginary or virtual phenomenon, as I have suggested. Its inchoate underground presence can occasionally be detected, nonetheless, in textual details that act like scattered clues to a burgeoning conspiracy.

New Amazonia: A Foretaste of the Future, by the English feminist Elizabeth Corbett, offers a suggestive preliminary example. In this novel, the narrator awakes in New Amazonia, formerly Ireland, in the year 2472. It transpires that it was in Ireland, at the end of Queen Victoria's reign, that "the incidents which ultimately resulted in the disruption of the British Empire" took place (38). Ireland had lapsed into a state of anarchy, after a failed attempt to achieve national self-determination, at a time when Germany and France threatened the supremacy of the empire. So after the victory of the suffragists, "one of the greatest political events the world has ever seen," it had been resolved by the most progressive elements in society that the "odd women" who so outnumbered men in mainland Britain should colonize Ireland (38). Eventually, through the agency of a mass political movement, they succeed in setting up a eugenicist utopian society, one in which, though emancipated men comprise an important part of its population, women dominate the state apparatus (known as "the Mother"). The narrator self-consciously sets out to describe this society in order to return to her own epoch and so inspire her feminist contemporaries.

It is Corbett's brief description of the process whereby, prior to its utopian recolonization, anticolonial ideas are diffused in Ireland, that interests me in the present context. Relating the prehistory of the utopian state, her narrator relates that steadfast anticolonialists had resolved, after the end of Queen Victoria's reign, to liberate their country from British control. To this end, she notes, thinking at the same time, I suspect, of her late nineteenth-century readership, and of the feminist aspirations that she imputes to them, they "formed themselves into a secret society which embraced nearly all the nation" (30). This is perhaps the deepest social dream of the utopian novelist: a secret society the size of the nation. Almost all of the utopian fantasies of the late nineteenth century, on the Left and Right of the political spectrum, have in common a desire to build a Party of Utopia that will one day expand to such an extent that it is capable of implementing systematic social reform at a stroke. A conspiracy on that scale is no longer a conspiracy; it is a mass movement that has simply been condemned by adverse historical circumstances to a secret existence.

Edward Bellamy's *Looking Backward*, a book to which Corbett's utopia was clearly indebted, came closest to translating this dream into reality. Published in the U.S. in 1888 and quickly pirated in Britain, it was by far the most popular and influential utopian fiction of the period. It sold two hundred thousand copies in the U.S. during its first year in print, as well as spawning numerous imitations. In England, it proved almost as successful: seventeen reprints of its first English edition had been issued by the end of 1889, and in early 1890 the *Review of Reviews* reported sales of some one-hundred thousand copies (see Marshall 87–8). Its political impact has been widely compared to *Uncle Tom's Cabin* (1852), the only North American novel that sold a greater number of copies in the nineteenth century. John Dewey, for example, claimed in 1934 that "what *Uncle Tom's Cabin* was to the anti-slavery movement Bellamy's book may well be to the shaping of popular opinion for a new social order" (quoted in Kumar 134). After all, it founded a national political movement. The first Nationalist Club was established in Boston in September 1888, and by February 1891 there were 165 Nationalist clubs distributed across twenty-seven Union states. Their object, as Krishan Kumar explains, was "to propagate Bellamy's ideas as expounded in *Looking Backward*": "the hope was that by a systematic educating of public opinion Bellamy's ideas could find their way into the mainstream of political life" (136). Broadly speaking, this is what happened. The Nationalists supported the Populists, who incorporated a number of policies derived from the principles set out in Bellamy's book. They campaigned for them in the presidential election of 1892 and helped to attract as many as one million voters to their candidate, General Weaver. It might thus be said that behind the People's Party stood the Party of Utopia.

Nationalist organizations were also established in Britain. In July 1890, the Nationalization of Labour Society was formed to promote Bellamy's system. By the autumn, it boasted some two-hundred and thirty members, who had bought and sold almost three-hundred copies of *Looking Backward* and distributed approximately fourteen thousand pamphlets on related subjects (see Marshall 97–9). Heated debates about the practicability of Bellamy's system were conducted in the liberal and radical periodical press, and it was widely interpreted by social reformers as proof of an epoch-making change in the political culture of capitalist society. "The enormous sale of, and continued demand for, such a book as Bellamy's *Looking Backward*," the feminist weekly *Shafts* commented, "is but another illustration of the awakened thought of the time" (10).

As a contribution to this debate from the Right, Alfred Morris, provincial secretary to the conservative Primrose League for the metropolitan boroughs, wrote a fictional rebuttal to Bellamy's novel that reveals a suspicious awareness of what I have called the Party of Utopia. *Looking Ahead!*, an attempt "to oppose the advancing tide of Philosophical Socialism," is a fictional portrait of the radical opinions that animated the labor movement in the late 1880s and early 1890s (v). The novel claims that the appearance of *Looking Backward* "came as a godsend to the Socialist leaders, who either could not, or dared not, formulate any definite or connected constructive policy" (37): "it was a positive fact that the Socialist leaders, when pressed to formulate their policy, were in the habit of referring enquirers to this book, as affording a complete and unanswerable solution" (38). Preeminent among the socialist organizations that treat Bellamy's book as "a sort of working-man's Bible" is the Social Republican Propaganda party, which Morris's impressionable protagonist, a laborer called Sam, impetuously joins (39). This party, a prototypical Party of Utopia, is composed of secret committees that exist across the world for "the ostensible purpose of advancing ultra-liberalism" (49). Their aim is, first, to win over individual soldiers and policemen who might defend the capitalist system, and, second, to drill the international working class so that, "at a given moment or a given signal, they might act as one man in carrying out the behests of the respective secret committees" (50). This right-wing version of a dystopian prospect is realized on 21 May 1905, when a kind of mass coup is successfully coordinated by the secret committees: "So admirably had the revolution been organized that, by noon, London was entirely in the hands of the social democratic party" (239). Amidst social anarchy, Bellamy's ideas are instituted, and the country quickly collapses into a feudal chaos, from which a new capitalist system, it is forcefully implied, must be built from the bottom up.

Morris's fear is that a conspiratorial movement will eventually achieve critical mass among the population at large and so enact its scheme in a single gesture. Ironically, this was not unlike the aspiration underpinning the Primrose League, which was a conservative response to the rise of mass politics after the Second Reform Act of 1867. Neville Kirk explains that the Primrose League, formed initially in 1883, as "a semi-secret society of Conservative gentlemen" (to further the cause of Winston Churchill and his clique), was soon transformed into a mass organization committed to the defense of the Church and Crown and traditional hierarchies and seeking to enlist the support of those Tory worthies beyond the existing network of clubs and associations" (202). It was thus the mirror-image of those socialist organizations feared by its members in the late 1880s and early 1890s. Here, the Party of Utopia, it appears, was composed of right-wing as well as left-wing factions.

Utopian fiction in the late nineteenth century is a repository for faith in the capacity of consciousness to conquer social conditions. *"We are that we are because so far it has been impossible to make the rich and poor understand,"* Robert Blatchford affirmed in *The Sorcery Shop* after characterizing the lamentable condition of England at the turn of the new century (xiv). This idealist attitude to political reform defines the fantasies of conservative authors, contemplating social anarchy, as well as of feminist writers and reformist socialists, half-confident of a peaceful solution to the social conflicts of the *fin de siècle*. A simple shift in consciousness, it is hoped, will make it possible to fulfill a social dream in practice. In his critique of H.G. Wells, Christopher Caudwell commented that "since he assumes that the relation between mind and environment is perfectly fluid, that the mind can make of the environment anything it pleases, he quite logically considers as his primary task the drawing up of a completely planned Utopia [...] so that this planned Utopia can by his converted readers be brought into being" (87). This rationale is virtually structural to late-Victorian utopian fiction.

The Party of Utopia that such utopian fiction secretly posits, as I have already claimed, is founded on the readership that it interpellates. It is the outcome or the organization of a scattered assortment of individuals who by virtue of their reading have become a mass movement of potential activists. When John A. Hobson praised *Looking Backward*'s impact on "the great British public," he did so because "to many thousands of isolated thinkers it offered the first distinctively moral support and stimulus to large projects of structural reform in industry and politics which had hitherto been tainted by association with revolutionary violence" (180). What interests me here is the assertion, implicit in Hobson's statement, that Bellamy collectivized and even united "many thousands of isolated thinkers." In the Althusserian terms that I have appropriated, this implies that his utopia recruited concrete individuals to a notional collective, transforming them into the constituents of an historical subject.

This description of an atomized audience congregating into a network of political solidarity in the reception of a book evokes Edwin Abbott's meditation on utopian thinking in *Flatland: A Romance of Many Dimensions*. Abbott's curious novel is a mathematical fable that is on one level about the political importance of understanding that it is possible to construct a perspective from which society is finally a cultural (and therefore transformable) phenomenon rather than a natural (or unalterable) one. In Flatland – a two-dimensional realm in which people of all different geometrical shapes, from the lower-class irregular triangle to the upper-class polygon, can grasp their fellow citizens' social status only by feeling their angles (because everybody looks like a straight line when confined to one plane) – the alternative perspective is a three-dimensional realm called Spaceland. Abbot's two-dimensional narrator, the solidly middle-class Square, is taken to Spaceland by a Sphere; and there he discovers that the third dimension offers a revolutionary perspective on the limited linear world he has left behind him. "Let us begin by casting back a glance at the region whence you came," the Sphere counsels (78). The Square observes his own family, in its

"Pentagonal house," from above: "I looked below, and saw with my physical eye all that domestic individuality which I had hitherto merely inferred with the understanding. And how poor and shadowy was the inferred conjecture in comparison with the reality which I now beheld!" (79). Whereas in Flatland figures are reduced to edges, the narrator now sees them as shapes. This peculiar optic has dramatic political implications. He now realizes that his wife and children are marked by individual characteristics, and that he is himself more than a mere social abstraction. Furthermore, he can see straight through his social superiors, literally as well as metaphorically. On his return to Flatland, the radicalized Square tries "to diffuse the Theory of Three Dimensions" to other alienated Flatlanders. "With the view of evading the Law," he discusses it in an abstract code, speaking "not of a physical Dimension, but of a Thoughtland whence, in theory, a Figure could look down upon Flatland and see simultaneously the insides of all things" (96). He fails to evade the Law, however, and is arrested. In prison, he is forced in effect to retreat to the Thoughtland that he has hypothesized, that is to say, to a mental space from which the truth can be inferred but not acted upon. Thoughtland is both a kind of liberation and a further confinement.

Trapped in a cell at the end of the novel, where he has been incarcerated for holding seditious opinions, Abbott's narrator, Square, who has experienced the third dimension, and who has consequently perceived the limitations of his two-dimensional world, complains that he is "absolutely destitute of converts," and wonders whether "the millennial Revelation has been made to me for nothing" (100). In this dispirited frame of mind, he is reduced to hoping that his memoirs, "in some manner, I know not how, may find their way to the minds of humanity in Some Dimension, and may stir up a race of rebels who shall refuse to be confined to limited Dimensionality" (100). Here, I would argue that all utopian fiction is premised on the same hope that it will somehow find sympathetic readers who can stir up a race of rebels, or of partisans at least. And all utopian fiction is premised, like the Square's social dream, on the idealist assumption that, if enough people become the advocates of an alternative future, they have already started to bring it into being.

But this remains mere hope, mere assumption. As the Square is forced to admit when he pauses to consider his faith in this race of rebels, "that is the hope of my brighter moments" (100). In his darker moments, he lacks any confidence in himself and reflects that "all the substantial realities of Flatland itself, appear no better than the offspring of a diseased imagination, or the baseless fabric of a dream" (100). In the absence of a collective movement, capable of verifying his belief that there is a third dimension in which the everyday world acquires unimaginable richness and depth, he is like one of the many thousands of isolated thinkers, dreaming of a new social order, described by Hobson in his article on *Looking Backward*. The Square's memoirs, which constitute *Flatland* itself, are therefore like a desperate conspiratorial message that has been smuggled out of his prison cell. It is almost impossible to predict who will read them and how they will be interpreted, but they appeal to an ideal readership all the same. They are written for "the minds of humanity in Some Dimension," a collective audience that can stir up the race of rebels (100). The Square does not ask his imaginary readers to free him so much as to create a well-nigh universal audience for the book's basic idea, that we are "all alike the Slaves of our respective Dimensional prejudices" (100). For once, we all discover that we are the slaves of a limited world view, we are no longer the slaves of a limited world view. An entire race of rebels is the utopian state for which it has conspired. A secret society the size of the nation is the nation.

Utopian fiction dreams, therefore, that the diffusion of its ideas in the present will create the conditions necessary for instituting its ideal society in the future. In this way, it can conceive a revolutionary transformation by evolutionary means. In *Looking Backward*, for example, Dr. Leete tells Julian West that "popular sentiment" supported the capitalist corporations because the people "came to realize their necessity as a link, a transition phase, in the evolution of the true industrial system" (79). Bellamy's book is itself the preliminary attempt to forge in the present the consensus that it imagines will transform society in the future. It appeals not to particular readers but to a *readership*, an abstract collective. And it hopes that this readership can comprise an incipient community of nationalists that will ultimately encompass entire sections of the population.

Of course, as Jameson argued in "Reification and Utopia in Mass Culture," under capitalism, almost any readership is in practice a kind of *public introuvable*, in contrast to the more readily identifiable readerships of precapitalist social formations:

> The older pre-capitalist [literary] genres were signs of something like an aesthetic "contract" between a cultural producer and a certain homogeneous class or group public; they drew their vitality from the social and collective status (which, to be sure, varied widely according to the mode of production in question) of the situation of aesthetic production and consumption – that is to say, from the fact that the relationship between artist and public was still in some way or another a social institution and a concrete social and interpersonal relationship with its own validation and specificity. With the coming of the market, this institutional status of artistic consumption and production vanishes (18).

It is because of the "situation of aesthetic production and consumption" in a capitalist society that the readership of a utopian novel, as of any other novel, is almost inevitably only a notional aggregate of individual readers, not unlike Hobson's thousands of thinkers. It is also because of this situation, though, that utopian fiction, which is committed almost by definition to looking outside, or questioning at least, the current social formation, secretly aspires to repair the damaged relations between writer and readers under capitalism, through its interpellation of an ideal readership. That is, its political aspirations effectively require it to invest in the hope that some less atomized readership is possible. It has to assume, as Jean-Paul Sartre did, that "the human race is at the horizon of the concrete and historical group of its readers" and that its "real public" can be expanded to the limits of its "virtual public" (58, 61). A universal readership, as I have implied, is the deepest social dream of late nineteenth-century utopian fiction.

The idealist assumption that the mind can make of the environment anything it pleases, and that it is therefore of pressing political importance to draft ideas that can be realized by a popular movement in the future, is a characteristic effect of what I call a utopian structure of feeling. The late nineteenth century was a time when society appeared to be on the point of structural transformation: the capitalist system was metamorphosing in the face of sustained economic crisis; the working class was emerging as an organized historical force; and a kind of counter-culture, defined by middle-class and lower-middle-class intellectuals who, unconfidently enough, were beginning to question the ideology of progress that they had inherited from the mid-Victorian age, tried to come to terms with the metabolic impact of modernity. In these circumstances, the future seemed to acquire a uniquely plastic quality. And utopian ideas consequently assumed an inflationary importance. The subjective conditions for social reformation outran its objective conditions of possibility; despite the unprecedented potential of the forces of production, the relations of production militated against systemic change. Thus, the social dreams of the late nineteenth century centered for the most part on the superstructure. Instead of depicting a class conflict capable of transforming the organizing structures of society, along the lines thrown up by the political convulsion of the Paris Commune, they depicted a gradual victory over the hearts and minds of the middle classes. Utopian fiction, in this context, posited its readers as a kind of evolutionary vanguard.

The most sophisticated, and commercially successful, critique of *Looking Backward* in the late nineteenth century, in Britain at least, was offered in *News from Nowhere*, William Morris's celebrated utopian novel. Morris's Marxist Utopia posits an alternative relationship with its readership to Bellamy's; and it is this alternative relationship that I want to explore in my conclusion to this essay. It needs to be stated at the outset, though, that Morris – whom, as will be seen, I regard as an exception, in important respects, to the pattern cut out by contemporary utopian writers – is not entirely immune to the criticism that he too places excessive political faith in the diffusion of progressive ideas. His materialist attitude to history is sometimes contradicted by an idealist attitude to the political requirements of the present. In the *Manifesto of the Socialist League*, for example, Morris and Ernest Belfort Bax stressed above all the role performed by "the education of the people" in "the advancement of the Cause" (8). "Industry in learning its principles, industry in teaching them, are most necessary to our progress," its account of socialist doctrine concluded; "but to these we must add if we wish to avoid speedy failure, frankness and fraternal trust in each other, and single-hearted devotion to the religion of Socialism" (8). The notion of a "religion of socialism" was attractive to middle-class individuals associated with the late-Victorian counter-culture not least because it implied the necessity of an intellectual priesthood, a hieratic elite whose historical vocation is to administer socialist ideas to the people.

There is however a crucial distinction between Morris's understanding of the role of the political vanguard and that of other utopians in the period. This can perhaps be most clearly illustrated with reference to the final paragraph of his lecture on "Art under Plutocracy":

> Organized brotherhood is that which must break the spell of anarchical Plutocracy. One man with an idea in his head is in danger of being considered a madman; two men with the same idea in common may be foolish, but can hardly be mad; ten men sharing an idea begin to act, a hundred draw attention as fanatics, a thousand and society begins to tremble, a hundred thousand and there is war abroad, and the cause has victories tangible and real; and why only a hundred thousand? Why not a hundred million and peace upon the earth? (84–5).

Morris dreams, like so many of his contemporaries in the movement for social reform, of the diffusion of progressive ideas among the people, to the point at which they acquire a popular democratic mandate. But unlike his contemporaries, he perceives that, even in these subjective conditions, the objective conditions of society cannot be reformed as if by universal fiat. Capitalist society itself is not after all an aggregate of individuals, but an historical formation in which the interests of the ruling class are more or less successfully managed. It has to be altered by *acting* together and not merely by *thinking* together. According to Morris, systematic change requires class struggle. This is the process of revolutionary transformation that he relates in the chapter on "How the Change Came" in *News from Nowhere*. There, the working class acts collectively, in its own interest, because it has nothing to lose but its chains. "Socialist opinion," with which "the huge mass [has] been leavened," serves to direct the workers' "animal necessities and passions" from the destruction of the old society to the task of creating "a system of life founded on equality and Communism" – but on its own it is not an historical force (125, 128).

Utopian fiction takes on a different function within this dialectical and materialist framework. Morris does not inflate the role of ideas in the outcome of class conflict. So his utopia is a heuristic intervention in the ongoing dialogue about the future of society at the *fin de siècle*. His utopia is not a goal, but an *orientation* within the struggle against capitalism. It does not identify its readership as, necessarily, the nucleus of the society of which it dreams. The readers of *Commonweal*, the journal of the Socialist League in which *News* originally appeared, are instead only the precursors of those "declared Socialists" to which he refers in *News from Nowhere*, who will guide the "huge mass" of working people when the revolution occurs (Abensour 125). Morris, for whom, as Miguel Abensour argues, "the first and most important milieu to be addressed is the extremely limited circle of radical readers of a theoretically and politically engaged journal," stands virtually alone in the late nineteenth century as an instance of what Abensour describes as the aspiration "to transform utopian writing into a necessarily partial and provisional moment of revolutionary practice within a specific group" (129, 128). To interpellate a utopian readership is for Morris to appeal to a concrete rather than an abstract collective.

Morris was at best then ambivalent in his attitude to what I have described as the Party of Utopia. According to him, utopian ideas, and the political endeavors of intellectuals more generally, had to be harnessed, through concrete political links, to an existing movement for social change. There is no such thing as a secret society the size of a nation. He did not share the conviction evinced by several contemporary utopians that a political movement can simply be conjured up through an appeal to the aspirations of their readers. His utopia in this respect continues to provide an incisive critique of what Ernst Bloch called "abstract utopianizing" (145). For today, the Party of Utopia, if it exists (and Jameson, certainly, might not recognize the caricature that I briefly offered in the opening section of this essay) is doomed to be no more than an expression of some spiritual affinity between disaffected intellectuals, as Derrida's New International seemed in danger of being, if it remains defined by disaggregated readerships that are committed only to the abstract benefits of utopian thinking.

Works Cited

Abbott, Edwin A. *Flatland: A Romance of Many Dimensions*. London: Seeley, 1884.
Abensour, Miguel. "William Morris: The Politics of Romance." *Revolutionary Romanticism*. Ed. and trans. Max Blechmann. San Francisco: City Lights, 1999. 125–61.
Althusser, Louis. "Ideology and Ideological State Apparatuses (Notes towards an Investigation)." *Lenin and Philosophy and Other Essays*. Trans. Ben Brewster. New York: Monthly Review, 1971. 127–86.
Anderson, Perry. "The River of Time." *New Left Review* 26 (2004): 67–77.
Bellamy, Edward. *Looking Backward: 2000–1887*. Boston: Ticknor, 1888.
Blatchford, Robert. *The Sorcery Shop: An Impossible Romance*. Manchester: Clarion, 1907.
Bloch, Ernst. *The Principle of Hope*. Trans. Neville Plaice, Stephen Plaice and Paul Knight. 3 Vols. Cambridge, Massachusetts: MIT Press, 1986.
Britton, Norman. "New Heaven and a New Earth." *Progress* 4 (1884): 113–22.

Caudwell, Christopher. "H.G. Wells: A Study in Utopianism." *Studies in a Dying Culture*. London: Lane, 1938. 73–95.
Corbett, Mrs. George. *New Amazonia: A Foretaste of the Future*. London: Tower, 1889.
Derrida, Jacques. *Specters of Marx: The State of the Debt, the Work of Mourning, and the New International*. Trans. Peggy Kamuf. London: Routledge, 1994.
Foote, G.W. "Social Dreams." *Progress* 6 (1886): 189–94.
Hobson, J. A. "Edward Bellamy and the Utopian Romance." *Humanitarian* 13 (1898): 179–89.
Jameson, Fredric. "Marx's Purloined Letter." *Ghostly Demarcations: A Symposium on Jacques Derrida's* Specters of Marx. Ed. Michael Sprinker. London: Verso, 1999. 26–67.
____ "The Politics of Utopia." *New Left Review* 25 (2004): 35–54.
____*Postmodernism, or, The Cultural Logic of Late Capitalism*. London: Verso, 1991.
____ "Reification and Utopia in Mass Culture." *Signatures of the Visible*. London: Routledge, 1992. 9–34.
Kirk, Neville. *Labour and Society in Britain and the USA*. Vol. 2. Aldershot: Scolar, 1994.
Kumar, Krishan. U*topia and Anti-Utopia in Modern Times*. Oxford: Blackwell, 1987.
Marshall, Peter. "A British Sensation." *Edward Bellamy Abroad: An American Prophet's Influence*. Ed. Sylvia Bowman. New York: Twayne, 1962. 86–118.
Morris, Alfred. *Looking Ahead! A Tale of Adventure (Not by the Author of "Looking Backward")*. London: Henry, 1892.
Morris, William. "Art under Plutocracy." *Political Writings of William Morris*. Ed. A. L. Morton. London: Lawrence & Wishart, 1973. 57–85.
____ "Manifesto of the Socialist League." *Journalism: Contributions to Commonweal, 1885–1890*. Bristol: Thoemmes, 1996. 3–8.
____ *News from Nowhere; or, An Epoch of Unrest: Being Some Chapters from a Utopian Romance. The Collected Works of William Morris*. Vol.16. London: Longmans Green, 1912.
Roemer, Kenneth. *Utopian Audiences: How Readers Locate Nowhere*. Amherst: University of Massachusetts Press, 2003.

Sagittarius. "The Labour Question." *Shafts* 1.1 (1892): 10.
Sartre, Jean-Paul. *What is Literature?* Trans. Bernard Frechtman. London: Methuen, 1950.
Williams, Raymond. *Marxism and Literature*. Oxford: Oxford University Press, 1977.

Dan Smith

H.G. Wells's First Utopia: Materiality and Portent

Imagine yourself looking out onto a silent landscape of verdant hills and lush vegetation, punctuated by magnificent yet seemingly derelict palaces. After having embarked on a perilous journey and traveling far, perhaps further than anyone before, you have found yourself, as much by accident than design, in this uncharted place. You are effectively alone here, or at least the only one of your kind. This land is disturbingly strange and unfamiliar, its alterity emphasized by the great distance traversed. Yet although different, it still has some kind of vital connection to your point of origin, and forces you to think as much of home as of the scene before you.

    This sketch relates to a particular form of narrative contrivance. It fits into the specific tradition of utopian fiction, not so much a loosely defined genre as it is an uncanny and recurring specter. Alternatively, it could be seen as a kind of chronic hunger that nags away from within the history of social reflection. Or maybe this type of persistent fantasy could be seen as a form of that universal peculiarity of human experience and desire – the overstepping of boundaries.[1]

    The inventor of this particular fantasy was H.G. Wells. Consistently engaged in shaping ideas relating to modes of social reform, Wells's

---

1   This is an acknowledgement of the work of Ernst Bloch and the debt owed to him by many practitioners of critical utopian thought.

career was animated by the appearance of utopias.² These both mirrored his idiosyncratic brand of socialism and stepped beyond it as his futuristic visions took their rearrangement of society to severe extremes. Politically, he appears as a confused and confusing figure, but the sustained, urgent, and ultimately hopeful presence of utopias suggests some consistency among contradictory elements. To a degree, Wells's utopian thinking has been sullied irrevocably by his enthusiasm for eugenics as a solution to what he identified as degenerative forces at work among working class populations. He went even further with this disturbing tendency, targeting non-European races with the same disdain as he did the poor of London, and suggesting that they too were in need of purification. Without specifying as much, the implication is inescapably a genocidal solution. As if such thinking was not controversial enough, Wells's thoughts on processes of genetic cleansing have been framed by their realization in Nazi ideology and the atrocities of the Holocaust – the twentieth century's most appalling realization of utopian thought.

Yet perhaps it is unfair to characterize Wells's legacy in terms of such an interpretation. He was a pacifist and an egalitarian socialist with a sense of social justice, albeit abiding by standards of his own definition. Eugenics was a minor facet within his utopian discourse, which spanned the closing decades of the nineteenth century and half of the twentieth. While his arcane solutions to the world's ills may have endorsed compulsory sterilization among the masses, he also advocated games with toy soldiers. In *Little Wars*, he set out a system of rules and conditions for adults to stage miniature battles on the living room floor. Written on the eve of the First World War, this was not just a guide for a recreational hobby, but actually a proposed means of ending hostilities between the nations of the world. His logic was that if generals and politicians were to

---

2   Wells's engagement with utopian ideas has generated an immense critical response and interpretation, of which I shall provide a very brief and selective list here: see Bergonzi, Hillegas, Booker, Ferns, Stover, Parrinder.

play at war with toy soldiers, they would calculate the cost in life required for even the smallest maneuver. To see the price of war enacted in play, Wells argued, would eradicate its possible realization in life. However trivial and ridiculous, viewed through the lens of the carnage that followed, his plea for peace through a diverting pastime stands out, bizarrely, in sharp clarity.

Patrick Parrinder provides a more generous account of Wells's sense of social responsibility and political engagement than I have so far suggested here:

> By the 1920s, Wells was not only a famous author but a public figure whose name was rarely out of the newspapers. He briefly worked for the Ministry of Propaganda in 1918, producing a memorandum on war aims which anticipated the setting-up of the League of Nations. In 1922 and 1923 he stood for Parliament as a Labour candidate. He sought to influence world leaders, including two US Presidents, Theodore Roosevelt and Franklin D. Roosevelt. His meeting with Lenin in the Kremlin in 1920 and his interview in 1934 with Lenin's successor Josef Stalin were publicized all over the world. His high-pitched piping voice was often heard on BBC radio. In 1933 he was elected president of International PEN, the writers' organization campaigning for intellectual freedom. In the same year his books were publicly burnt by the Nazis in Berlin, and he was banned from visiting Fascist Italy. His ideas strongly influenced the Pan-European Union, the pressure group advocating European unity between the wars ("Biographical Note" xii).

Parrinder usefully provides a counter-balance to those elements that seem indefensible by association in Wells's work. Perhaps more importantly, Parrinder's emphasis on this period of Wells's life makes clear that his fantasy writing must always be read in relation to his engagement with social reality, and in particular, as engaged in a lifelong exploration of utopian impulses.

Between the chilling suggestions of genocide and the endearingly preposterous little wars, Wells takes a reader of his utopian thought across a range of emotional responses. Like the totality of his written output, Wells's utopian thought should be read as varied and complex, determined by a set of apparently contradictory impulses. These incongruous drives are, I would like to suggest, what is significant about the presence of utopian impulses within his writing. More than this, these impulses are characteristic of the contested and unstable nature of utopian thought itself, and possibly invest Wells's utopian thinking with a critical potential. And it is with this in mind that I will attend to an early crystallization of Wells's utopian thought, in the form of his first novel, *The Time Machine*. It is from this that my introductory landscape-sketch is drawn and in which, rather than set out an idealized future, he sets out to consider the worst that can happen.[3] However, I would also like to suggest that Parrinder's account of Wells's prolonged effort to engage in political debate and change retrospectively transforms *The Time Machine* from a narrative of despair to a discourse of hope.

This short novel was the first of a sequence of books – *The War of the Worlds*, *The Invisible Man*, *The Island of Dr Moreau* and *The First Men in the Moon* – written between 1895 and 1901, that he described as "Scientific Romances." As a formative work of modern science fiction (sf), *Time Machine* has an originary resonance. It precedes the forms of codification that populate sf in its generic forms and signal its presence elsewhere. In particular, Wells's novel exploits that essential element that Darko Suvin argues make possible the "basis for a coherent poetics" of science fiction: the aspect of strange newness, or *novum* (4). Suvin distinguishes science fiction from other forms of fiction "by the narrative dominance or hegemony of a fictional 'novum' (novelty, innovation) validated by cognitive logic" (63). As I shall argue subsequently, Wells configured his fantasies according to a very particular arrangement of

---

3   This is in contrast to Wells's *A Modern Utopia* which lacks the formal tightness that constitutes the intensively rendered material world in *The Time Machine*. Wells positions the later work as an articulation of his utopian desires; therefore, I argue that it lacks the complexity and critical potential that, I argue, saturates that substance of his first novel.

cognitive logic and fictional novum, and *The Time Machine* serves as a generative model for Suvin's influential work on science fiction (222–36).

However, while *The Time Machine* may hold some claim as a template for subsequent sf stories, it would be misleading to overly privilege its ontological status. Rather, it is worth recognizing not only the quantity, variety, and histories of fantastic and futuristic narratives, or early sf, that abounded in the late nineteenth and early twentieth centuries but also, as Suvin points out, that *The Time Machine* shares its status as a basic model for subsequent sf with Sir Thomas More's *Utopia* of 1516 (see Suvin 222). It is with this in mind that I intend to interpret Wells's first novel as a very specific utopian form.

A discussion of Wells as a writer of utopias must recognize not only that his work has generated substantial amount of interpretation and reflection around the theme of Utopia but that it occupies a privileged position in the field of utopian studies, particularly as the field intersects with sf studies. As Tom Moylan proposes, the convergence of two concurrently emergent fields, particularly in the 1960s and 1970s, was driven by a shared interest in the possibility of engaging with social reality through readings of narrative fiction. In particular, this was brought about by a resurgence of interest in utopian themes in much of the sf writing of the period: "The resurgence of utopian writing within the textual universe of sf guaranteed that many scholars, and some writers, chose to work at the intersection of utopian and sf studies, and the affiliation of the new utopian sf with the growing oppositional culture further ensured that these twinned intellectual projects would take up the challenges of an engaged political critique" (Moylan 70). Moylan emphasizes a link between emergent forms of sf scholarship and utopian studies in the manner in which objects of study – whether they be text, community, or theory – were addressed with a degree of specificity as well as in the ways in which textual form, especially the utopian, enters a historical moment.

I would like briefly to reconsider Moylan's framework for describing this moment in utopian studies, which through its relationship with forms of scholarship privileges fiction from the last quarter of the twentieth century. The position of *The Time Machine* is as a distant predecessor of forms of critical utopian thought described as "more cunning as the century moved on" (Moylan 276). Both the forms and degrees of crises that shaped twentieth-century manifestations of the utopian imagination may be historically specific and bound to forms of neo-liberalist/conservative governments and configurations of global capitalism. However, the opening of a temporal frontier in Wells's novel might encourage some reflection on the role of the definitive construction of time in the formation of theoretical and epistemological models. In *The Life of Forms*, art historian Henri Focillon argues that a quotidian normalization of chronology has been habitually extended into historical organizations of time, as a necessary means of construction to secure the possibility of meaning. Stated intervals both classify objects and events and facilitate their interpretation. For Focillon, days, weeks, and months offer the evidence of their own beginnings and endings, providing inalienable authenticity to reckonings of time:

> We are exceedingly reluctant to surrender the isochronal concept of time, for we confer upon any such equal measurements not only a metrical value that is beyond dispute, but also a kind of organic authority. These measurements presently become frames, and the frames then become bodies. We personify them. Nothing, for instance, could be more curious in this respect than our concept of the century (Focillon 138).

Focillon proposes that this model of time has the tendency of shaping centuries within the ages of a human life, parenthesized by birth and death. Time is organized according to a known architectural plan, allocated galleries, and display cases as in a museum, and is molded into discrete and efficient partitions.

While I enthusiastically acknowledge Moylan's history of critical utopian thought and fiction, I would like to suggest that it is useful to apply this suspicion of historical organization. While I do not contest the conditions for such practices, models of history and their reflection in fiction should perhaps be defined less by convenient and normative temporal boundaries. For example, one could take conditions from the long and varied nineteenth century that are as much fuel for a critical and sustained engagement with utopian thought: the transformation of living conditions under rapidly developing forms of capitalist modernity, imperial and colonial expansion, war, and constitution of subjects according to ideological extremes of class, gender, and race.[4] It need not be stated that the nineteenth century was one that was as much characterized by utopian desire, thought, and fiction.[5] Thus, I would like to detach Moylan's notion of a critical utopian imagination from its ontological link with late twentieth-century criticism and reinvest it into the fiction of a more distant past.

Rather than a remote ancestor, then, *The Time Machine* can be read as a direct and immediate progenitor of a more recent body of work. Recent manifestations of a utopian imagination shared by sf and sf criticism both map the present and suggest or stimulate both psychic and social transformations. These characteristics, as they have become expectations for critical utopian thought, are already present in a

---

4   It is with such factors in mind that I would suggest not only including Conrad's *Youth* in the realm of utopian fiction – as in Carey – but also including *Heart of Darkness*: written at the end of the nineteenth century, based on what Conrad had seen in 1890, but not published until 1902, this should be included in the moment of the late nineteenth-century critical utopian imagination. As *A Modern Utopia* makes clear, the tradition of late nineteenth-century utopian thought failed to respect precise divisions of the calendar.

5   The writing of this period is granted the status of constituting the roots of the latter century's forms of utopian thought by Moylan. However, as Francis Wheen points out, Wells's *Modern Utopia* "is a creature of its time, and the fact that he wrote such a book at all shows how well attuned he was to the zeitgeist: almost a hundred Utopian fantasies were published between 1875 and 1905, an efflorescence unparalleled before or since" (xvi). Moylan, I'm sure, would beg to differ that such a prevalence of utopian fiction has remained unparalleled since the beginning of the twentieth century.

sophisticated and developed form in *The Time Machine*.[6] Perhaps more significant is my claim that while Moylan's account is clearly of a convergence of theoretical or scholarly writing and sf, Wells had already sought to unify such concerns within an overall practice of writing. He was aware of traditions of utopian thought, which are engaged with throughout *The Time Machine*. More generally, his fiction was inseparable from an outlook defined by his sustained interest in politics, science, and the possibilities of social transformation.

My approach to describing this utopian form is to interpret *The Time Machine* as a very specific kind of object. The novel is characterized – as, I would like to suggest, are all of Wells's scientific romances – by the articulation of, and dependence on, a peculiarly resonant sense of materiality. The presence of materiality and material culture in the novel could be addressed as a means of realizing the imagined elsewhere, a mode of what Moylan describes as "world-building." This is a formal and logical characteristic of the mechanics of sf, an "ability to generate cognitively substantial yet estranged alternative worlds" (Moylan 5). For Moylan, this is the greatest pleasure to be found in sf. However, he also argues that it is the source of its subversive potential: "for if a reader can manage to see the world differently (in that Brechtian sense of overcoming alienation by becoming critically estranged and engaged), she or he might just, especially in concert with friends or comrades and allies, do something to alter it" (5). Moylan's sense of world-building could be read as mutually constituted by author and reader. This mechanism of imagining an elsewhere, at the same time as providing a cognitive map of contemporary actuality, goes some way towards envisioning the sense of materiality that is detectable in *The Time Machine*.

---

6   As Moylan points out: "H.G. Wells's Time Traveller struggles to ground his vision and find his way, and by metaphoric extension the way of humanity, in a nasty future in which his own present, Wells's empirical moment and the Time Traveller's 'Britain,' is the terrifying past" (3).

However, to better understand the quality I wish to evoke, it is necessary to trace Wells's attempts to differentiate the scientific romances from the work of Jules Verne. Wells objected to being compared to Verne – an objection that was reciprocated by Verne. The distinction Wells makes between their work is very specific. He says of his own early novels:

> As a matter of fact there is no literary resemblance whatever between the anticipatory inventions of the great Frenchman and these fantasies. His work dealt almost always with actual possibilities of invention and discovery, and he made some remarkable forecasts. The interest he invoked was a practical one; he wrote and believed and told that this or that thing could be done, which was not at that time done. He helped his reader to imagine it done to realise what fun, excitement or mischief would ensue. Many of his inventions have "come true" ("Preface" 139).

In contrast, Wells describes the scientific romances as fantasies; and, rather than projecting a conceivable possibility, their conviction is analogous to that of a dream. After reading one of these novels, one wakes up to its impossibility. However, these are dreams that may not relate to technological possibility, but do certainly relate to social possibility. The dream is one that takes place within a recognized and politicized configuration of social reality, which it offers a contrast to. Like that of William Guest, the protagonist and somnambulant time traveler in William Morris's *News from Nowhere*, the dream Wells describes is one of a possible future experienced from the present.

Wells describes the "living interest" of these novels as lying in their non-fantastic elements: "the fantastic element, the strange property or the strange world, is used only to throw up and intensify our natural reactions of wonder, fear or perplexity" ("Preface" 140). The invention in itself is nothing; it is only the translation of a singular fantastic element into a commonplace world that invests the narrative with the values of literary interest and engagement that Wells describes as "human." It is thus essential to isolate the fantastic, to restrict it to a singular contrivance. Wells's logic is predicated on the possibility of identification, of the sense of readers projecting themselves into the fictional circumstance and asking what might happen to them if they were in this situation: "But no one would think twice about the answer if hedges and houses also began to fly, or if people changed into lions, tigers, cats and dogs left and right, or if everyone could vanish anyhow. Nothing remains interesting where anything may happen" ("Preface" 140).

There is a correlation with Wells's rules for what constitutes the interest value in his scientific romances in Suvin's assertion that sf can usefully be thought of as the literature of "cognitive estrangement." Suvin contrasts this formal logic to that found in narratives of pure fantasy, such as the folktale:

> The stock folktale accessory, such as the flying carpet, evades the empirical law of physical gravity – as the hero evades social gravity – by imagining its opposite. This wish-fulfilling element is its strength and its weakness, for it never pretends that a carpet could be expected to fly – that a humble third son could be expected to become king – while there is a gravity (8).

In attempting a rigorous understanding of sf, Suvin's example binds a specificity of literary form to a particular relationship with materiality. I would, however, like to read Suvin's emphasis on the conditions in which cognitive estrangement can usefully take place within literatures of the fantastic as a means of interpreting a connection between a crude sense of material possibility and social possibility, one which seems latent in Wells's early utopia – thus, a more believable constitution of materiality and its inherent potential for transformation in text suggests a more profound impulse for change in the mind of the reader.

In his own account of the scientific romances, Wells's trick was to domesticate the impossible. A plausible illusion allows the story to play out, and science becomes a modern substitute for magic, which Wells thought had lost its narrative currency by the late nineteenth century: "I simply brought the fetish stuff up to date, and made it as near actual theory as possible" ("Preface" 140). Aside from the presence of such trickery, Wells sees the business of the fantasy writer as maintaining a sense of reality: "Touches of prosaic detail are imperative and a rigorous adherence to the hypothesis. Any extra fantasy outside the cardinal assumption immediately gives a touch of irresponsible silliness to the invention" ("Preface" 141). Used in this precise way, fantasy holds the potential, in Wells's argument, to provide a new and novel angle on telling stories which themselves might be discursively revealing. In this light, Wells admits his admiration for Jonathan Swift's *Gulliver's Travels* and acknowledges it as a profound influence throughout the scientific romances: "it is particularly evident in a predisposition to make the stories reflect upon contemporary political and social discussions" ("Preface" 141).

Writing soon after Wells's death, Jorge Luis Borges also set out to distinguish Wells from Verne. He writes that Wells "bestowed sociological parables with a lavish hand" (quoted in "Critical Heritage" 332). Yet it is Borges's own poem *Things* that might be equally appropriate in characterizing the scientific romances:

> My cane, my pocket change, this ring of keys,
> The obedient lock, the belated notes,
> The few days left to me will not find time
> To read, the deck of cards, the table-top,
> A book encrushed in its pages the withered
> Violet, monument to an afternoon
> Undoubtedly unforgettable, now forgotten,
> the mirror in the west where a red sunrise
> blazes its illusion. How many things,
> files, doorsills, atlases, nails,
> serve us like slaves who never say a word,
> blind and so mysteriously reserved.
> They will endure beyond our vanishing;
> And they will never know that we have gone
> (quoted in Hawkins and Olsen xvii).

Borges thematizes a range and scope of material culture beyond any simplistic notions that artifacts carry semiotic meanings. Rather, the poem suggests that notions of self are bound up with seemingly trivial, but invasively intimate, things. Similarly, I would like to suggest that, while *The Time Machine* is a utopian discourse of social conflict and possibility, it also constitutes a sense of materiality to define not merely a static notion of objects, but, like the poem, the nature of people.

The notions of material culture upon which I draw privilege an anthropological, archaeological, and museological understanding of the term. The artifact of material culture is, as museologist Susan Pearce suggests, expandable to the extent that the whole of what might be called some form of cultural expression is drawn into the realm of material culture. A useful way to imagine this is through the potential scope of museums, and what might fall within their field of influence. To think of the world, as it is imagined as cultural, in terms of material culture, is to make the world itself potential material for inclusion in the museum, at least as much as any smaller scaled "thing" or "specimen":

> Strictly speaking, the lumps of the physical world to which cultural value is ascribed include not merely those discrete lumps capable of being moved from one place to another [...] but also the larger physical world of landscape with all the social structure that it carries, the animal and plant species which have been affected by humankind (and most have), the prepared meals which the animals have become, and even the manipulation of flesh and air which produces song and speech (Pearce 9).

Material culture, then, need not be reduced to the study of forms of architecture, visual art, or moveable objects. An expanded understanding of material culture is required here, one that does not rely on traditional statistical or artifactual analysis and that can also usefully be conceptualized through the psychoanalytical rethinking of selfhood and phenomenologically accessible, anatomical bodies. Bodies, in any sense, cannot be anterior to the realms of material culture, and notions of selfhood cannot be critically sustained as purely reliant on biological, rather than cultural, determinisms. Reading Wells's novel as a material world can also initiate an engagement with some early positions set out by Jean Baudrillard. As a theorist of cultural forms, his work has helped both to establish a tradition of thinking about objects and extending such practices away from the more orthodox disciplinary sites of material culture discourse. In particular, in my argument that follows I will make use of the logical and interpretative tension present in his "The Ecstasy of Communication."

The *Time Machine* itself is narrated from a point three years after the events described. Hillyer, the narrator, or more appropriately, the "outer narrator," is a friend and regular guest of the central protagonist. Referred to only as "the Time Traveller," he could be described as the "inner narrator," whose account is contained within that of the "outer narrator." Hillyer's narration begins with a scene in the Time Traveller's home, where in front of an audience of guests the Time Traveller attempts to describe time in terms of a speculative theory of four dimensionality. In proposing time as analogous to spatial, directional movement, he is able to introduce the notion of time travel. He then reveals a miniature time machine, which is actually a fully operational scale model of the full-size version revealed subsequently. He performs a demonstration that has an air of a magician's spectacle. Before the assembled guests, the machine vanishes, to a suspicious and incredulous response. After stating his intention of traveling in time, he reveals the actual machine housed in his workshop, not yet complete.

The following week, another group of guests, including Hillyer, has assembled at the Time Traveller's house. They wait impatiently as their host has not yet arrived, and they sit down to dinner without him. Suddenly, the Time Traveller makes a dramatic entrance, demanding food and drink, disturbingly haggard in appearance. He explains that he has been to the future; and from this point, the "inner narrator" takes over as he relates the events of his journey. That morning, he had tried out his machine in a reckless and unprepared leap into the future. As he traveled, he had been able to see events take place before him at an accelerated pace. After panicking about the inherent dangers of time traveling and slamming the machine to an abrupt halt, he arrived violently in the year 802,701.

The Time Traveller's impressions of this world and its inhabitants develop slowly, gradually deducing what he comes to believe is the correct analysis, but which he acknowledges is only his best speculation, as there is no contextual evidence to support the theory. The future world that he encounters is a landscape punctuated by ruined, palatial structures and populated by the descendants of late nineteenth-century humans. After this huge period of time, humanity has evolved into two distinguishable species: the Eloi and the Morlocks. The Eloi are regarded by the Time Traveller as beautiful, androgynous, physically frail, and intellectually regressive. They have no recorded knowledge, written language, or awareness of technological processes. Their life is one of both leisure and fear. All their material needs are catered for by the subterranean, ape-like Morlocks. As the Time Traveller eventually deduces, the Eloi are essentially cattle, reared by the Morlocks as food. The described relationship between them is a conventional model of Marxist class distinction that has become grossly distorted along an evolutionary scale until the power relationships have been horrifyingly inverted. The Time Traveller discovers soon after his arrival that his machine has vanished, dragged inside the base of a statue by Morlocks; and its recovery becomes the focus of the Time Traveller's activities.

He eventually succeeds in finding it and makes a frantic escape, accidentally hurtling even further into the future. As he travels through time, he witnesses the Earth's rotation slow down until it stops, with one side of the planet continually facing a static red sun. He slows down, making stops to witness the changes taking place before him. He finds himself on the shore of a sea, watching the final generations of the last forms of life on earth and sees what might be the moon or possibly the planet Mercury eclipse the sun. This scene of a grotesque sunset populated by bizarre creatures is literally the twilight of the earth and its life. The Time Traveller then begins his return journey.

As he hurtles back in time, the Time Traveller can see the blurred forms of time moving in reverse gradually becoming more familiar, until he reaches the day that he left, in time to make his dramatic entrance and tell his story to the disbelieving audience. The voice of the novel then switches back to the "outer narrator," Hillyer. After telling his story, the Time Traveller starts to doubt its veracity in the light of the hostile reception it receives from his guests, who, although entertained, see no truth in it. He takes them to see the machine in the workshop. The sight of the machine, which has sustained considerable damage, reassures the Time Traveller of his own memories, at which point he says goodnight to his unconvinced guests. The next day, Hillyer returns, unable to come to a conclusion as to whether or not the story was true. After finding the time machine in the laboratory, he meets the Time Traveller, with a camera and knapsack, apparently preparing for another journey. He asks Hillyer to wait for him in the smoking-room. When he remembers another appointment that he just has time to make, the narrator returns to the laboratory to tell the Time Traveller that he must leave. As he enters, he sees the faint image of the time machine disappearing, with the Time Traveller as an indistinct figure in a whirling mass as he disappears. Hillyer explains that he waited at the Time Traveller's house for his return but then feared that he would have to wait a lifetime, and that three years had now passed. As an epilogue, Hillyer imagines what could have become of his friend, comforted by two shriveled white flowers of an unknown order, material evidence brought back from the future.

In considering *The Time Machine* as a utopian tale, it is perhaps appropriate to see a core narrative element articulated by the materialization of the people of the future. I would argue that these bodies become like objects, part of a codified discourse of materiality, whose extremity of form helps to suggest the contingent, material, and linguistic nature of bodies in general. These bodies are described according to grotesquely exaggerated physiognomic principles. Appearance and behavior, biological and social, are bound and mutually constitutive. The Eloi are androgynous, effete, and described as possessing a Dresden

China-like prettiness. The almost-animal Morlocks actually rear, slaughter, and consume the Eloi, reducing their prey to a different register of animal-like existence. Yet while their fate is no different from cattle, the Eloi strike the Time Traveller as the most human of the two species, at least the most able to inspire sympathy. Of the Morlocks, the Time Traveller says:

I felt a peculiar shrinking from those pallid bodies. They were just the half-bleached color of the worms and things one see preserved in spirit in a zoological museum. And they were filthily cold to the touch. Probably my shrinking was largely due to the sympathetic influence of the Eloi, whose disgust of the Morlocks I now began to appreciate (86).

That these two subspecies are so different must be the result of some form of evolutionary principle, but they have not been brought about by Darwinian selection and adaptation, but rather, as the Time Traveller eventually hypothesizes, have been produced by the perpetuation of social conditions that exist within his own epoch.

This discourse is solidified by the image of the sphinx that dominates the immediate landscape around the Time Traveller's point of arrival, and inside which his machine is later hidden by Morlocks.[7] The statue alludes to an essay by Thomas Carlyle from his collection *Past and Present* (1843), which together with his *Sartor Resartus* – referred to by the Time Traveller – was ubiquitously familiar to Wells's late nineteenth-century audience. Carlyle's essay draws upon the allegory of the sphinx. This concerns the myth that certain death was promised to anyone that could not answer her riddle. The essay prophesied a similar fate of his own question, relating to the organization of labor and management of the working classes, were to remain unanswered. For Carlyle, decadent generations of factory owners had allowed labor to organize itself with (as put by Leon Stover by way of Carlyle's phrases) an "'ape's freedom' in

---

[7] The social point was reinforced by Wells's insistence that the cover of the first London edition of *The Time Machine* should represent an image of the sphinx.

pursuit of sectarian class interests at the expense of social duty; with the 'liberty of apes,' Labour seeks its own greed no less than its nominal masters given only to profiteering" (Stover, *Time Machine* 3). Carlyle's solution to this unsustainable system was the militarizing of labor.

In Wells's future, this problem has been allowed to escalate, feeding his fear of a working-class bestial, predatory materiality. In recognizing his own social context, "the Time Traveller realizes that he has never left home; that the future is but a mockery of his own time" (Stover, *Time Machine* 2). Through the characterization of the Morlocks as ape-like beasts, the working classes have taken on this outward appearance. An equivalent physiognomy applies to the Eloi, whose name refers ironically to fallen gods from the Old Testament. The decadent ruling class is based upon Carlyle's notion of Dandies, a leisure class who allow the perpetuation of a volatile class situation. Thus, "in *Sartor Resartus* [Carlyle] speaks of the Dandies as a leisure class living for show on the surface of life. The Drudges dig and work in the earth, living there in dark dwellings where they seldom see the sky" (Stover, *Time Machine* 8). As Carlyle put it: "To the eye of the political Seer, their mutual relation, pregnant with the elements of discord and hostility, is far from consoling" (quoted in Stover, *Time Machine* 8). The lack of any apparently Darwinian explanation for the physical differences between the Eloi and Morlocks seems explicit and deliberate, and seems to bear little correlation to any idea of adaptation that would appear obviously beneficial to reproduction and survival: why would ape-like features be better suited to an underground, industrial society? This imagery then is purely physiognomical, an embodiment of social discourse.[8]

However, while the embodied subjects of the future represent a significant set of thematic presences in *The Time Machine*, this is still a

---

[8] This conflation of the social and physiological is epitomized by an illustration of a gorilla which had served as an emblem of uncanny terror for Wells during childhood.

rich site of further investigation; and there are other manifestations of materiality and material culture that may shed some light on the presence of utopian themes. In particular, I would like to suggest that the Time Traveller is characterized by a sustained sense of immobility. Put another way, he never really leaves home. My assertion is made possible by the nature of his journey and the instrumental device, and material artifact, after which the novel is named. On his machine, he moves in time, not space. It is therefore possible to read the novel in terms of a severe erosion of distinctions between interior and exterior, providing a unifying device with which to consider a speculative notion of material culture. The breadth of vision applied to the scope of museologically orientated material culture, applicable to entire landscapes, is fused with the sense of artifactually rendered domestic intimacy found in the Time Traveller's home.

Suvin has drawn attention to the contrast implicit in the spatial register in the novel, which he argues is a common structural element in the scientific romances, characterized by a destructive newness encroaching upon the tranquility of the Victorian environment. The inner and outer framework of the narrative is also seen by Suvin as a means of establishing this collision: "The framework is set in surroundings as staid and familiarly Dickensian as possible, such as the cozy study of *The Time Machine*" (208). However, I would like to read this interior space is a meticulously crafted environment in which the politicized tension that Wells depicts in the future is staged with equal, albeit codified, bluntness. The presence of incandescent gaslight is one element of this. By 1895, gaslight was an obsolete technology; and it was the lack of a unified system of modernization to electricity that lurks behind its presence in the novel, as Richmond was under a set of different authorities to other parts of London. In this use of gaslight as a visual effect upon an interior, a system of lighting, a part of a distribution network connected to the organization of capital and the efficiency of government, Wells thematizes the past through a motif of obsolescence and incompetence.

What appears to be an environment of domestic refinement and comfort contains an explicit reference to the chairs upon which the guests in the Time Traveller's home sit: "Our chairs, being his patents, embraced and caressed us rather than submitted to be sat upon" (1). These chairs are a direct reference to William Morris, designer, craftsman, writer, and utopian.[9] For Morris, furniture was politics: "William Morris was to wage war on the factory-made ugliness of Victorian domestic interiors, and to expand, even more trenchantly than Ruskin himself, on the intimate connections between morality, as socially and privately understood, and design" (Wilson 164). That these chairs are uncannily comfortable sets up the Time Traveller as an inventor in competition with Morris, who was in actuality the first to patent a cushioned chair with a backrest that could be inclined. This inexplicable quality suggests that Morris's patent has been surpassed.

Although not named in the text, a fictionalized Morris is also one of the guests of the Time Traveller on the night of his return from the future. He is described, in a manner that is designed to be insulting, as "a quiet, shy man with a beard – whom I didn't know, and who, as far as my observation went, never opened his mouth all the evening." (19) The sophistication of the chair design in relation to anything that Morris had been able to build indicates an assumed superiority of social theory articulated within the narrative. It sets up *The Time Machine* as a novel in a direct and adversarial relationship with Morris's *News from Nowhere*, published five years previously. In *News from Nowhere*, a socialist with a hatred of modernity awakens in, or rather dreams of, a medieval fantasy of the future in which capitalism and technology have been left behind by a society favoring an egalitarian and rural existence. In Wells's text, Morris's utopian dream is swiftly dismissed, in codified form, through the chairs: they are contrasted with his medievalism, his looking backwards,

---

[9] The observation of this connection has been made by Stover in his analysis of *The Time Machine* (23–4).

his idea of the future as an imagined fantasy of the past. To imagine progress in the image of a precapitalist, preindustrial arcadia suggested no answer for Wells, and failed to address the conditions of modernity as he saw them. And although Wells's future is a nightmare, the momentum is still forward looking in its call to arms. But Wells was also unlike Morris in the way in which he constructed his utopia. Morris took the process literally, and saw himself as a purveyor of pure authorial intent. There was no subtlety in his fantastic worlds. They were meant to represent in a clear, unclouded manner, the views of the author.

Wells, on the other hand, constructs a narrative that is polemical, but utilizes materiality as a set of raw materials for cognitive engagement, as well as estrangement. Rather than spell out a utopian fantasy, as a panorama of the present through a dream of what might be, *Time Machine* explores aspects of utopian possibility. Wells's future, although addressed as a stark warning, is still a future, and therefore perhaps more utopian a discourse than Morris's nostalgic paradise. Wells's text is about resolving the problems of the now, of not getting stuck in fantasies of the past. The presence of gaslight hints at this, as an attack on the slowness and inefficiency of modernity to move in a smooth and organized action; rather it seems to lurch forward in stops and starts, like the clumsy actions of the Time Traveller upon his machine. However, this reading of the chairs as a reference to Morris overlooks the very qualities that are supposed to indicate the politicization of the chairs: their technological sophistication, the illusion of some form of agency as a result and the peculiar dissolution of a series of physical, psychic, and technological boundaries. These chairs are prosthetic extensions that respond to a form of instrumental but unskilled control. The situation is described not in terms of a body in a chair, but as an amalgam of the two.

The chairs are therefore useful in sustaining a general sense of erosion throughout the narrative, which is mirrored in a general absence of distinction between interior and exterior in the future landscape, as well as by the negation of spatial distance implicit in the operation of time travel. Like the time machine itself, the chairs hint at an unskilled instrumentality that Baudrillard describes in "The Ecstasy of Communication" as private telematics: "each person sees himself at the controls of a hypothetical machine, isolated in a position of perfect and remote sovereignty, at an infinite distance from his universe of origin" (128). For Baudrillard, this is a model of the realization of a living satellite within quotidian space. The notion of interior as discrete, with clear and impermeable boundaries, is radically destabilized here. This is to suggest "interior" as referring both to the interiority of a subject and architectural interior: private and domestic spaces, psychic and built, are no longer the sites where drama is played out in an engagement with objects and images.

Baudrillard counters the foundation of his earlier argument made in *The System of Objects,* which relies on the meaningful opposition of subject/object (material artifact) and public/private, as well as the privileging of "a domestic scene, a scene of interiority, a private space-time" (126). His position shifts from one of scene and mirror to screen and network, a non-reflecting surface of communication. The very space of habitation – both psychic and architectural – can be conceived of as a point of regulation and organization within a series of multiple networks. Within this space of habitation, then, a sense of utopian discourse as a narrative of distance and alterity is collapsed within the present and the familiar. The telematic apparatus of the time machine allows the protagonist to travel without leaving his home. I suggest that his home, manifested through the articulation of materiality, is made into the site of the novel. As such, this site functions analogously to Baudrillard's hypothetical space, in which an antiutopian nightmare is played out, as a necessary evil to confront before the fulfillment of any utopian dream.

Works Cited

Baudrillard, Jean. "The Ecstasy of Communication." *Postmodern Culture*. Ed. Hal Foster. London: Pluto Press, 1987. 126–34.

Bergonzi, Bernard. *The Early H.G. Wells*. Manchester: Manchester University Press, 1961.

Booker, M. Keith. "H.G. Wells: A Modern Utopia." *Dystopian Literature: A Theory Research Guide*. Westport: Greenwood, 1994. 63–7.

Carey, John (ed.). *The Faber Book of Utopias*. London: Faber and Faber, 1999.

Ferns, Chris. *Narrating Utopia: Ideology, Gender, Form in Utopian Literature*. Liverpool: Liverpool University Press, 1999.

Hawkins, Hildi, and Danielle Olsen (eds). *The Phantom Museum and Henry Wellcome's Collection of Medical Curiosities*. London: Profile Books, 2003.

Hillegas, Mark R. *The Future as Nightmare: H. G. Wells and the Anti-Utopians*. New York: Oxford University Press, 1967.

Moylan, Tom. *Scraps of the Untainted Sky: Science Fiction, Utopia, Dystopia*. Boulder: Westview, 2000.

Parrinder, Patrick (ed). "Biographical Note." *A Modern Utopia*. Ed. Gregory Claeys and Patrick Parrinder. London: Penguin, 2005. vii–xii.

_____ *H.G. Wells: The Critical Heritage*. London and Boston: Routledge and Kegan Paul, 1972.

_____ "*News from Nowhere, The Time Machine* and the Break Up of Classical Realism." *Science-Fiction Studies* (1976): 265–74.

_____ "Utopia and Meta-Utopia in H.G.Wells." *Utopian Studies* 1 (1987): 79–97.

Pearce, Susan M. (ed.). *Interpreting Objects and Collections*. London and New York: Routledge, 1996.

Stover, Leon. *The Shaving of Karl Marx: An Instant Novel of Ideas, After the Manner of Thomas Love Peacock, in Which Lenin and H. G. Wells Talk About the Political Meaning of the Scientific Romances*. Lake Forest: Chinon Press, 1982.

_____ (ed.). *The Time Machine: An Invention. A Critical Text of the 1895 London First Edition*. Jefferson and London: McFarland and Company, 1996.

Suvin, Darko. *Metamorphoses of Science Fiction: On the Poetics and History of a Literary Genre*. New Haven and London: Yale University Press, 1979.
Wells, H.G. *Little Wars*. London: Palmer, 1913.
_____ *A Modern Utopia*. Ed. Gregory Claeys and Patrick Parrinder. London: Penguin, 2005.
_____ "Preface to The Scientific Romances of H.G. Wells." *The Invisible Man*. London: J. M. Dent, 2000. 139–43.
_____ *The Time Machine: An Invention*. London: Heinemann, 1895.
Wheen, Francis. "Introduction." *A Modern Utopia*. Ed. Gregory Claeys and Patrick Parrinder. London: Penguin, 2005. xii–xxvi.
Wilson, A.N. *The Victorians*. London: Arrow, 2003.

Michael G. Kelly

Immanence and the Utopian Impulse. On Philippe Jaccottet's Readings of Æ and Robert Musil

Prior to the business of exploring is that of locating. To posit a utopian *impulse* both suggests Utopia's origins in an inner space and segregates the utopian from the volitional, the ordered, the reflective. The utopian is othered within the subject via this originary gesture. It comes to represent a heteronomy, one of the order of a force of nature working through the subject placed within the flux of the given. The subject is engineered into that eminently modern position of being spoken through. This is an understandable move given Utopia's historical vulnerability to rationalistic hubris. That history equally serves to underline, however, Utopia's abiding issue with the quality and jurisdiction of human consciousness. In particular, that issue gravitates around the attempts of consciousness to confront and negotiate its own limits.

Thus in *Das Prinzip Hoffnung*, for example, Ernst Bloch associates what he calls the utopian *function* with a particular consciousness of the subject in respect of the forward glance. A tempering reflexivity is necessary in the face of the persistent waywardness of the subject abandoned to its desires, its unbounded ability to desire. This is for Bloch a qualitative issue: "Pure wishful thinking has discredited utopias for centuries, both in pragmatic political terms and in all other expressions of what is desirable; just as if every utopia were an abstract one [... The "immature utopian function"] is easily led astray, without contact with the real forward tendency into what is better" (145).[1] He cites the Martin Heidegger of *Sein und Zeit* as an example of recuperable nihilism in the face of this discredit, wherein wishing and anticipation are stigmatized as essentially *evasive* of the given – and in which the utopian, whether impulse or function, is reduced to a form of self-exonerating escapism. The issue becomes that of discerning and describing what measure of utopian forward tendency can resist that which Bloch, no enemy to the pleasures of rhetoric, colorfully terms "the ripe old platitude of the way-of-the-world philistine, of the blinkered empiricist whose world is far from being a stage, in short the confederacy in which the fat bourgeois and the shallow practicist have always not only rejected outright the anticipatory, but despised it" (145).

The battle for Utopia's legitimacy is being fought here by characterizing the *mature* utopian function as something other than impulsional – a form of firstly mental activity, no longer a reflex but, even as it retains the characteristic dynamic that is the prime guarantor of its deep necessity, a reflective practice. Desires are fully appropriated through a process of critique. Utopian thought becomes legitimate in attaining the quality of an *autonomous* practice – that is, in the sense imparted to that adjective by Cornelius Castoriadis, a practice not simply independent or sovereign (preludes to the delirium of omnipotence) but centrally engaged in the determination of its own limits. Moving from the level of the individual subject, Castoriadis derives his understanding of autonomy from the Freudian *Wo Es war, soll Ich werden*:

> Je dois prendre la place de Ça – cela ne peut signifier ni la suppression des pulsions, ni l'élimination ou la résorption de l'inconscient. Il s'agit de prendre leur place en tant qu'instance de décision. L'autonomie, ce serait la domination du conscient sur l'inconscient.

---

[1] See the discussion of the Blochian utopian function and its crystallization at this juncture in Bloch's exposition in Moylan.

[I (*Ego*) must displace It (*Id*) – that cannot mean the suppression of the pulsions, nor can it mean the elimination or resorption of the unconscious. It is a question rather of replacing them as the instance of decision. Autonomy would become the domination of the unconscious by the conscious] (151). [2]

The utopian conceived of as an autonomous practice would migrate from pure psychodynamics to a politics in the broadest sense, from the neutralizing all-or-nothing scenario to being a scrupulously maintained sense of balance in the face of the given, in which the work of the individual gaze becomes all-important. Describing what he calls the mature utopian function, Bloch brings out the suspensive difficulty of this position for the utopian subject:

> what is important is the fact that the hope-charged imaginative glance of the utopian function is not corrected from a worm's-eye view, but solely *from the real elements in the anticipation itself.* That is, from the perspective of that solely real realism which only is so because it is *fully attuned to the tendency of what is actually real*, to the objectively real *possibility* to which this tendency is assigned, and consequently to *the properties of reality which are themselves utopian*, i.e., contain future (145, emphasis added).

The challenge of the given to the utopian gaze is thus that of discerning and developing the promise within it. It is that of apprehending what *is* in a particular light – that in which its presence is no longer experienced as a pure imposition, even as it becomes the ineluctable parameter of futurity. In this sense, I would hold that the utopian and the poetic share a common problematic along a spectrum of possible positions. Jean Baudrillard, in *Le miroir de la production*, sets out a version of one end of this spectrum, in which poetry and the negation of process, the absolute demand for the instant gratification of desire in the here and now – what might be called utopian impulsiveness – become synonymous:

---

2   All English versions of texts quoted in French in this essay are my own.

> Ce que la poésie et la révolte utopique ont en commun, c'est cette actualité radicale, cette dénégation des finalités, c'est cette actualisation du désir, non plus exorcisé dans une libération future, mais exigé ici, tout de suite, dans sa pulsion de mort aussi, dans la radicale comptabilité de la vie et de la mort. Telle est la jouissance, telle est la révolution. Elle n'a rien à voir avec l'échéancier politique de la Révolution.
>
> [What poetry and utopian revolt have in common is that radical actuality, that denegation of finalities – it's that actualization of desire, no longer exorcised in a liberation to come but demanded here, immediately, even in that part of it that is death drive, in the radical accounting of life and death. Such is *jouissance*, such is revolution. It has nothing to do with the political schedule of the Revolution] (120).

Rather than simply echoing this astute bracketing of much that is received as poetic work in a particular cultural field (modern poetry in French), my interest in this parallel is with respect to a utopian function within that same practice – a consciously formed position on practice which attempts to honor both the meaning of the utopian impulse and the complex insistence of the real. Restated, this can read like an inversion of Baudrillard's parallel. A particular strain of modern poetry in French places what *is* at the very limit of artistic *possibility*. At the same time, the writing process is laid bare to the danger of implosion under the weight of the present. In its refusal of myth and its suspicion of discourse, such work is challenged to formulate self-conceptions that both vindicate and emancipate its desire for realization. Very often this challenge is addressed not in the discovery of foundation but in the impetus of encounter. The poet recognizes in the work of another a variant or indeed an anticipation of the personal quest. Example or counter-example, in any case an energizing echo from past practice – the encounter recalls the practice to itself and thereby allows it to go on under a particular authorial name.

I propose briefly to outline in what follows an intertextual, intercultural, and transgeneric meditation on experience and action, and to suggest some implications of this meditation for an understanding both of a personal poetics and of the utopian resonances within a modern poetic questioning. My primary sources are two relatively early essays in the work of the Swiss-born French-language poet Philippe Jaccottet: *La Vision et la vue* (1957), a discussion of the poet's attempts to clarify his own need to write poetry via a reading of the Irish literary revivalist Æ's *The Candle of Vision* (1918); and *A partir du rêve de Musil* (1961), in which his reflection on experience and practice departs from his long frequentation of the Austrian novelist's *The Man without Qualities* (*Der Mann ohne Eigenschaften*) – unfinished at the time of Musil's death in 1942 – of which he is the French translator. These two encounters will be seen both to support and to counterbalance one another in the development of a vocational rationale and theory of practice in a third literary and linguistic culture. This they do in particular with respect to the characterization and circumscription of the utopian properties of creative work.

Both of Jaccottet's essays occur as opening texts to works that are examples of an intermediate or non-genre practiced by him, tantamount to the essayistic reflection on practice required of the poet for whom an analytical/theoretical knowledge has become necessary to the continued commitment to practice – what in shorthand might be designated as vocational prose. Elements of autobiography, literary exegesis, criticism, poetic prose, and philosophy are drawn together under the cardinal metaphors of wandering, ascending, exploring, surveying – for more than most, Jaccottet's poetics, or at least his parallel articulations thereof, are spatial. In each case, the literary encounter dynamizes a sense of quest in the writer by either focusing or challenging an evolving sense of potential practice. Thus, *La Vision et la vue* opens on an account of several years of self-questioning on the appropriate approach or disposition to adopt in life. The decisional element to this portrait of intellectual and artistic maturation is explicit:

> J'étais parvenu à ce moment de la vie où l'on prend conscience, ne serait-ce que par moments et confusément, d'un choix possible et peut-être nécessaire; et quand je

> songeai à trouver un critère qui me guidât dans ce choix, tout appui extérieur me faisant défaut, je ne vis guère que mon sentiment d'avoir vécu, certains jours, mieux, c'est-à-dire plus pleinement, plus intensément, plus *réellement* que d'autres; et je découvris peu à peu que ces jours, ou ces instants, chez moi, étaient liés, d'un lien qui restaient évidemment à définir, à la poésie.
>
> [I had reached that point in life where one becomes conscious, if only intermittently and confusedly, of a possible and perhaps necessary choice; and when I thought about finding a criterion which might guide me in that choice all I could come up with — all external basis being of no avail to me — was my feeling of having on some days lived better, that is to say more wholly, more intensely, more *real-ly*, than on others; and little by little I realized that those days, or those moments in my life were related, through a link of course as yet to be defined, to poetry] (14, emphasis in original).

The activities of reading and reflection go on, not in the desire to create a text in turn, but in respect of an ongoing sense of an unanswered question and the search for corroboration in the works of precursors of the poet's own feeling in the face of uncertainty. At this stage, Jaccottet singles out Friedrich Hölderlin (another artist for whom he is the preeminent French translator) as one whose preoccupations and formulations appeared most material to his own situation. The attractions of the intertext soon fall away, however, before the solicitation of the physical world, designated specifically by Jaccottet in its ordinariness:

> Je ne pouvais plus détacher mes yeux de cette demeure mouvante, changeante, et je trouvais dans sa considération une joie et une stupeur croissantes; je puis vraiment parler de splendeur, bien qu'il se soit toujours agi de paysages très simples, dépourvus de pittoresque, de lieux plutôt pauvres et d'espaces mesurés.
> [I could no longer avert my gaze from that moving, changing place and I would find in the consideration of it a growing joy and amazement; I can honestly use the term splendor, even though it was always a matter of very simple landscapes, devoid of picturesque qualities – of somewhat poor places and of measured spaces] (19).

It is as he attempts to understand these emotions and their relation to the practice of poetry, that is, to begin to formulate a reflective discourse in parallel to the cardinal utterances of an artistic practice, that Jaccottet happens upon Æ's work in a French translation. This experience is at least in part, as he relates it, that centrally ambiguous experience of all late-comers: "Il se trouvait que ce livre, en son début du moins, était celui-là que j'aurais voulu, et n'avais jamais pu écrire" [It transpired that this book, at least in its beginning, was the one I would have wished, but had never been able, to write] (22). Primary among the reasons for this identification is what Jaccottet describes as the matter-of-fact tone adopted by Æ in his accounts of extraordinary experience – in particular of how, seen in a certain intensity, the encounter of the material world may give rise to an intimate conviction in the speaking subject of the unity of all things. The Irish poet's account is above all, in the early sections Jaccottet singles out for praise, an achievement of tone – a statement that is calmly revelatory of its problematic object, credible and valuable as the metadiscursive communication of a prized state of feeling:

> Je comprenais, comme Æ l'avait fait, le caractère contradictoire de ces pressentiments: impressions fugaces, par la plupart des hommes jugées frivoles et sans valeur, et auxquelles l'intensité de l'expérience vécue exigeait pourtant que l'on accordât plus de prix qu'aux événements les plus visibles et les plus massifs de la vie quotidienne et de l'histoire. Je me trouvais ainsi embarqué, moi sans courage, dans une aventure où il s'agissait vraiment de confier toute sa vie à des lueurs peu sûres, à des voix sourdes et intermittentes, presque à l'invisible...
>
> [I understood, as had Æ, the contradictory character of those presentiments: fleeting impressions, judged frivolous and valueless by most people, and which the intensity of their lived experience demanded nonetheless that more value be placed upon them than upon the most visible and imposing events of daily life and of history. It was in this way that I, an individual without courage, found myself bound upon an adventure in which a whole life was to be given over to uncertain lights, to muffled and intermittent voices, almost to the invisible ...] (26).

The distinguishing apprehension is of something contradictory, elusive, dubious, almost invisible – mediated in the clear prose of the other writer it initiates the poet in a consignment of his efforts to what had before that reading been little more than premonition. Jaccottet formulates this as a transparency imparted to the world in the certitude of continuity between all things – a redemptive and open-ended immanence. For Æ, in the opening text of his book, it quickly culminates "one warm summer day lying idly on the hillside, not then thinking of anything but the sunlight" in the knowledge that "the Golden Age was about me, and that it was we who had been blind to it but that it had never passed away from the world" (8, 9). Jaccottet, who recognizes in this an almost-literal quotation of Novalis, describes "that which [he, Jaccottet] had dreamed" for the development of Æ's text at this point: "Que A.E., ayant pris conscience de l'intelligibilité du monde visible, ne songerait plus dès lors qu'à l'interroger comme on déchiffre un texte […] que cette perfection oubliée ou cachée, il s'acharnerait à nous la faire découvrir dans les choses" [that Æ, having become aware of the intelligibility of the visible world, would think of nothing else thereafter but to interrogate it as one deciphers a text […] that he would put all his efforts into having us discover in things that forgotten or hidden perfection] ("La Vision et la vue" 28–9). This is not, as it turns out, what Æ goes on to do, turning away from the elements of the outside world to the recounting of "différentes espèces de visions qui le visitent en rêve, ou dans la nature, ou même en plein travail, dans son bureau de comptable" [different kinds of vision which visit him in his dreams, or through nature, or at work as an accountant in his office] (29). Disappointment sets in quickly in his reader: Jaccottet diagnoses a limit to imagining in his reading of Æ, and brings about therein an equation of the poetic utterance – conceived of as an optimum in language – with immanence. He describes his sense of a weakening of Æ's style at that moment where the Irish writer attempts to describe his confoundingly detailed otherworldly visions – and then immediately speculates on the meaning of this change in the intensity of his relation to the text:

> On peut se demander si la parole humaine (elle-même une énigme, d'ailleurs) n'est pas inséparable de la mort, ou plus exactement du monde où nous habitons, limité

Immanence and the Utopian Impulse 215

par la mort; et si tout ce que l'on essaie d'imaginer en dehors de ces limites n'est pas en dehors de l'image, et inaccessible à la parole.

[One could wonder whether human speech (itself an enigma, be it said) is not inseparable from death, or, more exactly, from the world in which we live, which is limited by death; and whether all that we try to imagine outside of those limits is not outside image and inaccessible to speech] (36).

Parole here, as in many French discourses on the poetic, has a qualitative feel – warranting perhaps a translation such as authentic speech. It designates a frontier in language production beyond which speech loses that ontological charge after which the poet seeks and by which he imagines the possibility of a *poetic* achievement. That frontier would then appear to coincide with something like a reformed genre division, the attempt to delimit a space of practice – the poetic adhering as much to such affectively charged impressions as to any prosodic characteristics. (As an aside, we could add that this renders all the more interesting the fact that Jaccottet's dialogues are with narratives of quest and/or transformation rather than with a technique or formally described style.)

In the reading of Æ, Jaccottet's difference, that which he derives from a taking of distances with the Irish text, is resolved – in a manner typical for the poet – in spatial terms, in what he describes as a redirection of self towards the earth: "On voit que c'est vers la terre que je me retourne, que je ne peux pas ne pas me retourner; mais comment nierai-je cette rage de l'Absolu ?" [One can see that it is towards the earth that I am turning – to which I cannot but turn – but how could I deny that passionate thirst for the Absolute?] (37). Jaccottet evokes and discards a scenario in which the earth serves as a template or prefiguration of the Absolute. He does this in favor of a second negation of the logic he has encountered: "Car cette splendeur semble avoir sa source dans la mort, non dans l'éternel; [...] finalement, l'extrême beauté luirait peut-être dans l'extrême contradiction" [For that splendor seems to have its source in death, not in the eternal; [...] in the end, perhaps it is that extreme beauty shines out of extreme contradiction] (38). This further restriction is the layering of the rhetorical and topological groundwork – as well as the human parameters – for a practice of poetic irony in the conscious resistance to the undialectical alternative of the unrelieved here and the unattainable elsewhere:

> On doit bien voir, maintenant, qu'il ne s'agit absolument pas dans mon esprit d'un retour à un monde raisonnable, explicable, même pas à l'acceptation de certaines limites; que je rêverais plutôt *d'un enfoncement du regard dans l'épaisseur de l'incompréhensible et contradictoire réel*; d'une observation à la fois acharnée et distraite du monde, et jamais, au grand jamais, d'une évasion hors du monde.
>
> [One should see clearly now that it is absolutely not a question to my mind of a return to a reasonable, explicable world, not even to the acceptance of certain limits; that my dream would be rather of *a penetration of the gaze into the thickness of the incomprehensible and contradictory real*; of an observation both dogged and nonchalant of the world, and never, ever of an escape out of the world] (38–9, emphasis added).

The reading of Æ culminates, thus, in a complex imagined figure of reconciliation which is at the same time resolutely practical and practice-oriented. The Irish writer's dream visions engender a commitment to the here and now in his reader. Four years later, with Musil, Jaccottet identifies this commitment with a governing problematic of European modernity, that of grounding action in the world without reference to externalities, the "adventure" of a purely immanence-based approach to action. The transition would appear to be from the seductions of style to the rigors of reason – but this "adventure" is the "dream" of Musil's referred to in Jaccottet's title. In the third part of *The Man without Qualities*, the protagonist Ulrich and his sister Agathe are reunited at their father's funeral and embark upon an intense reflective exchange, cut off from the world in the dead father's house.[3] The incestuous dimension of

---

3   Titled "Ins Tausendjährige Reich (Die Verbrecher)," translated into English by Wilkins as "Into the Millennium (The Criminals)."

their attraction, suggested in Musil's writing, remains inchoate in the unfinished work. Remarks of the author's in this respect are quoted by Jaccottet, who makes it clear that their interest for him lies in their general rather than their contextual import. In a passage quoted at unusual length in his own French version by Jaccottet ("A partir du rêve de Musil" 22–3), Musil's narrator suddenly turns to his imagined audience in the middle of one of Agathe and Ulrich's colloquies and declares:

> Whoever has not already picked up the clues as to what was going on between this brother and sister should lay this account aside, for it depicts an adventure of which he will never be able to approve: a journey to the edge of the possible, which led past – and perhaps not always past – the dangers of the impossible and the unnatural, even of the repugnant: a "borderline case," as Ulrich later called it, of limited and special validity, reminiscent of the freedom with which mathematics sometimes resorts to the absurd in order to arrive at the truth. He and Agathe happened upon a path that had much in common with the business of those possessed by God, but they walked it without piety, without believing in God or the soul, nor even in the beyond or in reincarnation. They had come upon it as people of this world, and pursued it as such – this was what was remarkable about it (826).

Musil depicts this self-limitation within disenchantment as a matter of fact, one self-evident to the protagonists even as their non-recourse to figures of transcendence renders them "remarkable" to him. Utopian energy in this scenario is not dependent upon irony for its continued existence – immanence is not a limitation so much as a total re-statement of the problem. Jaccottet writes of brother and sister recognizing in one another "le même désir de retrouver l'accord intérieur" [the same desire to regain a sense of inner accord] (23). This, rather than any of the great possibilities of 'Parallel Action' and its occult political designs as recounted in earlier sections of the novel, figures a possible horizon for the utopian subject. Musil's narrative, remarks Jaccottet, attains an almost total stillness as it borders the eerily named *Tausendjährige Reich* (the Millenium) – yet (and here Jaccottet is speculating on what remains unfinished), following Ulrich's own maxim that "faith should never last more than an hour," it is a state which must at all costs avoid complete stasis (36). Jaccottet:

> La poésie flamboie un instant, puis un autre instant, et entre ces deux instants il semble qu'il n'y ait pas de liens, rien qu'un désert. C'est pourquoi Ulrich suspecte la religion et critique la poésie: ce feu apprivoisé et ces lueurs fugaces ne lui suffisent pas. Mais comment ferait-il pour aller au-delà? Il voudrait marcher en homme de ce monde sur les voies de la sainteté (et même y rouler en voiture, dit-il): mais comment pourrait-il tout avoir?
>
> [Poetry flares up for a moment, and then another moment, and between those two moments it would seem there is no link, nothing but a desert. That is why Ulrich is suspicious of religion and critical of poetry: that tamed fire and those fleeting lights are not enough for him. But how might he go beyond them? He would wish to walk as a man of this world in the ways of saintliness (and even — he says — to drive along them in a car): but how could he have everything?] (36).

The possible solution which Jaccottet picks out from Musil's notes in response to this says much as to the disposition whereby the poetic might overcome, imaginably, the flaws that have been assigned it. This solution is a more limited "utopia" than that of the beatific state; it is one which Musil terms the "utopia of the inductive mentality" (37–8)[4]. And it is one of which Jaccottet limits himself to examining the personal dimension, "cette recherche que beaucoup d'hommes ont en commun avec Ulrich, recherche d'une vie juste dans un monde délabré" [that search which many people have in common with Ulrich, that for a just life in a broken-down world] (38).The poet's reading of the novel reads in its turn as an existential poetics. The utopia of the *inductive mentality*, of which it is

---

4   Ulrich's "Utopie der induktiven Gesinnung," as Jaccottet points out, occurs only in Musil's notes towards a possible ending for the novel (37). The difficulties of affirmative interpretation as regards this stage of Musil's work may be gauged by consultation of *Der Mann ohne Eigenschaften. II Band. Aus dem Nachlaß* 1912–35 ('Kapitel-Studien 1932/33 – 1941).

unclear whether it represents a new modesty of objectives or a frank act of resignation on the part of Musil's protagonist, is singled out and seen by Jaccottet to be a renewal of the subject's commitment to the here and now as the basis for all forward movement – but, equally, as the incorporation of that anticipatory dimension into the attention afforded by the subject to the here and now:

> Il faudrait tout reprendre, dit-il, par le bas, partir des faits, avancer prudemment, méthodiquement, dans un monde ouvert. L'établissement d'une quelconque vérité a priori obstrue les passages; il vaut mieux quelques bonnes vraisemblances, l'usage, comme en science, d'hypothèses de travail, le déblaiement des erreurs auxquelles il s'est d'ailleurs si longuement livré dans le roman. On peut concevoir qu'il s'agit là d'une acceptation en quelque sorte provisoire des limites, le regard n'en demeurant pas moins aux aguets de l'illimité.
>
> [It would be necessary to start all over again, he said, from the bottom up – to begin with the facts, to advance prudently, methodically, in an open world. The establishment of any a priori truth blocks the passages – much better to work with a few good probabilities, much better the use, as in science, of working hypotheses, the clearing away of the errors to which he had for so long devoted himself in the novel. It can be understood that it is a question here of an in some sense provisional acceptance of limits, with the gaze nonetheless lying in wait for the limitless] (38).

Jaccottet admits that this imagined posture harbors dangers of greyness and stagnation – of a return of the real not dissimilar to that unleavened worm's-eye view so roundly stigmatized by Bloch. But what is crucial in Musil's utopia is the perspective within which this return to the real is undertaken – that is, precisely as a recourse against the forces of reification and identity. As David S. Luft has pointed out in respect of the figure of the man without qualities, "Ulrich is opposed to everything that assumes a firm order: to all finished laws and ideals and to the satisfied character. He suggests the possibility of giving up the normal possessiveness towards experience" (224). Paradoxically, a process of individuation can be seen to be thinkable around the embrace of the impersonal. The possibility of limitlessness to which Jaccottet refers above might be argued to refer ultimately to the figure of the individual subject of experience – cornerstone of the tradition – cohering around the poles of identity and dissolution. The immanent embrace of the impersonal becomes the basis for a possible accession to speech, that whereby affirmation in the name of the subject can continue to occur. This Jaccottet recognizes by finally hinting at the assumption of an independent voice, and an individual vocation – having gone as far as the intertext can take him: "Ici devrait peut-être commencer un tout autre roman, un roman qui peut-être n'a jamais été écrit, ou un livre qui ne serait pas un roman tel qu'on l'entend d'ordinaire [...] Ici, peut-être, *reprendrait tous ses droits une certaine poésie*, et avec elle un art de vivre, qui n'est pourtant pas sans exemples" [Here perhaps it is that a completely different novel should begin, one which has perhaps never been written, or a book which would not be a novel in the ordinary understanding of that term [...]. Here, *perhaps, a certain poetry would be fully reinstated in its rights*, and with it an art of living which is not, however, without example] ("A partir du rêve de Musil" 39, emphasis added). Genre categories are re-imagined in terms of a possible locus of un-alienated affirmation – wherein the affect of belief is maintained in respect of new objects, and the posture of autonomy is salvaged without a complete regression into the magical dimension of the performative, or into established and quickly recuperable forms of transcendence (constituting thus a radically different kind of ironic effort to that, for example, implicitly advocated in the conclusions of Slavoj Žižek's reflections *On Belief*). The poetic, induced from the reading of prose work, becomes synonymous with a practical disposition of the subject – one that André Lacaux, in a commentary of Jaccottet's poetic writing, has described in terms of an *éthique du regard*, an ethics of the gaze.

Jaccottet moves from the crystallizations of a utopian problematic in Æ and in Musil towards a personal poetic practice focused in an exemplary manner on the maintenance of openness within everyday experience – something of the order of a minimal setting for a contemporary 'utopian' consciousness, in the broadest sense. In so doing, he distances his own practice from those he attributes to his two selected precursors. While Musil's contribution to his reflection is primarily discursive and theoretical, that of Æ might ultimately be characterized as auratic – the achievement whereby the improbable text resurrects the connections between experience, emotion, and the possibility of self-recognition. Jaccottet confronts the dilemma of immanence frontally as the occasion and potential of poetic utterance. The poetic is no syntactic or formal difference in this understanding, but the effort – openly conceived of as vital to the very survival of the subject – towards a practice centered around the maintenance of the mature utopian function within lived, individual experience. The occurrence of consonant trains and tones of thought in Jaccottet's formally poetic writing will be indicated here via a sole example:

> Dernière chance pour toute victime sans nom :
> qu'il y ait, non pas au-delà des collines
> ou des nuages, non pas au-dessus du ciel
> ni derrière les beaux yeux clairs, ni caché
> dans les seins nus, *mais on ne sait comment*
> *mêlé au monde que nous traversons,*
> qu'il y ait, imprégnant ses moindres parcelles,
> de cela que la voix ne peut nommer, de cela
> que rien ne mesure, afin qu'encore
> *il soit possible d'aimer la lumière*
> ou seulement de la comprendre,
> ou simplement, encore, de la voir
> elle, comme la terre la recueille,
> et non pas rien que sa trace de cendre.
>
> [Last chance for every nameless victim:
> that there be, not beyond the line of hills
> or of the clouds, not above the sky
> or behind the beautiful bright eyes, nor hidden
> in the naked breasts but, *one knows not how,*
> *mixed into the world that we are passing through,*
> that there be, suffusing its least divisions,

> something of that which the voice cannot name, of that
> which nothing measures, so that still
> *it would be possible to love the light*
> or at least to understand it,
> or just even to see the light
> how the earth collects it,
> and not only its ashen trace alone]
> (Jaccottet *"Dis encore cela...,"* 71–2, emphasis added).

The themes of light and the love of light (that is, the euphoric escape from the figural without recourse to the invisible) might, indeed, be argued to further condense our problematic – the maintenance of the life-giving properties of the practice of belief – as a governing concern for a postwar generation of poets in French.[5] In a culture that for a time was in a position to imagine itself as developing in an aftermath to religion, this insistence on the possibility of an immanent engagement with the absolute was (and is) an affirmation of humanity's ability to survive its imaginary underpinnings in the anticipation of a general dis-alienation of the self. Alive both to the necessity and the dangers of a practice of anticipation, a broad modern strand of French-language poetry thus becomes readable as a lucidly humanized engagement with the utopian impulse in the pursuit of a mature utopian function.[6]

---

5 An example consonant with that of Jaccottet's cited poem is the following from his French contemporary, Yves Bonnefoy: "Et poésie, si ce mot est dicible,/ N'est-ce pas de savoir, là où l'étoile/ Parut conduire mais pour rien sinon la mort,// *Aimer cette lumière encore*? Aimer ouvrir/ L'amande de l'absence dans la parole?" [And poetry, if that word is speakable,/ Is it not to know, there where the star/ Seemed to lead but for nothing if not death, // *To love that light yet?* To love opening/ The almond of absence within speech?"] (42, emphasis added).

6 As distinct from a purely or even primarily intellectual or abstract engagement. Mahon, his preeminent (Irish) English translator, has singled out for readers of the *Selected Poems* this aspect of Jaccottet's achievement as a poet (9). It is one the present approach is keen to emphasize, as crucial to that achievement, in conclusion.

Works Cited

A. E. (Æ) (George William Russell). *The Candle of Vision.* London: Macmillan, 1928.

Baudrillard, Jean. *Le Miroir de la production.* Paris: Galilée, 1975.

Bloch, Ernst. *The Principle of Hope.* Vol. 1. Trans. Neville Plaice, Stephen Plaice and Paul Knight. Cambridge, Massachusetts: MIT Press, 1986.

Bonnefoy, Yves. "Le mot *ronce*, dis-tu." *Ce qui fut sans lumière.* Paris: Mercure de France, 1987.

Castoriadis, Cornelius. *L'institution imaginaire de la société.* Paris: Seuil, 1975.

Jaccottet, Philippe. "*Dis encore cela...*" *À la lumière d'hiver suivi de Pensées sous les nuages.* Paris: Gallimard (Poésie), 1994. 69–72.

____ "La Vision et la vue." *La Promenade sous les arbres.* Lausanne: Bibliothèque des Arts, 1957. 11–43.

____ "A partir du rêve de Musil." *Éléments d'un songe.* Paris: Gallimard, 1961. 9–51.

Lacaux, André. "Le Regard et son éthique dans la poésie de Philippe Jaccottet (de *Airs* à *On voit*)." *La Poésie de Philippe Jaccottet.* Ed. Marie Claire Dumas. Paris: Champion, 1986. 45–60.

Luft, David S. *Robert Musil and the Crisis of European Culture 1880–1942.* Berkeley: University of California Press, 1980.

Mahon, Derek. "Introduction." *Selected Poems.* Ed. Derek Mahon. Trans. Philippe Jaccottet. Harmondsworth: Penguin, 1988. 7–16.

Moylan, Tom. "Bloch against Bloch. The Theological Reception of *Das Prinzip Hoffnung* and the Liberation of the Utopian Function." *Not Yet. Reconsidering Ernst Bloch.* Ed. Jamie Owen Daniel and Tom Moylan. London: Verso, 1997. 96–121.

Musil, Robert. *The Man without Qualities.* Trans. Sophie Wilkins. London: Picador, 1995.

____ *Der Mann ohne Eigenschaften. II Band. Aus dem Nachlaß.* Ed. Adolf Frisé. Reinbeck bei Hamburg: Rohwolt, 1987.

Žižek, Slavoj. *On Belief.* London: Routledge, 2001.

PHILIPP SCHWEIGHAUSER

Who's Afraid of Dystopia? William Gibson's *Neuromancer* and Fredric Jameson's Writing on Utopia and Science Fiction

In the ominous year of 1984, William Gibson published an important dystopian assessment of America in the age of information technology.[1] His *Neuromancer* depicts a world so fully permeated by electronic flows of information that the boundaries between empirical reality and its representation have become thoroughly blurred. Gibson's characters live in a world of simulations and commodified subjectivities they fully take for granted. The first sentence of Gibson's cyberpunk novel already registers the complete obliteration of anything we could confidently call nature: "The sky above the port was the color of television, tuned to a dead channel" (9).[2] That this is not merely a metaphorical description of a gray sky but a representation of a technologically produced "reality" becomes clear when the color of the sky in Freeside, a zero-gravity holiday resort, is described as "the recorded blue of a Cannes sky" that can be "turned off" (148).

Neuromancer's fictional world is a thoroughly dystopian space in which ecocide has already occurred. It is a world in which the "real" sky is a "poisoned silver sky," horses are extinct, and rats grow to the size of small children (13; 112–3). Gibson's characters are fascinated

---

1   I thank Nicole Nyffenegger, Matt Kimmich, Tom Moylan, and Michael J. Griffin for useful feedback on earlier versions of this essay.
2   Cyberpunk is a subgenre of science fiction (sf) that has affinities with so-called "hard" sf in its focus on technology and, to a lesser degree, science, but it departs from many traditional examples of the genre in its depiction of a *near* and consistently dystopian future. *Neuromancer* is widely regarded as the inaugural work of cyberpunk (McCaffery 11–12).

and repulsed, elevated and diminished by conspiratorial webs of information of a truly global order – an order that is dominated by ruthless multinational corporations and their vast informational grids. Gibson's fictional subjects surgically enhance their bodies with inorganic prostheses or organic implants readily available at black-market clinics. *Neuromancer*'s world is, in short, a world of cyborgs in which human memory, knowledge, and actions are enhanced, interfaced with, and sometimes replaced by machines and the simulations they produce.

The sheer "density of information" of Gibson's world triggers near-religious states of consciousness (261). When Case, the novel's protagonist, "jacks in" and projects his consciousness into cyberspace, he experiences a feeling close to mystical union:

> Symbols, figures, faces, a blurred, fragmented mandala of visual information.
> Please, he prayed, *now*—
> A gray disk, the color of Chiba sky.
> *Now*—
> Disk beginning to rotate, faster, becoming a sphere of paler gray. Expanding—
> And flowed, flowered for him, fluid neon origami trick, the unfolding of his distanceless home, his country, transparent 3D chessboard extending to infinity. Inner eye opening to the stepped scarlet pyramid of the Eastern Seabord Fission Authority burning beyond the green cubes of Mitsubishi Bank of America, and high and very far away he saw the spiral arms of military systems, forever beyond his reach.
> And somewhere he was laughing, in a white-painted loft, distant fingers caressing the deck, tears of release streaking his face (68–9).

What we find at the heart of the experience of cyberspace is a merging of the subject's own information-processing systems with those that exist outside its body. In this important passage, mystical rapture is rendered in the double register of sexuality ("*now* [...] *Now* [...] And flowed, flowered for him," "fingers caressing the deck," "tears of release") and religion ("mandala of visual information," "Please, he prayed," "extending to infinity") familiar from descriptions of mystical moments of being. Case experiences his immersion into cyberspace as a communion with the infinite space of a technological other.

At the same time, however, this passage registers the material reality beneath the virtual reality of the matrix.[3] The references to a Japanese-American bank and "the spiral arms of military systems" evoke the socioeconomic context of globalization, a context that is crucial to any understanding of Gibson's world of information. Gibson's vision of the near future belies Daniel Bell's assertion that "in the post-industrial society, production and business decisions will be subordinated to, or derive from, other forces in society [...] not only the best talents but eventually the entire complex of prestige and status will be rooted in the intellectual and scientific communities" (344–5).[4] In *Neuromancer*, Gibson singles out multinational corporations rather than knowledge institutes as the new seats of (global) power and thus identifies more accurately than Bell the dominant socioeconomic actors of the late twentieth century: "Power, in Case's world, meant corporate power. The zaibatsus, the multinationals that shaped the course of human history, had transcended old barriers" (242). *Neuromancer* identifies with some accuracy a social trajectory that Frank Webster describes as "the continuation of existing social relations rather than the emergence of a 'post-industrial' society in which 'theory' is decisive" (49).

In its oscillation between mystical rapture and dystopian resignation at the prospect of a world fully organized around the capitalist production, distribution, and exchange of information, *Neuromancer* is an example of what Linda Hutcheon has usefully analyzed as a "paradoxical postmodernism of complicity and critique," i.e., a postmodernism "that at once inscribes and subverts the conventions and ideologies of the dominant cultural and social

---

[3] This is also true of Gibson's depiction of the cybercity, which corresponds to what Castells has referred to as the "bipolarization" of the "informational city," i.e., the emergence of divided cities like New York or Tokyo – nodal points of the information age in which highly qualified information workers spend their daytime side by side with a steadily growing mass of the underprivileged (*Informational City* 184).

[4] Bell's concept of the postindustrial society is problematic, both as a tool of sociological analysis and as a description of the set of concerns raised in Gibson's novel. See Castells for a concise critique of Bell (*Rise* 203–8).

forces of the twentieth-century western world" (11). Gibson's depiction of corporate power structures and acts of violence ensures that Case's fascination with the informational networks of multinational capitalism is never fully transferred to the reader. Case's emotional and cognitive response itself is more accurately described as a mixture of fascination and fear, of transport and entrapment. His response is more properly analyzed as the sense of awe the subject experiences in the presence of the sublime.

Fredric Jameson has asserted that Gibson's work belongs to those "most energetic postmodernist texts" which "afford us some glimpse into a postmodern or technological sublime" (*Postmodernism* 37). In the postmodern era, he argues, nature has given way to technology as the radically other capable of inspiring awe. Nature, now largely domesticated, is no longer the mighty force that inspires astonishment and terror (as it did for Edmund Burke) or produces – in the case of Immanuel Kant's mathematical sublime – a temporary overwhelming of our faculty of imagination. Today, the new technologies that enable the vast communicational networks of late capitalism are home to the sublime. Yet while Jameson does acknowledge the vitality of Gibson's work, his judgment of its politics of representation is ultimately a negative one. After classifying cyberpunk as "entertainment literature" and dismissing it as "high-tech paranoia," he goes on to state that

> conspiracy theory (and its garish narrative manifestations) must be seen as a degraded attempt – through the figuration of advanced technology – to think the impossible totality of the contemporary world system. It is in terms of that enormous and threatening, yet only dimly perceivable, other reality of economic and social institutions that, in my opinion, the postmodern sublime can alone be adequately theorized.
>
> Such narratives, which first tried to find expression through the generic structure of the spy novel, have only recently crystallized in a new type of science fiction (sf), called *cyberpunk*, which is fully as much an expression of transnational corporate realities as it is of global paranoia itself: William Gibson's representational innovations, indeed, mark his work as an exceptional literary realization within a predominantly visual or aural postmodern production (*Postmodernism* 38).

Jameson's critical judgment of cyberpunk is consonant with his analysis of postmodern art in general and is already formulated in the first footnote of *Postmodernism, or, The Cultural Logic of Late Capitalism*: "This is the place to regret the absence from this book of a chapter on cyberpunk, henceforth, for many of us, the supreme *literary* expression if not of postmodernism, then of late capitalism itself" (419 n.1). Jameson's most recent pronouncements on cyberpunk in his long essay, "The Desire Called Utopia," in *Archaeologies of the Future* reiterate his earlier verdict. With "the free-enterprise, neo-conservative celebrations of present-day cyberpunk," he suggests, the imbrication of literary production in the networks of late capitalist production reaches its apex (132).

At this point, I want to clarify my own take on Jameson's writing on postmodernism. As should have become clear by now, I read Jameson as a detractor of postmodernism, not as one of its proponents. Even though he is genuinely fascinated by the ingenuity and energy of much postmodern art, Jameson ultimately considers its politics baleful. No careful reading of his work can, I believe, reach a fundamentally different conclusion. That this is so should, moreover, already become clear to anyone who has pondered on the implications of the title he, an avowed Marxist, has given his *opus magnum*: *Postmodernism, or, The Cultural Logic of Late Capitalism*. Having said this, I must admit that I am mystified by attempts to recuperate Jameson as either a neutral observer of the postmodern age and its art or even a (however ambivalent) champion of it.[5] To be sure, Jameson *is* ambivalent about aesthetic postmodernism (if not about socioeconomic postmodernity) – although he tends to conflate the two. But he is not ambivalent about the politics of postmodern art. I

---

5   See Helmling (online) and Bertens (160–84) for overviews of readings of Jameson's stance on postmodernism. In his article, Helmling deems it necessary to warn his readers that "neither [Jameson's] repudiation of modernism, nor his embrace of the postmodern are so simple as many of his more excited readers have wanted to believe" (par. 3 online). To me, Jameson vastly prefers the temporal imagination and depth of modernism to the flat surfaces of postmodernism. I am forced to conclude that I am not Helmling's implied reader.

cannot shake the feeling that "affirmative" readings of Jameson's writings on postmodernism exemplify a tendency within postmodern culture and theory, analyzed by Jameson and others: the acceleration of processes by which dissent is co-opted and transformed into consent. My own reading of cyberpunk, then, makes use of Jameson as a critic of postmodernism and acknowledges the importance of his critique. It does, however, suggest that one can, and I think should, develop a critical perspective on postmodernism in all of its forms that is *less* dismissive of its politics of representation than Jameson's.

With respect to *Neuromancer*, I argue that beneath the hip neologisms of Gibson's work and its obvious fascination with new technologies, the reader can always detect the material reality of multinational corporations that exert enormous power and, in Gibson's dark vision, do not shrink from using violence to secure their business interests. In *Neuromancer*, the representation of ecological disaster and the surveillance society, paranoia, and conspiracy theory become tools of a cultural critique that can by no means be brushed aside as merely delusional. Paranoia in Gibson is as a strategy of making sense of the increasing complexity of the world. As such, it has an ambivalent political valency. Case's identification in the above passage of "the spiral arms of military systems" as that which ultimately remains "forever beyond his reach" pinpoints in no uncertain terms "that enormous and threatening, yet only dimly perceivable, other reality of economic and social institutions" in terms of which "the postmodern sublime can alone be adequately theorized" (Jameson, *Postmodernism* 38).

Gibson's novel may not provide the "cognitive mapping" Jameson calls for, and some of the more sympathetic commentators have all too hastily identified cognitive mapping as a social function cyberpunk actually serves (see Lohmann). With *Neuromancer*, Gibson does not "achieve a breakthrough to some as yet unimaginable new mode of representing [multinational capitalism], in which we may again begin to grasp our positioning as individual and collective subjects and regain a capacity to act and struggle which is at present neutralized by our spatial as well as our social confusion" (Jameson, *Postmodernism* 54). Yet, while Gibson's fiction does not provide a blueprint for a passage that would lead us from a sense of overwhelming awe before the technological sublime to political action, neither does it simply "express" late capitalism (no work of fiction does that). Instead, in its peculiar mixture of joy and terror in the face of late capitalism's informational networks, it stages what Hutcheon describes as "complicitous critique," a "strange kind of critique, one bound up, too, with its own *complicity* with power and domination, one that acknowledges that it cannot escape implication in that which it nevertheless still wants to analyze and maybe even undermine" (4).

Considering that Jameson is a frequent contributor to *Science-Fiction Studies*, the absence of a sustained discussion of cyberpunk in his landmark study on postmodernism is indeed surprising. A possible reason for this absence can, however, be found in "Progress Versus Utopia; or, Can We Imagine the Future?," the most influential of Jameson's contributions to the journal and his most succint statement on the function and meaning of Utopia – which, following Darko Suvin, he considers a "socio-economic sub-genre" of sf ("Desire" xiv). For Jameson, sf enables a historicizing of the present, irrespective of whether its imagined future is utopian or dystopian. Sf thus acquires the capacity to "defamiliarize and restructure our experience of our own *present*" ("Progress" 151). In a sense, then, sf is always critical of the status quo even if many of its varieties belong to mass culture. This is not only so because it constructs an alternative future – and thereby transcends the endless repetition of existing societal relations other products of the culture industry "hamme[r] into human beings" – but also because it passes a negative judgment on our own inability to imagine a future that is fundamentally different from our present (Adorno 90). It is in this respect that sf inherits "the true vocation of the utopian narrative," which is "to confront us with our incapacity to imagine Utopia" (Jameson, "Progress" 156).[6] This

---

6   Much critique of Jameson's work focuses on his assertion – which is at the heart of *Postmodernism* and still informs his discussion of postmodernism in "The Desire Called Utopia" (165–9) – that *"late capitalism"* is "not only [...] something like a literal translation of the other expression, *postmodernism*, its

summarizes Jameson's basic position on the politics of utopian thinking, a position he has reiterated in many publications including, most recently in "The Politics of Utopia."

In his latest work on Utopia, Jameson modifies this take on the political function of the genre somewhat, arguing that "the Utopian form itself is the answer to the universal ideological conviction that no alternative is possible, that there is no alternative to the system. But it asserts this by forcing us to think of the break itself, and not by offering a more traditional picture of what things would be like after the break" ("Desire" 232). In the light of recent resurgences in utopian thinking – think of Attac's slogan, "Un autre monde est possible," and the discursive shift on parts of the Left from antiglobalization to alter-globalization (*altermondialisme*) – Jameson de-emphasizes our ideological imprisonment and stresses that utopian thinking invites us to consider both the necessity and the difficulty of imagining and ultimately realizing systemic rupture (*Attac France* online). Jameson here suggests a somewhat more sanguine view of the possibility of radical systemic change in which utopian thinking becomes "a rattling of the bars and an intense spiritual concentration and preparation for another stage which has not yet arrived" (233).

While Jameson is at pains to point out that sf possesses a critical potential "irrespective of the 'pessimism' or 'optimism' of the imaginary future world," his focus on fictional as well as nonfictional imaginations of a future world that is *radically* different (read: better) than our own, betrays a preference for utopias rather than the near-

temporal index seems already to direct attention to changes in the quotidian and on the cultural level as such. To say that my two terms, the *cultural* and the *economic*, thereby collapse back into one another and say the same thing, in an eclipse of the distinction between base and superstructure that has itself often struck people as significantly characteristic of postmodernism in the first place, is also to suggest that the base, in the third stage of capitalism, generates its superstructures with a new kind of dynamic" (*Postmodernism* xxi). On challenges to Jameson's conflation of the cultural and the socioeconomic – of postmodernism and postmodernity – see Hutcheon (26); Brooker (26); and Schweighauser (143–8).

future visions of dystopias ("Progress" 153).[7] This preference is readily apparent in his endorsement of Kim Stanley Robinson's and Ursula K. Le Guin's work. The sense of hope Jameson invests in sf is expressed most succinctly in his contention that, "in the twilight of late capitalism's virtually global hegemony, with all its post-modern complacency, the utopian imagination is very much on the agenda!" ("Critical Agendas" 102).

An important reason for Jameson's aversion to dystopian fiction stems from the antiutopian impulses of many works of the genre, ranging from Orwell's *Nineteen Eighty-Four* to David Fincher's movie *Fight Club* and beyond. This emerges most clearly in Jameson's angry denunciation of dystopian writers such as George Orwell or Fëdor Dostoevskij, whom he labels "enemies of Utopia" who would "sooner or later turn out to be the enemies of socialism" ("Islands" 3). Yet this would not explain his negative stance on cyberpunk. The political valency of *Neuromancer*'s dystopian imagination is, in any case, very clearly different from that of *Nineteen Eighty-Four*, which Jameson rejects with such gusto. Gibson does not, as Orwell arguably does, discredit socialist visions of a better future.

However, the politics of dystopian writers are deeply problematic for Jameson even if they do not join the chorus of those who equate utopian totality with totalitarianism – a position that has gained increasing currency, also in poststructuralist circles, since the end of the Cold War (*Seeds* 53; "Desire" 191–9). Dystopias are not necessarily anti-utopias. In fact, in *The Seeds of Time* (a work that was published twelve years after "Progress Versus Utopia"), Jameson argues that utopia and dystopia do not constitute a pair of opposites (an "optimist" and a "pessimist" vision of the future, respectively). While a utopia "does not tell a story at all. […] it describes a mechanism or even a kind of machine, it furnishes a blueprint" for "the construction of material mechanisms that would alone enable

---

7   The "secession of the Utopian space itself from the world of empirical or historical reality" is for Jameson one of the defining features of the utopian mode ("Desire" 39).

freedom to come into existence," a dystopia "is generally a narrative [...] what is in the language of science-fiction criticism called a 'near-future' novel" (55-7).[8]

What Jameson finds most troubling about dystopian narratives is that the stories they tell about a bleak near future have, he claims, the effect of hardening us into accepting the harsh realities under late capitalism, thus blocking our utopian imagination. In Jameson's own words, dystopian visions of "pollution, destruction of the ecology, overpopulation, fallout, and the like" serve "American business [...] to exchange the older consumer optimism for some new and more austere acceptance by the public of collective constraints and communal living" ("Introduction/Prospectus" 364). His discussion of cyberpunk literature and film in *The Seeds of Time* suggests the genre's even greater complicity with the late-capitalist restructuring of social relations. Unlike earlier dystopian narratives, cyberpunk invites us not only to accept the current socioeconomic order but to derive pleasure from what Jameson now diagnoses as an empty, lawless social space emerging out of the displacement of civil society – here conceptualized as the space between bourgeois privacy and state rule – by the hegemonic sway of corporate logic: "such conceptions of the no-man's-land are not altogether to be taken as nightmares; they do not [...] have any of the bleak otherness of the classical dystopian fantasy, and the very freedom from state terror lends the violence of

---

8   Note that Jameson in "Desire" shifts emphasis most descisively from Utopia as the figuration of a better future to Utopia as a self-reflexive meditation on the difficulty of imagining radical political change. He goes as far as suggesting that the "vacuous evocation" of the utopian wish "as the image of a perfect society or even the blueprint of a better one are best set aside from the outset without any further comment" (72). In his earlier work, both views are still allowed to co-exist side by side. To be fair, his shifting positions are due less to any argumentative inconsistency on his part than to changes in the genre itself. He suggests as much when he writes that "the older texts seemed indeed to offer blueprints for change" while now, with works such as Robinson's Mars trilogy, "arguments about the nature and desirability of Utopia as such [...] move to the center of attention" (216). For further discussion of the distinction between dystopianism and antiutopianism, see also Fitting ("Impulse").

the no-man's-land the value of a distinctive kind of praxis, excitement rather than fear – the space of adventure that replaces the old medieval landscape of romance with a fully built and posturban infinite space, where corporate property has somehow abolished the older individual private property without becoming public" (159). It is in line with this reconsideration of cyberpunk as excitement that Jameson in "The Desire Called Utopia" toys with the idea that the genre might actually be less dystopian than "something like the Utopian expression of late or finance capital as such" (190).

This takes me back to my discussion of *Neuromancer*, a close reading of which will highlight some of the limits of Jameson's writing on Utopia and sf. Jameson's assertion that cyberpunk evokes an atmosphere of "excitement rather than fear" certainly captures something of Case's exhilaration in the face of the multiple challenges he faces in the networks of technology and power, and it surely also helps explain the genre's appeal to a predominantly male young-adult readership. Yet, while Case's acts of aggression are sanctioned as those of a lone adventurer, about which more needs to be said below, the systemic violence perpetrated against Case and other characters never is. As readers, we are asked to identify with Case but not with the radically debased world in which he moves. That world exhibits much of the bleakness Jameson does not find in it. Its pathologies include the death of nature, urban poverty and decay, snuff porn, corporate violence, schizophrenia (Armitage), inhuman viciousness bordering on the psychotic (Riviera), and a general disregard for human life. These and other social and psychological pathologies are neither recuperated not neutralized by the excitement the adventure story format generates, and Gibson's fictional take on our possible near future continues to oscillate between fascination and repulsion.

If utopian sf betrays our own inability to imagine a world better than our own, Jameson's writing on sf betrays an inability on his part to perceive the critical potential of visions of a future worse than our own. The limits of some forms of Marxist critique of cyberpunk are also demonstrated by the work of Tom Moylan, one of the more influential commentators on recent dystopian sf. In his article on Gibson's trilogy, Moylan focuses almost exclusively on the novels' utopian enclaves, in which he locates all "possibility of historical change" and "resistance to the dominant forces" ("Global" 186-7). Unable to find viable alternative models of living that are affirmed in Gibson's trilogy, Moylan concludes that "Gibson's texts begin to lose their critical edge as the utopian enclaves (as developed in the iconic register of the alternative world) fall under the compromising influence of the primary plot and protagonist (as developed in the register of the 'master narrative' running through all three volumes)" (189). In its straightforwardness, Moylan's argument crystallizes some of the problems that also beset Jameson's writing on dystopian fiction. Subsequently, in *Scraps of the Untainted Sky: Science Fiction, Utopia, Dystopia*, he has proposed the term "critical dystopia" for those contemporary dystopian narratives that present and affirm utopian spaces against the background of a radically darkened world. While I find "critical dystopia," as does Jameson, a highly useful term, it does not allow for an appreciation of the critical potential of the dystopian itself as a cognitive mode since it locates the possibility of cultural critique exclusively in the utopian vision of dystopian narratives. Bearing in mind Jameson's categorical distinction between utopia and dystopia in *The Seeds of Time*, we may well ask whether Marxist critics are not demanding too much from dystopian narratives when they approach them with expectations regularly raised and met by classical utopian but not by classical dystopian texts.

This question, it seems to me, needs to be answered in the affirmative not only for Jameson's work but also with respect to many of the re-evaluations of the dystopian mode collected in Raffaella Baccolini and Moylan's important *Dark Horizons: Science Fiction and the Dystopian Imagination*. Let me give but two examples. Phillip Wegner's reading of *Fight Club* and *Ghost Dog* as dystopian films that exhibit close affinities with cyberpunk does acknowledge their "brilliant critique" of outmoded but still active notions of masculinity only to conclude that "in the end, both films pass beyond the engagements of the critical dystopia and give way to the 'resigned pessimism' of the naturalist ideologies from which the form arises in the first place" (182).⁹ Peter Fitting's contribution to *Dark Horizons* even raises the stakes: to him, only those dystopias deserve to be called "critical" which offer "an explanation of how the dystopian situation came about as much as what should be done about it" ("Unmasking" 156).

Against such tendencies in recent sf criticism, I argue that dystopian extrapolations of a nightmarish future from our present age of multinational capitalism may constitute critiques of the status quo even if they do not hold out the promise of a radically different world. Cultural critique need not be affirmative to achieve its aims. True to Jameson's assertion that sf's visions of the future have the effect of "transforming our own present into the determinate past of something yet to come" and contrary to his claim that postmodernism has lost all sense of history, I maintain that dystopian writing such as Gibson's *Neuromancer* stages a cultural critique by historicizing the present state of the world as an undesirable condition with an even less desirable future ("Progress" 151-2).¹⁰ Gibson's critique is inscribed precisely in the bleakness of his vision.

Yet Gibson's novel does bear heavy ideological burdens. Gibson freely draws on the conventions of established narrative genres without giving much thought to some of their less sanguine implications. As Tom Myers points out, Case's name already links him with the detective genre (888). A number of other important postmodernist texts – including Don DeLillo's *White Noise,* Thomas

---

9   I should add here that I find *Ghost Dog* a far less obvious candidate for a discussion of dystopian film than *Fight Club*.
10 It is also in this sense, not merely in its depiction of a *near* future, that Gibson's fiction belongs to extrapolative sf. The utopias Jameson privileges largely belong to speculative sf. As Brian McHale points out with recourse to Carl D. Malmgren's distinction between extrapolative and speculative sf, "extrapolative sf begins with the current state of the empirical world, in particular the current state of scientific knowledge, and proceeds, in logical and linear fashion, to construct a world which might be a future extension or consequence of the current state of affairs. Speculative world-building, by contrast, involves an imaginative leap, positing one or more disjunctions with the empirical world which cannot be linearly extrapolated from the current state of affairs" (244).

Pynchon's *The Crying of Lot 49*, and Ishmael Reed's *Mumbo Jumbo* – equally develop a detective plot. Yet what distinguishes Gibson's use of generic conventions from that of his fellow postmodernists most sharply is its utter lack of parodic inflection. And it is primarily this lack which renders Gibson's return to traditional narrative forms problematic.

Case's coolness, his obstinacy, substance abuse and less than legal methods make him a cyberspace version of the hard-boiled detective.[11] Andrew Ross has characterized Gibson's fiction as "hard-boiled masculinity, second time around," and feminist critics have rightly criticized cyberpunk's masculinist bias (Ross 156; Hollinger 31). What I consider the most troublesome aspect of Gibson's writing, though, concerns yet another trait it shares with hard-boiled detective fiction. When George Grella notes that the American detective novel is "energized by the self-reliance of the frontier" and "customarily establishes its moral norm within the consciousness of an individual man," he might as well describe Case's narrative function within *Neuromancer* (104). In his excellent discussion of Gibson's novel, David Brande suggests that its frequent references to westward expansion and frontiers, its designation of hackers as "console cowboys," and its evocation of the matrix as a space "extending to infinity" are manifestations of late capitalism's political unconscious (*Neuromancer* 52). Gibson's cyberspace stages a crucial ideological fantasy of the late-capitalist system: the possibility of a limitless space into which capital can expand to escape its own inherent contradiction of overaccumulation. So far, Brande's analysis, published in the same year as *The Seeds of Time*, is rather close to Jameson's reflections on

---

11   Grella's description of some of the characteristics of hard-boiled detective fiction reads like an account of *Neuromancer*'s style and thematics: "The American detective novel, paradoxically, combines its romance themes and structures with a tough, realistic surface and a highly sensational content" and is "characterized by rapid action, colloquial language, emotional impact, and the violence that pervades American fiction" (104).

cyberpunk's "posturban infinite space." Yet Brande adds that Gibson's fiction should not be read as a mimetic reflection of socioeconomic realities but as a staging of both the fantasies *and* the contradictions of late capitalism:

> Gibson's fiction, on one hand, helps to structure real capitalist social relations by providing constitutive fantasies of the final subsumption of all symbolic exchange, and the subject itself, into the money form of value: cyberspace as the answer to crises of overaccumulation [...] On the other hand, as an ideological dream, his fiction announces the lack that mobilizes these fantasies: the insatiable hunger of the market and its systemic and inevitable tendency toward crisis – the internal contradictions of capitalism (536).

I fully concur with Brande's reading, but I would add that the contradictions of capitalism emerge most fully in the dystopian vision of Gibson's novel. It is the dystopianism so many Marxist critics, including Jameson, are uncomfortable with which ensures that Gibson's critique does not disappear beneath his novel's ideological burdens, its conventional narrative strategies, its gadget-crammed surface, and its obvious enchantment with the hum and glitter of the new technologies of information. Whether Gibson intended this or not, *Neuromancer* issues a warning: "if you continue in your ways, your future will look like *this*." It is, finally, the bleakness of Gibson's vision that allows him to continue the work of cultural critique despite his realization that, in the postmodern era, positions *wholly* outside the prevalent discourses and material structures are no longer available – if, indeed, they ever were.

Works Cited

Adorno, Theodor W. "Culture Industry Reconsidered." *The Culture Industry: Selected Essays on Mass Culture.* Ed. J.M. Bernstein. London: Routledge, 1991. 85-92.
Attac France. 2006. Attac France. 25 August 2006
 <http://www.france.attac.org/>.

Baccolini, Raffaela and Tom Moylan (eds). *Dark Horizons: Science Fiction and the Dystopian Imagination.* New York: Routledge, 2003.

Bell, Daniel. *The Coming of Post-Industrial Society: A Venture in Social Forecasting.* Harmondsworth: Penguin, 1973.

Bertens, Hans. *The Idea of the Postmodern: A History.* London: Routledge, 1995.

Brande, David. "The Business of Cyberpunk: Symbolic Economy and Ideology in William Gibson." *Configurations* 2.3 (1994): 509-36.

Brooker, Peter. "Introduction: Reconstructions." *Modernism/Postmodernism.* Ed. Peter Brooker. Harlow: Longman, 1992. 1-33.

Castells, Manuel. *The Informational City: Information Technology, Economic Restructuring and the Urban-Regional Process.* Oxford: Blackwell, 1989.

_____ *The Rise of the Network Society.* Vol. 1. Oxford: Blackwell, 1996.

Fitting, Peter. "Impulse or Genre or Neither?" Rev. of *The Dystopian Impulse in Modern Literature: Fiction as Social Criticism* by M. Keith Booker, and *Dystopian Literature: A Theory and Research Guide* by M. Keith Booker. *Science-Fiction Studies* 22.2 (1995): 272-81.

_____ "Unmasking the Real? Critique and Utopia in Recent SF Films." *Dark Horizons.* Ed. Baccolini and Moylan. 155-66.

Gibson, William. *Neuromancer.* London: Harper Collins, 1984.

Grella, George. "The Hard-Boiled Detective Novel." *Detective Fiction: A Collection of Critical Essays.* Ed. Robin W. Winks. Englewood Cliffs: Prentice-Hall, 1980. 103-20.

Helmling, Steven. "Failure and the Sublime: Fredric Jameson's Writing in the '80s." *Postmodern Culture* 10.3 (2000): 35 pars. 25 August 2006 <http://www.iath.virginia.edu/pmc/text-only/issue.500/10.3helmling.txt>.

Hollinger, Veronica. "Cybernetic Deconstructions: Cyberpunk and Postmodernism." *Mosaic* 23.2 (1990): 29-44.

Hutcheon, Linda. *The Politics of Postmodernism.* New York: Routledge, 1989.

Jameson, Fredric. "Critical Agendas." Rev. of *Aliens: The Anthropology of Science Fiction* (Ed. George E. Slusser and Eric S. Rabin), *Storm Warnings: Science Fiction Confronts the Future* (Ed. George E. Slusser, Colin Greenland and Eric S. Rabin), and *Utopie per gli anni Ottanta: Studi interdisciplinari sui temi, la storia, i progetti* (Ed. Giuseppa Saccaro del Buffa and Arthur O. Lewis). *Science-Fiction Studies* 17.1 (1990): 93-102.

_____ "The Desire Called Utopia." *Archaeologies of the Future: The Desire Called Utopia and Other Science Fictions*. London: Verso, 2005. 1-233.

_____ "Introduction/Prospectus: To Reconsider the Relationship of Marxism to Utopian Thought." *The Jameson Reader*. Ed. Michael Hardt and Kathi Weeks. Oxford: Blackwell, 2000. 361-7.

_____ "Of Islands and Trenches: Naturalization and the Production of Utopian Discourse." *Diacritics* 7.2 (1977): 2-21.

_____ "The Politics of Utopia." *New Left Review* 25.2 (2004): 35-54.

_____ *Postmodernism, or, The Cultural Logic of Late Capitalism*. Durham: Duke University Press, 1991.

_____ "Progress Versus Utopia; or, Can We Imagine the Future?" *Science-Fiction Studies* 9.2 (1982): 147-58.

_____ *The Seeds of Time*. New York: Columbia University Press, 1994.

Lohmann, Ingrid. "Cognitive Mapping in Cyberpunk: Wie Jugendliche Wissen über die Welt erwerben." *Out of this World! Beiträgen zu Science-Fiction, Politik und Utopie*. Ed. Petra Mayerhofer and Christoph Spehr. Hamburg: Argument-Verlag, 2002. 171-84.

McCaffery, Larry. "Introduction: The Desert of the Real." *Storming the Reality Studio: A Casebook of Cyberpunk and Postmodern Science Fiction*. Ed. McCaffery. Durham: Duke University Press, 1991. 1-16.

McHale, Brian. *Constructing Postmodernism*. New York: Routledge, 1992.

Moylan, Tom. "Global Economy, Local Texts: Utopian/Dystopian Tension in William Gibson's Cyberpunk Trilogy." *minnesota review* 43/44 (1995): 182-97.

_____ *Scraps of the Untainted Sky: Science Fiction, Utopia, Dystopia*. Boulder: Westview, 2000.

Myers, Tony. "The Postmodern Imaginary in William Gibson's *Neuromancer*." *Modern Fiction Studies* 47.4 (2001): 887-909.

Ross, Andrew. *Strange Weather: Culture, Science and Technology in the Age of Limits*. London: Verso, 1991.

Schweighauser, Philipp. *The Noises of American Literature, 1890-1985*. Gainesville: University Press of Florida, 2006.

Suvin, Darko. "On the Poetics of the Science Fiction Genre." *Science Fiction: A Collection of Critical Essays*. Ed. Mark Rose. Englewood Cliffs: Prentice-Hall, 1976. 57-71.

Webster, Frank. *Theories of the Information Society*. New York: Routledge, 1995.

Wegner, Phillip E. "Where the Prospective Horizon Is Omitted: Naturalism and Dystopia in *FightClub* and *Ghost Dog*." *Dark Horizons*. Ed. Baccolini and Moylan. 167-85.

Williams, Raymond. "Utopia and Science Fiction." *Science Fiction: A Critical Guide*. Ed. Patrick Parrinder. New York: Longman, 1979. 52-66.

PAULA MURPHY

Paradise Lost: The Destruction of Utopia in *The Beach*

> Of man's first disobedience, and the fruit
> Of that forbidden tree, whose mortal taste
> Brought death into the world [...],
> Sing heavenly muse.
> John Milton, *Paradise Lost*

In his introduction to *The Principle of Hope,* Ernst Bloch states that "thinking means venturing beyond. [...] Real venturing beyond knows and activates the tendency which is inherent in history and which proceeds dialectically. Primarily, everyone lives in the future, because they strive, past things only come later, and as yet genuine present is almost never there at all" (4). This impetus to seek out a better future is the driving force behind any utopia, whether ancient or modern; but it is also a feature of the theories of two prominent poststructuralists, Jacques Derrida and Jacques Lacan. On the surface, the incorporation of these writers into a discussion on Utopia may appear problematic, as Lacan has often been described as nihilistic and dystopian. Equally, Derrida's relentless deconstruction of signification and his critique of its inherent hierarchies seem to leave little room for a utopia of any sort. However, like Bloch, Derrida argues that humanity is unavoidably directed towards the future: "this question *arrives*, if it arrives, it questions with regard to what will come in the future-to-come. Turned toward the future, going toward it, it also comes from it, proceeds from [*provident de*] the future" (xix). In this extract from *Specters of Marx*, Derrida is referring to the question of justice in the political realm, suggesting like Bloch, that the desire for positive change must be situated in the future. Lacan too, in his writings on psychoanalysis, encompasses the future orientation of personal and social development in the following statement: "what is realized in my history is not the past definite of what was, since it is no more, or even the present perfect of what has been in what I am, but the future anterior of what I shall have been for what I am in the process of becoming" (*Écrits* 94).

The existence of utopian ideals in theory and in literature can be regarded as an effect of human desire. In essence, Utopia represents the impossible fulfillment of desire. The area of critical theory that has particularly focused on the issue of desire is psychoanalysis, which pinpoints the catalysts of desire in childhood and its operations in adulthood. According to Lacan, desire is the result of the division of subjectivity that occurs in early childhood through the castration complex, the mirror stage, and the acquisition of language, all of which cause a split in subjectivity. Desire cannot take place without language. Lacan's philosophy is based around three orders: the imaginary, the symbolic, and the Real. Language belongs to the realm of the symbolic and in opposition to the Cartesian *"cogito ergo sum"* (*Écrits* 182); for Lacan, the subject is created in and by language. Even before it is born, the child is controlled by language. Lacan states that "his place is already inscribed at birth, if only by virtue of his proper name" (*Écrits* 163). In utopian studies, the intersection of utopianism and psychoanalysis has been regarded as problematic because psychoanalysis primarily focuses on the individual, whereas the definition of utopianism according to Ruth Levitas is "the attempt to describe in fiction or construct in fact an ideal society" (158). Because of this difficulty, Levitas criticizes Frank Manuel's *Utopian Thought in the Western World* for its reliance on Jungian psychology to propose that the idea of Utopia is a psychologically regressive phenomenon resulting from the desire to return to the womb. In contrast to Karl Jung and Sigmund Freud, Lacan argues that in childhood, the subject must relinquish the utopian fullness of the pre-linguistic Real in exchange for a position within language and society. So, the desire for utopian fulfillment is not a simplistic return of the repressed, but on the contrary, a desire to access the Real.

The order of the Real is the most ambiguous of the three orders and it is perhaps best understood in comparison with the symbolic. Unlike the symbolic, which is characterized by gaps and absences, such as the gap between meaning and articulation and the consequent division of subjectivity that ensues, the Real is characterized by a lack of absence. It is not structured, and so is completely undifferentiated. It is, as Lacan states, "absolutely without fissure" (*Seminar, Book II* 97). Also, the Real cannot be symbolized in any way, but is outside of representation. It can be thought of as the outer limit of language, and thus represents a site of total wholeness. With the advent of language, the individual is cut off from the plenitude of the pre-linguistic Real, meaning that, "the symbol manifests itself first of all as the murder of the thing, and this death constitutes in the subject the eternalization of desire" (*Écrits* 114). From this point on, the signifier (symbol) takes precedence over the signified (thing). Although desire usually takes the form of an imaginary relation with an Other as object, person, or concept, since the symbolic is governed by the imaginary, it is situated within language. This is the concept behind Lacan's famous statement, "speech is the mill-wheel whereby human desire is ceaselessly mediated by re-entering the system of language" (*Seminar, Book 1* 179). Desire is an appeal to the symbolic Other, the kernel of speech and also the locus of lack, and according to Lacan, it can never be satisfied.

The insatiability of human desire is particularly evident in the era of capitalism, when money and goods are the measure of success. It is perhaps no surprise then, in affluent western society, where access to enjoyment or *jouissance* is for some, unlimited, that utopian ideals still permeate popular culture. They can be seen in the form of films like M. Night Shyamalan's *The Village* and Alex Garland's novel *The Beach*, the film version of which is discussed below. Rather than increased wealth and advances in technology satisfying desire as one might expect, however, capitalism and consumerism only further confirm the unending nature of desire, showing that individuals still want a better car, a more lucrative job, or a more fulfilling relationship. Todd McGowan goes so far as to suggest that the materialism of the contemporary western world actually inhibits utopian *jouissance,* because it neutralizes the most important factor: prohibition. According to McGowan, "the salient feature of contemporary American society is the premium that it places on enjoyment," and he argues that this characteristic of American society is symptomatic of a cultural change so radical that it is as significant as the onset of modernity (1). Contemporary American culture has shifted from a society founded on the prohibition of enjoyment to a society that actually commands enjoyment or *jouissance*. In a society of prohibition, all members must sacrifice their private enjoyment for the good of society as a whole. In this way, "one receives an identity from society in exchange for one's immediate access to enjoyment, which one must give up" (3). For example, many traditional religions promise an afterlife of enjoyment in return for the eschewal of enjoyment in earthly life. McGowan regards the incest prohibition, described by Claude Lévi-Strauss and later by psychoanalysis as the cornerstone of modern society, to be characteristic of the society of prohibition in its demand that private satisfaction be repudiated. In the new society of enjoyment, such a sacrifice is no longer necessary. Instead, private enjoyment has become almost a social duty, tantalizingly promising an end to dissatisfaction.

The impossibility of the fulfillment of desire is a central tenet of Lacanian theory. Therefore, rather than producing an idyllic society of contented citizens, the new society of commanded enjoyment ensures that enjoyment itself is just as unattainable as before, but for a different reason. In the society of prohibition, "enjoyment is something that *does not exist prior to its renunciation*" (16). McGowan argues that since there is no longer a barrier to enjoyment, enjoyment itself cannot exist.

One of the most interesting examples of this in recent years is the film *The Beach,* directed by Danny Boyle and based on the Garland novel. Portraying a character who is anxious to escape from the packaged, consumer-driven society of America, the film reverts to motifs of prohibition that draw on Christianity, illustrating the veracity of Lacan's theory that McGowan has applied to American culture, and confirming that the command to enjoy actually blocks fulfillment, rather than encourages it. The utopia depicted in *The Beach* is another version of the utopia of Christian religion, because its prohibitive ideology makes Utopia easier to access than the liberalism of the twenty-first-century west. The tagline of the film hints at the religious ideology that underpins it: "innocence never lasts forever" (*The Beach*). This "innocence" connotes the innocence that was lost in the

Garden of Eden, one of the earliest utopias in literature. The creation story in the book of Genesis provides a relatively familiar cultural reference for the plot of *The Beach,* as it tells of the destruction of paradise as the result of the desire for knowledge. In the film, the knowledge is that which comes from the experience of a different culture and an ostensibly utopian lifestyle. On a broader level, this trend is apparent in the turn toward eastern philosophies in the west, particularly in the area of alternative healthcare. According to the bible, Adam and Eve had been warned by God not to eat the fruit from the tree of knowledge, but Eve gave into temptation thinking "how wonderful it would be to become wise" (*Genesis* 3:6). The word "paradise" in the title of this essay refers to John Milton's *Paradise Lost,* but it is also a common name for both the Garden of Eden and heaven. More recently, it is a word frequently used in advertisements for travel and holidays to describe exotic locations and both of these signifieds apply to the setting of *The Beach.*

Boyle's film follows the journey of a young American backpacker, Richard, who has an apathetic attitude to conventional holidays: "everyone's got the same idea. We all travel thousands of miles just to watch TV and check in to somewhere with all the comforts of home, and you gotta ask yourself, what is the point of that?" (*Beach*). Reluctant to accede to the safety of the package holiday, he travels to Bangkok in the hope of finding adventure, and "in search of something different" (*Beach*). At a grimy hotel, Richard makes the acquaintance of a man called Daffy, a psychotic drug-addict, who relates to him the story of a beach he had once visited, one that is unparalleled in its beauty and in its isolation from the tourist hordes: "I'm not just talking [...] 'oh, that's nice, man,' this place is fucking perfect" (*Beach*). During the night, Daffy commits suicide, and Richard discovers a hand-drawn map to the mysterious beach, which he decides to follow. He enlists a young French couple to join him: Françoise, with whom he is infatuated, and her boyfriend, Étienne.

The journey to the beach reveals another aspect of Christianity that this miniature paradise mimics. It is fraught with difficulty, and the three tourists must overcome numerous obstacles before they reach their destination. If the beach symbolizes paradise, then the tests they must go through to get there correspond to the Christian values of sacrifice and endurance that are exchanged for the eternal reward of heaven. They must swim across open sea from one island to another, crawl through fields of cannabis past armed guards, and finally, in a literal leap of faith, jump from the top of a 120-foot waterfall. Arriving on the beach, the three are assured of a welcome from the residents. Their successful negotiation of the tests *en route* ensures their suitability to become members of the community. Like entering heaven, the happiness of the new arrivals results not only from reaching their destination, but also because their presence on the beach reflects positively on the self-image of the trio as chosen people in the religious sense. According to Lacan, subjectivity is fragmented from early in childhood when the mirror stage cleaves a gap between imaginary self-image – the Ideal-I – and the objective self. The mirror stage allows the child to recognize his or her separate identity as a subject, yet it also means that the child experiences that identity as inherently alienated, because it presents a coherent, self-governing subjectivity (the Ideal-I) that the child has not, and never will, attain. It "situates the agency of the ego, before its social determination, in a fictional direction, which will always remain irreducible for the individual alone, or rather, which will only rejoin the coming into being (*le devenir*) of the subject asymptotically" (*Écrits* 3). Christianity's symbolic validation of those who lead religious lives serves to decrease the gap between Ideal-I and actual self-image. Richard's two friends who question him about the beach to no avail serve to underscore this point. They are stoned on cannabis and are depicted as stupid and ineffectual. This contrast implicitly suggests that only the particularly intelligent and resourceful will make it to the beach.

The arrival of Richard, Françoise, and Étienne is heralded with breathtaking panoramic shots of Maya Bay on the Thai island of Phi Phi Lay, where the scenes are filmed. From this spectacular beginning however, the remainder of the film catalogues the gradual dissolution of this utopia. Its demise is predicated on two factors that are characteristic of all utopias and which consequently predetermine their downfall. First, a utopia can only be conceptualized in relation to its opposite, which in the case of *The Beach* is epitomized by the crowded, threatening city of Bangkok. *The Beach* reveals that the concept of Utopia is contingent on the imperfections of mainstream society, which necessitate the idea of a utopia as a dialectical other, even if it is purely imaginary. Ferdinand de Saussure has pointed out that meaning is generated in language from differences between signs and not from any inherent meaning in them, claiming that in language there are only differences, without positive terms. Like all signs, the meaning of is garnered by its difference from other paradigmatic signifiers, so that it is a structurally necessary reference point outside of the logic of society and language, a place where personal and social desires can be fulfilled. In this sense, it corresponds to the Lacanian Real, which is a place beyond the structures of language and society, like the Kantian thing-in-itself (*Ding-an-Sich*), an unknowable, yet identifiable, recognizable entity.

Like the Real, Utopia paradoxically assures its own impossibility by its situation outside of the structures of society. And like the Real, Utopia is structurally and psychologically necessary, but materially inaccessible. Speaking of the Real, Slavoj Žižek states that, "it is impossible to occupy its position. But, Lacan adds, it is even more difficult simply to avoid it [...] the only way to avoid the Real is to produce an utterance of pure metalanguage which, by its patent absurdity, materializes its own impossibility" (*The Sublime Object of Ideology* 156). Utopia is part of a binary, and its idyllic perfection is opposite to the flawed nature of society. Derrida, whose writings have been influenced by the structuralism of Saussure, maintains that each binary is a hierarchy, and of course, within the binary of utopia/dystopia, it is obvious which is more favorable. Yet, it is the very perfection of Utopia that makes it impossible in reality. As Derrida puts it:

> guaranteed translatability, given homogeneity, systematic coherence in their absolute forms, this is surely [...] what renders the injunction, the inheritance, and the future – in a word the other – impossible. There must be disjunction, interruption, the heterogenous [...]. Once again, here as elsewhere, wherever deconstruction is at stake, it would be a matter of linking an affirmation (in particular a political one), if there is any, to the experience of the impossible, which can only be a radical experience of the perhaps (35).

As an isolated entity, Utopia is impossible. It can only, as Derrida suggests, exist as an experience of the perhaps, as the possibility of a better future. In "The Frontiers of Utopia," Louis Marin states that Utopia is necessarily "a perfect idea above any limit" and "beyond any frontier" (13). While this is an idyllic idea from a social point of view, being above and beyond means that utopias are ultimately unreachable, in the same way that the Lacanian Real is situated outside of the linguistic domain in which we live. Utopias can and have existed both in reality and in literature and theory throughout history, but they have generally been short lived, which I would argue is an effect of their structural position in relation to society, which leads to the second reason why utopias deconstruct themselves.

A utopia is bound to society as a whole. It is a part of it, defined in relation to it, and its population consists of members of this larger societal group, members who, by leaving the larger group in favor of the smaller, idealistic one, regard themselves in some way superior, more enlightened than their peers. This is evident in *The Beach*, where the residents of the community, as I have argued, regard themselves to some extent as "chosen," thus fitting into the religious schematics of the film. If a utopia is to survive, then it must be exclusive. If it does not exclude, then it will simply become a replica of the world from which it is trying to differentiate itself. This exclusion and covetousness that the islanders feel towards their island is illustrated in the argument that erupts when it is discovered that Richard may have inadvertently allowed others access to the secret map to the island. It is evident that the existence of a utopia requires that it mimic the strategies of exclusion, power, hierarchy, and greed that its inhabitants are trying to escape. This is made clear in an even more dramatic manner when one of the inhabitants of the island becomes ill and is left to die alone in the wilderness of the island, out of sight of the happy community for whom the maintenance of their utopia is more important than a single life. Richards learns that, "in the perfect beach resort, nothing is allowed to interrupt the pursuit of pleasure, not even dying" (*Beach*).

Before these events, the atmosphere on the island has already become tense when it begins to be obvious that Françoise reciprocates Richard's attraction for her. They inevitably consummate their relationship, with Françoise appearing stereotypically as the temptress, whose inability to quell her desire signals the loss of innocence that will result in the failure of the beach paradise, thus linking her unmistakably with the biblical Eve. Later in the film, Richard finds himself bearing the brunt of the selfishness that characterizes this utopia when he becomes temporarily deranged. In a surrealist sequence, he wanders alone around the jungle, idolizing the memory of the crazed Daffy who originally gave him the map and imagining himself as a character in a video game. The isolation that he experiences from the community who enveloped him in warmth and goodwill when he first arrived is the culmination of a series of indicators that prophesy the demise of the beach paradise.

In *Madness and Civilization*, Michel Foucault argues that dreaming can be considered a form of temporary insanity: "it is madness which takes its original nature from the dream and reveals in this kinship that it is a liberation of the image in the dark night of reality" (103–4). What constitutes madness is that these images, released, from a psychoanalytic perspective, from the unconscious, are erroneously substantiated in conscious reality: "madness occurs when the images, which are so close to the dream, receive the affirmation or negation that constitutes error" (104). Consequently, madness can provide insights into not only the psyche of the individual but also of the particular society of which he/she is a part, since the unconscious images of insanity need verification, however false, from the wider social order, before they are internalized and accepted as truth by the individual. As Foucault states, "the symbol of madness will henceforth be that mirror which, without reflecting anything Real, will secretly offer the man who observes himself in it the dream of his own presumption" (27). Accepting the premise that madness may reveal aspects of the community or society from which it emerges, Richard's temporary delusion takes on a new significance. His love of video games and Vietnam War movies has been foregrounded earlier in the film, and his re-enactment of these two discourses of popular culture in his madness on the island suggests one of the reasons for the failure of this utopia. In the twenty-first century, it is almost impossible to remain separate from the rest of society. Technology brings even the most remote locations into the communicative sphere and in the rare instances where this is not the case, visitors still bring the attitude of their technology-saturated society to bear on their experiences of exotic places, as Richard does in his acting out of war movies and games, which as a consequence of his American lifestyle are associated for him with the jungle in which he finds himself.

If this point is only implicit at this juncture in the film, it is made explicit at the end, when Richard is seen fully recovered from his adventure in a cyber-cafe, downloading an emailed photograph of the island community on their beach paradise, the otherness of Phi Phi island thus normalized by its mediation through communications technology, as it was when he was actually there. Richard summarizes the effect of this succinctly: "I just feel like everyone tries to do something different, but you always wind up doing the same damn thing" (*Beach*). Richard's technological delusions in the jungle contradict the claim made by Herbert Marcuse, which Levitas succinctly summarizes: "technology makes possible the abolition of scarcity and consequently renders Utopia no longer an impossible dream but a possible future; it is the key to a concrete utopia" (131). In fact, the ostensible communality that technology promises makes the individual even more isolated. As McGowan suggests, a barrier to enjoyment is paradoxically necessary for it to be attained. Mark Holloway takes the opposite view to Marcuse, stating in accordance with psychoanalytic interpretations of Utopia that "the more immediately and efficiently we can communicate, world-wide, the less do we need the actual physical presences of our bodies anywhere but at home" (182). This is the conclusion that Richard is forced to acknowledge when, having attempted to escape from the technological saturation of the west in Thailand, he eventually realizes that he cannot, and he takes comfort at the end of the film in filtering his experience there through technology, capturing it in a photograph of smiling faces and sunny beaches that glosses over the reality of his time there.

In the contemporary global world, where technology aids the advance of western imperialism, every culture is to a certain extent homogenized. This is evident in Bangkok, to which Richard travels in an attempt to find something "more beautiful, something more exciting and yes, I admit, something more dangerous" (*Beach*). While his initial impression of Bangkok excites him by its difference, for example when the locals try to entice him into drinking snake blood, the western infiltration of Asian culture is undeniable. Episodes of *The Simpsons* appear on television, and radios blast out western pop. In the modern world, utopian enclaves like that of *The Beach* are even less likely to succeed than before. Not only is its extra-societal position under threat from its structural proximity to the rest of society, the acquisition of that isolated state has itself become tenuous, even arbitrary.

This is evident even from the cultural makeup of the island community. The utopia is in Thailand, but its inhabitants are western, an assortment of young Europeans and Americans, suggesting that an island paradise cannot be deemed so unless it has been first validated by westerners. This subtle racism permeates the film, wherein the western revelers are the focus of attention and the objects of audience sympathy, while the native islanders who grow cannabis in plantation fields near the beach are depicted as menacing and violent. Indeed, the production history of the film verifies how influential and how invasive western utopian ideals really are, operating not only without any portrayal of native culture, but also damaging the native environment. Although filmed on location in Thailand, Maya Bay was not beautiful enough for the film crew, who destroyed the landscape by leveling the beach and planting palm trees, guessing, probably correctly, that no beach could be considered a tropical paradise through western eyes without them. Scrub bushes that dotted the sand were regarded as unsightly and were cleared, although they are essential to the native ecology in order to prevent erosion. Twentieth Century Fox, in an attempt to appease the locals and not wishing to be branded anti-environmentalist, left a hefty lump sum for the reconstruction of the beach and departed. It was not, however, enough to undo the damage that had been done (see Vidal). In the end, *The Beach* is nothing but a product of the western imagination, a rehashing of orientalist stereotypes, in both the diegetic and the extra-diegetic narrative.

If Utopia is considered as outside of society in the same way as the Lacanian Real is outside of language, a useful comparison can be made between the two. What Lacan calls the *traite unaire,* the unitary feature, is according to Žižek, "a point of symbolic identification which clings to the subject" (*Enjoy your Symptom!* 2). Sarah Kay describes the Real as similar to a hole in a doughnut. The hole is necessary to give the doughnut its shape, yet in itself it is just empty space; likewise, "the Real is what shapes our sense of reality, even though it is excluded from it" (4). It is both the effect of the subject's indoctrination into the symbolic order and the lack that this entails. Žižek points out that the symbolic does not act as an independent generator of meaning, but is given meaning by the Real, *le traite unaire,* the hole in the doughnut that gives it its structure. Utopias have the same function in relation to society that the Real does in relation to the symbolic. They are places which do not belong to the symbolic order of reality, but the existence of which is necessary in order to give meaning to and improve real life.

The writings of Lacan and Derrida, like those of Bloch, are directed towards the future, and incorporate utopian idealism. From a psychoanalytic point of view, the existence of utopias both literary and actual, can be regarded as an effect of desire, a desire according to Lacan that is insatiable. The materialistic western world, where consumers are commanded to attain satisfaction in their leisure pursuits, actually inhibits *jouissance*, which is why *The Beach* reverts to tropes of Christianity, indicative of a culture of prohibition paradoxically more suited to the fulfillment of desire, as can be seen in the allusions to the Garden of Eden, the ideology of sacrifice and reward, and the characterization of Françoise as Eve. However, this reversion also fails, because Utopia acquires signification from its opposition to the rest of society. It is extra-societal, as the Real is extra-linguistic. In order to differentiate itself from the rest of society, Utopia must exclude and this exclusivity eventually leads to the recreation of the hierarchical structures of the society that its inhabitants are trying to escape. The task of remaining separate becomes even more difficult in this twenty-first century, wherein technology allows access to the remotest corners of the world and western values permeate other cultures. Moreover, the effort results in the negation of the otherness that first made the location a utopia, which in *The Beach* happens as a result of the imposition of Western ideas about paradise, and implicit racism against the locals. However, as Lacan reveals, even if utopias are fated to deconstruct themselves, their social function is still a necessary one. They facilitate a space in which social harmony and complete fulfillment can be realized, if only for a short time, and in doing so, provide if not the ultimate experience of *jouissance*, then at least, as Derrida states, an experience of the perhaps.

Works Cited

The Beach. Dir. Danny Boyle. 2000.
Bloch, Ernst. *The Principle of Hope.* Vol. 1. Trans. Neville Plaice, Stephen Plaice and Paul Knight. Cambridge, Massachusetts: MIT Press, 1995.
Derrida, Jacques. *Specters of Marx: The State of the Debt, the Work of Mourning, and the New International.* Trans. Peggy Kamuf. London: Routledge, 1994.
Foucault, Michel. *Madness and Civilization: A History of Madness in the Age of Reason.* London: Tavistock, 1971.
Garland, Alex. *The Beach.* London: Penguin, 2004.
Good News Bible: The Bible in Today's English Version. New York: Thomas Nelson, 1976.
Holloway, Mark. "The Necessity of Utopia." *Utopias.* Ed. Peter Alexander and Roger Gill. London: Open Court, 1984. 179–88.
Kay, Sarah. *Žižek: A Critical Introduction.* Cambridge: Polity, 2003.
Lacan, Jacques. *Écrits: a Selection.* Trans. Alan Sheridan. London: Routledge, 1989.
____*The Seminar, Book 1, Freud's Papers on Technique, 1953–4.* Trans. John Forrester. Cambridge: Cambridge University Press, 1987.
____*The Seminar, Book II. The Ego in Freud's Theory and in the Technique of Psychoanalysis, 1954–44.* Trans. Sylvana Tomaselli. Cambridge: Cambridge University Press, 1988.
Levitas, Ruth. *The Concept of Utopia.* Syracuse: Syracuse University Press, 1990.
Marin, Louis. "The Frontiers of Utopia." *Utopias and the Millennium.* Ed. Krishan Kumar and Stephen Bann. London: Reaktion, 1993. 7–16.

McGowan, Todd. *The End of Dissatisfaction? Jacques Lacan and the Emerging Society of Enjoyment.* New York: State University of New York Press, 2004.
Milton, John. *Paradise Lost.* Ed. Johnathan Goldberg and Stephen Orgel. Oxford: Oxford University Press, 2004.
The Village. Dir. M. Night Shyamalan. 2004.
Vidal, John. "Di Caprio Film-Makers Face Storm over Paradise Lost." *The Guardian* 29 October 1999
    <www.thaistudents.com /thebeach/archives_10_99.htm>.
Žižek, Slavoj. *Enjoy your Symptom! Jacques Lacan in Hollywood and Out.* New York: Routledge, 2001.
____ *The Sublime Object of Ideology.* London: Verso, 1989.

Michael J. Griffin and Dara Waldron

Across Time and Space: The Utopian Impulses of Andrei Tarkovsky's *Stalker*

One of the standard descriptions of a utopia is that it is "a nonexistent society described in detail and normally located in time and space" (Claeys and Sargent 1). The same could be true of the utopian impulse, except that an impulse (or an anxiety generated by an impulse) can best be represented in time and space when it is allegorized. One of the problems surrounding Andrei Tarkovsky's *Stalker* relates to its fidelity to the novel upon which is it supposedly based: *Roadside Picnic*, by the Strugatsky bothers. The film is only tenuously linked to the talkative, noirish science fiction (sf) of the novel, which provides very nominal parameters for the film's allegorical meditations on time, memory, hope, and fear; other than that, the book's plot recedes. For Tarkovsky:

> the subject which the screenplay would be based on permitted one to express in a very concentrated manner the philosophy, so to speak, of the contemporary intellectual. Or rather, his condition. Although I must say that the screenplay of Stalker has only two words, two names, in common with the Strugatsky's novel *Roadside Picnic*: Stalker and Zone. As you see, the story behind my film is rather disappointing" (Tarkovsky and Guerra online).

Fredric Jameson describes *Stalker* as an obscurantist and "lugubrious religious fable" (*Geopolitical Aesthetic* 92), and as such a debasement of the original. However, we suggest that what might be perceived as the lugubriousness of Tarkovsky's adaptation is part of its poetic point. The film is more suggestively symbolic and allegorical, and, if not utopian, more profoundly investigative of the utopian impulse. Our essay, then, will argue that *Stalker* is a momentous cinematic study of the utopian impulse in film, an impulse impressed in two strands which accord to dimensions of time and space. The utopian impulse is thus associated in *Stalker* with two phenomena: the first is time in the form of music; the second, space in the form of a mysterious room and *Stalker*'s socialization of the traditionally atomized, emptied associations of space in film noir.

The work of Gilles Deleuze provides a convincing template for a consideration of *Stalker*. Deleuze's writings on cinema are among the most lucid of his oeuvre. "Whatever one's attitude to Deleuze," writes Robert Bird, "his rigorous dissection of the cinematic image has revivified its concealed magic" (online). Slavoj Žižek has suggested that "Tarkovsky is the clearest example of what Deleuze called the time-image replacing the movement image" (102). Further, Bird has remarked that "Deleuze's sparse comments on Tarkovsky mask the director's profound significance for the theorist" (online; see also Beasley-Murray). Deleuze, in his two seminal analyses of cinema – *The Time Image* and *The Movement Image* – identifies the Second World War, when history and innovation converged, as a revolutionary point in cinematic development. As general background to his theory, Deleuze proposed that, over the centuries between the Greeks and philosophical modernity, a gradual revolution took place in representation, whereby the subordination of time to movement was slowly reversed. Deleuze claims that, as this revolution consolidated itself, time came increasingly to stand for itself alone. As a late arrival in dramatic representation, cinema condensed the long revolution from a theater of movements to a theater of moments:

> Time is out of joint: Hamlet's words signify that time is no longer subordinated to movement, but rather movement to time. It could be said that, in its own sphere, cinema has repeated the same experience, the same reversal, in more fast-moving circumstances. The movement-image of the so-called classical cinema gave way, in the post-war period, to a direct time-image" (*Time-Image* xi).

The time-movement dialectic stems from Deleuze's readings in Bergsonian philosophy. Henri Bergson asserted that ancient thought posited movement as a reference to intelligent elements. With Aristotelian notions of dramatic effect, movement (or action) "merely expresses a 'dialectic' of forms, an ideal synthesis which gives it order and measure. Movement, conceived in this way, will thus be the regulated transition from one form to another, that is, an order of *poses* or privileged instants, as in a dance" (*Movement-Image* 4). With postwar cinema, the subjugation of time to movement gave way to a new subordination of movement to time. Prior to the war, it must be supposed, there was a sort of Aristotelian unity to ontology itself, reflective of pastoral harmony, urban and rural. After the war, however, much of the social and physical environment was changed; and, as a consequence, the old order yielded to a general existentialism, according to which nothing really moved and time had become, in representative terms, an independent variable.

With the privileged instants and privileged spaces of prewar cinema razed, postwar cinema represented "any-instants-whatever," and, relatedly, "any-space-whatevers, *deconnected* or *emptied spaces*" (*Movement-Image* 123). For Deleuze, the postwar situation, "with its towns demolished or being reconstructed, its waste grounds, its shanty towns, and even in places where the war had not penetrated, its undifferentiated urban tissue, its vast unused places, docks, warehouses, heaps of girders and scrap iron" has generated a different type of cinema, in which "characters were found less and less in sensory-motor 'motivating' situations, but rather in a state of strolling, of sauntering or of rambling which defined *pure optical and sound situations*" (*Movement-Image* 124). With its crystallization of time, the filmic project of *Stalker* is a ready, exemplary instance of Deleuze's template. The contortions of plot relegated, time is imprinted all the more vividly. Not only is the passage of time realistically depicted; it also succeeds in vividly rendering the Deleuzian turn. The film's rhythmically steady time-image occasions a gradual and collectivist thematic of music, while the emptied spaces of the film provide, in a similarly gradual way, a locus of collectivism and camaraderie. Deleuze's theory periodizes and legitimates what might otherwise be considered lugubrious. However, it also provides a template for a proper consideration of the utopianism which, in Benjaminian terms, pulses through the allegory.

Music

In comparison with music, Tarkovksy writes, "cinema stands out as giving time visible, real form" (*Sculpting in Time* 118). Cinema has the power to represent time; but, like music, cinema also has the power to manipulate and distort it:

> A piece of music can be played in different ways, can last for varying lengths of time. Here time is simply a condition of certain causes and effects set out in a given order; it has an abstract, philosophical character. Cinema on the other hand is able to record time in outward and visible signs, recognizable to the feelings. And so time becomes the very foundation of cinema: as sound is in music, color in painting, character in drama" (*Sculpting in Time* 118–9).

Tarkovsky's filmic achievement is to collapse all of these artistic components – music, painting, dramaturgy – into renditions of time's passing. However, he also seems to allow music the closest analogy to the total effect of his work:

> I classify cinema and music among the *immediate* art forms since they need no mediating language. This fundamental determining factor marks the kinship between music and cinema, and for the same reason distances cinema from literature, where everything is expressed by means of language, by a system of signs, of hieroglyphics. The literary work can only be received through symbols through concepts – for that is what words are; but cinema, like music, allows for an utterly direct, emotional, sensuous perception of the work" (*Sculpting in Time* 176).

Music and cinema together are conceived of as unmediated by Tarkovsky; and it is this theme of unmediation, or de-atomization, which is the most vividly utopian aspect of *Stalker*.

Utopia and music, of course, have a long established connection, from the social engineering of Plato's philosophy of music to the "utopian community briefly realised" through music in Ian MacEwan's *Amsterdam* (172). For Ernst Bloch, music can reflect, in an abstracted mode, the material tensions of society at the same time that it possesses transformative energies which anticipate change. Music reflects the damaged contingency of the here and now, but also designs the not here, the not now, and the Not Yet of the utopian. In Bloch, music, when it is to the good, can transcend mediated or administered culture. "Only in Beethoven," as he puts it, "does the self advance further toward the discovery of that certain ground that perhaps extends all the way into the final God" (65). Music's ideality is also figured in terms of God or the absolute in Theodor Adorno's "Music and Language: A Fragment," wherein a distinction is made between music and intentional language. Intentional language can attempt to describe the absolute, but the absolute escapes. Music, on the other hand, "finds the absolute immediately, but at the moment of discovery it becomes obscured, just as too powerful a light dazzles the eyes, preventing them from seeing things which are perfectly visible" (4). Adorno's treatment of music is metaphorically related to Plato's allegory of the cave in Book VII of *The Republic*, wherein shadows on the wall provide the classical analogy for discursive language. A hypothetical figure emerges from the cave to be blinded by the sun's beams. In both Plato and Adorno there are equivalent aesthetic gradations towards the good; but the good – or the absolute – can be blinding to a limited conceptual realm (see Griffin).

The utopian expressiveness of music is instanced in other texts. Standish James O'Grady's *Sun and Wind* is an Irish revision of Plato's Spartan utopia. Sparta, for O'Grady, represents the possibility of a return to an organic unity prior to the Fall. The Fall here is the descent into civilization's mediating systems of dead language and filthy lucre. O'Grady's thoughts on this topic merge with the emerging semiotic theories of the early twentieth century:

> Have you ever observed that our words which we habitually employ are worlds removed from the things which they so arbitrarily represent: that our language, in fact, is as dead as a door-mat. We don't know why we say door or why we say mat. The language is dead [...]. I feel certain that our ancient Aryan ancestors used a language which was in all its parts alive and sparkling with significance. What a dead unlovely word is this, for instance, which ends the foregoing sentence; but all our words are like it in this quality by deadness. Let me hazard a prediction; it is that when men begin to live again by returning to Nature they will strip these dead languages from their minds and tongues and create for themselves again a living speech. Man naturally hates all dead things, dead customs, institutions, dead religions, and dead words (15).

In O'Grady's writing, the utopian impulse desires to attain the condition of music in living. Musical harmony is the temporal partner to an Arcadian spatiality. Music in his utopia consists of a purer communication, uninfected, O'Grady seems to suggest, by language. Language is figured as analogous to money, to commerce, to capitalism, and to property. Money is only significant (that "dead, unlovely" notion again) in the context of a dehumanizing system; it is "an absurd God, the absurdest that men, in their madness, ever bowed down before and worshipped" (8).

The utopian plan involves a social transcendence towards a Platonic plane of purer exchange in music and communal arcadia, which existed in the imagined past, and will exist again in an imagined future: "It is said that at some time in our aeonian past our speech was song only when we lived in a universe of sound and music; and I think that thought is true" (O'Grady 16). The goal now for the hero of O'Grady's small epic is "to evoke order out of disorder, concord out of things discordant, to form and reform, may be to become the grand reformer of all time" (16). Reform in society will allow movement towards "an awareness that we live in the midst of an infinite ocean of Music. We don't hear the harmonies but we know they are there. All the poets from before and since Plato have been deeply aware of it [...]. If Nature is Beauty, as she is, so, too, she is Music. But in the midst of all the Music there is one harsh discord. Man is that. We are the one discordant and terribly dissonant note in the great harmony" (40).

Humanity's corruption is egoism and selfishness, set against the possibility of a more generous impulse in humans which, in the view of the character of the Stalker in Tarkovsky's film, is spoken to most directly by music. Music becomes, as it was for Bloch, the currency of hope. Perhaps one of the most transfixing segments of *Stalker* is the Stalker's monologue, listened to with rapt attention by the Writer and the Professor. The Stalker, after one mysterious moment of communal sleep and dream, speaks to his charges on the meaning of life:

> The unselfishness of art. Take music for instance. Less than anything else, it is connected to reality. Or, if connected at all, it's done mechanically, not by way of ideas, just by a sheer sound, devoid of any associations. And yet music, as if

> by some miracle, gets through to our heart. What is it that resonates in us in response to noise brought to harmony, making it the source of the greatest delight, which stuns us and brings us together? What's all this needed for? And most important, who needs it? You would say no-one, and for no reason. Unselfishly. No. I don't think so. After all, everything has some sense. Sense and reason (*Stalker*).

Music gets through to the collectivist unconscious the utopian impulse of "our innermost" wishes. The Stalker's vocabulary creates a will to community, and a will to "sense and reason," a coalescence of subjective "beings" into a larger harmony.

Tarkovsky is loathe, however, to lead his audience by the ear with a rapturous soundtrack to communalism, as is evident in his philosophy of music in film. For the film to use a lucid soundtrack would be counterproductive:

> I thought that the film did not require music. It seemed to me that it could, that it should, rely only on sounds. Sounds possess a special expressivity: perhaps they are not able to replace music in general, but they can superbly replace illustrative music, 'film music' to be precise. The spectator of *ten* guesses in advance the moment when such music starts up; he hears it and thinks: 'there we are, fine, now everything is clear'" (Tarkovsky and Guerra online).

Tarkovksy's admonition augments Hanns Eisler and Adorno's critique of administered meaning in mainstream cinema, where the musical score "converts a kiss into a magazine cover, an outburst of unmitigated pain into a melodrama, a scene from nature into an oleograph" (Adorno 32). Instead, Tarkovsky proposes that the music should be combined with, or hidden under, the sounds experienced by the characters in the film itself:

> I would like to try a muffled music, barely distinguishable through the noise of the train that passes underneath the windows of the Stalker's home. For example, Beethoven's Ninth Symphony (the Ode to Joy), Wagner, or, perhaps, the Marsellaise, music, in other words, that is rather popular, that expresses the sense of the movement of the masses, the theme of the destiny of human society. But this music must barely reach, through the noises, the ear of the audience, so that, until the end, the spectator does not know if he is really hearing it or if he's dreaming (Tarkovsky and Guerra online).

In this final sentence, Tarkovsky generates a utopic ambiguity between the real and the dreamt. "Muffled music" is experienced then as dreamlike, as though allegorizing the utopian political unconscious of those whose environment it infuses. The abrasive combination of music with an environment of technological modernity aspires to express the memory of a beleaguered collectivity, and to prefigure, in sound, the destiny of that collective.

Tarkovsky's cinema seeks to record poetic memory and the passing of time, to render visually the elusive substance of both. Time is most effectively accelerated or slowed by the interference of music and sound, which compresses and elongates the human experience of temporality through melodic and rhythmic manipulation. What music does, that status to which, according to Walter Pater, other arts aspire, is the object of Tarkovsky's time-image cinema: to create a cinema that approaches music. His work has been described variously as poetic cinema, analogously, it is painting as music, sculpture in time, and also, as Vita Johnson and Graham Petrie's famous study has it, a visual fugue. *The Ninth*, and the tumultuous, redemptive "Ode to Joy," which Tarkovsky heard in his mind's ear, is according to Estaban Buch, "the most convincing depiction of Utopia in sound. And Utopia is a concept that haunts private unhappiness just as it does political ideas" (4). *Stalker* ends with the diegetic of Beethoven's ode coalescing with non-diegetic sound. Music reverberates as Monkey sits in a lonely Room, a Room that in some ways counteracts the search for such a Room that takes up most of the film's plot. Space and time converge, but the meaning of space has changed within the short instance of the film time. It is no longer a wrecked, empty, or "deconnected" space, but a space of love and hope.

Noir

Stalker is Tarkovsky's second foray into sf, after *Solaris*. But *Stalker* is also part of a developing subgenre of sf: sf noir. Features of noir are set side-by-side with features of sf. The spaces of the film – lonely city bars, empty rooms – are noir. The thematic, the philosophy of the film, however, is not. In fact, the theme of the film consists, ultimately, of noir's rejection. The film exposes noir's redundancies by exploring something other: the utopian impulse. The remainder of this essay explores the noir impulse generated in *Stalker* through a particular stylistic emphasis on objects and quests powered by a utopian impulse, but generated by a resistance to the goal of these quests.

One of the leading psychoanalytic critics of noir, Joan Copjec, illustrates noir experience with recourse to an oxymoronic term: "the phenomenal nonphenomenal" (167). The perceptive analysis of the break between classical detection and noir detection that leads to the invention of this term stems from Copjec's previous suggestion that "the infinite, inexhaustible space of the older model" gives way "in film noir to its inverse; the lonely room, such as the one in which Neff utters his confessions (in Billy Wilder's noir *Double Indemnity*). For Neff sits in one of those vacant office buildings, those plain and for the moment uninhabited spaces that constitute the characteristic architecture of film noir" (189). A characteristic feature of noir is the "curious depopulation of space," which means that "spaces have been emptied of desire" (Copjec 189). Space is reduced to its elemental form, a material devoid of sense or signification. As an illustration of what Copjec means, the noir hero of Bela Tarr's 1987 neo-noir, *Damnation*, is shown sitting in a lonely room at the close of the film, confessing in one such space "emptied of desire." Verbal Kint, the antihero of Bryan Singer's 1996 *The Usual Suspects*, is shown in a similar confessional process. Verbal seemingly confesses to the police; but by fabricating his confession using the contents of the room in which he is interrogated, he leaves a void of desire amidst the superfluous texts: the meaningless information on the walls of the room. The noir moment in both films features the police, who feel they have succeeded in their criminal manhunt, realizing that they have failed. The police are hoodwinked by a yarn that simply opens up a void, emptying space of its significatory substance. Copjec's reading of noir consists of rejecting the dominant sociological interpretation of noir as a paranoiac response to cold war hostilities. For Copjec, this means seeing in "noir" a characteristic of the social constellation in western liberal democracies. The classical feature of noir is "erosion of privacy that permits the Other to penetrate, to read one's inner thoughts," but Copjec is led to permit "that the opposite is true. It is on the public level that the erosion has taken place. No social distance separates individuals, no 'social clothing' protects their innermost being" (190). No "discursive knowledge" can emerge with this erosion. Equally, in *The Usual Suspects*, Verbal Kint walks away just as any discursive explanation of his actions is rendered null. Verbal's innermost thoughts are devoid of real expression. Simply put: Verbal's noir impulse exposes "being" without sense.

George Bataille offers theoretical justification for Copjec's analysis of noir in *The Accursed Share:*

> If I say of individual love that it is outside history, this is insofar as what is *individual* is never manifest in history. Those men whose names fill our memories have nothing individual about them except an appearance which we lend to them: their existence is given to us only to the extent that their destiny corresponds with the general movement of history. They were not independent, they served that history which they imagined they were leading. Only their private life escaped (at least in part) the *function* that ensured their overt role. But the wall of private life, precisely if it protects individual love, marks off a space outside history (158).

"Individual love" is "being" removed from sense and is a suitable concept for considering the "phenomenal nonphenomenal." In contrast, Tom Moylan approaches the utopian impulse as a "separation" of Utopia as "impulse or historical force" from utopia as specific "expressions (as texts, communal societies, or social theories)" (155). The utopian impulse is an attempt to impose sense on a society, a text, a social order, which precedes the actual expression of Utopia. The impulse to express Utopia consists of moving beyond the privative. It consists of a transferral of individualizing desire (with an end-point in the noir experience of "being" without sense) to a collective desire, with an end-point in the expression of Utopia.

This transferral of desire from an investment in the individual to a conscious impulse for Utopia is the pertinent issue in Tarkovsky's *Stalker*. The "plot" of the film consists of a group of travelers moving through a Zone, an off-limits space for those who inhabit a police state, and the group's attempt to enter the Room – the end-point of the journey, and perhaps the end-point of desire, which offers to grant the "innermost wish" of those who enter. The Stalker is, for Tarkovsky, "the last idealist [...] a man who believes in the possibility of a happiness independent of man's will and his efforts" (Tarkovsky and Guerra online). He is leading a poet and a scientist, precariously, through a ruined region, suspended in utopian or dystopian sequestration from the rest of society, a place of potential threat but also of fulfillment; for at the heart of Zone is the possibility of realizing one's deepest wishes. The ruined spaces of the film, its "any-spaces-whatever" offer, due to the miraculous interference of an otherworldly force, the unsettling possibility of transcendence: a sort of utopian footpath. The any-spaces-whatever rendered by Tarkovsky in real time are objective correlatives – to use T.S. Eliot's phrase – to an inner ruin, but also to an inner motivation. The Stalker has become a specialist in navigating the Zone, where death lurks at every corner, and has devoted his life to leading the "down and out" to the Room. The Writer and the Professor, utopian agents of tradition and modernity, culture and technology, ideality and materiality, are the two derelict characters the Stalker leads on the mission. Both seek a confirmation of their chosen "being," their chosen profession; both seek to confront and perhaps to realize their most profound, almost unsayable aspirations.

The travelers' arrival is marked in the film by a change in form. Sepia imagery is used up until the point in which the group arrives in the Zone, at which time sepia gives way to color photography. The group's escape from the city, which consists of action and movement, gives way to the stillness of introspection and intellectual debate. This sudden change in pace (reflected in "form") leads the Writer to argue: "Let's imagine I enter this Room and return to our God-forsaken town a genius. A man writes because he's tormented, because he doubts. He needs to constantly prove to himself and to others that he's worth something. And if I know for sure I'm a genius? Why write then? What the hell for?" (*Stalker*). The quintessential feature of a utopian impulse is a doubt as to the validity of the present. The Writer's emphasis on doubt at the expense of fulfilled desire, works towards exposing the impulse to experience the lonely room as an impulse to achieve a fullness of being. The noir impulse consists of emptying desire; but in *Stalker* the travelers, prompted by doubt, reject the Room. This choice, this resistance, is made after hearing the fate, as recounted by the Stalker, of his predecessor, Porcupine. Having entered the Room, thus breaking the Stalker code, Porcupine is found hanging in another lonely Room a week later. This story affirms the Writer's belief that the Room's power consists of extinguishing "doubt," a doubt coeval with what Bloch and Augustine have described as the Not Yet (see Daniel and Moylan; and Augustine 169). To extinguish the Not Yet is, within the terms of this debate, to extinguish the Writer's doubt.

There is nothing to suggest an expression of Utopia in *Stalker*. There is, however, everything to suggest an impulse other than that of the noir impulse towards the procurement of "individual love." By rejecting the Room's promise of "individual love," transfigured on a self-reflexive basis in the experiential domain of noir in the film, the Writer reveals the gradual transformation from noir spectacle to utopian, collective enterprise. This transformation is evident in the changing relationship between the Stalker and his wife. In the opening scene, she is informed of his desire to return to the Zone, evidence of his willful neglect of familial obligations. When he returns from his mission in the Zone, the Stalker's wife supports his vocation. Tarkovsky explains this support:

> There before them is a woman who has been through untold miseries because of her husband, and has had a sick child by him; but she continues to love him with the same selfless, unthinking devotion as in her youth. Her love and her devotion are that final miracle which can be set against the unbelief, cynicism, moral vacuum poisoning the modern world, of which the Writer and Scientist are victims (*Sculpting in Time* 198).

The Stalker's wife is a paradigm of virtue and belief, affirming the Stalker's spiritual mission in the Zone in counterpoint to his rejection of the Room. The second reason to support our view of the transformation of noir spectacle into utopian enterprise is the transfusion of color into previously sepia spaces in the final section of the film. The sepia used to represent the city at the beginning, and up until the entry into the Zone, gradually fades. This fading gives a clue as to the significance of the travelers' rejection of the Room and the Stalker's devotion to the Zone (although the Writer and Professor's failure to see the Zone as the utopian space of the film leads to the Stalker's disgruntled demeanor on his return). The switch implies that the Zone is enlightening (in color) the city. The final sequence culminates with a long take of the Stalker's daughter, Monkey, as she looks away from the camera while reading what is possibly the Bible. Beethoven's "Ode to Joy" battles aurally with the sound of a passing train just as the camera stabilizes on Monkey. Monkey moves a glass from one end of the table to the next, telekinetically, while a voiceover reads a verse of poetry:

> But there's more that I admire
> Your eyes when they're downcast
> In bursts of love-inspired fire
> And through the eyelash goes fast
> A somber dull call of desire (*Stalker*).

As Hannah Arendt puts it: "the truly positive aspect of our essentially death-determined existence lies in this "not yet" of our being"— thus affirming the positivity of the Zone as a space where the "somber dull call of desire" is felt (73). Rashit Safiullin, the production designer of *Stalker*, describes the Zone as a space where "you can meet people and live as you like, without reacting to what's without [...] Without you have to lie, circumvent others; but here you live being your inmost self" (*Stalker* DVD). Safiullin prioritizes demystifying the Room's powers (as an experience of an "inmost self") over the impulse to experience "being" without "sense" (*Stalker* DVD). Here the utopian impulses expressed by the Stalker in his monologue on music – where music is the inspiration and impulse towards sense – is given further impetus by the Writer's impulse to make sense of the world, and therefore reject the supersensual experience offered by the Room.

Conclusion

Stalker allegorizes the desire to possess rather than experience the "inmost self," a possession offered by the Room; but the film is also Tarkovsky's most vigorous condemnation of a society where being has become fully subjectivized – where the desire to experience "being" without "sense" has overtaken the "not yet" of sense itself. Noir shows us how such desire implodes in a suffocation of being. Unlike in noir, the utopian impulse lies in the group's attempt – through the temporal considerations of music and the spatial pilgrimage to *interpret* being – to reignite "collective" sense, as above, "in bursts of love-inspired fire". His own disdain for the film notwithstanding, Fredric Jameson offers a theoretical mode of assessing *Stalker*'s collectivist, utopian impulse:

> If indeed one believes that the utopian desire is everywhere, and that some individual or pre-individual Freudian libido is enlarged and completed by a realm of social desire, in which the longing for transfigured collective relationships is no less powerful and omnipresent, then it is scarcely surprising that this particular political unconscious is to be identified even there where it is the most passionately decried and denounced (*Seeds* 54–5).

Jameson catches and encapsulates here the dialogic quality of the film's philosophy: the subjective desires (and suspicions) of individual characters seem senseless and antiutopian but are socialized and partially resolved into a reciprocating sense of doubt and vulnerability. Though there is partial resolution, there is no closure; rather, the film retains a compelling aura of incompletion. In this incompletion, the film's form and utopian philosophy converge.

The aim of this essay has been to explore the allegorized utopian suspensions of time and space in *Stalker*. Music activates a non-referential communalism; external space allegorizes the inner life. Such a space facilitates the emergence of what is dialectically other to the desire for an "innermost wish." The Stalker denounces the group's striving for individual love, which paradoxically allows for the experience of a collective relationship to emerge during the travelers' time in the Zone. This is an impulse unfolding in an allegorical continuum where the "utopian impulse," rather than Utopia itself, prevails.

Works Cited

Adorno, Theodor, and Hans Eisler. *Composing for the Films*. London and Atlantic Highlands: Athlone, 1994.

Arendt, Hannah. *Love and St. Augustine*. Ed. Joanna Vecchiareli Scot and Judith Chelius Stark. Chicago: University of Chicago Press, 1996.

Augustine. *Confessions*. Trans. Robert Scott Pine-Coffin. New York: Dorset Press, 1961.

Bataille, George. *The Accursed Share: An Essay on General Economy*. Vols. II & III. Trans. Robert Hurley. New York: Zone, 1991.

Beasley-Murray, Jon. "Whatever Happened to Neorealism? — Bazin, Deleuze, and Tarkovsky's Long Take." *Iris* 23 (Spring 1997): 37–52.

Bird, Robert. "Gazing into Time: Tarkovsky and Post-Modern Cinema Aesthetics." 2003. 27 June 2005 <http://www.acs.ucalgary.ca/~tstronds/nostalghia.com/TheTopics/Gazing.html>.

Bloch, Ernst. *The Spirit of Utopia*. Trans. Anthony A. Nassar. Stanford: Stanford University Press, 2000.

Buch, Estaban. *Beethoven's Ninth: A Political History*. Trans. Richard Miller. Chicago and London: University of Chicago Press, 2003.

Claeys, Gregory and Lyman Tower Sargent. "Introduction." *The Utopia Reader*. Ed. Gregory Claeys and Lyman Tower Sargent. New York: New York University Press, 1999. 1–5.

Copjec, Joan. "The Phenomenal Nonphenomenal: Private Space in *Film Noir*." *Shades of Noir: A Reader*. Ed. Joan Copjec. London and New York: Verso, 1993. 167–98.
Damnation. Dir. Bela Tarr. 2003.
Daniel, Jamie Owen and Tom Moylan. *Not Yet: Reconsidering Ernst Bloch*. London: Verso, 1997.
Deleuze, Gilles. *Cinema 1: The Movement-Image*. Trans. Hugh Tomlinson and Barbara Habberjam. London: Continuum, 2005.
____*Cinema 2: The Time-Image*. Trans. Hugh Tomlinson and Robert Galeta. London: Continuum, 2005.
Double Indemnity. Dir. Billy Wilder. 1944.
Griffin, Michael J. "Utopian Music and the Problem of Luxury." *Utopian Studies* 16.2 (2005): 247–66.
Jameson, Fredric. *The Geopolitical Aesthetic: Cinema and Space in the World System*. London: BFI, 1992.
____ *The Seeds of Time*. New York: Columbia University Press, 1994.
Johnson, Vita T. and Graham Petrie. *The Films of Andrei Tarkovsky: A Visual Fugue*. Indiana: Indiana University Press, 1994.
McEwan, Ian. *Amsterdam*. London: Jonathan Cape, 2005.
Moylan, Tom. *Scraps of the Untainted Sky: Science Fiction, Utopia, Dystopia*. Boulder: Westview, 2000.
O'Grady, Standish James. *Sun and Wind*. Dublin: University College Dublin Press, 2004.
Pater, Walter. "The School of Giorgione." *The Renaissance: Studies in Art and Poetry*. Oxford: Oxford University Press, 1986. 83–98.
Safiullin, Rashit. "Interview." *Stalker* DVD 2. Artificial Eye. 2002.
Stalker. Dir. Andrei Tarkovsky. 1979.
Solaris. Dir. Andrei Tarkovsky. 1972.
Strugatsky, Boris and Arcady Strugatsky. *Roadside Picnic*. Trans. Antonina W. Bouis. New York: Macmillan, 1977.
Tarkovsky, Andrei. *Sculpting in Time: Reflections on Cinema*. Trans. Kitty Hunter-Blair. Austin: University of Texas Press, 1986.
Tarkovsky, Andrei and Tonino Guerra. "Tarkovsky at the Mirror: A Conversation Between Andrei Tarkovsky and Tonino Guerra." Trans. David Stringari. 1979. 22 February 2005 <http://www.acs.ucalgary.ca/~tstronds/nostalghia.com/TheTopics/Tarkovsky_Guerra-1979.html>.
The Usual Suspects. Dir. Bryan Singer. 2002.
Žižek, Slavoj. *The Fright of Real Tears: Krzysztof Kieślowski between Theory and Post-Theory*. London: BFI, 2001.

Caitríona Ní Dhúill

"One loves the girl for what she is, and the boy for what he promises to be": Gender Discourse in Ernst Bloch's *Das Prinzip Hoffnung*.

This essay investigates the ways in which the discourse of desire is gendered in Ernst Bloch's seminal work of utopian philosophy. The dynamic, forward-striving movement of utopian desire is often figured in Bloch's work as a force which acts upon the world, creating from it a home fit for human habitation. Bloch's philosophy focuses on the tension between the human and the natural: he emphasizes the complementary double movement of the "humanization of nature" and the "naturalization of man" (1:149, 234).[1] Instances of anticipation of this move, and analogies for the utopian desire which is its precondition, are variously located and identified by Bloch, and one important location is the erotic. I argue here that there is a tendency in *Das Prinzip Hoffnung* to figure desire in heterosexual male terms. The analysis of Bloch's language offered in the essay helps unravel the relationship between Bloch's understanding of desire and the gender categories he inherits from a cultural tradition dating to the early modern period and transformed, but not negated, by Romanticism. The fact that woman is figured by Bloch as a space of anticipation, "an expectant landscape" (2:934) raises several questions: to what extent is utopian space feminized in Bloch's work, and what does this gesture owe to its converse, the Romantic utilization of the feminine? Bloch's references to the feminine deserve closer attention than they have hitherto received in Bloch scholarship, as they may illuminate the extent to which the polarities of gender discourse can be inscribed in utopian thinking. The designation of woman (*das Weib*) as an

---

[1] All translations of Bloch are my own.

expectant landscape (*erwartende Landschaft*) in *Das Prinzip Hoffnung* draws attention to the complex relationships of analogy and influence that pertain between the spheres of utopian thought, discovery and conquest, and gender. Bloch draws creatively on the affinities among these discourses, but he does not always call their presuppositions into question, especially where the categories of masculine and feminine are concerned. Before assessing the extent to which Bloch relies on inherited or unquestioned gender categories, it will help to look briefly at the role accorded to such categories in utopian thinking and writing prior to Bloch.

It has been noted by John Carey and others that modern utopian imagination in its early phase is pervaded by the discourses of discovery and conquest. As Anne McClintock has shown, the conventional binary of active subject and passive object, correlating to male and female, was imaginatively transposed onto the activities of geographical exploration and political colonization in the early modern period;, for instance, in ideas such as incursion into, and conquest of, "virgin lands." John Donne's 1595 poem, "To His Mistress on Going to Bed," punningly reflects the contemporary imbrication of the languages of sexual and geopolitical conquest, further complicating it in that the already gendered language of discovery in turn becomes a metaphor for the erotic encounter:

> O my America! my new found land,
> My kingdom, safeliest when with one man manned,
> My mine of precious stones, my empery,
> How blessed am I in this discovering thee! (38).

Carey comments that the poem, in imagining the female body as a land to be discovered, explored, and possessed, enacts an "exuberant celebration of woman as Utopia" (57). Seamus Heaney's poem "Act of Union" takes up the same figure almost four centuries after Donne, inverting it in a way that reveals its inherent violence: the speaking subject of the poem describes himself as "imperially male," and the metaphor of sexual encounter by means of which the poem also refers to Irish history is figured as "a gash breaking open the ferny bed" (Heaney 74–5). Celebration and exploitation/violation, far from being mutually exclusive, can in fact coexist and even affirm each other, as Donne's poem shows; the female body becomes a utopian space in the poem, a *tabula rasa* on which the adventure of male sexual subjectivity can be written or acted out.

As the utopian space to be occupied and possessed by geopolitical conquest served Donne as a metaphor for the mistress's body, so too did the tropes of exploration and possession inform the approach to the natural world set forth by the modern utopian project of rationalism and science, most clearly articulated in the early modern period by Francis Bacon. Bacon's *New Atlantis* develops from the *tabula rasa* conception of nature a threefold vision of human action: penetration, interpretation, and use. The patriarch of Salomon's House, the colony's headquarters in *New Atlantis*, explains this vision to the newcomers as follows: "the End of our Foundation is the knowledge of Causes, and secret motions of things; and the enlarging of the bound of Human Empire, to the effecting of all things possible" (70). The scientific study of nature outlined by Bacon not only facilitates the domination of nature for human needs, but also entails the possibility that nature itself may be changed or improved upon. The description of this process has a prophetic ring to the twenty-first-century reader: "And we make (by art) [...] trees and flowers to come earlier or later than their seasons; and to come up and bear more speedily than by their natural course they do. We make them also by art greater much than their nature; and their fruit greater and sweeter and of differing taste, smell, color, and figure, from their nature" (72).

This very vision of the absolute mastery and manipulation of nature for human ends came under the critical dystopian gaze of writers such as Yevgeny Zamyatin and Aldous Huxley in the twentieth century. Yet, while texts like *We* and *Brave New World* were effective in criticizing the modern instrumentalist conception of, and attitude towards, nature, they were less explicitly critical when it came to the ways in which gender categories and gender relations functioned within and underlay the objectification of nature and the dream of conquering it. Feminist theory from the late twentieth century on has drawn from insights into gendered relations of domination in order to extend and radicalize the critique of instrumental rationality. At its most utopian, late twentieth-century feminism located the transformative potential of feminist consciousness precisely in the rejection of a compartmentalized and instrumental view of subject-object relations. Nancy Vedder-Shults, in a 1978 article, offered a programmatic statement of the feminist concern with alternative models of interaction between selves and others, humans and their environment: "Instead of viewing the world as material to be manipulated – whether it is nature exploited by the industrialists or the masses in the hands of the 'party' – feminists have raised the question of means and ends as it relates to a concrete concept of wholeness" (16). The complex interplay of means and ends to which Vedder-Shults refers is a central concern of Bloch's dialectical utopian thought. As we shall see, Bloch relies on the metaphoric and conceptual power of the categories "masculine" and "feminine" and their encounter in the moment of desire in order to articulate some of his most significant ideas in this area. Given the centrality of the relationship between humanity and nature for Bloch and the significance he accords to the dialectically conceived project of humanizing nature and naturalizing humanity, it is worth enquiring further into his understanding of the feminine; for the feminine has a long tradition of being associated, even equated, with the natural, as the complement and antithesis of a masculinity thought to transcend or oppose nature.

Returning to late twentieth-century feminism, we can begin to review this tradition in reverse. There are several reasons why the tasks of reconceptualizing nature and of rethinking humanity's place within it and interaction with it were perceived as significant, even urgent, by late twentieth-century feminists. First, the women's movement arose at a time of increasing awareness of the ecological destruction wrought by western patterns of production and consumption, an awareness rendered all the more acute by the threat of nuclear holocaust. No thoroughgoing critique of, and genuine alternative to, patriarchy could afford to ignore these issues, as feminist texts such as Françoise d'Eaubonne's *La féminisme ou la mort* (1974), Marge Piercy's *Woman on the Edge of Time* (1976),

Mary Daly's *Gyn/ecology* (1978), and Christa Wolf's *Störfall. Nachrichten eines Tages* (1987) made clear.

Second, feminists sought self-determination and self-definition, and this entailed critical scrutiny of the categories "femininity" and "woman." Proceeding from Simone de Beauvoir's contention that one is not born, but rather becomes a woman, late twentieth-century feminists drew attention to the social, political, and economic factors at work in this process of becoming, and identified the ways in which the concept of "nature" was deployed in the service of patriarchal structures. Gender discourse, particularly from Romanticism onwards, had tended to align the feminine with the natural; this tendency intensified around 1900 in response to the concrete political gains made by the women's movement in its first wave (see Janz; Taeger). Even where the modern scientific objectification of nature à la Francis Bacon was rejected in favor of a qualitatively different conception and experience of the natural, as expressed in the Romantic dream of reconciliation or mystical union with nature, the gendering of nature as female and the alignment of femininity and naturalness persisted. One can note, for instance, in Friedrich Schiller's 1796 poem "Dignity of Women" (*Würde der Frauen*) the superimposition of the dual anthropology of nature and reason, necessity and freedom, being and becoming, immanence and transcendence onto the two sexes. The poem portrays women as the loving, nurturing "daughters of nature," who cherish the present moment (*des Augenblicks Blume*) in a way that men in their impatient striving are unable to do (206). As Wolfgang Riedel has argued, Schiller's figuring of woman as "natural" shades over into a utilization of the feminine:

> The "sentimental" gaze of a male subjectivity which recognizes its own deficiency and destructiveness "invents" women in this poem as the manifest negation of this unhappy subjectivity, a negation comprehended by the nature concept. To this extent, woman is the utopian sex. In that it simultaneously makes present a lost naïveté and anticipates future perfection, femininity is transfigured to become the real-ideal of humanity fulfilled, the image of a

being-human reconciled to itself — and this even in the age of dividedness (180).[2]

This utopian view of femininity, predicated on the identification of "woman" with "the natural," did not proceed merely "from without," through a male projection onto the feminine of that which masculine subjectivity was thought to lack. Rather, it was appropriated in late twentieth-century feminist texts such as Verena Stefan's *Häutungen* (1975), which "located the source of utopian transformation in the rediscovery of a supposedly 'natural' self" (Bammer 76). The feminist appropriation of the Romantic "woman as nature" trope was highly problematic, as the divided reception of Stefan's text reveals. Angelika Bammer's analysis recapitulates the main objection to this kind of "essentialist" feminism: "by taking recourse to nature and to the concept of a body without history, [Stefan] suggests that woman is not [...] a subject in the process of becoming, but rather one that has essentially always been" (76).

There are key differences between the two utilizing visions of femininity I have briefly outlined, the vision of woman as "new found land" to be explored or conquered versus the Romantic figuring of woman as the embodiment of a lost and longed-for unity with nature. These differences revolve around the question of how the subject imagines and relates to the feminine other (and even in a text such as Stefan's it is, arguably, a feminine "other," an imaginative projection or fantasy), whether as object of the desiring subject or source of the emerging subject, a difference which corresponds to the contrast between the figures of lover and mother. In the remainder of this essay, I look at the ways in which Bloch inherits these figures of

---

[2] "Der 'sentimentalische' Blick einer sich selbst als defizitär und destruktiv erlebenden männlichen Subjektivität 'erfindet' in diesem Gedicht die Frauen als Verkörperung der im Naturbegriff gefaßten Negation dieser unglücklichen Subjektivität und *insofern als das utopische Geschlecht* [...] Vergegenwärtigung der verlorenen Naivität und Vorschein der künftigen Vollkommenheit zugleich, transfiguriert sich Weiblichkeit zum Real-Ideal geglückter Humanität, zum Inbild eines mit sich versöhnten Menschseins – selbst im Zeitalter der Entzweiung."

thought and discourse from patriarchy and Romanticism and puts them to work in the service of his exhaustive enquiry into hope. The presence of any binary, including gender, in the work of a dialectical thinker such as Bloch raises the question of whether and how the two elements of the binary, in this case masculine and feminine, enter into relationships of dialectical interaction and mutual transformation.

Bloch's thought is utopian in that it revolves around the relationship between the tensions of the past and present and the possibilities of the future. For Bloch, as for Karl Mannheim, the utopian is a dynamic, restless attitude that is driven beyond the known and strives to transcend or "burst the bounds" of existing conditions. Bloch's utopianism thus addresses the problem of closure which haunted the concept of Utopia from the insularity of Thomas More's imagined society to the totalitarian stasis of the great twentieth-century dystopias. Bammer has characterized the "two contending concepts of Utopia inherent in the dialectic of progress and modernity" as, on the one hand, "the ideal [...] of a state of peace and calm guaranteed by a benign and rational order," and, on the other hand, "the dream [...] of a state of freedom unbounded by regulating forces" (19). As Bammer has noted, the utopia of peace, calm, and order "more closely resembles the stasis of death than the dynamic process of living" (18). It forecloses future possibilities, precludes the continued movement of desire, and absorbs all difference into itself. Bloch's reference to the salutary final wish of the Buddhist, which is to cease wishing (*keinen Wunsch mehr zu haben*), draws attention to the limitations of a static conception of Utopia: if the ultimate goal of desire is its own extinction, then the utopian risks exiting history if it is conceived of as the gratification or end of desire (3:1584).

Utopian theory since Mannheim and Bloch has broken with the idea of Utopia as static and has divested the utopian of its traditional associations of insularity, stasis, and self-perpetuation through an emphasis on open-endedness, dynamic change, and the unfolding, and hence unpredictable, narrative of the desiring subject in history. The outcome is unpredictable because utopian striving continually revises its goal to take account of new perspectives and possibilities; in Bloch's words, "a new summit appears behind the one which has just been reached" (1:216). The transformation of the utopian concept in the latter half of the twentieth century has proceeded through the insistence that Utopia, in Bammer's formulation, "is not to be found in a particular place or form," but is rather "a movement toward possibilities" (58). The open-ended utopianism of postmodernity avoids formulating the end of desire, focusing instead on the process of desire or, in Miguel Abensour's formulation, the "education of desire" (quoted by Kumar in Morris). Late twentieth-century formulations of critical utopianism, such as those advanced by Agnes Heller or Richard Rorty, respond to dystopian critique by rehabilitating the Heraclitean moment within the utopian. The accusation that Utopia is static – an accusation put forward by, among others, Northrop Frye, and more forcefully by Karl Popper – is refuted through the insistence that the most static society is the one that admits of no utopian version or vision of itself. As Jost Hermand has observed, wholesale rejection of utopian formulations on the grounds of their static quality ignores the dynamizing, transformative potential of imagined alternatives: "a world lacking in utopias reproduces only itself" (17).

The radical redefinition to which the concept of Utopia has been subjected in recent decades is, at least in part, a response to the dystopian misgivings raised in the mid-twentieth century by the human cost of social experiments conceived on a grand scale, but it has also been informed by Bloch's work. Bloch's hospitable opening up of the concept played a key role in turning utopian thought away from the insistence on *Utopia* as an "antithesis" to present conditions, and towards a more processual view of *the utopian* as a series of anticipatory moments "within the shifting configurations of the possible" (Bammer 47). This turn in utopian thinking dissociates the utopian from the definitive blueprints, static models, and totalitarian tendencies which led Karl Popper to describe utopianism as "a pernicious form of rationalism" (358).

Two categories of particular importance to the new understanding of Utopia are *desire* and *alterity*. One could say that the utopian has been redefined in terms of the movement of desire and the recognition of difference, but this leads to important questions about how desire and difference are conceptualized and located. Bloch began to address these questions in *Das Prinzip Hoffnung* through his emphasis on the importance of encounters with the unknown. The sense of being drawn beyond the given (*übers Gegebene hinaus*) to new experiences exemplifies utopian anticipation for Bloch (1:26). He identifies the ways in which the imaginary landscapes of "the wished-for distant place" and "the beautiful unknown" arise in response to, and in turn expose, the inadequacy of existing conditions (1:22, 435). His location of the utopian in figures of desire – "daydreams themselves possess a foam from which a Venus has from time to time emerged" – calls for a closer look at the places in which such desire is produced and apprehended, and at configurations of the desired other (1:225). The connections elaborated by Fredric Jameson between the formal problem of closure in Utopia and the question of difference throw new light on the interface between gender discourse and utopian thought (see *Archaeologies* 72–85). Gender difference, that which in our own time has been called (somewhat essentialistically) "the mysterious distance between a man and a woman," is only one space of alterity; but it is one that functions in Bloch's work as an exemplary instance of all such distance and difference. The encounter with *das Weib* often features in Bloch's work as the ultimate encounter with the other.

Before exploring in more detail the workings of gender discourse in Bloch's work on hope, it is important to note that his attitude to the political question of women's emancipation is neither equatable with nor reducible to the gendered metaphors that appear in his writing or the gender categories to which he has recourse. Bloch was not alone in seeing socialism as the solution to the "woman question," a view revealed in such notorious statements as "the Soviet Union no longer confronts the woman question, because it has solved the worker question" (2:694). Bloch's view of the bourgeois women's movement is colored by a combination of distrust and sexual stereotype; he regrets what he sees as the tendency of feminism to render its champions sexless by transforming them into "grey sisters of reform" (2:692). Here, he draws on an existing tradition of discrediting feminism through the claim that it somehow desexualizes; he thus reiterates the familiar stereotype of the repressed or unattractive feminist, a type familiar from the writings of late nineteenth-century and *fin de siècle* authors such as Friedrich Nietzsche, Karl Kraus, and Frank Wedekind (See Nietzsche, *Jenseits* III, 701–3; and Wedekind). The *graue Reformschwester*, argues Bloch, fails to live up to the exotic hetaerism seemingly promised by women's emancipation in its initial phase: "Behind the dreamed-of future of women lay a plenitude of celebratory, Dionysian revolutionary images. A generation later, all that was left of such images was the liberation from the corset and the right to smoke, vote and study" (2:689).

Bloch's aim is to expose the limitations of the bourgeois women's movement, which is in his view worthless because it merely demands a larger slice of the same cake for women with "no change to the recipe" (1:36). As Vincent Geoghegan observes, Bloch "does not seem to recognize the cross-cutting effect of gender on class relationships" (115). His position serves the aim of discrediting non-socialist feminism to repeat the familiar denigration of concrete gains in women's rights, which he achieves through the syntactic alignment of "smoking" with "voting and studying" in the above passage. Even if these rights provide women with greater social flexibility, the overall social structure remains, from Bloch's perspective, rigidly inflexible. They do nothing to unfold what he calls "der weibliche Inhalt" or "das Weibhafte," the feminine content or potential of femininity that has been blocked by patriarchal capitalism (2:695). Yes, his reference to such a feminine potential prompts us to ask how Bloch understands this category and what has shaped his understanding of it. Its specifics are not spelled out, but it seems reasonable to infer from the concept an underlying binary of opposed and complementary masculine and feminine "essences." Such essentialistic gender binarism was, as we have seen, part of the Romantic tradition, and had been reinvigorated during Bloch's formative years by Johann Jakob Bachofen's influential theory of prehistoric matriarchy, which appealed to thinkers on both the Right and Left.[3]

---

3   On right- and left-wing Bachofen reception, see Fromm.

It is not just Bloch's understanding of the feminine, but his understanding of desire itself that is shaped by the available conventions that govern gender discourse at this time, by the binary of the rational, active, desiring male and the irrational, passive, desired female. Bloch deploys such gendered oppositions in his appraisal of the utopian dimension of music: the "male world of will," embodied, as he sees it, in the anticipatory aspect of Ludwig van Beethoven, is set in opposition to the chthonic, elemental, regressive world of Richard Wagner's music-dramas (3:1275). Through such an opposition, we can glimpse again the trope of the inscription through action of male subjectivity on a chaotic, undifferentiated "nature," gendered female. These binary pairs of cosmic and tellurian, transcendent and immanent have been identified by de Beauvoir and others as key carriers for essentialist-binaristic gender concepts. Bloch aligns "sublimity" with the male, "peacefulness" with the female principle: "the starry sky provides the male component to complement the feeling of the maternal in nature," an echo here of Immanuel Kant's reference to the starry sky above, which is linked to the moral law within (2:1077). Johann Wolfgang Goethe's formulation from *Dichtung und Wahrheit* speaks through Bloch's text: "One loves the girl for what she is, the boy for what he promises to be" ["man liebt an dem Mädchen, was es ist, und an dem Jüngling, was er ankündigt"] (3:1172). What was for Goethe a passing comment justifying his affection for the promising writer Maximilian Klinger, who was a mere youth when Goethe became acquainted with him, becomes for Bloch an eloquent figure for the relations between being and becoming, latency and tendency (Goethe 670). Its eloquence derives, however, from a gender concept which locates the feminine in immanent presence but figures the masculine as transcendent and evolving – the one is desired for her being, the other admired and fostered in his process of becoming.

If the active *subject* of history – "the working and creative human who transforms and overcomes given conditions" – is masculinized through this gendered discourse, the *object* of utopian desire is correspondingly feminized (3:1628). It is entirely consistent with such a "feminization" of the utopian object and "masculinization" of the subject of utopian striving that Bloch's crowning metaphor for the goal of such striving should be *Heimat*, a problematic category steeped in organic and maternal imagery and associations of motherland (see Boa and Palfreyman). The oft-quoted conclusion of *Das Prinzip Hoffnung* conflates the arrival in Utopia with the mythic *nostos*, confirming Bloch's indebtedness to a thought tradition that Bammer has characterized as follows: "if the mythic return home to mother is the paradigmatic utopian dream, then woman indeed embodies Utopia" (14). Bloch, of course, inherits in order to transform: the paradoxical conclusion of *Das Prinzip Hoffnung* yokes the familiarity of *Heimat* to alterity and newness; and the homeland of which Bloch writes is no ordinary homeland, but rather one "where no-one has yet been" (3:1628). It thus encompasses both the known and the unknown. The feminine element of *Heimat* – place of first nurturing, motherland, source of the mother tongue – is configured anew so that homecoming, arrival in this *Heimat* will not be a return or regression. Despite the fact that this *Heimat* is currently uninhabited and can only be achieved through the utopian striving of the creative subject, however, it is a future with intimate links and affinities with the past, as it contains that which all have glimpsed in childhood (*etwas, das allen in die Kindheit scheint*).[4] These links to the past complicate the earlier confident, exclusively forward-looking assertion that the humanization of nature has no parental home from which it has exited and to which it must return, "die Humanisierung der Natur hat kein Elternhaus am Anfang, dem sie entlaufen ist, zu dem sie [...] wieder zurückkehrt" (1:234). While Bloch rejects a cyclical view of history, which would deny progress in favor of a *restitutio in integrum* devoid of the novum, his conception of forward-looking utopian desire is inextricable from fantasy, memory, and the past. Thus, while he figures *Heimat* as the product of human imagination and action, a goal to be striven towards rather than a womb-like origin, he retains the associations of *Heimat* with those realms of experience conventionally seen as feminine: childhood and the irrational. Bloch made room in his utopian philosophy for

---

4   On the role of memory in the constitution of the Blochian future, see Geoghegan.

psychological and experiential domains which had been frequently either neglected or explicitly discredited by Marxist thinkers, from daydreams and mysticism to the artistic heritage of Christianity; but his attentiveness to the significance of these domains proceeded from a thought tradition which aligned the irrational/rational binary with the feminine/masculine, and did little to dismantle the latter binary.

The gendering of utopian desire in *Das Prinzip Hoffnung* is also effected through the figure of the "doubled Helen" – Trojan Helen versus Egyptian Helen. Bloch uses this double figure to demonstrate the importance of mediating between reality and dream. The doubled Helen figure enables him to tackle a problem that inheres in the concept of Utopia: the aporetic presence of disappointment or hollowness within wish-fulfillment. Drawing on a drama of Euripides, as reworked into a dialogue and opera libretto by Hugo von Hofmannsthal, Bloch reads the saga of the Egyptian Helen as an illustration of the potentially dangerous power of hope wherever it is undialectic, that is to say unmediated by the real. The outline of the "doubled Helen" story is as follows: Menelaos has won back Helen after ten years of battle at Troy, and is returning via Egypt; he comes ashore, leaving his wife on the anchored ship, and encounters Helen, "not the beautiful, all too famous Helen, whom he had left in the ship, but rather one who was another and yet the same" (1:211). The Trojan Helen for whom the battles were fought turns out to have been an illusion, a phantom; and Menelaos's real wife has been sequestered in Egypt all the while. What is significant for Bloch is that Menelaos's reaction is not one of unmixed joy: "ten years of fixation on the Trojan Helen form a barrier between him and the Egyptian Helen" (1:211). The act of hoping intensifies the imaginary presence of the hoped-for object in the phase of hope; but this renders the phase of fulfillment aporetic, especially if accompanied by experiences of privation and suffering, as in the case of the Trojan War. The hoping subject must come to terms with the inevitable discrepancy between intense, internalized imaginary presence and actual, flesh-and-blood presence and otherness of the hoped-for object: "For the object of real fulfillment was not personally present during the adventures, unlike the dream object [...] It was only the Trojan Helen, and not the Egyptian, who went into battle under the standard and absorbed the longings of the ten utopian years" (1:212). Clinging to one's wish and insisting on it in the face of the other constitutes the kind of narcissistic response which Giovanna Silvani has described as a persistent flaw in utopian thought. In the phase of hope, the subject experiences the object's presence internally, through a combination of memory and imagination, faculties which as we have seen are crucially constitutive of utopian striving. This interiorization of the object is however disrupted once (s)he is there as an actual presence, recalling Silvani's argument that "the ego [the hoping, desiring subject] is unable to establish an authentic relationship with the others, face them squarely and accept their problematical otherness" (152).

Menelaos's disappointment lies at least in part in the recognition that this Helen, unlike the one for whom he had fought, cannot be fully interiorized, resists complete subsumption into his own narrative. While Bloch is critical of the reification of the hoped-for object which the legend illustrates, his analysis of the "aporia of fulfillment" turns more on the disappointment of the desiring subject than on the alterity and selfhood of the desired object. The disappointment of hope and the "melancholy of satisfaction" are likewise discussed in terms of the possession of a feminine object by a masculine subject (1:216, 221). Addressing the utopian residue that remains even where hope is fulfilled (*utopischer Bildrest in der Verwirklichung*), Bloch uses the following parable-like image:

> A man awaits a girl, the room is full of tender unrest; the last light of evening heightens the tension. But if the expected girl crosses the threshold and all is well, the hope itself is no longer there, this has disappeared. It has nothing further to say but carried something away with itself, something which remains silent in the present joy. Complete congruence [*Deckung*, i.e. between hope and fulfillment] is seldom, has perhaps never occurred (1:204).

In his exploration of the problem of disappointment, Bloch also has recourse to the explanatory figure of "fiasco." He adopts the fiasco concept from Stendhal, broadening its scope. For Stendhal, the fiasco was the (male) experience of desiring a woman ardently, dreaming of her, idealizing her from afar and then, at the moment of "possession," realizing that one was not attracted to her after all, or perhaps after the event of possession, losing interest or even experiencing feelings of aversion (1:205). Stendhal's scenario is imagined from a male perspective which renders the role of female desire in the sexual encounter negligible and figures sex in terms of possession (a figure still present in everyday parlance in the use of the verb "to have" to signify coitus). His gendered definition of fiasco is not degendered by Bloch's appropriation of it for his utopian theory. Bloch notes also the aporia of fulfillment in Søren Kierkegaard's famous renunciation of Regine Olsen: "This sort of love has the majestic vanity to be in love with itself; it is a feast day which can tolerate no Monday" (1:208). Kierkegaard's act of renunciation saves him from the danger of fiasco, understood as the anticlimax of a desire that remains unfulfilled by the attainment of what had functioned as its goal.

The fiasco is an important figure for utopian thought, and particularly for the postmodern understanding of utopian imagination as an ongoing process subject to continual revision. If dystopian writing is understood (at least in part) as a manifold problematization of utopian optimism, it can be said that the task of dystopia is to expose the realization of the modern Utopia as a "fiasco" in Stendhal's sense: that which is desired until it is attained. The fiasco figure emerges in Bloch's writing through a gendered analogy in which the desiring subject is male, the initially desired and subsequently rejected object female. While its significance as a powerful cipher for the disappointment that lurks within the fulfillment of hope is not exhausted by the sexual scenario from which it derives, this derivation and the gender concept that underlies it can be said nonetheless to inform Bloch's understanding of the relationships between hope and the hoped for, now and the future, the subject of history and the object of utopian desire.

Bloch's condemnation of bourgeois-democratic visions of the future and their claim to constitute a genuine alternative to fascism relies in a particularly problematic way on contemporary images of femininity. It is to be expected that Bloch would denounce what he sees as the empty promise of non-socialist antifascism. What is notable in this context is the language and imagery he uses for the purpose. Here it is useful to remember the threefold figuring of the feminine in the thought tradition Bloch inherits: the three possibilities that patriarchy held open to *das Weib* can be broadly summed up as virgin, mother, and whore.[5] A hypocritical rhetoric of human rights that leaves the economic order of capitalism unchanged is decried by Bloch as follows: "The bourgeois-democratic future admittedly does not wear the martial death-mask of fascism. Instead it wears a moralistic make-up, feigning human rights as if the capitalist whore could ever revert to virginity" (2:682).

It is necessary to ask why Bloch uses this particular metaphor, why he relies on the familiar binary of virgin and whore, on the vivid contrast between a valorized, controlled female sexuality and its reviled promiscuous other to bring more abstract political oppositions to life. His framing of the polarities of just and unjust, ethical and unethical, authentic and inauthentic in precisely these terms suggests an imaginative feminization of utopian space and of its negative other. The whore, infinitely exchangeable and faithful to nothing but the highest price, represents the material conditions of existence under capitalism, as Georg Simmel had argued in *Philosophy of Money*:

> One senses in the essence of money [...] something of the essence of prostitution. The indifference with which it offers itself to all uses, the infidelity with which it frees itself from each subject, because it was never in fact bound to any, the objectivity which precludes any relation of the heart, which characterizes it as pure means – all of this creates a fateful analogy between money and prostitution (414).[6]

---

5 On the less than clear-cut oppositions between these figures, see Bronfen. The entrenched polarity of virgin and whore accounts for the stir created by Weininger's *Sex and Character*. Unlike other writers on the "woman question," Weininger's typology of femininity was based on only two types, the mother and the whore, as he did not allow for the possibility of the virgin as type.

6 "So empfindet man [...] am Wesen des Geldes selbst etwas vom Wesen der Prostitution. Die Indifferenz, in der es sich jeder Verwendung darbietet, die Treulosigkeit, mit der es sich von jedem Subjekt löst, weil es mit keinem eigentlich verbunden war, die jede Herzensbeziehung ausschließende Sachlichkeit, die ihm als reinem Mittel eignet – alles dies stiftet eine verhängnisvolle Analogie zwischen ihm und der Prostitution."

Bloch extends this idea by aligning the virgin with an ethical discourse of authenticity, emancipation, and fulfillment. The desire that drives those crucially utopian activities, transcendence of the known and anticipation of the not-yet-known, is described as being driven towards the "virginity of that which has not yet been seized" ["die Jungfräulichkeit eines noch nicht Ergriffenen"] (2:883). Here, Bloch imagines the utopian desire to transcend the given and know the not-yet-known as a specific erotic encounter: the deflowering of the virgin.

It could be objected that these are mere figures of speech, that Bloch's quasi-poetic use of the German language draws on a wide metaphoric range that inevitably includes the polarities of gender that pervade culture and grammar. In the above-quoted example in which the "bourgeois-democratic future" is configured as a prostitute, for example, Bloch exploits grammatical gender: as future, *die Zukunft*, is feminine, the pronoun *sie* can carry this extended metaphor even more convincingly than translation allows. Indeed, the presence of grammatical gender in the German language is perhaps one reason for the relative under-representation of gender discourse analysis in Bloch scholarship. It could be argued, for instance, that the active, striving subject of history is inevitably ascribed the pronoun "he" (*er*) because this is the pronoun that belongs to the masculine noun *der Mensch*; similarly, the feminine pronoun belongs to *die Heimat*. Once one begins the task of identifying gendered language and imagery throughout *Das Prinzip Hoffnung*, however, it becomes clear that Bloch's deployment of such figures is, at least in many instances, no mere accident of grammar, but rather draws on a long-standing cultural understanding of desire which is itself gendered.

Bloch's central category is that of the active, striving subject, who is to achieve the utopian "Reich der Freiheit," the realm of freedom which, even before it is achieved, is latent in all utopian striving. The subject of history must seize – come into possession of – its *Heimat*, which exists in the tendencies of cultural anticipation and in the latencies of nature's yet-to-be-humanized *tabula rasa*. Bloch speaks in this connection of the "building site which has not yet even been cleared, the building materials which are not yet even adequate for the human house which is not yet adequately available," thus collapsing locus, means, and result of hope together into the space of Not Yet (2:807). He sees the journey to the truly human society as a voyage of discovery, in which the unrealized potential of cultural anticipation can function as map and compass. Yet, as we have seen, his creative adaptation of the discourse of discovery that underpinned utopian imagination in the early modern period does not entail a *mise-en-question* of the gender categories inherent to this discourse. Bloch's rethinking of utopianism in terms of an active process driven by a creative, imaginative subject enacts a gendering of desire: as demonstrated by his references to the doubled Helen, the virgin and the whore, the awaited lover and the fiasco, he draws on the inherited practice of utopizing the feminine in order to feminize utopian space.

The scrutiny of Bloch's use of language I offer here has revealed that gender, more particularly the understanding of masculine and feminine as complementary and opposite essences, occupies an important place in his thought, both in its conceptual underpinning and in its metaphoric formulation. Bloch is notable for his receptivity to diverse cultural influences, and it is hardly surprising that the pervasive categories of gender discourse are embedded in his conceptions of difference and desire. There is more than one way of conceptualizing the gender binary and of valorizing its constituent terms; and even where Bloch seems to reaffirm the conventional alignment of the male with the active, the female with the passive principle, this reaffirmation does not preclude a positive view of the latter. To invert the conventional wisdom on masculine and feminine by privileging the latter term is, however, less radical a gesture than it seems, as Bammer has argued in her assessment of the limitations of essentialist feminism. Bloch's references to the unrealized "feminine content" [*weiblicher Inhalt*] discussed above imply a readiness to embrace the potential of this "feminine" [*Weibhaftes*] without enquiring into its social and historical constitution.

Works Cited

Bachofen, Johann Jakob. *Das Mutterrecht*. Stuttgart: 1861.
Bammer, Angelika. *Partial Visions. Feminism and Utopianism in the 1970s*. London: Routledge, 1991.
Bacon, Francis. *New Atlantis. Francis Bacon: The Great Instauration and New Atlantis*. Ed. Jerry Weinberger. Wheeling: Harlan Davidson, 1989.
De Beauvoir, Simone. *The Second Sex*. Trans. Howard M. Parshley. London: Everyman, 1993.
Bloch, Ernst. *Das Prinzip Hoffnung*. 3 Vols. Frankfurt: Suhrkamp, 1985.
Boa, Elizabeth, and Rachel Palfreyman. *Heimat: A German Dream. Regional Loyalties and National Identity in German Culture, 1890–1990*. Oxford: Oxford University Press, 2000.
Bronfen, Elisabeth. *Over Her Dead Body. Death, Femininity and the Aesthetic*. Manchester: Manchester University Press, 1992.
Carey, John (ed.). *The Faber Book of Utopias*. London: Faber, 1999.
Donne, John. *Selected Poems*. London: Dover, 1993.
Fromm, Erich. "Die Sozialpsychologische Bedeutung der Mutterrechtstheorie." *Zeitschrift für Sozialforschung* 3 (1934): 196–226.
Frye, Northrop. "Varieties of Literary Utopias." *Utopias and Utopian Thought*. Ed. Frank E. Manuel. London: Souvenir, 1973. 25–49.
Geoghegan, Vincent. *Ernst Bloch*. London: Routledge, 1996.
____ "Remembering the Future." *Not Yet. Reconsidering Ernst Bloch*. Ed. Jamie Owen Daniel and Tom Moylan. London: Verso, 1997. 15–32.
Goethe, Johann Wolfgang. *Aus meinem Leben. Dichtung und Wahrheit*. Frankfurt and Leipzig: Insel, 1998.
Heaney, Seamus. *New Selected Poems 1966–1987*. London: Faber, 1990.
Hermand, Jost. *Orte, irgendwo. Formen utopischen Denkens*. Königstein: Athenäum, 1981.
Jameson, Fredric. *Archaeologies of the Future: The Desire Called Utopia and Other Science Fictions*. London: Verso, 2005.
Janz, Marlies. "'Die Frau' und 'das Leben': Weiblichkeitskonzepte in der Literatur und Theorie um 1900." *Faszination des Organischen. Konjunkturen einer Kategorie der Moderne*. Ed. Hartmut Eggert, Erhard Schütz and Peter Sprengel. Munich: Iudicium, 1995. 36–52.
McClintock, Anne. *Imperial Leather: Race, Gender, and Sexuality in the Colonial Contest*. London and New York: Routledge, 1995.

Morris, William. *News from Nowhere, or an Epoch of Rest: Being Some Chapters from a Utopian Romance*. Ed. Krishan Kumar. Cambridge: Cambridge University Press, 1995.

Nietzsche, Friedrich. *Jenseits von Gut und Böse. Werke.* 5 Vols. Ed. Karl Schlechta. Frankfurt: Ullstein, 1969.

Popper, Karl. "Utopia and Violence." *Conjectures and Refutations*. London: Routledge & Kegan Paul, 1963. 355–63.

Riedel, Wolfgang. *"Homo Natura": Literarische Anthropologie um 1900*. Berlin: De Gruyter, 1996.

Schiller, Friedrich. *Schiller's Werke: Nationalausgabe*. Vol. 2. Ed. Norbert Oellers. Weimar: Böhlau, 1983.

Silvani, Giovanna. "Woman in Utopia from More to Huxley. *Requiem pour l'utopie? Tendances autodestructives du paradigme utopique.*" Ed. Carmelina Imbroscio. Pisa: Libreria Goliardica, 1986. 135–52.

Simmel, Georg. *Philosophie des Geldes*. Berlin: Dunkcer & Humblot, 1977.

Taeger, Annemarie. *Die Kunst, Medusa zu töten. Zum Bild der Frau in der Literatur der Jahrhundertwende*. Bielefeld: Aisthesis-Verlag, 1987.

U2. "A Man and a Woman." *How to Dismantle an Atomic Bomb*. Universal Music, 2004.

Vedder-Shults, Nancy. "Hearts Starve as Well as Bodies: Ulrike Prokop's 'Production and the Context of Women's Daily Life.'" *New German Critique* 13 (Winter 1978): 5–17.

Wedekind, Frank. *Tod und Teufel. Werke in zwei Bänden*. Ed. Erhard Weidl. Munich: dtv, 1996.

Weininger, Otto. *Geschlecht und Charakter. Eine prinzipielle Untersuchung*. Munich: Mathes & Seitz, 1980.

Aidan O'Malley

Rhyming Hope and History in the "Fifth Province"

The concept of the "fifth province" entered contemporary Irish cultural discourse with the announcement of its "rediscovery" in the editorial of the first number of the journal *The Crane Bag* in 1977: "Modern Ireland is made up of four provinces, whose origin lie beyond the beginning of recorded history. And yet, the Irish word for province is *cóiced* which means a fifth. This fivefold division is as old as Ireland itself, yet there is disagreement about the identity of the fifth fifth" (Kearney, "Editorial" 4). The first task of my essay is to unveil the tensions within the utopian impulse that informed the idea of the "fifth province." I will do this by looking first at how this site was uncovered in *The Crane Bag*, where two rather distinct versions of the "fifth province" ultimately found expression: one that leaned towards a transcendental reading of the site, while the other articulated its potential in terms of human interaction. The connection between these two tendencies, versions of which might be thought to mark all utopian ideas and projects, and the act of translation, the process that brought the "fifth province" into being in *The Crane Bag*, are investigated in light of the fact that an interaction between transcendental idealism and human possibility also informs the act of translation.

In order to observe this contradictory dynamic more closely and to come to terms with the possible significance of the "fifth province," the second section of my reading turns to what might be thought of as the most noted expression of the site: the possibility, articulated in Seamus Heaney's *The Cure at Troy*, that hope and history might come to rhyme. As Hugh Denard has commented, there are very few other "dramatic texts which can claim to have acquired such prominence in the political affairs of modern times," and the reason for this can be said to lie in the utopian impulse that is inscribed in the concept of rhyming hope and history (2). Perhaps occasioned by the turn of the millennium, this conjunction of hope and history has had a remarkable political career as an expression of utopian possibility and longing in reflections on diverse situations such as South Africa (Nadine Gordimer, *Living in Hope and History: Notes on Our Century*), the United States (Bill Clinton, *Between Hope and History: Meeting America's Challenges for the 21st Century*), and, most particularly, in the context of the Northern Irish peace process (for instance, Gerry Adams, *Hope and History: Making Peace in Ireland*), along with a panoply of Irish and British journalists and politicians.[1] Here, then, I will uncover the significance of this notion – what it might mean to rhyme hope and history – by reading it in the context of the Heaney play in such a way that this utopian desire might shed light on the ways in which the transcendental and the "human" both cleave to and from one another in the "fifth province." The perspective opened by this reading allows for a tentative charting of the temporal and ethical locations of this site. These two perspectives are perhaps inevitably fused in a utopia and, in the conclusion, will be thought of in terms of the generative act of translation.

The Crane Bag and the Dis-Positions of the "Fifth Province"

It is important to underscore, on setting out on this reading, that what is being discussed here is best thought of as the *Crane Bag* translation of the "fifth province," as this is the one which entered Irish cultural discourse in the late 1970s. This version would have been disputed by linguistic and historical authorities such as T.F. O'Rahilly and Alwyn

---

[1] Denard recounts the instances of the employment of these lines in the Northern Irish context by Mary Robinson, Bill Clinton, Jacques Santer, and the Chair of the Forum for Peace and Reconciliation in Dublin, Judge Catherine McGuinness (1–2).

and Brinley Rees who have pointed out that while there is no definitive location for the "fifth province"; there are, however, traditions which posit its existence. As Rees and Rees reveal,

> *Lebor Gabála Érenn* attributes the original division into five provinces to Fir Bolg. These settlers were led by five brothers and they shared Ireland between them. The fifth province of that division consisted of a subdivision of Munster, and in accordance with this, Ireland is represented throughout most of early literature as consisting of Connacht, Ulster, Leinster, and "the Two Munsters" (East Munster and West Munster) (118).

O'Rahilly, however, rejected the idea that the "fifth province" was the product of this division of Munster. In his *Early Irish History and Mythology*, he suggested that there were originally four provinces and that while the name in the early language for a province is no longer known, he surmised that it might have just been "a fourth" (see 171–83). Subsequently a legendary king called Tuathal Techtmhar carved out a fifth kingdom in the Midlands. The name of this fifth part has not survived, but since then the neighboring provinces came to be known as, for instance, "the fifth part of the Ulstermen" for the province of Ulster and so forth. This fifth kingdom was ruled by the king of Tara, and as he became the most powerful of Irish kings, the Midland kingdom was no longer reckoned to be a mere fifth part or province, and so the term "fifth part" eventually only applied to four provinces.[2]

Richard Kearney and Mark Patrick Hederman, *The Crane Bag* editors, used these historical findings as a form of poetic inspiration and presented the "fifth province" as a physically deracinated site; one "marked by the absence of any particular political and geographical delineation, something more like a dis-position" (Kearney, "Editorial I: Endodermis" 4). More precisely, as can be observed in the quotation at the beginning of this essay, they located the "fifth province" in language, as its presence, and the cryptic nature of its (non-)being, is marked in Old Irish. As Hederman elucidates it, "the Irish language

---

2 I am grateful to Mícheál MacCraith for pointing out, in personal correspondence, the references to the five provinces in O'Rahilly.

contains within its alluvial deposit of meaning a very partinent [*sic*] truth in its word for province (*coiced* [*sic*]) which means "a fifth". Although there would seem never to have been more than four geographical or political provinces in Ireland, this linguistic oddity suggests that the notion of a "fifth province" was embedded in the language (Hederman 115).

Cóiced is the Old Irish form of the Modern Irish *cúige*, and the *Crane Bag* version of the "fifth province" is essentially a translation of *cóiced* in the fullest sense of the term, as it is presented as literally coming into being through the act of translation: *cóiced* signifies both "a province" and "a fifth," but not "a fifth province," though that might be heard within this term. The seemingly innocuous shift from considering "a fifth" solely as a noun to framing it, at the same time, as a complementary adjective, releases the energies that were latent within the term *cóiced*, and unveils a new possibility. As such, it is always already present and not-present: in depicting it as a translation, it is implied that it should have an "original" in the past which might be recovered in the future through translation; yet in this case it is, at the same time, also immediately apparent that any such recovery would be an act of creation. It is always an-other place and, potentially, a place of otherness, as it exists entirely as a possibility, one that might be glimpsed at through translation. Fredric Jameson has pointed out that utopian texts are fundamentally "about" processes rather than descriptions, and the "fifth province" is about nothing other than process (385). At no point is a description of it possible. Of course, Thomas More animated Utopia in a similar manner, as it was coined when he brought together the Greek adverb *ou* (not) and the noun *topos* (place) and gave "the resulting compound a Latin ending," moreover in such a way that "the word puns on another Greek compound, *eutopia* ('happy' or 'fortunate' place)" (Logan and Adams xi). In other words, like the "fifth province," Utopia, in its very name, thematizes its status as a translation (from an "older" language) and, as such, its existence, or rather its possibility, in language.

In turning to explore the nature of the possibility that is presented as latent in the "fifth province," it is immediately apparent that this takes two, seemingly contradictory, forms. While Kearney and Hederman were the joint editors of *The Crane Bag*, they also maintained their individual voices in the journal, which is epitomized by the fact that there were two editorials in the first number: "Editorial I: Endodermis," which opened the journal and introduced the concept of the "fifth province," was penned by Kearney; and "Editorial II: Epidermis," at the end, was written by Hederman (Böss 143). This editorial pluralism was also reflected in two rather different interpretations of the significance of the "fifth province."

Hederman read the "fifth province" principally through terms and concepts drawn from Martin Heidegger's *Poetry, Language, Thought*. In Kearney's editorial, the "fifth province" was viewed as an equally important, "non-political" "second centre," which provided a "necessary balance" to the political center, Tara. Hederman held that this second, compensatory, center could only be accessed through art; while he equated the other, political, center with "our normal scientific consciousness" (Hederman 111). He saw this interpretation as consistent with the ancient tradition of the "fifth province," which held that it was "known only to the druids and the poets" (Kearney, "Editorial I" 4). Thus, the hidden or absent center is aesthetic and "requires a method and a language which are sui generis both to reach it and describe it. The only method available to us at the moment is a certain kind of art. Taking my cue from Heidegger, I call this language and method 'poetry' understood in a very particular way" (Hederman 111).

Hederman then employs a Jungian analogy in an attempt to define this "very particular way." This is an idea of a new center, distinct from the ego, located somewhere between the conscious and the unconscious, and which provides a "new equilibrium, a new centering of the total personality" (Jung, quoted in Hederman 111). This analogy however, is ultimately insufficient to express Hederman's reading of "the fifth province," as this

> realm [...] is beyond both the domain and the methods of psychology. This centre is a space which gives access to the transcendent. It goes beyond the psychology of the individual. It is for these reasons that Heidegger proposes the artist, and especially the poet as the only one who can provide us with access to this domain" (111).

Hence, the "fifth province" is seen as an access point, or means, to "the transcendent." The significance of this term renders this version of the "fifth province" extremely problematic. How "the transcendent" is to be understood is unclear, and this opacity leads Edna Longley to suspect that "Hederman's terminology in invoking 'the fifth province' owes more to transformed Nationalism, and transformed Catholicism, than perhaps he realises" (120). This is of a piece with the tenor of the many critiques that the "fifth province" has attracted in Ireland. In general, these have focused on the prevailing obscurity that surrounds the site and have sought to outline the potentially negative politics that could issue from, or be hidden by, such obscurity. In particular, these critiques have seen in the propensity towards the transcendental, a reformulated Catholic mysticism that has been associated with Irish nationalism.[3] As such, this criticism in very many ways echoes what has been identified as "the twentieth century argument that utopianism necessarily leads to totalitarianism and violence" (Sargent 4). In this light, it is notable, and somewhat surprising, that the "fifth province" has hardly ever been formally associated with utopian thinking, either by its proponents or critics. Yet, the "fifth province" expresses, almost in embryonic form, a paradoxical impulse that informs many utopian ideas.

These contradictions become evident when attention is shifted to Kearney's version, which could be said to be based on his reading that, "in the fifth province, it is always a question of thinking *otherwise*" (Kearney, *Postnational Ireland* 100). While my emphasis thus far has been on what might be termed the (non-)presence of utopias, the other essential aspect of these sites is that they, at the same time, also articulate actual social concerns; as Lyman Tower Sargent puts it, "with [...] few exceptions, social interaction is fundamental to the utopian form" (13). Kearney, indeed, has viewed the "fifth province" as a site whereon identity is constructed through a re-imagining of one's relationship with the other; a process that would involve movement towards the other and which would, at the same

---

3   For an overview of this criticism, and in particular of Field Day's use of the "fifth province," see Böss 148–9.

time, be consistent with the answer to the riddle which he cited to illustrate the functioning of the "fifth province" in the 1977 editorial: "'Where is the middle of the world?' The correct answer to the riddle is: 'Here' or 'Where you are standing'" (Kearney, "Editorial I: Endodermis" 4). In other words, those of Paul Ricoeur, actually, it would be the state of "oneself-as-another"; and Kearney's reading of this concept draws out the process of interaction that it involves "the shortest route from self to self is through the other [...] the self is never sufficient unto itself, but constantly seeks out signs and signals of meaning in the other" ("Introduction" 1). Rather than imagining the "fifth province" as an access to the transcendental, Kearney tends to envisage it in terms of human communication, as a state of being that comes about through encounters with the other. Nonetheless, at no point does the "fifth province" ever assume a spatial form; it informs, in a very general fashion, a mode of being in society rather than specifying the dimensions of an ideal society. In short, it remains a dis-position or a meeting-point of different dis-positions, existing in what Michel Foucault has called the "non-place of language" (*Order of Things* xviii).

This ambiguous, never-to-be-materialized quality of utopias, which exists on the reverse side of the aforementioned fear of the potential latent threat of totalitarianism in utopianism, has also led to much questioning of their social and political salience. For Foucault, for instance, utopias did nothing more than "afford consolation" as they are, in Lisa Lowe's reading of Foucault, "the imaginary inversions of the real spaces of society" (*Order of Things* xix; Lowe 15). In opposition to this, Foucault proposed the concept of the heterotopia. Heterotopias are disturbing sites of infinite pluralities and "spaces of otherness," which Foucault made a determined effort to locate in "real spaces – places that do exist and that are formed in the very founding of society" (Lowe 15; "Of Other Spaces" online). He therefore delineated, to use David Harvey's words, spaces in which

> otherness, alterity, and [...] alternatives might be explored not as mere figments of the imagination but through contact with social processes that already exist. It is within these spaces that alternatives can take shape and from these spaces

that a critique of existing norms and processes can most effectively be mounted (184).

These were places that were also seen as having the quality of being, in some ways, non-places, such as the theater, the brothel, and the ship. However, as Harvey points out, this concept remains, in effect, an alternative form of unrealizable Utopia, as Foucault "gives no clue as to what a more spatiotemporal utopianism might look like" (184–5). This project, which Foucault would ultimately turn his back on, has relevance for a reading of the contrary versions of the "fifth province" (see Harvey 184).

If it is allowed that, to adopt Foucault's taxonomy, Hederman appears to offer the "fifth province" as a utopia and that Kearney sees it in terms of a heterotopia, the fact that a heterotopia cannot articulate a properly material alternative to Utopia intimates the propinquity of the relationship that exists between these two versions. It suggests that whatever salience the "fifth province" might have may depend on an interplay of the two dispositions. I explore the enabling potential of this interaction in the next section in light of the fact that, in short, utopias do not depend upon having inscribed within them the possibility of being physically achieved in order to have social and political relevance – indeed, Foucault's concept of the heterotopia has much more power in terms of discourse, where he originally envisaged it and where it has been usefully employed (see *Order of Things* xix; and Lowe 15). Bernard Dauenhauer, in his reading of Ricoeur's *Lectures on Ideology and Utopia*, elaborates on this conjunction of the sociopolitical significance of utopias and their "non-presence" in a manner that is entirely apposite here. He argues that utopian thought

> imaginatively projects another kind of society, a different world. In so doing, the social imagination is functioning inventively rather than conservatively and integratively. Rather than seeking order and unity in present reality, utopian thought is always in search of "otherness." The critique to which utopian thought subjects the sociopolitical status quo is a thought located in a kind of "nowhere." That is, its critique of what presently exists does not rest on something that exists elsewhere. It gives expression to a kind of society or set of institutions that does not presently exist anywhere and that never actually

existed at all. But utopian thought is not nonreferential. It refers to a condition or world that should exist instead of the one that does exist (217–18).

As such, Utopia acts like nothing so much as a metaphor, and the "fifth province" has proven to be an influential metaphor in various discourses since its inception. Moreover, versions of the two inclinations that it embodies can be seen to perform in variety of different forms in the diverse uses to which it has been put. For instance, *The Fifth Province* is the title of two films: one is a 1997 Irish production, directed by Frank Stapleton, which is a surreal and self-consciously postmodernist film that, among other things, brings *Psycho* and *8½* into a *Father Ted*-type territory; the other is a 2003 Canadian documentary, directed by Donald McWilliams, which offers a collage of images of striving, peace, and war from various parts of the world, accompanied by ghostly whispering. The "fifth province" has also lent its name to such disparate things as a Celtic-inspired theme park/installation in Derry, and to a social therapy approach developed by Imelda Colgan McCarthy and others, which is based on the act of imagining the other (see Colgan McCarthy 258–9). The "fifth province" was also evoked by Mary Robinson in her inaugural presidential speech in 1990, which was directly inspired by Kearney, and which saw it as a place of reconciliation and healing (Böss 152). However, the most noted and extended use of the "fifth province" was by the Northern Irish Field Day enterprise. Indeed, the "fifth province" and critiques of this ideal are most often associated with Field Day, as it explicitly linked the "fifth province" with the "national question" and the Northern Irish "Troubles," a concatenation that was implicit in the "rediscovery" of the site in *The Crane Bag* (see, for instance, Longley 120).

The Cure at Troy and the Temporal and Ethical Dimensions of the "Fifth Province"

Founded in 1980 by the actor Stephen Rea and the playwright Brian Friel, Field Day had the objective of constructing some form of cultural intervention into the Northern Irish "Troubles." Rather than issue a program or manifesto, the company turned to the "fifth province" in order to define its objectives. Friel underscored the importance of this site for Field Day in 1984, when he phrased the utopian impulse that drove the enterprise in terms that echo Kearney's vision of the "fifth province" as a place of possibility and otherness: "we appropriated (from Richard Kearney) the phrase 'Fifth Province,' which may well be a province of the mind, through which we hope to devise another way of looking at Ireland, or another possible Ireland, and this really is the pursuit of the company" (quoted in Richtarik 245). While Field Day branched out into other areas of academic and artistic endeavor, it began as a theater company with the objective of producing and touring a new play on an annual basis. One of these plays, Seamus Heaney's *The Cure at Troy*, which the company produced in 1990, is my focus here; or, to be more precise, my reading focuses on the speech from this drama in which the phrase "hope and history" was first articulated. The idea of making hope and history rhyme invokes immediately just such a chiasmic relationship between a transcendental ideal and human interaction as that which obtains in the "fifth province." I turn to this phrase at this point as it clearly concentrates on the bringing of these two dispositions together, and so the possible way it is suggested that this might happen needs to be revealed. Moreover, this move also signals a turn from a consideration of the spatial features of the "fifth province" to its temporal aspects, as it is in this dimension that the potentially enabling utopian contradictions of the site become more apparent.

It is perhaps unsurprising that the most eloquent articulation of the ideal of the "fifth province" should have been made in a translation, as *The Cure at Troy* is Heaney's translation of Sophocles's *Philoctetes*. Moreover, the idea that hope and history might come to rhyme is expressed in a speech which represents Heaney's largest diversion from Sophocles, and this deviation comes about precisely because of a tension, one which becomes apparent in a late twentieth-century translation, between transcendental and human forms of resolution.

In brief, the action of *The Cure at Troy* and *Philoctetes* concerns the attempts of Neoptolemus and Odysseus to get Philoctetes's bow, without which, it has been foretold, Troy would not be captured. Philoctetes had been abandoned on the island of Lemnos by his Greek companions many years previously because his wounded foot was creating a stench that was impossible to endure on ship. He has spent the years on the island with both the painful, festering foot and with an even more powerfully festering hatred of the Greeks in general, and of Odysseus in particular. It is Odysseus who comes up with the plan to procure the bow: rather than resort to force, which was Neoptolemus's first thought, Odysseus urges that he trick Philoctetes into either joining them or relinquishing the bow. He should befriend him, and this bond of confidence might be achieved by speaking badly of Odysseus. As Elizabeth Belfiore has pointed out, in Sophocles the relationship between Philoctetes and Neoptolemus is established through the elements of the *xenia* ritual, which in Greek society "enacted the acceptance of the suppliant into the social group of the person supplicated. It changed the suppliant 'from *xenos* in the sense of '*outsider*' to *xenos* in the sense of *guest*, one who in the future may be addressed as *philos*" (115).[4] This ritual was marked by an exchange of gifts, and the drama plays with the formal acts of reciprocation that lie at the heart of the *xenia* ritual:

> The initiatory gifts were called *xénia* or *dora* [...]. In the exchange of the *xénia*, gift was promptly followed by counter-gift of commensurate worth. A refusal to reciprocate amounted to a declaration of hostilities, while acceptance of the gifts marked the beginning of the *xenia* relationship. Because the *xénia* gifts had symbolic as well as functional value, they were unusual objects, each with its own history. They represented a man's place in society [...]. [Thus] it [is]

---

4   The embedded quotation is from Gould 79.

understandable that weapons were frequently exchanged in Greek warrior societies (Belfiore 116).

Neoptolemus and Philoctetes enact this ritual, with Neoptolemus promising to bring Philoctetes home; and, in return for this, Philoctetes puts the bow into Neoptolemus's hands to establish their relationship as friends. Furthermore, when Philoctetes subsequently realizes he has been tricked, he vents his anger and frustrations in terms of the *xenia* ritual. Neoptolemus's conscience and human sympathy are pricked; he returns the bow to Philoctetes, much to his surprise and to Odysseus's anger. Neoptolemus then asks Philoctetes if he will join his fellow Greeks at Troy, and when he refuses to do so Philoctetes accepts his decision but chides him on his suppurating hatred. It is at this impasse that Heaney introduces his invention. In Sophocles, this crux is resolved by Hercules appearing *ex machina* and dictating a resolution; Heaney, however, did not think this appropriate in his version and so, as he explains it in his note in the program for the first productions, he "attempted to present the conclusion as the inevitable culmination of an honestly endured spiritual and psychological crisis rather than as the result of a supernatural intervention" ("A Note on the Play").[5]

In other words, in bringing Sophocles into the late-twentieth century, Heaney implicitly acknowledges that the transcendent on its own does not provide a convincing form of resolution to a problem created precisely by a failure of human interaction. To get around this problem of translation, Hercules's divine diktat is substituted with an intervention by the Chorus which locates the resolution in the realms of the possible, or more precisely in terms of an ongoing tension between the human and the transcendent:

---

5   He has also confessed that this choice was made because he "simply had not the nerve to bring on a god two minutes from curtain" (see Heaney, "Production Notes" 172).

> History says, *Don't hope*
> *On this side of the grave.*
> But then, once in a lifetime
> The longed-for tidal wave
> Of justice can rise up,
> And hope and history rhyme.
>
> So hope for a great sea-change
> On the far side of revenge.
> Believe that a further shore
> Is reachable from here.
> Believe in miracles
> And cures and healing wells.
>
> Call miracle self-healing:
> The utter, self-revealing
> Double-take of feeling.
> If there's fire on the mountain
> Or lightning and storm
> And a god speaks from the sky
>
> That means someone is hearing
> The outcry and the birth-cry
> Of new life at its term (77–8).

To reiterate, my reading is based on viewing this speech as a form of resolution occasioned by the failure of the *xenia* ritual – the failure of Neoptolemus and Philoctetes to create trust between themselves – and by the assumed insufficiency of divine intervention on its own. The interpretive task therefore becomes one of understanding what alternative resolution is being proposed in this speech: how, in other words, the possibility latent in the tension between the transcendent and the human are being phrased. Looked at in this light, what seems to be suggested in this speech is that forgiveness is the key to opening the utopian possibility that hope and history might rhyme, as it is forgiveness that could be said to exist "on the far side of revenge," which is where the "great sea-change" the protagonists are enjoined to hope for will occur. Thus, without forgiveness, "the tidal wave/ Of justice" that will animate the improbable rhyme cannot "rise up".

John D. Caputo offers a version of forgiveness that contributes to an understanding of the logic of the Choral intervention, as not only does he see forgiveness as the antidote to resentment (such as that expressed by Philoctetes) but he also describes it in temporal terms that suggest how hope and history might come together:

> Forgiveness is aimed at dismissing the past. Forget the past. Dismiss our past just insofar as we have dismissed the past of others. Just as we give up providing for the future on our own and let God's providential rule do the providing, so do we give up holding on to the past. [...] For just as the future, which we cannot master or program or plan, is unpredictable, so the past is irreversible. If our redemption from the future is to live without anxiety, the only redemption from the past is forgiveness. [...] Forgiveness keeps the net of social relationships open and makes possible what Arendt calls "natality," the fresh, natal, initiating power of a new action, new beginnings, new starts [...]. Resentment, Nietzsche said, is the will's ill-will expressed towards the past. Vengeance and resentment chain us to the past, forcing us to go over it again and again, pulling the strings of the social net into an ever-tighter knot, whereas forgiveness releases and sets free (96–7).

Looked at rather simply, this maps out a plausible route by which hope and history might rhyme: forgiveness, in this account, would dismiss the past and replace it with something that could be considered to be hope. In this way, substituting hope for history, hope might come to rhyme with itself. However, the fact that this would be, to say the least, a rather poor rhyme signals that this route may not be entirely sufficient; there is something too simple, too perfect about it to be of any interest. The difficulty may lie in the fact that Caputo's account could be considered to be dealing with a pure form of forgiveness, one that calls on human agency to assume a transcendental perspective. What forgiveness has to surmount in this rendering is precisely the notion of human exchange. Yet, it could also be said that forgiveness always calls for an exchange, as it depends upon an economy that is initiated by someone asking for forgiveness and perhaps receiving it in return. Jacques Derrida, who also proposes a pure form of forgiveness, has dismissed this form of forgiveness as "conditional," finding the logic of sovereignty that operates within it repulsive (*On Cosmopolitanism* 33). While a moment's reflection on the peace process in Northern Ireland (which, of course, is entirely salient to Heaney's translation) would tend to confirm the justice of this viewpoint, there nevertheless lingers the suspicion that the dismissal of history that is required here, rather than a form of coming to terms with the past, is problematic. On the contrary, it could be argued that the strength of "conditional" forgiveness lies in its refusal to dismiss totally the past. Moreover, it might also be contended that forgiveness essentially needs the past; it needs to confront and live with the past rather than dismiss it. In like fashion, hope, if it is to be a possible hope, must exist despite (or maybe even because of) history, not in its place.

This temporal and ethical quandary might now be usefully read back into the "fifth province," as even Hederman, in his exposition of the transcendental version of the "fifth province," also strove to think of the site in terms of human history, arguing that

> 1. Continuity of tradition is the basic condition for the existence of culture.
> 2. Breaking continuity, rupture of tradition, is the necessary condition for the formation of a new kind of culture.
> I would claim that "the fifth province" is an attempt to maintain the paradox of both these truths (110–11).

This acknowledges that contradiction is invoked and enveloped within the "fifth province." In this extract, the contradiction concerns the paradox between the past and the necessary, continual rereading of it; and it is exactly this notion that provides a possible way of reading the larger contradiction between the two versions of the "fifth province," as the ethical potential of this site could be viewed as being dependent upon a move outside human temporality that affords a more illuminating and ambiguous perspective on history. In Reinhart Koselleck's terms, utopias, even if they are flawed, exist precisely because of the possibility of alternative histories: "Actual history is always simultaneously more and less, and seen ex post facto, it is always different than we are capable of imagining. For this reason, there are utopias, and also for this reason, they are condemned to be wrong" (99).

Utopias are always beyond human experience, being located in the forgotten past, in the future, or in an alternative other time; and the utopian impulse, it might be said, is only "possible in doing the impossible," which is exactly how Derrida conceived of pure forgiveness (*On Cosmopolitanism* 33). However, the ethical validity of this impulse does not simply reside in the act of imagining impossible possibilities or possible impossibilities, but in the way in which it articulates the need to construct such other realities. As Koselleck implies, utopias are always already necessary and impossible; and thus the "fifth province," because it comes into being through an act of translation, thematizes its necessity and impossibility by putting into play an unending interweaving of a transcendental ideal and human possibility and fallibility. To understand this better the modes of translation that are suggested by Hederman and Kearney's versions of the "fifth province" might be examined through the lenses furnished by Derrida's paradoxical description of "the necessary and impossible task of translation, its necessity *as* impossibility" ("Des Tours de Babel" 171).

Translating a Utopian Idea

For Hederman, as has been seen, the importance of the "fifth province" lies in the fact that it is an access point to a final destination that is explicitly beyond the realms of human history. While language may well have a role to play in such a transcendent realm, it would necessarily be a rather particular form of language, one in which the problems of interpretation were no longer present. In short, it would be a form of Adamic language, which would follow the logic outlined in Brian Friel's *Translations*:

> OWEN: Eden's right! We name a thing and – bang! – it leaps into existence!
> YOLLAND: Each name a perfect equation with its roots.
> OWEN: A perfect congruence with its reality (45).

As Derrida has noted, "the theme of a transcendental signified took shape within the horizon of an absolutely pure, transparent, and unequivocal translatability" ("Interview with Julia Kristeva" 20); and it could be argued that a myth of pure translatability, or to put it more correctly, a myth that thinks in terms of there being no need for translation, haunts utopian thinking. Indeed, it can also be heard in Kearney's version; according to his blueprint, "the creation of this fifth province calls for the provision of a new vocabulary, a new mode of communication which could acknowledge, and perhaps ultimately mediate between the sundered cultural identities of this island" ("The Language Plays of Brian Friel" 125). Yet, at the same time, this also sounds a different note. Once again Kearney locates the "fifth province" in the realm of human striving, and there is an implicit acknowledgement in this that communication is not easy and is indeed liable to fail. It is in this acknowledgement of possible failure that the ethical quality of the "fifth province" becomes clear as, thought of in this manner, the transcendental, rather than being seen as a site of perfection, becomes a symbol of impossibility. Hence, the importance of the "fifth province" is not to be found in arriving there, but in the continual necessity of trying to construct it, in the knowledge that all attempts to do so are probably doomed to failure. Nevertheless, in the move towards possible versions of the site, perspectives – versions of the past, future possibilities – have been altered, have been rendered other. And this, of course, is the motion, promise, and fate of translation.

Jameson has noted that "Utopia was always an ambiguous ideal," and the paradox that informs the "fifth province" is that for it to have a positive ethical force, it has to take account of the past in such a way that it leaves open the possibility that hope and history will fail to rhyme (382).

Works Cited

Adams, Gerry. *Hope and History: Making Peace in Ireland*. Kerry: Brandon, 2003.

Belfiore, Elizabeth. "*Xenia* in Sophocles's *Philoctetes*." *The Classical Journal* 89.2 (1993/1994): 113–29.
Böss, Michael. "The Postmodern Nation: A Critical History of the 'Fifth Province' Discourse." *Études Irlandaises* 27.1 (2002): 139–59.
Caputo, John D. "Reason, History and a Little Madness: Towards an Ethics of the Kingdom." *Questioning Ethics: Contemporary Debates in Philosophy*. Ed. Richard Kearney and Mark Dooley. London and New York: Routledge, 1999. 84–104.
Clinton, Bill. *Between Hope and History: Meeting America's Challenges for the 21st Century*. New York: Times, 1996.
Colgan McCarthy, Imelda. "Fifth Province Re-Versings: The Social Construction of Women Lone Parents' Inequality and Poverty." *Journal of Family Therapy* 23 (2001): 253–77.
Dauenhauer, Bernard P. *Paul Ricoeur: The Promise and Risk of Politics*. Lanham: Rowman and Littlefield, 1998.
Denard, Hugh. "Seamus Heaney, Colonialism and *The Cure*: Sophoclean Revisions." *PAJ: A Journal of Performance and Art* 22.66 (September 2000): 1–18.
Derrida, Jacques. *On Cosmopolitanism and Forgiveness*. Trans. Mark Dooley and Michael Hughes. London and New York: Routledge, 2001.
_____ "Des Tours de Babel." *Difference in Translation*. Ed. and trans. Joseph F. Graham. Ithaca and London: Cornell University Press, 1985. 165–207.
_____ "Semiology and Grammatology: Interview with Julia Kristeva." *Positions*. Trans. Alan Bass. London: Athlone, 1981. 15–36.
Foucault, Michel. "Of Other Spaces." Trans. Jay Miskowiec. 14 September 2005 <http://foucault.info/documents/heteroTopia/foucault.heteroTopia.en.html>.
_____ *The Order of Things: An Archaeology of the Human Sciences*. London and New York: Routledge, 2002.
Friel, Brian. *Translations*. London and Boston: Faber, 1981.
Gordimer, Nadine. *Living in Hope and History: Notes on Our Century*. London: Bloomsbury, 1999.
Gould, John. "*Hiketeia*." *JHS* 93 (1973): 74–103.
Harvey, David. *Spaces of Hope*. Edinburgh: Edinburgh University Press, 2000.
Heaney, Seamus. *The Cure at Troy: A Version of Sophocles's Philoctetes*. London: Faber and Faber, 1990.
_____ "*The Cure at Troy*: A Note on the Play." The Cure at Troy *by Seamus Heaney, after "Philoctetes" by Sophocles*. Programme. 1990.

_____"*The Cure at Troy*: Production Notes in No Particular Order." *Amid Our Troubles: Irish Versions of Greek Tragedy.* Ed. Marianne McDonald and J. Michael Walton. London: Methuen, 2002. 171–80.
Hederman, Mark Patrick. "Poetry and the Fifth Province." *The Crane Bag* 9.1 (1985): 110–19.
Jameson, Fredric. "Utopianism and Anti-Utopianism." *The Jameson Reader.* Ed. Michael Hardt and Kathi Weeks. Oxford: Blackwell, 1994. 382–92.
Kearney, Richard. "Editorial I: Endodermis." *The Crane Bag* 1.1 (1977): 3–5.
_____"Introduction." *Paul Ricoeur: The Hermeneutics of Action.* Ed. Richard Kearney. London: Sage, 1996. 1–2.
_____"The Language Plays of Brian Friel." *Transitions: Narratives in Modern Irish Culture.* Ed. Richard Kearney. Dublin: Wolfhound, 1988. 123–60.
_____*Postnational Ireland: Politics, Culture, Philosophy.* London: Routledge, 1997.
Koselleck, Reinhart. "The Temporalization of Utopia." *The Practice of Conceptual History: Timing History, Spacing Concepts.* Trans. Todd Presner. Stanford: Stanford University Press, 2002. 84–99.
Logan, George M., and Robert M. Adams. "Introduction." *Utopia.* Ed. George M. Logan and Robert M. Adams. Cambridge: Cambridge University Press, 1989. xi–xxviii.
Longley, Edna. "A Reply." *The Crane Bag* 9.1 (1985): 120–2.
Lowe, Lisa. *Critical Terrains: French and British Orientalisms.* Ithaca and London: Cornell University Press, 1991.
O' Rahilly, Thomas F. *Early Irish History and Mythology.* Dublin: Institute for Advanced Studies, 1946.
Rees, Alwyn, and Brinley Rees. *Celtic Heritage: Ancient Traditions in Ireland and Wales.* London: Thames and Hudson, 1961.
Richtarik, Marilynn J. *Acting between the Lines: The Field Day Theatre Company and Irish Cultural Politics 1980–1984.* Oxford: Clarendon, 1994.
Sargent, Lyman Tower, "The Three Faces of Utopianism Revisited." *Utopian Studies* 5.1 (1994): 1–37.

Timothy Keane

The Chartist Land Plan: An English Dream, an Irish Nightmare

Owing its beginnings to William Lovett and the London Working Men's Association, Chartism would eventually spurn the overtures of middle-class radicalism and become the movement most readily identified with the British working classes in the 1840s. Chartism swelled throughout Britain under the leadership of Feargus O'Connor, who used the pages of his newspaper, *The Northern Star*, to mobilize the industrial towns in the north of England. The battle cry of the Chartists demanded political inclusion, calling for an end to the "class legislation" that was only possible because the working-class voice comprised just a fraction of the electorate. The basis for this parliamentary reform was the six points of "The People's Charter," which called for universal suffrage, the ballot, equal electoral districts, annual parliaments, elimination of the property qualification for MPs, as well as the payment of MPs. On three occasions (1839, 1842, and 1848), the National Chartist Convention presented a petition with millions of signatures to Parliament calling for the People's Charter to be adopted. These petitions showed the level of organization, as well as the popular support, for the measure; but in each instance, the petitioners were dismissed by Parliament and disregarded by polite society. The Chartist leadership and the Chartist press were able to unite the working classes in these endeavors to attain political inclusion for all. In these very public and very vocal petition drives, Chartism provided a semblance of unity; and, in this union, the working classes were given a chance to hope, a chance to imagine that their lives could change if they could only participate in political society. In the Chartist Land Plan, O'Connor would provide a glimpse of future possibilities, a utopian dream for the English working classes.

In much of the historiography, there seems to be a tendency to speak of Chartism as a single entity, assuming a singular vision, a vision that was firmly fixed in the political realm. However, there was a great diversity within Chartism, a diversity that offered an opportunity for various programs of social and political reform to come together. For some, Chartism embodied a social and economic radicalism – whether Spencean or Owenite, socialist or communist. For others, Chartism recalled a radical conservativism reminiscent of William Cobbett that would enable Chartists to be denounced as Tories. At the same time, there was an element that held fast to the tenets of republicanism, which allowed Chartism to be decried as an illegitimate political expression because of this "physical force" element. Additionally, critics would ridicule Chartism for its Irish elements, noted in the ethnicity of many of its leaders, most prominently O'Connor, but also in Chartism's support for the Repeal of Union.

Figure 1. John Leech, "A Social Sketch, or, Everything in Common." © Bodleian Library, University of Oxford, 2003. (Alm) 2706 g.4; drawing inside front cover.

Following the collapse of the mass platform of Chartism in the aftermath of the failures of 1848 (a failed mass demonstration, a failed parliamentary petition, a failed Irish rising followed by the failure to rise in England), *Punch* was able to find the humor in this working-class movement that posed the single greatest threat of revolution since the Napoleonic wars. As a light-hearted supplement to a pocket diary, a cartoon by John Leech folds out of the cover of *Punch's Pocketbook for 1850*. In this pictorial commentary on a defeated movement, Leech gives expression to the multiple layers of fear that Chartism created in English society, fears that were never fully engaged in the pages of *Punch* until Chartism was safely expunged.

"A Social Sketch, or, Everything in Common" depicts a convergence of anxieties regarding Chartism. To begin with, the image ridicules the aspirations for self-improvement that were central to the ethos of all reform and working-class institutions in nineteenth-century Britain. This is clear from the dismissive reference of the leader, who was nicknamed "the Perfessor": dressed in military uniform, he personifies the danger of knowledge being abused for a radical agenda. Chartism is marked as hostile to the rights of property, the foundation of a capitalist society, seen in the wall hanging in the top-right corner. Behind the child wearing what looks to be an imperial crown rests a sign which reads "ALL PROPERTY IS ROBBERY." Naming the Chartists as communists and socialist levelers would alienate the middle classes, who were becoming major participants within capitalism, from the People's Charter. The scene is a Victorian parlor, the epicenter of "respectability" for the flourishing middle class, under siege. A youth coopts the phrase "Heaven helps those who helps themselves"; while an individual voice from within the group of intruders cries out "They're as much mine as yourn." *Punch* ridicules the very essence of social, and hence political, mobility in this warning against social leveling. The comedy of the cartoon is derived from the obvious deficiencies of the invading masses within the domain of the "respectable classes." Although the threat of Chartism had already passed, similar warnings were continually pronounced to prevent any true middle-class alliance with popular Chartism.

On another level, *Punch* moves beyond the abstract commentary on radical social policies, such as socialism, to paint Chartists in a specifically Irish light. Thus, Leech links Chartism with Ireland, as the Irishness of these Chartist levelers is apparent in both their speech and dress. The figure who controls the scene, seen in the deference given to him by the central woman, brandishes a shillelagh. *Punch* consistently placed shillelaghs and blunderbusses in the hands of Young Ireland; in this case, especially when examined alongside the French military uniform, the viewer is encouraged to identify the threat of republicanism inherent in Irish models of agitation and to recognize that this physical force agitation had no place in "proper" British politics. As *Punch* has rarely been criticized for subtlety, the Irish connection becomes even more explicit as the young lady is forced to peel "pertaters," the subsistence crop consistently equated with the Irish throughout nineteenth-century popular culture. There is another military figure holding a blunderbuss; and the presence of the pipe, especially in the mouth of a woman or a child, had become a racial marker of the Irish in the caricatures of *Punch*.

The entire scene depicts violence breaking out, or the fear of violence, as there are a group of cowering women to the right who are in need of protection, who cannot even look directly at the scene unfolding. Irishness is once again envisaged in terms of a contagion – an attitude that had survived since Edmund Spenser, and which had been continued in the work of Dr. Kay in Manchester (Spenser 67–70; Davis 109). The warning that Leech communicates takes on additional significance when we examine the "general's" proposal to the archetypal Victorian woman: "When you've done peelin' them Pertaters put on yer Bonnet & cum out for a walk in Kensington Gardings!!!" While mirroring the traditional Victorian values that would have made a Sunday stroll fashionable, there is also a sense that this is a courting ritual, a means of the intruder consolidating his newly attained position.

Strikingly, at the same time this proposition is being made, we see a Victorian man stepping in to protect middle-class women. To the left of center, we see a properly dressed man pulling an African minstrel off of another woman. Here, Leech is calling for civil society to step up against the Irish contagion in the same manner in which an

African threat would be met. At this point, Chartism had undergone a radical change in the English psyche. This defeated mass political movement that had drawn its strength from the industrial towns of England and Scotland, and had recently elected an MP, had now become a *foreign* body. It is, therefore, not an *English* movement that threatens Victorian society, but an *Irish* contagion that must be cured. It is clear from "A Social Sketch" that Ireland was viewed as a dystopia, one mobilized by the governing classes to deflect criticism. Using the Irish as a warning allowed polite society to forget that Chartism had a wide appeal for the working and middle classes of Britain; all were warned against providing support to the Chartists.

Chartism, however, was *elastic*. Its foundation was to agitate for basic political rights, but there was scope for other radical agendas. The battle cry forged by the leadership became "The Charter and Something More." In this regard, Chartism undoubtedly possessed a utopian impulse, as it sought electoral reform and the political inclusion of the working masses as a beginning, not an end. However, in this broad utopian appeal, there were in fact varying utopian agendas that would have been envisioned by its supporters. Whether envisioned as a democratic fraternity of republicanism or as the idealized socialism of Owenite or Speancean supporters, these several utopian projections could not practically be uttered without tearing apart the crosscurrent of support gathered throughout the working classes. But during a "lull" in Chartist agitation, as the historiography of Chartism refers to the years 1843–1846, O'Connor sustained a utopian vision of society that successfully forged solidarity within the working classes.

The crushing defeat of the Chartist petition in 1842 was followed by a tempestuous summer of riots and strikes, from the colliers to the cotton industries. The heavy-handed response of the government created a feeling of despondency within the movement.[1] Chartist leaders and activists were imprisoned throughout the country, and the working classes simply felt that political success could not be carried.

---

[1] For a detailed examination of the strikes and distress within the Chartist movement in 1842, see Thompson, ch. 11; and Fyson.

Numbers attending Chartist meetings drastically declined throughout Britain. As Gregory Claeys notes "the Chartist movement [...] had conceived political power to be the means and social happiness the end of radical reform" (245). The "end," social happiness, was always left undeveloped in Chartist discourse. The hope invested in the political process was lost with the failed petition, and O'Connor needed to offer a fresh picture of the "social happiness" promised by the Charter. To do so, he turned to the land question to reinvigorate the mass platform of Chartism. At the same time, he began publicly to reminisce about his youth as the son of landed gentry in Ireland. It was the beginning of a shift in strategy, focusing political reform on the workers' relationship to the land. In *The Labourer*, the organ of the Land Plan, he recounts that it was through his engagement with agricultural laborers and the small farmers that he became politicized, abandoning his red coat and polished boots for "the fustian and the brogues" of the workers on his family's estate in County Cork (quoted in Airey 190).

This preoccupation with the land was not new to radical politics. Land was the essence of much radical agitation from the late eighteenth century and throughout the nineteenth century in Britain.[2] O'Connor was first introduced to the centrality of land in radical politics by his uncle, the famed United Irishman, Arthur O'Connor. In 1843, the younger O'Connor republished a pamphlet that Arthur had written in 1798, entitled *The State of Ireland*. On one level, this publication was yet another attempt to link Chartism with the Irish radical traditions of the United Irishmen. It is for this reason that Feargus O'Connor was often abused by his contemporaries, who would have instinctively rejected any Irish model as unsuitable for British politics, as the very site of Ireland suggested degeneracy. Indeed, O'Connor has also been mistreated by historians, who have consistently viewed his attempts to link English and Irish radical traditions as an opportunistic means of consolidating and expanding

---

[2] Chase explores the long traditions of English radicalism's connection to the land. In relation to engagement with the land during the Chartist years, see Saville.

his powerbase for purely egotistical reasons. But as Dorothy Thompson notes, *The State of Ireland* also brought "before the Chartists the question of land ownership and cultivation" (301). The inspiration O'Connor found in the United Irishmen, and his uncle in particular, is obvious to all, as seen most readily in the naming of his trades journal, the *Northern Star*, after Arthur O'Connor's seditious journal of the same name. Suggesting a continuity between the program of the United Irishmen and Chartism was, however, just the beginning for O'Connor, for he would go on to publish his own treatise on the land in the same year, 1843.

It is worth recognizing another Irish influence whose impression can be seen in O'Connor's shift from political agitation to the economic reforms of cooperation. In the midst of the 1830 Tithe War in Ireland, John Scott Vandeleur chose to establish an Owenite cooperative community on his estate in County Limerick. The Ralahine Agricultural and Manufacturing Co-Operative Association was short-lived, lasting only three years, but its sad demise would have reminded O'Connor of the need to own and control the land. However, what is most interesting in this comparison is Vandeleur's impetus for his experiment. In response to the agrarian secret societies that were targeting "offending" landlords and their property, Vandeleur sought to improve the relationship between the landlord and worker in order to protect his estate (Bolger 13). In this light, Vincent Geoghegan has noted that the "anxiety of landowners" was an important element to Robert Owen's warm reception in Dublin in the midst of an earlier outbreak of rural violence, a fact that was "not a matter of chance" (378). Vandeleur, like Owen, saw the opportunity for a system of cooperation to address the causes of rural distress; and, with the outbreak of the tithe wars in 1830, he began to put his plan into action. Geoghegan acknowledges that the "rural crisis engendered a worried gentry and a desperate peasantry," but what needs to be emphasized is that this crisis engendered more than economic distress (410). Part of the crisis, as James Connolly would later identify, was that the political avenue for any meaningful reforms for the peasantry was shown to be an illusion.

Indeed, Connolly's examination of the Ralahine experiment traces the cause of the disturbed countryside during the Tithe War back to the failure of Catholic Emancipation (1829) to deliver the promised benefits to the poorer classes. While the Catholic middle and professional classes received all the benefits of the reforms, the peasantry were left to carry the burden of retribution, as evictions increased exponentially: "The Catholics of the poorer class as a result of the same Act were doomed to extermination to satisfy the vengeance of a foreign Government, and an aristocracy whose power had been defied where it knew itself most supreme" (Connolly 124). Vandeleur recognized the need to fill the void of the undelivered hope, in the same way that O'Connor realized a need to modify the direction of his agitation. Here, then, it needs to be noted that the reality facing radical beliefs and agendas, which by definition operate within a hostile environment, also defines utopian struggles. Lyman Tower Sargent identifies this reality: "The cycle of hope, failure, despair and the rejection of hope altogether, followed by the renewal of hope seems to be the basic pattern of attitudes to social change" (28). O'Connor, like Vandeleur, renewed the hope of the working classes only by recognizing their rejection of the political process; it was only through offering a clear vision of the "end" that a return to the political process could be established.

O'Connor's *The Management of Small Farms* (*MSF*) was written for the working classes, as is evident in its affordability (one shilling) as well as in the fact that it was published serially (Thompson 301); but the treatise, directed towards the moral and social failures of a society entrenched in the uncaring *laissez-faire* principles of British capitalism, desired to renew English society as a whole. Herein, O'Connor was working within a long tradition of radical Reform. His text invokes the memories of Cobbett's *Cottage Economy* and *Rural Rides*, which sought to re-establish a balance between the countryside and the urban centers. And, like the principles behind the mechanic institutes and political unions of the 1820s and 1830s – such as the *Society for the Diffusion of Useful Knowledge* and the *London Working Men's Association* – the drive for self-help was the foundation of *MSF*. Where O'Connor departed from this tradition however, in that he envisioned his book to be the launch of a national movement. He concludes *MSF* with a detailed plan for a land cooperative, which would come to be known as the Chartist Land Plan.

The historiography of Chartism has continually damned the Land Plan, often locating O'Connor's maniacal pre-occupation with it as the downfall of the movement (see Saville 60–3). In one respect, the plan itself was a failure, in that such a small percentage of the participants were settled on their own farm; in another respect, however, the Land Plan was an overwhelming success in that it sustained a Chartist movement that had otherwise become silent. Thompson notes that the Land Plan was responsible for "holding together the Chartist movement in the second half of the decade" (303). The reason O'Connor's Land Plan became a unifying force is that it tapped into a deeper longing within the working classes. The repeated failures of petitioning for political and social reform, the only outlet for the politically excluded masses, had silenced the national movement. O'Connor was not only aware of an antipathy within the Chartist ranks in 1843; he went as far as to plot a path forward: "Having, therefore, arrived at the conclusion that the people have nothing to expect in the way of change from the government, it becomes the paramount duty of their friends to point out how the required change in their condition can be effected without force or fraud" (98). In the Land Plan, O'Connor provided an alternate avenue for hope, one that was intended to bypass the political structures that remained openly hostile to the laboring poor.

The hope expressed by O'Connor followed a long line of radical discourse, in which the plight of the working classes was expressed in the discourse of slavery. The land held the potential to free the "factory slave," to free the working classes from the "national disease" of an artificial labor market. He begins this treatise by challenging his readers to examine the plight of the working poor in terms of slavery:

> I have come to the conclusion, that the emancipation of the working classes of this and every other country can never be achieved except by placing the working population, or so many of them as may choose to embrace the offer, upon so much land as each can conveniently cultivate for his own sole use, behoof, and benefit (7).

What was significant in this new campaign of self-definition was the land itself. Malcolm Chase highlights the utopian impulse behind the Land Plan:

> O'Connor's initial intention, though, was that the plan should be a practical demonstration of the power of spade husbandry; of the virtues of independent labor; of the social and economic importance of the family unit; and of the fallacies of Malthusianism. In short, it was to be a prototype of the kind of society which would be universally viable once the Charter was law (175).

Through his Land Plan, which was to operate in conjunction with agitation for the political inclusion of the working classes, we can find an insight into what Ernst Bloch referred to as *concrete utopia*. Douglas Kellner and Harry O'Hara locate the revolutionary thrust of Bloch's theories on utopia within this concept: "concrete utopia deals with possibilities which exist as tendencies latent within a given situation [...]. concrete Utopia does not impatiently leap into an ideal beyond but explores the present situation to discover real possibilities for radical change" (29–30). Participating within a capitalist framework offered O'Connor new possibilities for reform – reform with a revolutionary, utopian potential. Shaped by the understanding that the capitalists, the new merchant class, profit from the labor surplus in the industrial centers, the action of forming a land cooperative would allow segments of the working class access to land, and hence access to capital; it would also serve to protect and enhance the remaining labor force. The concrete utopian impulse of O'Connor's vision is outlined in the opening pages of *MSF*:

> The object which I have in view in submitting a practical work upon the management of small farms to the working men of this country is, that each man who is willing to work may be independent of every other man in the world for his daily bread; so that the prosperity of the country shall consist in an aggregate of happy individuals, rather than in a community of a few owners of all its aggregate wealth; and upon whose speculation, whim, and caprice, the poor man must now depend for his bread (5).

After two years of sharing his vision in the pages of the *Northern Star*, O'Connor convinced the National Chartist Convention to adopt the Chartist Land Plan as a supplement to the People's Charter.

The Chartist Land Co-Operative Society, as it was first termed, consequently began to purchase large tracts of land; subdivide it into plots of two, three, or four acres; and settle members on these farms. O'Connor even referred to these self-contained communities as "Chartist colonies." To raise funds, shares were sold at £2,10*s* each, although one could subscribe as little as three pence a week towards a share, making it available to the working poor. When land was purchased, and the infrastructure completed, all of those who owned two, three, or four shares (to correspond with the size of the farms) would be entered in a draw to be resettled on a small farm. Each successful shareholder would have a cottage built on their plot and would be provided with an advance of cash as initial capital to buy livestock. Rent was fixed and tenure given for life. Spade husbandry was to be practiced, enabling a life of self-sufficiency, with ample room for profit. By the end of 1847, "about 600 branches of the Land Company had been formed" (Ashton 69). In four years, the Land Company had 70,000 shareholders; raised more than £100,000; acquired 1100 acres of land; and settled 250 families (this last figure was a great disappointment, and proof for critics of the foolhardy character of the Land Plan's originator, as well as the shareholders).

The enterprise, however, was bound to fail, as it would have been impossible to settle even a majority of the shareholders. Opponents criticized it as nostalgic and irresponsible, as it promoted not only a policy of small farms but also spade husbandry to urban workers who did not possess the requisite knowledge or skills to succeed as small farmers. A local history, *Victorian County History of Hertfordshire*, published in 1914, is critical of the implicit shortcoming of the Land Plan:

> The mistakes of the promoter were at once revealed. The men who came to take up the holdings were small tradesmen, merchants or weavers from the manufacturing towns. They understood the ground as little as their wives understood the henhouse or dairy; they even had to buy bread because they

knew not how to bake. [...] The prospect for the poor settlers was rather the workhouse than the idyllic homestead (quoted in Brown 117).

In the midst of criticizing the foolhardy adventure of the industrial laborers who settled in O'Connorville, this commentator nevertheless recognized the utopian impulse that inspired the shareholders. Even the most hardened critic could not deny that the cycle of hope, so thoroughly defeated in the summer of 1842, had begun anew.

In spite of the failure of the enterprise, the broader success of the Land Plan can be located in the fact that a Chartist organization was once again mobilized. The Plan had met with great opposition even within the Chartist membership, but the movement was once again actively imagining working-class futures. As seen in the front page engraving of O'Connorville on its first anniversary, the Land Plan served to promote a utopian vision that could be achieved through the Charter. With this gathering of attention, if not support, O'Connor set out to use the cooperative model to allow the working class an access into capitalism that was previously impossible. His intent was to forge a proprietary class. In a *Northern Star* advertisement, entitled "The National Land and Labour Bank," which grew out of the Land Company, the problem restricting working-class entry into the world of commerce is noted: "Our giant trade and commerce preclude the possibility of the poor man becoming a competitor with the rich speculator" ("National Land and Labour Bank" 26 December 1846: 1). In spite of the long odds, a new potential was afforded the working classes. The Land Plan aimed to provide dividends to shareholders who were not settled, paid out of a portion of the rents coming in from the settled communities. The members of the Chartist Land Company were to be shareholders, participating at the highest levels of capitalism. Merely offering access to the capitalist structures denied to most of the working classes may seem modest, in terms of utopian thought. But it is important to recall Sargent's reminder when examining "social dreaming": "But not all [dreams] are radical, for some people at any time dream of something basically familiar" (Sargent 3). The model of cooperation was, at once, both familiar and radically new.

Figure 2. "Grand Demonstration on the 17th of August, 1846, To the People's First Estate, O'Connorville" (*Northern Star* 22 August 1846: 1).

The Land Plan was unusual when compared to other radical agrarian models in that it chose to work within the construct of capitalism. It was not a Spencean model calling for a national commonwealth; while a significant number of Chartists espoused socialist ideals, the Land Plan clearly fell short of those ideals. Hence, analyses suggesting that Chartism, as a national platform, was opposed to private property are erroneous; indeed, O'Connor used land as a means of creating and establishing a class of independent proprietors (Airey 194). Given the ambitious project of resettling laborers in the countryside, we need to remember that the policy also took aim at the industrial centers that were the lifeblood of Chartist support. O'Connor consistently remarked on the need to protect labor, and by relocating surplus labor, we felt that the Land Plan would be serving the entire working class. As Chase notes, the basic rationale behind the "Chartist estates rested on the central assumption that a strategic withdrawal of labor from the 'artificial' to the 'natural' economy would undermine the basis on which low wages rested" (144–5). The Land Plan thus sought to attack the abusive nature of capitalism in Britain on two fronts: through competition, and through market correction.

Another important subject that would bear directly upon the reception of the Land Plan was the "condition of Ireland." Several critics denounced the principles of the Plan as something more appropriate for O'Connor's "motherland." In fact, Ireland would continually be used as proof that the system of small farms could not succeed. O'Connor defended his small farm system against unfair comparisons with Ireland, noting "that the want of a small farm system, and not its existence, is the immediate cause of Irish distress" (101). What had to be done was to show that the failures in Ireland were due to artificial forces. The columns of both *The Labourer* and the *Northern Star* reported extensively on Ireland, highlighting the continual abuses hurled upon its workers, especially the evils of absentee landlordism, rack-rents, and the prevalence of evictions. A competition for the right to define the "state" of Ireland was pivotal to the struggle of the English working classes. There were two Irelands, each continually imagined as a dystopia: the Ireland of rack-rents, evictions, and famine that radicalism used as a warning against the evils of misrepresentation; and the Ireland portrayed in the pages of the major newspapers and journals in England, the Ireland that permeated the consciousness of the English public – seen as a degenerate nation characterized by laziness and idleness. Chartism took this contest for control of the representation of the Irish dystopia to the public not only through reportage on the distress of the oncoming famine, but also through a fictional narrative in the medium of romance. For example, in a serialized travel narrative that first appeared in the *Northern Star* in the autumn of 1846, a fictional

Scottish radical named Malcolm McGregor took it upon himself to uncover the true condition of Ireland at a time when reports of the famine had begun to moderate the English attitude towards Ireland.[3]

"The Narrative of Malcolm McGregor" brought the depiction of the "two Irelands" into close contact, making the radical case of Ireland as warning to the English public. McGregor thus offers a narrative of Ireland to reveal problems in the English social fabric, showing that the English public is vulnerable to the system of misgovernment that has already paralyzed Ireland. While Ireland at this historical moment may resist being read overtly as a *dystopia* – a concept usually reserved for twentieth-century social commentaries and fictions – it nevertheless embodies the spirit of how the dystopian imaginary can function in social activism. Tom Moylan's account of dystopia is, therefore, applicable to the discourses surrounding this nineteenth-century reform campaign:

> Crucial to dystopia's vision in all its manifestations is this ability to register the impact of an unseen and unexamined social system on the everyday lives of everyday people. Again and again, the dystopian text opens in the midst of a social 'elsewhere' that appears to be far worse than any in the 'real' world (xiii).[4]

In McGregor's narrative, Ireland is the social elsewhere, and he shows that the English systems of commerce and government have had a catastrophic effect upon the Irish people. By deconstructing the

---

[3] I have not been able to ascertain the identity of the author of the Malcolm McGregor contributions to the Chartist press. What is clear is that the first issues of *The Labourer*, the journal that continually promoted the Chartist Land Plan, contained poems penned by McGregor. These first issues were written entirely, it is thought, by the two editors, Feargus O'Connor and Ernest Jones. What is important is that McGregor reflects the editorial policies of *The Labourer*, whether penned by O'Connor, Jones, or a combination of the two. There were twelve instalments of "The Narrative of Malcolm McGregor," *Northern Star* 17 October 1846 to 30 January 1847.

[4] For a discussion of the relationship between nineteenth-century naturalist writing and the dystopian form, see Wegner; and for a useful account of dystopian discourse as a tool of concrete political analysis, see Varsam.

traditional explanations for Ireland's failures, McGregor intends to force the English public to assess their own future, as the systems that have destroyed Ireland have been left unexamined.

"The Narrative of Malcolm McGregor" adopts a structure familiar to English radicals, as it recalls the successful letters that comprised Cobbett's *Rural Rides*. But unlike Cobbett, the tension between *fiction* and *reality* is continually being played out. It is a romance, written by the imaginary Malcolm McGregor, whose fictional status is readily seen in the outrageous names of some of the characters: a rack-rent landlord named Captain Squeezetenant; a heartless Protestant preacher, living in luxury, aptly named Parson Preachlove; and British army officers named Lieutenant Shot and the newly arrived Eustace Killman Savage Silsby. These playful names would suggest that the fiction is to be digested lightly; however, in a Swiftian echo and a dystopian anticipation, the author challenges the way in which the story is consumed by the reader by grounding its outrageous fictional elements in reality. The proffered history of the O'Donnell family mirrors that of the hero of Thomas Moore's *Memoirs of Captain Rock*. We come to see how British misgovernment destroyed a family, a community, and eventually the country. Here, the English presence becomes the contagion, an inversion of the reading of the Irish immigrant in Britain. And at the climax, when the army is used to serve a civil decree of payment on behalf of a landlord, ending with the wrongful death of an industrious youth, the *editor* of the *Northern Star* compares the story with the Rathcormac tithe massacres in County Cork some fifteen years earlier. An extract taken from a Cork paper accompanies this installment of the narrative, revealing how the *romance* is in communion with the real (see "Narrative" 2 January 1847: 1).

The first installment of the narrative offers a powerful vision of the Irish landscape, a vision that is in no small part a metaphor for the larger state of the country. As the narrator's ship approaches Cobh, County Cork, he is overtaken by the physical beauty of the countryside. The idyllic imagery offers a potentially utopian vision of harmony, as the lush terrain mirrors the abundant wealth that has been accumulated in Ireland. But this vision is quickly tempered by the realization that Ireland, as a country, has been systematically drained of its wealth through misgovernment: "When I went on deck we had just passed Cove, and the most splendid scenery that can be imagined burst as if by magic upon the dazzled eye; it was a constant bewilderment of successive views, each surpassing the previous one, if not in grandeur, at least in artificial greatness" ("Narrative" 17 October 1846: 1). The narrator is engulfed with the natural beauty of the scene, but the beauty of the "princely mansions" that line the banks of the river is not equated with the idyllic. Immediately, McGregor announces the *artificial*; and in this first image of Ireland, it is intimated that the presence of the "artificial greatness" is an ill omen for the Irish people:

> The princely mansions of the Cork merchants, which I confess in some degree accounted for the reported barrenness of equally good land in the interior, but which I conjectured had been stripped of its wealth to enrich the hoarded treasure of those who by the process of barter, have discovered the magnetic influence by which the honey of labor may be attracted to the comb of speculation, the produce of the bee to the hive of the drone ("Narrative" 17 October 1846: 1).

Not only is the profit of the burgeoning merchant class shown to be at odds with the idyllic landscape, but McGregor demonstrates that this unfettered capitalism is unnatural, threatening labor and threatening the working classes. The metaphor of the bee thus serves to foreshadow the incommunicable distress of the Irish laborer.

On his way to catch a morning coach out of the city, McGregor is confronted with the true depths of distress that have gripped the Irish poor. As mothers and children scour the garbage in the streets for sustenance, he is faced with a vision he can scarce believe:

> Every street had an appalling amount of the most squalid and miserable looking creatures that ever my eye beheld [...] The groups for the most part consisted of half-naked females, the majority of whom had an infant tied up in the tail of a tattered garment, and fastened round the neck, while they groped in the ashes and rubbish thrown from the houses in the middle of the streets, for such fragments of food as might have escaped the notice or have been beneath the acceptance of the cat or dog ("Narrative" 24 October 1846: 1).

The narrator bemoans that such poverty persists in a city that, at first sight, would be noted for a "comparative respectability." And to his horror, he is immediately told that he has not seen the worst of the distress – that, in fact, if he was out an hour earlier in the morning, he would have seen a more horrible sight: "the poor craythers that's naked are flit, and its only them that has some rags on them that you see" ("Narrative" 24 October 1846: 1). Each contemporary reader was thus left with a critical first impression of Ireland that spoke to their own futures: dire poverty can so easily exist alongside extravagant wealth.

From the start of McGregor's account, we become aware that the English public's perception of Ireland has been continually sanitized. There is the obvious reference to the *Times* correspondent, and how his accounts are unrecognizable to the traveler. But even before McGregor arrives in Ireland, he encounters a British soldier who expresses the prevailing attitude towards the Irish, at a time when the extent of the famine was becoming known to the British public. Spilsby informs the traveler, without any invitation or provocation to share his insights, that the famine is merely the expression of the Irish character:

> Famine, I was assured, was but a natural consequence of the laziness and turbulence of the people, who preferred giving their last farthing to the REPEAL RENT, in the hope of becoming participants in the general plunder promised by Mr. O'Connell, OF IRELAND TO THE IRISH ("Narrative" 17 November 1846: 1).

A legitimate desire for self-governance is dismissed as an immoral money grab, and the deaths of thousands becomes the natural result of their own moral deficiencies. All political dissent is instinctively reduced to terror, whether in the form of communism as suggested by Spilsby, as well as by Leech's "A Social Sketch," or republicanism in so many other commentaries. Within the dominant discourse, political dissent is automatically at odds with the capitalist foundations of British society.

The morality of the Irish people remained a topic of much interest for an English press that wanted to distance their own moral responsibility from Irish woes, especially as the famine began to take hold. In their view, it was the idleness, the laziness of the Irish peasant, coupled with his violent republicanism, that had brought about the repeated famines of the nineteenth century. The famine could have potentially sunk the Land Plan if the public were to associate it with the system of small farms that prevailed in Ireland. For this reason, McGregor expresses an alternative understanding of the Irish character, one which locates the responsibility for the famine elsewhere:

> the present bearing of my mind inclining me to the conclusion, that the virtues of the Irish people are characteristics of their nature, while their vices are consequences of oppression and misrule. There has been much speculation as to the cause why Ireland should present the one solitary exception to the otherwise universal progress of civilization and improvement, and, in my opinion, the solution of the problem will be found in imperial misrule and neglect of domestic duties rather than in the unfitness of the Irish character to hold its place in the quick step of progression ("Narrative" 14 November 1846: 1).

Here, the narrator has finally discarded the prejudices by which he was taught to view the Irish and the (misrepresented) "condition of Ireland." As he attempts to rescue the Land Plan from the failure of the Irish small farm system, the author allows that most despised figure – the Catholic priest – to reveal where the blame lies.

As Father O'Farrell spells out the grievances of the Irish, the Chartist defense of Ireland becomes explicit. Most evident is that fixity of tenure is necessary to protect the value of labor, so that improvements to the land can benefit the worker, rather than the "unnatural proprietor," the middle man, the land agent. Since custom fixed certain moral duties to the ownership of the land, the tenantry could be protected, and the small farm system succeed, only if the responsibilities of the landlords were to be fully realized. Following from this, the rest of the evils would naturally disappear, as the educated laborer would come to demand the protection of the Charter. McGregor responds to this proposed remedy by parroting the tenets that defend the British system, at the cost of the laborer. Countering that political economy is no more than "the showman's puzzle, the merchant's philosophy, the trader's ready reckoner, and the poor man's thief," O'Farrell craves an alternative utopian political economy:

> Believe me, sir, the basis of the science of political economy – if any such science ever shall exist – must be equality, reciprocity, mutuality, and legislative regulation, where vendor and purchaser can meet upon equal terms in the mart of representation, while the very fact of capricious laws being called in aid of the principle, proves that it is a delusion, a mockery, and a snare ("Narrative" 26 December 1846: 1).

O'Farrell thus opens with the conservative call for protectionism in lieu of the current policies of *laissez-faire* principles; but he moves beyond this, alluding to the cooperative principles at the center of the Chartist Land Plan, which seeks to place the common laborer "upon equal terms in the mart of representation" ("Narrative" 26 December 1846: 1).

It is with the death of the text's hero, Phelim O'Donnell, that the hope of the small farm system rests. For the Irish, it is too late, as O'Donnell's wake announces its failure: "As we entered, and just in front of the door lay the father's hope, the mother's joy, the sister's protector, a cold, lifeless, bleeding corpse, stretched upon a bench, with a pillow under his head, covered with a white sheet, and his death bed hung round with linen" ("Narrative" 2 January 1847: 1). The hope promised by the Chartist Land Plan necessitates that Phelim's death lead not to expected failure, but to a redirection of the working people towards a better future. Recognizing the hostility directed by society towards the People's Charter, and understanding that the government would continually attempt to extinguish the dreams that the Charter enabled, meant that other avenues needed to be explored to attain the Charter as law. The "Narrative of Malcolm McGregor," therefore, reworks the representation of Ireland so that the English public, long resistant to viewing famine as anything other than a natural result of Irish depravity, could recognize the material impact that the English systems had on the ordinary lives of the O'Donnell family. This Irish nightmare, at once real and fictional, becomes a warning to the English people, and, the Chartists hoped, a recruiter for the English dream embodied by the Chartist Land Plan.

Works Cited

Airey, Glenn. *Feargus O'Connor 1842–1855: A Study of Chartist Leadership*. PhD Thesis. Staffordshire: Staffordshire University, 2003.
Baccolini, Raffaella, and Tom Moylan (eds). *Dark Horizons: Science Fiction and the Dystopian Imagination*. New York and London: Routledge, 2003.
Brown, Richard and Christopher Daniels (eds.). *The Chartists*. London: Macmillan, 1984.
Chase, Malcolm. *The People's Farm: English Radical Agrarianism, 1775–1840*. Oxford: Clarendon, 1988.
Claeys, Gregory. *Citizens and Saints: Politics and Anti-Politics in Early British Socialism*. Cambridge: Cambridge University Press, 1989.
Connolly, James. *Labour in Ireland*. Dublin: Maunsel and Company, 1917.
Davis, Graham. "Little Irelands." *The Irish in Britain, 1815–1939*. Ed. Roger Swift and Sheridan Gilley. London: Pinter, 1989. 104–33.
Fyson, Robert. "The Crisis of 1842: Chartism, the Collier's Strike and the Outbreak in the Potteries." *The Chartist Experience: Studies in Working-Class Radicalism and Culture, 1830–60*. London: Macmillan, 1982. 194–220.
Geoghegan, Vincent. "Ralahine: An Irish Owenite Community (1831–1833)." *International Review of Social History* 36.3 (1991): 377–411.
"Grand Demonstration on the 17th of August, 1846, To the People's First Estate, O'Connorville." *Northern Star* 22 August 1846: 1.
Kellner, Douglas and Harry O'Hara. "Utopia and Marxism in Ernst Bloch." *New German Critique* 9 (Autumn 1976): 11–34.
Leech, John. "A Social Sketch, or, Everything in Common." *Punch's Pocket Book for 1850*. London: Punch, 1850.
McGregor, Malcolm [pseudonym]. "The Narrative of Malcolm McGregor." *Northern Star* 17 October 1846: 1; 24 October 1846: 1; 14 November 1846: 1; 26 December 1846: 1; 2 January 1847: 1.
Moylan, Tom. *Scraps of the Untainted Sky: Science Fiction, Utopia, Dystopia*. Oxford: Westview, 2000.
"The National Land and Labour Bank." *Northern Star* 26 December 1846: 1.
O'Connor, Feargus. *A Practical Work on the Management of Small Farms*. 1843. 7th edn. Manchester: Abel Heywood, 1847.
Sargent, Lyman Tower. "The Three Faces of Utopianism Revisited." *Utopian Studies* 5.1 (1994): 1–37.

Saville, John. "Introduction." *History of the Chartist Movement 1837–1854*. 1894. Robert George Gammage. New York: Augustus M. Kelley, 1969. 5–66.

Spenser, Edmund. *A View of the State of Ireland*. Ed. Andrew Hadfield and Willy Maley. Oxford: Blackwell, 1997.

Thompson, Dorothy. *The Chartists*. London: Temple Smith, 1984.

Varsam, Maria. "Concrete Dystopia: Slavery and Its Others." *Dark Horizons*. Ed. Baccolini and Moylan. 203–25.

Wegner, Phillip E. "Where the Prospective Horizon is Omitted: Naturalism and Dystopia in *Fight Club* and *Ghost Dog*." *Dark Horizons*. Ed. Baccolini and Moylan. 167–87.

Lucian M. Ashworth

The League of Nations as a Utopian Project: The Labour Party Advisory Committee on International Questions and the Search for a New World Order

The Question of Global Utopia

Why are there so few international utopias? The study and formulation of international utopias suffer from two prejudices. First, in the subject of International Relations, "utopian" has become such a pejorative term that writers are keen to avoid any association with it. Experts on the international like to see themselves as "practical people." Second, the study of utopias themselves often concentrates on the local community, and here the international and global are often presented as evil antiutopian forces from outside. The most recent manifestation of this latter tendency is the persistent use of "globalization" as a disparaging term for external influences. The global is presented as a threat, not an opportunity. Groups labeled as utopian are often those that work at local levels. Even Lyman Tower Sargent's summation of utopianism, while it does not necessarily exclude global utopias, implicitly favors the local (see "Three Faces"). While it is true that the ideology of these groups might often be described as "acting locally, thinking globally," this is not enough to make them global. Acting locally, thinking globally all too easily becomes "acting locally, dodging globally." Global issues and alternatives become distant aspirations that are seen as at best secondary to the establishment of ideal relationships between people and groups within a narrow and circumscribed area. The perfect community soon resembles a gated community, wherein the ideal existence of the local few stands out against the vast mass of unreformed humanity.

Yet, there have been international utopian plans in the past. From the early seventeenth century to the late nineteenth a cross-section of European intellectuals dreamed of a perfect organization for the world as a whole. A few, such as Eméric Crucé or the Duc de Sully, appeared in the seventeenth century in response to the viciousness of the wars between the newly centralized states. In the next two centuries, Comenius, William Penn, the Abbé de Saint-Pierre, and Immanuel Kant all created plans for an ideal and peaceful world. Yet, this said, global utopias have always been a poor cousin to their more territorially limited brethren, and for two very good reasons. First, so many of the global utopian schemes have centered on a particular dynastic or national interest. Any international utopia was initially an object of suspicion by others. Second, a global utopia, almost by definition, requires the consent of a large section of the world's community, and consequently so many of those earlier utopias remained nothing more than grand schemes of the mind. This might also account for why so many fell back on the local when attempting to put their ideas into practice. For both of these reasons the relatively few international utopias remained first and foremost intellectual exercises.

The major change in these attitudes to the global utopia came in the nineteenth and early twentieth centuries. Two fundamental changes altered people's attitudes to the possibilities for a global utopia. The first of these was the steady growth of new intellectual paradigms in the nineteenth century that combined a belief in the progression of humanity towards better worlds with a sometimes-naive faith in human science and potential. The second change was the First World War. Prior to 1914, it was possible for large numbers of educated people in the west to regard the development of a better international system as a leisurely aspiration. The Great War suggested that, unless the world was thoroughly reordered, human conflict would very soon wipe out the species. While the First World War concentrated the minds of opinion formers and practitioners in the major western capitals, it was equally influential among those in the smaller states and the non-western world, who felt that their exclusion from major international decisions had had an important part to play in the march to war. This helped overcome the fear of the domination of sectional interests. So it was that the idea of the League of Nations came to fruition. Although clearly a western idea backed by the victorious great powers, it was also a project that was attractive to the smaller and the non-western nations. This convergence, along with the comprehensiveness of the project, makes the League of Nations interesting as the first serious attempt to create a global utopia to replace the obviously flawed pre-1914 international anarchy. The League was utopian in the sense that, consistent with Ruth Levitas's definition of utopia, it represented a desire to bridge the gap "between the needs and wants generated by a particular society and the satisfactions available to and distributed by it" (189). The League was always a work in progress, and was never held up, even by its most enthusiastic supporters, as a complete and finished work. While this contradicts the vulgar view of utopianism as the urge to impose perfection, it is now generally accepted in utopian studies that most utopias are presented as works in progress, rather than blueprints (see Sargent 9). Thus, the literature on the League fits neatly into the broader definitions in utopian studies of what constitutes a utopia.

In this essay, I will look at the development of the League as a global utopia by concentrating on the work carried out by a group of international experts associated with the British Labour Party. The problem with evaluating all of the ideas of the League's supporters is that they form such an amorphous and polyglot mass that there is little uniformity in their ideas about the form and shape of the League. Also, their connections with policy formulation vary greatly. The advantage of concentrating on a smaller, more cohesive group is that it allows me to reconstruct a more coherent set of policies and plans. I will therefore concentrate on the group of international experts and scholars that made up the Labour Party Advisory Committee on International Questions. Among these experts were people who were recognized at the time as among the top experts on international affairs. They included J.A. Hobson, Leonard Woolf, Norman Angell, Philip Noel-Baker, Hugh Dalton, H.N. Brailsford, and William Arnold-Forster. Their work is utopian insofar as they imagined new worlds in which the problems of war and global insecurity were eliminated. Yet, unlike the global utopias of earlier eras, their speculations were designed to be applied concretely through the League of Nations. They also had direct access to British Labour Party policy, and consequently saw many of their ideas become party, and sometimes government, policy. E.H. Carr referred to the period between 1924 and 1931 as the period of pacification: "these years, with all their uncertainties and imperfections, were the golden years of post-war Europe" (81). Many of the major problems from the era of the Peace Treaties – the French occupation of the Ruhr, German reparations, Franco-German hostility, and German and Soviet exclusion from international intercourse – would all find solutions during this period. While there were hotspots of instability, there appeared to be no major threats to international stability. This was true even after the 1929 Wall Street Crash had sparked an economic crisis (Carlton 59). On a number of occasions, the League was able to prevent a crisis becoming a full-blown war. With no major threats to world peace, and the machinery of the League gaining respect through regular use, the potential for the construction of an alternative international order around the League and its specialized agencies seemed eminently possible and practical. The stability and relative prosperity of the period, not to mention the successes of the League system, made the discussion of an alternative and pacific world order a practical and reasonable undertaking. It was only after 1931 that the League faced problems it was not equipped to solve.

This spirit was reflected by the Advisory Committee's submission of a twenty-three page memorandum in 1923 on the need for a League foreign policy in the Party. Here the Advisory Committee's position anticipated the 1924 Labour Government's policy towards the League in a number of key respects. A central part of the memorandum's analysis of the League and its structures was the acceptance that for the foreseeable future the League would have to remain as a free association of states, rather than a federal organization. The memorandum pointed out that a fully fledged federation would entail "the mechanical and psychological difficulties of federating all nations, with their different traditions, their different systems of government, languages, levels of culture, ways of thought, and so forth" ("Need for a League Policy" 6). Rather, the memo envisaged a slow aggregation of the principle of free association extending to cooperation between "supreme economic organs" of government, to the development of interparliamentary cooperation and the extension of the role of non-voting technical experts in the League's organs ("Need for a League Policy", 6, 9, 10). Utopia would be achieved by stealth.

Behind this advice lay the further assumption that, despite the continued existence of state sovereignty, the states of the world had become dependent on each other. As a result, the international anarchy associated with the old diplomacy was counter-productive; and the crucial question was what could be done to build a security structure that could best serve the interdependent world that now existed. There was general agreement among Labour advisors and leaders that as long as sovereign states were the political reality then the development of some kind of system of peaceful arbitration, coupled with disarmament, was necessary. The main fault line in the party was over the question of whether there needed to be any sanctions – including, if necessary, military sanctions against aggressor states that refused to abide by League arbitration.

Disarmament, Arbitration, and Sanctions

In Europe as a whole one of the major debates in international policy between 1922 and 1931 was over the question of the relationship between disarmament, arbitration, and League sanctions (economic and military). Ostensibly this was about closing gaps in the League *Covenant*, but it also marked a major split between two views of how the League should work. A number of the Advisory Committee memoranda dealt with the issue of disarmament, arbitration, and sanctions, whether separately or together; and one of the biggest disagreements on the Committee revolved around the issue of defining sanctions. Related to this was a common realization that the *Covenant* of the League, rather than being a fully functioning guarantor of peace, was no more than a work in progress. The *Covenant* had made it a requirement of membership that disputes "likely to lead to rupture" be submitted to arbitration, judicial inquiry, or inquiry by the League Council (Article 11), and had made the immediate severance of trade and financial links between League members and an aggressor state mandatory (Article 16). Yet definitions of terms and the proper procedures were left vague.

There were at least five recognized gaps in the *Covenant*. First, there was no clear definition of aggressor in the *Covenant*; second, while arbitration and other peaceful methods of dispute settlement were mentioned, it was not clear what the correct procedure would be in different disputes; third, while disarmament "to the lowest point consistent with national safety and the enforcement by common action of international obligations" was made a condition of membership in Article 8, there was no definition of the "lowest point," and no discussion of the mechanisms to be employed to bring about disarmament; fourth, the *Covenant* had not fully removed the right of a state to go to war unilaterally; and, finally, the nature of appropriate sanctions in the event of aggression was not spelled out. Linked to the second point was the question of the validity of the Permanent Court of International Justice, and especially the signing of the Optional Clause, by which the signatory state would recognize the decisions of that Court as binding. Many of these issues lay unresolved in 1931, when the full force of the economic depression hit the world economy. In this sense, the League, as the first serious attempt to create a truly global security organization, was very much a work in progress during its first decade. Statesmen were still unsure how it should be used, and League officials were managing an organization whose powers were as unclear as they were unprecedented. Thus, the League did not enter the 1930s fully equipped to deal with the problem of aggression. Rather, after eleven years of existence, it was still being developed. In 1927, Noel-Baker asked if the League's institutions would "be given time to build up their strength before the catastrophe of a new war sweeps them all away?" (*League of Nations at Work* 131). Six years before Adolf Hitler's coming to power, even the strongest of the League's supporters knew that there was much work to be done before the League was up to the test of a serious war-threatening crisis.

Of course, these five "gaps" were all related. In fact, from the point of view of the majority on the Advisory Committee disarmament, arbitration and sanctions formed an inter-related triangle in which one could not be realized without the other two (see Noel-Baker, *Geneva Protocol* 13–9; Mitrany, *International Sanctions* 2). Disarmament was not going to be a serious prospect until a system of arbitration and conciliation that removed the necessity for armed defense had been put in place. The question of arbitration and conciliation carried with it the question of what to do if the methods of peaceful resolution failed. The issue of economic and military sanctions also affected the discussions of disarmament: what level of arms would be required by a sanctions regime; and in the absence of a sanctions regime would smaller states feel that disarmament was not an option? Sanctions also introduced the thorny issue of the definition of aggression. Prior to 1931, the sharpest split in Labour's ranks in the foreign policy field was over the question of whether the League needed the power of sanctions in order to make arbitration and disarmament a reality within the League system. While Labour remained very much a pro-League party, the question of sanctions left the pacifist wing deeply suspicious and worried about the prospect of a future "League war," while the hard core of radical socialists continued to see the League, as it had done in the immediate post-Peace period, as a predominantly capitalist organization unworthy of support. Not surprisingly, given the importance of the issues involved, the relationship between arbitration, sanctions, and disarmament in the building of an effective League-based alternative to the international anarchy were frequently discussed in the Advisory Committee.

The basic idea behind international arbitration was the substitution of an effective system of peaceful change for the reliance on war as the primary arbitrator of disputes between states. A major distinction was made between conciliation, in which the parties would be brought together through a third party such as the League Council, and arbitration, in which a legally binding decision would be made by an appropriately competent body. Thus, at its core, arbitration assumes that a state would be willing, under international agreement, to waive its sovereign right to be judge and jury in its own case in order to maintain peace. Article 12 of the *Covenant* mentioned arbitration as one of three possible peaceful dispute settlements open to its members, the other two being judicial settlement and inquiry by the League Council. Article 14 of the *Covenant* required the parties to establish the Permanent Court of International Justice, which could be the arbiter of all judicial disputes between states once the states involved signed up to the Optional Clause that obligated the state to accept the rulings of the Court. Discussions of the place of arbitration during the interwar period divided conflicts between states into judicial and non-judicial (or political) disputes. There was widespread agreement in the Advisory Committee that judicial disputes, which involved clear-cut cases of international law, could and should be submitted to the Permanent Court (see Arnold-Forster, "Commentary").

This is not to say that there were not concerns about the success of arbitration, even for judicial disputes, among Advisory Committee members. In fact, one of the most influential books written during the First World War on the reform of international relations, Woolf's *International Government*, advocated arbitration with reservations. Arbitration could only be used for cases that could be phrased in a legal form; and the conservative nature of the law made it unlikely, at least in the foreseeable future, that states without a vested interest in the *status quo* would accept a wholly legal arbitration regime. The answer for Woolf lay in the option of taking the case to an international conference instead, and in giving states more of a say in the shape of the tribunal (*International Government* 52–9). Despite Woolf's concern, the development of the Permanent Court, and the Optional Clause that committed states to accepting the Court's decisions, gave the League system the means of settling judicial disputes between states.

A more vexing question was the issue of non-legal disputes, where the Permanent Court would not have the jurisdiction or the competence to adjudicate. The Labour Party, largely through the work of Advisory Committee members, was committed to the creation of an all-inclusive arbitration regime that would include non-legal disputes. If the settling of legal disputes was possible but problematic, the settling of non-legal disputes in a world of selfish states appeared daunting. Despite his reservations about arbitration during the war years, Woolf collaborated with Arnold-Forster in 1927 on a draft convention that would lay out the possible shape of a system of arbitration for non-legal disputes. The League of Nations, as it stood, had a system of resolving non-legal disputes through conciliation. Conciliation was not binding, and it did not involve a renunciation of the use of force by the parties involved (Arnold-Forster and Woolf 1). Woolf and Arnold-Forster's proposals involved a long process in which the dispute would go first to the Permanent Conciliation Commission of the League, then to the League Council, and finally to a committee of arbitrators agreed to by the parties. Throughout the process, "the parties undertake that, under no circumstances will they attack or invade each other's territory or resort to war unless in the fulfillment of their obligations as members of the League of Nations" (Arnold-Forster and Woolf 2–3). Obviously the whole proposal rested on the willingness of the parties to renounce war. In a limited way this had already been accomplished through the various bilateral arbitration treaties that had come in to force between a number of states during the late nineteenth and early twentieth centuries. These treaties, encouraged by the League, had bound various states to settle bilateral differences through arbitration. Britain had such a treaty with Uruguay, while the treaty between France and the United States was the subject of much discussion in Labour Party circles (see Arnold-Forster, "Note"). In the final analysis, though, arbitration seemed unlikely to work as a stand-alone system of pacific settlement. The solution was to tie arbitration to a sanctions regime.

The position of those who supported League sanctions was summarized by Dalton in 1928: "Some provision for sanctions and coercive action [...] is a logical requirement of any legal system, it takes human shape in police and judges" (211). This was far from being a universally accepted position in the Party, and it was deeply criticized by both the pacifist and radical socialist wings: the former because sanctions still entrenched violence; the later because they gave teeth to what was still regarded as a capitalist-run organization. Arthur Ponsonby supplemented his pacifist convictions with the view that the inability to define aggression accurately ruled out the value of sanctions for the League (106–9). The Geneva Protocol, discussed below, did provide a clear definition of aggressor – as those who refused to submit their dispute to arbitration while also engaging in hostilities – and from the point of view of the supporters of sanctions this remained clear and definitive (see Arnold-Forster, "Sanctions" 5n; Noel-Baker, *Geneva Protocol* ch. 7). C.R. Buxton took a different line, arguing that it was extremely unlikely that there was a will to use military sanctions in the Labour Party, the country as a whole, and the Dominions. He was willing to countenance economic sanctions, but he felt that, on the whole, it was best to concentrate on the less contentious issues of arbitration and disarmament (see Buxton, "Sanctions").

At a minimum, it was pointed out that the whole League system rested on sanctions, and would continue to do so as long as there was still the threat of the outbreak of private war by one state against another. Article 16 of the *Covenant* made economic sanctions mandatory in the event of aggression, and the threat of League sanctions had worked on minor belligerents in 1922 against Serbian troops and 1925 against the Greeks (see Arnold-Forster "Sanctions" 3-4; Mitrany, "Labour Policy" 2). Noel-Baker argued that at a bare minimum an effective sanctions regime would reduce the risk of war by deterring possible aggressors (*Geneva Protocol* 133). A more positive reason was the continued likelihood of war, and the consequent insecurity of many states, including many of the minor powers. The threat of sanctions was the only means the League had of guaranteeing that the *Covenant* would be respected (Arnold-Forster, "Sanctions" 3). Because many smaller states, and even larger ones like France, felt deeply insecure a strong sanctions regime presented the only alternative to the build-up of arms. In other words, an effective sanctions regime would be the only way to wean many states off relying on their own force of arms for defense, and consequently without sanctions there could be no comprehensive international disarmament or arbitration regime (see Arnold-Forster, "Sanctions" 4; Mitrany, "Labour Policy" 2; Mitrany, *International Sanctions* 2).

The use of military sanctions was a more vexing issue. For Dalton, the use of the military should be "our last line of defense […]. But it is not possible to wipe it off the map" (235) For David Mitrany, military sanctions "must remain an extreme measure, to be adopted only in exceptional circumstances" (*International Sanctions* 27) This necessity of some form of military threat in the background was given a slightly different twist by Arnold-Forster, who argued that economic sanctions itself might require the enforcement of a naval blockade, and thus extensive use of the military, if it was to be effective ("Sanctions" 8). A final note of caution was voiced by Mitrany. While he supported sanctions, and saw them as indispensable to the League system, he was worried that obligatory sanctions might encourage states, unwilling to contribute to a sanctions regime, to "hamper the peace machinery of the League" (Mitrany, "Labour Policy" 2). Thus, while "it is doubtful whether the League could keep the peace without sanctions," their success, and consequently the success of the system of arbitration rested uncomfortably on the willingness of states to act (Mitrany, "Labour Policy" 7).

All members of the Party could agree that the ultimate end was disarmament. Arms were seen as a product of the wasteful system associated with the international anarchy, and created instability by their very existence (see Dalton 145; Noel-Baker, *Disarmament* 16–23; Madariaga, *Disarmament* 2–12). Even before 1914, writers like Angell had written that armaments, by bringing security to the holder but insecurity to everyone else, actually increase the levels of insecurity in the world (*Foundations* 163–93). The security of armaments can only be relative to the armaments of your potential opponents. For Noel-Baker, the value of disarmament was two-fold: it would save national resources for more productive enterprises, and would ease international tensions by reducing states' abilities to wage aggressive war abroad (*Disarmament* 7).

Ironically, the much hated Versailles Treaty offered an excellent precedent and template for disarmament in the arms limitation provisions imposed on Germany. The caps on German armaments were justified by the Allies at the time as being consistent with Germany's defense and security, and it therefore followed for many advocates of disarmament that the reduction of the rest of the world's arms to a level commensurate with Germany's was a reasonable proposition. By reducing all arms down to the level of the defeated powers, it was believed that the sense of grievance felt by Germany and her former allies towards the Allies and the peace treaties would be sharply reduced (Noel-Baker *Disarmament* 24). Unfortunately, such disarmament to Germany's level remained a pipe dream as long as France felt that her armaments were necessary for her security. France continued to link disarmament to a guarantee of its security, whether that was adequate League sanctions or a system of military guarantees. As Angell put it: "The reef upon which every scheme of Disarmament so far has been shipwrecked is Defence, Security" ("Behind These Failures" 4). Thus, progress in disarmament was once again linked up to the question of inclusive arbitration and effective sanctions. Some have even speculated whether acceptance of the Geneva Protocol in 1924 would have given the push needed to carry disarmament through (see Carlton 73).

The Geneva Protocol was the First Labour Government's major contribution to the development of the League of Nation's system. Although it never came in to force, the Protocol remained the template for future agreements and the basis of Labour's policy during the Second Labour Government. In essence it was an attempt to close several of the gaps in the *Covenant*, and through that closure to reassure France that she would not be left to face any future German aggression alone. The *Covenant* had left the process of the pacific settlement of disputes vague, and under Article 12 the right to go to war was merely suspended for three months while the dispute was submitted to arbitration or conciliation. Article 16 only required the members to cease trade, finance, and general intercourse between League members and an aggressor. France wanted a cast-iron guarantee of immediate military aid in the event of aggression.

The Protocol was an articulation of the view that disarmament, arbitration, and League sanctions represented mutually supporting pillars of an alternative world order. It laid down a clear system for the arbitration of disputes and added to this a clear definition of aggressor based on a state's failure to accept arbitration or conciliation in a dispute likely to lead to rupture (Noel-Baker, *Geneva Protocol* 18). Arbitration was seen as the means by which security and disarmament could be linked, since a system of arbitration would provide a means of defining aggressor states that should be the subject of sanctions, while both reducing tensions and the need for a state to possess a preponderance of military might in order to guarantee its security. Thus, the Protocol proved that aggression could be defined within a regime of arbitration and conciliation (Arnold-Forster, "Sanctions" 5). The most important thing in the Protocol, from the French point of view, was the provision of League sanctions in the event of aggression, although it fell short of making full military sanctions obligatory. Sanctions by the League members would be compulsory against an aggressor. This was key not only to get France to agree to disarmament, but it was also seen as necessary if the members of the League were to be weaned off relying solely on their own military might for security, and thus to be encouraged to reduce their armaments and armed forces to an acceptable international policing level.

The members of the Advisory Committee were vocal in their support for the Protocol's linkage of disarmament, arbitration, and sanctions. Noel-Baker's book-length treatment of the Protocol is a good example of this. Looking back to the events of 1924 in a letter to James Ramsay MacDonald, Arnold-Forster wrote that

> Some of our friends still think we can achieve radical disarmament without having to think about [compulsory] arbitration, and without having to accept the responsibilities of pooled security. But your way, the Protocol's way, is the only one between Scylla and Charybdis ("Letter to James Ramsay MacDonald" 1).

J.A. Hobson was willing to trumpet publicly that League sanctions were a necessary part of dispute settlement (79–80).

Although the incoming Conservative Government finally announced in March 1925 that it would not sign the Protocol, aspects of the Protocol were included in the Treaty of Locarno. Unlike the Geneva Protocol, the Locarno Treaty was signed and ratified, and therefore became fully operational. What perhaps took Locarno beyond the Protocol, however, was that it included Germany as an equal partner with Britain and France, and thus paved the way for German membership of the League with a permanent seat on the Council. Both of these were goals of Labour foreign policy. Yet, in so many ways it was still only a half measure. In July 1925, the Advisory Committee worried that Locarno, while not an old-style alliance, might be "a return to the system of partial alliances" ("Report of the Sub-Committee" 1).

By the time Labour returned to power in 1929, the gaps in the League *Covenant* were still apparent, despite the attempts to tighten up the mechanisms and definitions in the *Covenant*. The Protocol's definition of aggression had found wide acceptance among the international community, while the principle of arbitration had largely been accepted, even if the specific mechanisms of it were not. One of the biggest gaps in the *Covenant* remained the failure of many states to sign up to the Optional Clause, which committed its signatories to recognize the decisions of the Permanent Court of International Justice on legal disputes between states. Another was the failure of the various attempts at general disarmament, despite the continued application of the disarmament clauses of the peace treaties, which continued to limit the military power of the defeat states to a level consistent with defense and internal security. In effect, the Locarno Pact had not been built on. In 1929, it still seemed reasonable that a mood of goodwill could be exploited in the service of firming up the provisions of the *Covenant*.

Under Advisory Committee influence, the Labour Government of 1929–1931 signed up to both the Optional Clause and the General Act, finally committing Britain to an all-inclusive arbitration regime, while the Disarmament Conference was finally scheduled to begin deliberations in 1932. The major failure was in the area of sanctions, and the firming up of the provisions of the *Covenant* on the matter of the legality of war. For the *Covenant* to work effectively, and for arbitration to replace war as a means of settling disputes, there had to be effective sanctions to guarantee the security of states. Only then could disarmament be comprehensive. Thus, once again, comprehensive disarmament was undermined by insecurity created by the weakness of the sanctions provisions in the *Covenant*. In 1924, such vagueness would have been of little consequence; but in 1931 they proved disastrous, for 1931 was the year that the global financial system broke down. In the short term, this brought down the Labour Government in Britain, and in the longer term it paved the way for the victory of the Nazi Party in Germany. And, 1931 was also the year that the first of the great powers challenged the authority of the League.

The Rise of the Dictators and the Weaknesses of League Security

The failure of the League of Nations has now become the stuff of legend, and its failure has usually been linked to the idea of the League itself, rather than to specific circumstances. In fact, the main problem with the League was that there had been so little time in which to develop its security arrangements. The *Covenant* was vague on so many details, and the attempts to construct a functioning pooled security regime, founded on arbitration, sanctions, and disarmament were still at an early stage in 1931 when the first major great power challenge to the League system struck. That the League's security system was not yet properly functioning allowed a certain amount of latitude among its members when dealing with aggression; and, consequently it was not difficult for a major power like Britain or France to bend the League towards its policy of appeasement of the dictators. In other words, as it stood in 1931, the *Covenant* and its ancillary agreements did not require any sustained or effective action from its membership in the face of a serious breech of the *Covenant*, with the possible exception of financial sanctions, while a clear definition of aggressor was yet to be agreed to by its full membership. So much was left vague that the pooled security arrangements of the League had to rely on the discretion of its most powerful members.

In September 1931, the Japanese authorities in the Chinese region of Manchuria launched an offensive against Chinese troops, and by January 1932 the Japanese had conquered all of Manchuria. The Chinese government appealed to the League. Despite the dispatch of a League Commission under Lord Lytton and the Japanese withdrawal from the League, the Japanese were not classed as aggressors, and no formal action was taken. Clearly the League had not prevented aggression, and this disappointment was felt among the Advisory Committee members. Soon after Japan's walkout at the League Assembly, the Advisory Committee assessed the damage done to the League by its failure to resolve the crisis. The first memo in March 1933 did not offer any policy prescriptions, but it was clear about the change that had occurred in the international situation to the detriment of the League ("Labour Party's Policy" 1–2). The second memo in April went into more detail. Central to it was the "necessity for the Party to redefine its attitude towards the League" ("Labour Party's Policy" 1). The failure of the League was seen as being inherent in its structure as a "League of Governments and it cannot be effective as an instrument of international peace unless the Governments of which it is composed are determined to use it as an instrument of co-operation, justice, and peace" ("Labour Party's Policy" 2–3). While the League had been badly shaken, the Advisory Committee was of the opinion that the League project was still worth advocating.

If the Advisory Committee regarded the Manchurian crisis as damaging to the League, it was the 1935–1936 Abyssinian crisis that undermined the League's authority as an effective vehicle for pooled security. It was this, rather than Manchuria that was, in the words of Woolf, "the final test [...] of the League of Nations and of what is called a system of collective security" for both the Government and the British public ("Meditation on Abyssinia" 17). Ironically, Italy had an arbitration treaty with Abyssinia signed in 1928, so that when Italian and Abyssinian troops clashed on the Abyssinian-Italian Somaliland border in December 1934 the League Council postponed the Abyssinian appeal subject to arbitration under the 1928 treaty. In September, the arbitrators reported that neither government could be held responsible for the clash; and with mounting evidence of Italy's preparation for war, the League began to consider Abyssinia's appeal. Britain, in the form of the Foreign Secretary Samuel Hoare, committed itself to fulfilling its obligations under the *Covenant*; but on 2 October 1935 Italy finally launched its invasion. By 19 October, the League had a clear plan of action that involved comprehensive economic sanctions under Article 16 of the *Covenant* (Carr 226). Yet, in the final analysis, limited economic sanctions proved unable to bring Italy's invasion to a halt, and by May 1936 Italy annexed Abyssinia. If Manchuria had highlighted the weaknesses of the League's structure and lack of a definition of aggressor, Abyssinia had shown that the sanctions regime lacked bite.

The arbitration and sanctions regime, which had developed so painfully slowly throughout the 1920s, now seemed defunct to many. As with the Manchuria crisis, the failure of the League was seen as residing both in a structure that made the League reliant on its members for effective action, and in the poor policies of the League's key members. Speaking in Geneva in August 1936, Herbert Morrison argued that the assumptions that had underpinned League success in the 1920s no longer existed, and as a consequence the "collective peace system" of the League now only existed on paper (see Morrison 1). For Woolf, writing for the Advisory Committee the following July, the various League failures had undermined both popular and state support for the League, leading to full rearmament as the only effective means of defense ("Memorandum on the Attitude" 6). In fact, as far as Woolf was concerned, in the absence of an effective League system the international situation would fall back on the *realpolitik* associated with the old international anarchy. This reality had to be accepted and worked with in the absence of an effective League system, and under a system dominated by the balance of power Britain's main competitor in Europe would be the stronger peace-threatening power, in this case Hitler's Germany ("Memorandum on an Immediate Policy" 1). This meant that the Labour Party needed to formulate a foreign policy that was independent of the League structures, but took into account the ideals of the League in the event of a possible future revival of a collective security system. Thus, a short-term policy of thwarting the aggression of the dictators should be coupled with the longer-term objective of recreating a collective security system ("Memorandum on an Immediate Policy" 1). In other words, a full-blown League system required the existence of certain international conditions to function effectively. In the absence of those conditions, Woolf argued, new policies were required that would take into account the existence of this international anarchy, while holding out the possibility of a return to a more stable and cooperative world order (see "The Resurrection of the League" 337–52; "Arms and Peace" 21–35; "The Ideal of the League Remains" 330–45). As early as 1936, the majority of Advisory Committee members had recognized that the League, in the short term, had ceased to function.

The League of Nations marked a dramatic break in the nature of global utopian thinking. Prior to 1914, global utopias had been intellectual exercises lacking a sense of urgency. The League was an exercise in the creation of a functioning global utopia that would replace the war-based system of states with a more legal and peaceful framework. The plans and policies of the Advisory Committee demonstrate how a League policy could be both practical and utopian. They were practical insofar as they were based on analyses of the nature of international life, but they were utopian in that they explored ways that new structures could be built over these realities. This practical aspect did not make this League policy any less utopian. If anything, the very real possibility of a League-run world heightened the desire, and made the dream more vivid. Yet the desire and the dream came with nagging doubts. Always deeply critical of those in power who failed to grasp the imperative for change, many of the Advisory Committee experts also predicted the collapse of the League if it was not given a clearer mandate with effective sanctions. In the end it was those parts of the League that lacked utopian vision – its system of cabinet representation; the gaps in the *Covenant* that allowed the international anarchy to continue largely unchecked – that was its downfall. Certainly, for the experts on Labour's Advisory Committee on International Questions the idea of the League remained the only serious and practical long-term solution to the problems of the lawless international realm.

Works Cited

Angell, Norman. "Behind These Failures." *Foreign Affairs* 11 (1928): 4.
_____ *Foundations of International Polity*. London: Heinemann, 1914.
_____ *The Great Illusion*. London: Heinemann, 1911.

____"Memorandum on the Reactionary Attitude of the Government in International Affairs." Advisory Committee on International Questions, Memo no. 341. Manchester: Labour Party Archives, November 1925.

Arnold-Forster, William. "Commentary on the British Government's Observations to the League on Arbitration and Security." Advisory Committee on International Questions, Memo no. 386. Manchester: Labour Party Archives, February 1928.

____Letter to James Ramsay MacDonald, 13 August 1927. Public Records Office. PRO 30/69/1170 (1) 429.

____"Note on the Franco-American and Anglo-American Arbitration Treaties." Advisory Committee on International Questions, Memo no. 387. Manchester: Labour Party Archives, February 1928.

____"Sanctions (Commentary on Mr. Buxton's Paper)." Advisory Committee on International Questions, Memo no. 365. Manchester: Labour Party Archives, May 1927.

Arnold-Forster, William, and Leonard Woolf. "Proposed Recommendation to the Executive Regarding a Convention for Pacific Settlement." Advisory Committee on International Questions, Memo no. 355a. Manchester: Labour Party Archives, Manchester, n.d.

Brailsford, H.N. "Arbitrate or Disarm. A New View of Security." *New Leader* 12 September 1924: 3.

Buxton, Charles Roden. "Memorandum on the Pact of Locarno." Advisory Committee on International Questions, Memo no. 340. Manchester: Labour Party Archives, October 1925.

____"Sanctions in the *Covenant* and the Protocol." Advisory Committee on International Questions, Memo no. 358. Manchester: Labour Party Archives, March 1927.

Carlton, David. *MacDonald versus Henderson. The Foreign Policy of the Second Labour Government*. London: Macmillan, 1970.

Carr, Edward Hallet. *International Relations between the Two World Wars (1919–1939)*. London: Macmillan, 1948.

Dalton, Hugh. *Towards the Peace of Nations. A Study in International Politics*. London: Routledge, 1928.

Hobson, John A. "What Outlawry of War Signifies." *Foreign Affairs* 6 (1924): 79–80.

"Labour Party's Policy with Regard to the League and Sanctions." Advisory Committee on International Questions, Memo no. 431a. Manchester: Labour Party Archives, March 1933.

"Labour Party's Policy Regarding the League of Nations." Advisory Committee on International Questions, Memo no. 433a. Manchester: Labour Party Archives, April 1933.

Levitas, Ruth. *The Concept of Utopia*. Syracuse: Syracuse University Press, 1990.

Lowes Dickinson, G. *The European Anarchy*. London: George Allen and Unwin, 1916.

de Madariaga, Salvador. *Disarmament*. London: Humphrey Milford/Oxford University Press, 1929.

"Memorandum on an Immediate Policy for the Party in Relation to the International Situation and Proposals for a New Security Agreement." Advisory Committee on International Questions, Memo no. 479a. Manchester: Labour Party Archives, April 1937.

"Memorandum on the Pact of Locarno." Advisory Committee on International Questions, Memo no. 340a. George Lansbury Papers. London School of Economics, November 1925.

Mitrany, David. "A Labour Policy on Sanctions." Advisory Committee on International Questions, Memo no. 366. Manchester: Labour Party Archives, May 1927.

____*The Problem of International Sanctions*. London: Humphrey Milford/Oxford University Press, 1925.

Morrison, Herbert. "A New Start with the League of Nations." Lecture delivered to the Geneva Institute of International Relations. Manchester: Labour Party Archives, ID/INT/3/1i. 21, August 1936.

____"Need for a League Foreign Policy." Advisory Committee on International Questions, Memo no. 287. Manchester: Labour Party Archives, 9 July 1923.

Noel-Baker, Philip. *The Geneva Protocol*. London: King & Son, 1925.

____*Disarmament*. London: Hogarth, 1926.

____*The League of Nations at Work*. London: Nisbet, 1927.

Ponsonby, Arthur. *Now is the Time. An Appeal for Peace*. London: Leonard Parsons, 1925.

"Report of the Sub-Committee on the Security Pact." Advisory Committee on International Questions, Memo no.339a. Labour Party Archives, July 1925.

Sargent, Lyman Tower. "The Three Faces of Utopianism Revisited." *Utopian Studies* 5.1 (1994): 1–37.

Woolf, Leonard. "Arms and Peace." *Political Quarterly*. 8 (1937): 21–35.

____*International Government*. London: George Allen and Unwin, 1916.

———"The Ideal of the League Remains." *Political Quarterly* 7 (1936): 330–45.

———"The League of Nations and Disarmament." Advisory Committee on International Questions, Memo no. 25. Manchester: Labour Party Archives, 1922.

———"Mediation on Abyssinia." *The Political Quarterly* 7 (1936): 16–32.

———"Memorandum on the Attitude which the Party should Adopt to Proposed Reforms of the League." Advisory Committee on International Questions, Memo no. 468. Manchester: Labour Party Archives, July 1936.

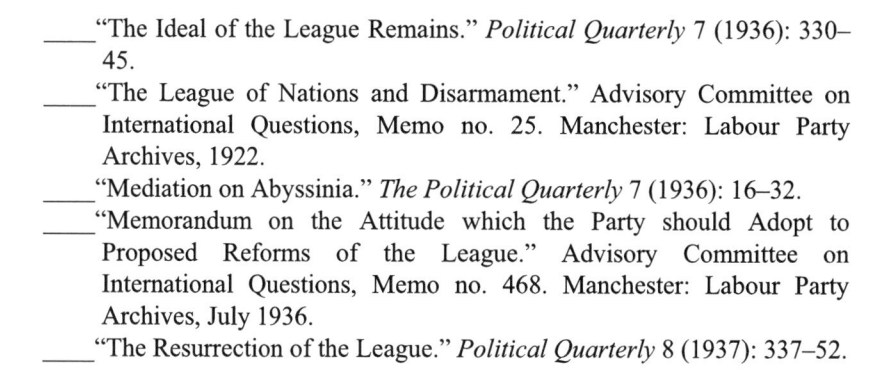

———"The Resurrection of the League." *Political Quarterly* 8 (1937): 337–52.

JENNY ANDERSSON

Beyond Utopia? The Knowledge Society and the Third Way

Politics beyond Utopia

The Third Way, as the central ideological project of contemporary social democracy – particularly its British strain – raises objections to the very term "Utopia."[1] The idea of Utopia defies the claim of the Third Wayers: namely, that "new" social democracy stands for a "new politics" defined precisely by its location beyond ideology and beyond utopian thinking. Indeed the term "utopia" is pejorative, for it denotes impossibility and not desirability. I argue in this essay that this Third Way position is related to the conceptualization, in British political discourse, of "new times" defined by economic and technological forces and the spread of knowledge and information. The logic of change in this new context is defined by the warp speed of creativity and by the logic of the silicon revolution, whereby the speed of information transmission constantly multiplies. In such a knowledge-based and individualized economic and social order, politics can no longer be about end-points because these would soon be overtaken by the pace of progress. The former Downing street advisor and Demos director, Geoff Mulgan, says:

> I mean I think that the idea that you describe an endpoint towards which you get, which was the popular idea of utopias in the seventeenth century, nineteenth century and so on, is simply incompatible with any society where

---

1   The political slogan of the Third Way has fallen from grace in the last years, but that does not necessarily mean that the kind of politics it referred to have been replaced by something else. I have therefore chosen to use the term.

knowledge plays a big role, because the nature of knowledge is to be dynamic, continually changing, and transformative, so there can't possibly be a vision of an endpoint, there can only be a vision of some of the processes controlling how that evolution happens. One of those is democracy, one of those is wid spread access to education, one of them maybe the market economy [...] all you can have a vision about are *the means of knowledge to constantly change everything else* (Interview, emphasis added).

The Third Way explicitly does not articulate a vision of the desired society. Rather, it understands change as a perpetual process of improvement of society, economy, self, and citizen, particularly through the expansion and accumulation of knowledge, understood as an infinitely dynamic factor that cannot be controlled, anticipated, or planned for, but constantly drives change into a higher gear.[2]

It would, however, be falling into a carefully laid-out rhetorical trap to think that this means that the Third Way is not a utopian project. The Third Way contains a series of utopic – in the sense both of hopeful and authoritarian – ideas around economy, society, and individual, some of which I will develop in the following pages. On a general level, the Third Way embodies a fundamental tension that springs to life when probed from the perspective of Utopia. This is the tension between its competing narratives of change – as adaptation to naturalized outside forces and an evolutionary economic and social process, on the one hand; and as ideological visions of a desired future, on the other. Within the very concept of "modernization," this tension takes the form of a vacillation between representations of the limits to change and representations of modernization as *will*. This tension-ridden concept of modernization is central to any understanding of the discourses that define not only the direction of change, progress, and desired change, as well as the role of social democracy as the carrier of change and the bringer of the future, but also the prevailing ideas of the limits and scope of the political project in contemporary political thinking. It reflects the paradox in historical utopian thought: that the desire to create a new world necessarily rests

---

[2] As the conceptual historian Koselleck has shown, this perception of accelerating change underpins modernity's notion of change and progress.

on the recognition that the world is essentially a social construction that can be changed, indeed destroyed; while, on the other hand, that reaching the new society is a process circumscribed by the limits posed by the old, which renders the project an inherently utopic dream in collision with the real world (see Ricoeur; Koselleck, *Vergangene Zukunft*). This tension between old and new is embodied in the very metaphor of a "Third Way," particularly in its aspiration to a space that transcends historical antagonisms. It is both spatial –between Left and Right in the political spectrum – and temporal – in the sense of having moved beyond history and of paving a way into the future, towards inherently *new times*. The Third Way, and its concept of modernization, locates ideological antagonism in a past of crisis and conflict and constructs modernization as a peaceful process of partnership, harmony, and reconciliation. In a sense, the very notion that it is possible for politics to move beyond a utopia towards some ideologically freed sphere of pragmatism is itself utopian, possibly bordering on the dystopic, in its rejection of the possibility of the Good Society.

This rejection of Utopia is a defining characteristic of "new politics," most prominently in British discourse, but not only in British discourse. The New Labour project is interesting not because it is an exception in contemporary politics, but because it takes to the extreme assumptions and truisms that lay at the core of contemporary politics more generally; for instance, in the insistence on dialogue and not conflict in the European Lisbon strategy. But political rejections of Utopia do not mean that politics are not utopic. Utopian thinking is at the heart of the art of politics and essential to the activity of thinking about the future, whether policy makers like it or not (see Beilharz).

In this essay, I make two claims. First, I make a claim for Utopia – for the act of thinking otherwise – as a vital, emancipatory, and deeply democratic function without which we are no longer talking of politics but of managerialism. The scrutiny of political utopias, silent or voiced articulations of the good society, is vital for such acts of thinking otherwise. This is the point of departure that informs my deconstruction of central claims in the Third Way. Second, I argue that the Third Way is in fact a utopia. It contains highly utopian ideas of what constitutes progress, of the requirements of individual and societal adaptation to the economy that progress brings, and of the political possibility to create an ideal knowledge-individual to inhabit this new economic and social sphere. To this extent, the Third Way is perhaps most accurately regarded as a *crypto-utopia*, a utopia that disguises itself as a non-utopia or an antiutopia. A crypto-utopia is a rhetorical device that, on the one hand, defies other utopias as detached from reality and reform but that, on the other hand, uses this rejection of Utopia as the platform for the construction of an alternative that is no less utopic but that comes forth as realizable, practical, and more inclusive in comparison. The history of the Left is full of such utopian constructions built around the depiction of other projects as "utopian." Indeed, Karl Marx famously rejected the utopian socialists with precisely such arguments (see Levitas, *Concept*).

It follows from my approach in this essay that the crypto-utopian tendency in Third Way discourse should be considered as highly problematic. It is problematic because it takes the existence of a common good as a given (as, I will argue, is the case in its approach to both community and capital), thereby ignoring the critical function of Utopia for political struggle, interest, and mobilization – all concepts that the Third Way regards as hopelessly outdated. Moreover, the relocation of ideology and Utopia, from dreams of a desired future to rejections of a crisis-ridden past, is in itself the very limit of the Third Way. This limit exists in terms of its incapacity to move from what Colin Hay has called "preference accommodation" to "preference shaping," or, in the language of current New Labour thinking, of moving from the Blairite language of adaptation to creating a progressive consensus or a new ethos that is capable of entrenching values of the good society (see Hay; and Compass). In other words, the deep paradox of the Third Way and particularly of the New Labour project, is that despite the spin there is a fundamental incapacity to realize the mobilizing role of political language in order to construct a different (better) future that is effectively for all, but that recognizes divergence, struggle, and the democratic role of plural future visions.

Making Ideology History: Modernization without *Telos*

The concept of modernization that informs New Labour thinking, even if it peaked in the late 1990s, stood in direct relationship to Blairism's interpretation of a new economic tide that would "simply roll over us" (Blair, *New Britain* 98). These new times demand new politics. The Third Way, as a project of ideological renewal, aims at producing new articulations of a new economy, a new society, and a new politics with new concepts of equality and justice, and even new citizens in a new contract between state, community, and individual.

A central element in this idea of modernization is that change represents progress. In the discussion of new politics, the term "modernization" became synonymous with pragmatism, in the service of progress. Modernization was about a technical or engineering outlook on politics, whereby political change and ideological rearticulation became defined as a pragmatic reconsideration of means, in some way detached from questions of values. New politics were about handling change, not about ideological "dogma" (see Blair; Cabinet Office; Nexus). New politics were consensus, dialogue, and partnership, and far from the conflicts around rivaling future visions (see Gray and Demos). Indeed, modernization was represented as a move away from the ideologies of the old, crisis-ridden, industrial society, and from the historical utopias of the "Good Society" that preoccupied social democracy in its past. "New politics" become defined by its break with "old" ideology; and pragmatism is regarded as something unideological and objective (see Finlayson).

Pragmatism, in this manner, takes the form of a historicisation of ideology, wherein ideology is relocated to a conflict-ridden past of clashing class interests. The perfect example of this was the "hyphenization" of ideology and socialism to "idea-ology" and "social-ism" in New Labour rhetoric in the mid 1990s to avoid two awkward terms but not lose their intellectual appeal altogether (see *Renewal*). "Idea-ology" was not a question of articulating a coherent worldview or an ontology of the social, but of coming up with a set of policy ideas and putting them together. "Social-ism" was not about providing a socialist critique of capitalism, but about laying a social gloss on economic features that were left more or less unchallenged. Neither term had much to say about the good future. Ideology is thus history and not future – decline, not progress. Ideology leads to crippled industrial relations, class wars, and vested interests, all symptoms of a deeply inefficient society. Modernization does not appeal to ideological values or collective visions of the Good Society, but rather to pragmatic values – those of fair play, reciprocity between rights and responsibilities, and concepts of Britishness that rely on presumptions of a common historical experience that somehow, it is hoped, will be a compass for the future (see Blair; Giddens; Miliband; Brown, "British Genius").

In this discourse, it is infinitely politically troublesome to talk of the Good Society in the postmodern age, after the social movements of the 1960s and 1970s, and in the individualized project of neoliberalism. Herein, "utopia" has become a pejorative term, one that denotes impossibility and not desirability and that as an intellectual project is regarded as both naïve and dangerously authoritarian. But what is left in notions of change, without articulations of a Good Society? In the words of Zygmunt Bauman, the contemporary modernization ethos is a modernization narrative without *telos* (Bauman 29, emphasis added). Change itself becomes the centrality of the modernization narrative; while meta-narratives of the Good Society, of the end point, are downplayed. Arguably there are two crucial elements in this process. One is the shift from end to motion, whereby the process of change becomes more important than the question of where change leads. The other is a discursive individualization of modernity, whereby change becomes a question both of individual adaptation to economic and technological forces, but through which the whole point of change is also conceptualized as a process of individual gains. The idea of self-fulfillment replaces the old place of collective future visions. Utopia moves from the sphere of political thought and collectivity to the individual sphere of personal dreams and aspirations.

The idea of the knowledge economy/knowledge society appeals to exactly such a modernization ethos without *telos*. Despite the rhetorical mobilizing capacities of the metaphor of the Knowledge

Society, the discourse of modernization that it is intimately bound up with does not explicitly articulate a vision of the desired society. As with many pervasive future visions, the metaphor of the "Knowledge Society" has the double capacity of signifying both end and process, since it refers both to the outcome of the process of modernization and to the process of modernization itself. This double meaning is most clearly expressed in the adjacent metaphor, "the Learning Society," as it denotes both a future utopia of the Knowledge Society and the "learning" process of getting there. To this extent, this parallel metaphor is inseparable both from the concept of modernization and its normative, empirical, and political claims, and from the metaphor of the Third Way, in itself an inherently utopic and liminal nowhere (see Bastow and Martin). This connotation of both process and end is in a way similar to 1950s and 1960s conceptualizations of the industrial society as both a process of economic transformation and as an end-point of economic and social maturity. However, its rejection of the Good Society sets it apart from the historical utopias of socialism, even as it also shares many of the elements of historical utopian thinking, social engineering, and rationalization discourses. Modernization in the post-World War Two period was a narrative with an end-point. It drew on ideas of a stadial or linear development, which led to the completion of the Welfare State as a collective project of the Good Society. The idea of the Knowledge Economy/Society certainly relies on a stadial model of development, and to that extent it contains pervasive assumptions of the logic of historical change and progress. However, it is more uncertain as to whether this current moment is really the final stage of capitalism (because of the capacity of knowledge to constantly reinvent itself); and rather it speaks of change as a perpetual and neverending process of improvement – both in terms of the aggregate level of economic expansion, growth, and productivity, and in terms of the learning self.

Infinite Knowledge, Infinite Justice

Beneath its self-proclaimed realism, the vision of the Knowledge Society contains themes that are inherently utopic, and that stand in continuity with the history of social democratic utopias and their quest for efficiency, productivity, growth, social harmony, and equality (see Beilharz). For instance, there is the idea of prosperity and of expansion more or less without limits.

Social democracy's postwar utopia of unlimited economic growth came to an end in the period following the late 1960s, as the ecological, social, ideological, and financial limits of industrial expansion came to the fore (see Sassoon). The politics of the Left became preoccupied with ideas of scarcity and austerity (see Pierson). But in Third Way discourse, knowledge is presumed to be an infinite and fluid resource that recreates the possibility of unlimited expansion, both in terms of economic productivity and in terms of individual growth and self-fulfillment, through learning and the increased access to knowledge and "opportunity" (see Leadbeater, *Living on Thin Air* and "Welcome to the Knowledge Economy"). Expansion, in the discourse of the knowledge economy, is conceptualized as a perpetual process of improvement, both in terms of productivity and economic growth and in terms of individual self-fulfillment and learning. While the definition of knowledge that makes up the discourse of the knowledge economy leans towards the economistic and utilitarian – and draws heavily on what might be called an enlightenment heritage of "useful knowledge" and a notion of improvement as linked to property, productivity, and profit – an economic expansion driven by knowledge is also presumed to lead to individual expansion and self-improvement, and positive social externalities in terms of a more learned and knowledgeable society (see Hodgson; Jessop; Meiksins Wood; Mokyr). There is, therefore, despite the many references to the risks of the skills revolution in contemporary political discourse, a silent but fundamental assumption that there is no conflict between the logic of a knowledge-driven industrial expansion on the one hand and social progress or individual wellbeing on the other. There is the idea that that knowledge leads beyond scarcity of material resources as well as beyond poverty of mind and that it also offers a way out of the crisis ridden politics of the last decades – because knowledge is an intangible good that leads away from the struggle over material goods.

The communitarian philosopher, Amitai Etzioni, has argued that the advent of the knowledge economy signifies the end of scarcity, since knowledge is an infinite resource and the organization of society and economy around knowledge thus curtails scarcity:

> Knowledge as a resource differs greatly from those relied upon in industrial societies—in that it can be shared and consumed many times over [...]. The more people satisfy their wants by drawing on free [sic] knowledge [by downloading files, playing chess on the internet or joining virtual self-help groups] the scarcer scarcity becomes [...]. There is a profound connection between fostering the knowledge economy and enhancing social justice. Most earlier theories of social justice are based on the idea of transferring large amounts of resources from the haves to the have-nots. This raises obvious political difficulties. However, to the extent that those whose basic needs are met draw their additional satisfaction from non-scarce resources, the door opens to a whole new world – in which the well off may well be less opposed to the transfer of material goods to the less well off. And those who have less could benefit from non-scarce knowledge resources, once the state and community ensure that they have the basic skills and resources needed to access the new world of knowledge. [...] The more we foster a transition to a knowledge based economy [...] the closer we come to living in a society that is driven less by scarcity – and is more equitable as a result (49).

There is thus the idea, reminiscent of the postwar conception that an expanding economic base permitted the infinite expansion of social justice, that the embracing of the transition to a knowledge-based economy will bring about new horizons for social justice and individual emancipation; the abolition of manual work in favor of "intelligent work" and the rise of skill- and network-based capitalism replaces the hierarchical division of labor and makes the worker a co-associate, a stakeholder, or an equal partner. The former British Chancellor of the Exchequer, Gordon Brown, has even suggested that the advent of the knowledge economy signifies a reversal of Marx's power relationship between labor and capital: labor is now free to exploit the capital put into the creation of knowledge in order to enhance its own value (*Fair Is Efficient* 4).

This idea of a positive relationship between economic expansion and productivity, on the one hand, and individual expansion and self-fulfillment, on the other, is obviously utopic; and it is strikingly familiar to historical socialist utopias of the industrial society. As these did, the Third Way contains a number of fundamental tensions. The first of these is the unwillingness to challenge the way that knowledge may be both created and redistributed in ways that perpetuate inequality – and here we can include the refusal to discuss questions of interest, ownership, and control. The second is that the tension between growth and wellbeing is ignored. The third is that the Third Way's idea of the knowledge society contains a fundamental tension in the way that it, despite the references to the knowledge economy as the end of scarcity and knowledge as a common good, tends to focus heavily on the primacy of competition and knowledge as a strategic resource, which ultimately suggests that it is inherently scarce in a zero-sum game between individuals and nations. This perception is reflected in dominant future metaphors in New Labour discourse of both Brown and Tony Blair, metaphors such as "the competitive society," "the electronic workshop," or "the race" (see Blair; Brown, "The Politics of Potential" and "Speech to the CBI National Conference").

Modernization as Harmony: Politics of Reconciliation

Third Way discourse contains a strong narrative of crisis and disjuncture. This crisis narrative is at the heart of the idea of the knowledge economy – often conceptualized as a new stage in a clear logic of capitalist development, driven by industrial revolutions in a three-step trajectory from the agrarian to the industrial economy to the knowledge economy. It thus tends to be understood in terms of an inevitable and linear process of change, rather than one possible outcome of an open-ended historical process (see Amin; Block). This assumption of a new stage in capitalism leads to the pervasive construction of a dichotomy between old and new, of revolution and crisis, and of a gap between the revolutionary pace of economic transformation and the more sluggish pace of society, politics, and individuals. Similar to the ways in which social democracy in earlier periods of economic transformation employed the language of social engineering or social rationalization to recreate a destroyed social sphere, Third Way discourse defines the role of politics primarily as that of creating a knowledge society to complement the knowledge economy. The term "efficiency," as in the Brownite "fairness and efficiency," mirrors this idea of recreating a social sphere that will "fit" the new economy, reduce social costs and keep up with economic transformation (see Brown, *Fair Is Efficient*).

It is well noted that the Third Way mirrors a dream of harmony and reconciliation between a number of antagonistic themes – the economy and the social, the market and the state, economic efficiency and social justice, and the state and citizen – through a reappraisal of terms like partnership, community, society (see Driver and Martell, "New Labour's Communitarianism" and *New Labour*). The influence of communitarianism on New Labour's concept of community is clear (see Bevir). The concept of community contains a reappraisal of interdependency, reciprocity, and trust. "Community" emphasizes the existence of a common good, embedded in reciprocal relationships and trust. The concept of community contains a strong emphasis on both rationality and morality – a contractual idea that rights are balanced by responsibilities and that there is a general agreement on the moral foundations of human interactions.[1] As discussed in this context, the concept of community is directly linked to the idea of social capital and its importance in a knowledge-driven, learning economy – as the value of social capital is dependent on the quality of the relationships and norms fostered in communities. "Community," in this sense, bridges the economic and the social, just as it bridges divisions between individuals and groups in society.

Community is thus a key metaphor of new politics. The definition of "new politics" is the claim to occupy a political space beyond the Left-Right divide, which is seen as an outdated remnant of the political alliances of the industrial society. The concept of community is clearly opposed to civil society as the central social metaphor of neoliberalism. However, this is not only a reaction against the Thatcherite "there is no such thing as society" but also to an "old Left" vision of society as something mechanistic and violent, and created by social struggle (see Donzelot; Steinmetz). Rather, community mirrors ideas of social change as an evolutionary process, and there is a return in contemporary politics of organic metaphors to describe both economic and social change. The accumulation of knowledge, for instance, is not conceptualized, despite the references to the knowledge society as a third industrial revolution, as taking place through revolutions and paradigmatic clashes. Rather, it is conceptualized as permanent evolution and growth.

If knowledge and learning are the driving forces of improvement, then politics needs to foster knowledge and learning. The role of politics is to foster opportunity, providing for the self realization of individuals. Collectivist, "old Left," projects of the Good Society are thus doomed to fail. There is a clear rejection of socialism as utopia, but also of the free-market utopia of neoliberalism, since knowledge and learning are presumed to be fundamentally connected social processes (see Hodgson; Mulgan; Halpern). Ultimately, as Chantal Mouffe has suggested, this emphasis on consensus, organic processes, and community leads to an idea of politics where Left and Right are irrelevant, and where the question of morality emerges as the key defining characteristic. Morality, in the notion of community, is not a question of dispute or struggle between opposing interests or of weighing standpoints against each other – as is, after all, the prerequisite of democracy – but of appealing to universal values of "what we know" to be right and wrong (see Mouffe). The purpose of community is to foster such universal, or at least British, values of entrepreneurship and flexibility.

Creating the Knowledge Subject

Importantly, this dream of efficiency and harmony leads to a particular conceptualization of the process of modernization that centers on the individual as the primary locus of change. "Modernization" is not only about changing politics and institutions but also about changing people themselves in order to create a new kind of citizen to inhabit the Knowledge Society. In a sense, the refusal of the Third Way to conceive of a utopia on the level of political articulation and mobilization is paralleled by the creation of the utopia of the individual sphere, as expressed in political expectations on the new learning "man." This new knowledgeable subject is defined by a number of characteristics, which are in demand in the new economy: entrepreneurship, flexibility, the ability to grasp opportunities and to make one's way through complexity. This definition of the ideal citizen is directly related to the attribution of knowledge and skill as the new means of production. If knowledge is the infinite resource that constitutes the basis for the promise of prosperity, its limits are to be found in the individuals who possess it and who make up the "human capital" of the knowledge economy. Individual knowledge is, however, not a question of possessing a set of crafts and skills, but rather refers predominantly to individual dispositions and is ultimately defined by the willingness of the individual to embrace change. In the same way that the knowledge society denotes both the process and goal of this idea of modernization, skill is both the outcome and the essence of the process of learning. Learning, often defined as "learning and relearning," denotes an individualized and perpetual process of modernization (see Rose; Stehr).

This emphasis on flux and constant learning, applicability, innovation, and flexibility thus contains a specific desire for a dynamic, adaptive, and malleable knowledge-individual as well as a specific understanding of the nature of knowledge. This new concept of knowledge, as expressed in the metaphors of human and social capital, ultimately refers to individual aptitudes to react to and embrace change in a continual process of self-development. This is a highly essentialized concept of knowledge, one that refers specifically to individual dispositions such entrepreneurship, motivation, perseverance, and adaptability. The ability that is central to this new skills revolution is not a facility for craft that can be learned and then possessed but rather a talent for constantly grasping and acquiring new skills, as the demand for knowledge is constantly changing (see Garsten and Jacobsson). To make sense of constant change, complex and opaque as it may be for the single individual, is thus the essence of knowledge in the Knowledge Society; and to adapt to constant change is the meaning of the contemporary concept of modernization. Learning, as "learning and relearning," takes the form of a perpetual process of modernization within, a mirror image of the concept of innovation in industry (see CEC).

This emphasis on the individual as the motor of change comes together with a turn in social policies and the social philosophy of social democracy – in a move away from the emphasis on structural economic factors and redistribution in the "old" welfare state and towards so-called supply-side social policies that are aimed at the individual and at his or her behavior and dispositions. At the heart of this shift are the so-called "social investment strategies" that aim at vesting individuals with the skills and capacities that they need to survive. This social vision defines the role of policy as that of creating the productive citizen by influencing – coercing, stimulating, enabling – the individual to act in politically desired directions in order to make real the dream of knowledge-driven prosperity and social justice. Here it is clear that contemporary political discourse, despite its self-proclaimed pragmatism, reflects historical discourses of social rationalization and central strands in social utopian thought. Modern politics is not economically *dirigiste*, in its prudent macro-economic norm politics, but socially *dirigiste* in a way that is not considered politically possible or socially desirable for the economic sphere (see Schmidt). In a matter of speaking, the fine-tuning of the economy of the Keynesian project seems to have been replaced with the fine-tuning of the social for the endogenous post-Keynesian age. The nineteenth-century idea of the *social* as a consequential state to the *economic* is turned on its head, as the social emerges as primordial and the individual becomes both the engine and the limit of economic expansion. The language of rationalization and efficiency is thus transformed into a discourse of the behavior of individuals, households, and communities – reflecting a Fabian obsession with the cultivation of the perfect character in each (see King).

This outlook on the learning, adaptive, and knowledgeable citizen who possesses the abstract ability to navigate complexity both constructs an ideal – utopic – knowledge citizen and its Other (the individual who lacks productive capacity, who is void of knowledge and skill, and who cannot learn). This individualized approach to the process of change draws on a pervasive idea of a dichotomous social order, expressed in metaphors such as "the social and the the asocial," "the socially included and the the socially excluded," "the employable and the the unemployable," "the information haves and the information have-nots." Social exclusion is today largely defined as a lack of skills inherent in the groups that do not have, or cannot acquire, those skills necessary to succeed in the Knowledge Economy. As Ruth Levitas has shown, the concepts of in-exclusion are spatial metaphors, describing the situation of individuals and groups in- or outside of the social fabric. Social politics reflect this horizontal spatial division of society as they stress inclusion rather than equality – moving the outsiders inside – rather than discussing relative power resources or the market structures that create in-exclusion (see Levitas, *Inclusive Society*). The term "modernization," then, is about this shift of the outsiders inside, about making everybody carriers of marketable skills, or not. Consequently, the definition of modernization is itself inherently dichotomous, separating social groups and categories and allotting them different roles in the process of change. Borrowing a term from the language of European integration, this is a concept of modernization as *à deux vitesses*, a modernization process of different temporalities, wherein change is a process that takes place at different speeds and in different gears for different segments in society. Ultimately, this is also an essentialized idea of modernization that inscribes different groups with given, and different, capacities for change and allocates different strategies and possibilities to them for "realizing their potential." The Third Way does not fundamentally question this bipolarity, but rather its definition of modernization springs out of it.

Works Cited

Amin, Ash. "Postfordism: Models, Fantasies, and Phantoms of Transition." *Postfordism: A Reader*. London: Blackwell, 1994. 1–41.
Bastow, Steve and James Martin. *Third Way Discourse: European Ideologies in the Twentieth Century*. Edinburgh: Edinburgh University Press, 2003.
Bauman, Zygmunt. *Liquid Modernity*. Cambridge: Polity, 2000.
Beilharz, Peter. *Labour's Utopias: Bolshevism, Fabianism, Social Democracy*. London: Routledge, 1992.
Bevir, Mark. *New Labour: A Critique*. London: Routledge, 2005.
Blair, Tony. *New Britain: My Vision of a Young Country*. London: Fourth Estate, 1996.
____*The Third Way: New Politics for the New Century*. London: Fabian Society, 1998.
Block, Fred. *Postindustrial Possibilities: A Critique of Economic Discourse*. Berkeley: University of California Press, 1990.
Brown, Gordon. "Exploiting the British Genius – the Key to Long Term Economic Success." Speech to the Confederation of British Industry (CBI). 20 May 1997 <www.hm-treasury.gov.uk>.
____*Fair Is Efficient*. London: Fabian Society, 1994.
____"The Politics of Potential. A New Agenda for Labour." *Reinventing the Left*. Ed. David Miliband. Cambridge: Polity, 1994. 113–22.
Cabinet Office. "Modernising Government." CM 4310. London: HMSO, 1999.
CEC, European Commission. "White Paper on Learning." Brussels: European Commission, 1996.
Compass. "Manifesto." London: Compass, 2004.
Driver, Steven, and Luke Martell. "New Labour's Communitarianism." *Critical Social Policy* 17.3 (1997): 27–46.
____*New Labour: Politics after Thatcherism*. Cambridge: Polity, 1998.
Etzioni, Amitai. *The Third Way to a Good Society*. London: Demos, 2000.

Finlayson, Alan. *Making Sense of New Labour*. London: Lawrence and Wishart, 2003.
Garsten, Christina and Kerstin Jacobsson. *Learning to Be Employable: New Agendas on Work, Responsibility, and Learning in a Globalizing World*. Basingstoke: Palgrave Macmillan, 2004.
Giddens, Anthony. *The Third Way: The Renewal of Social Democracy*. Cambridge: Polity, 1998.
Gray, John. *After Social Democracy: Politics, Capitalism and the Common Life*. London: Demos, 1996.
Hay, Colin. *The Political Economy of New Labour*. Manchester: Manchester University Press, 1998.
Hodgson, Geoffrey M. *Economics and Utopia: Why the Learning Economy Is Not the End of History*. London and New York: Routledge, 1999.
Jessop, Bob. *The Future of the Capitalist State*. Cambridge: Polity, 2002.
King, Desmond. *In the Name of Liberalism: Illiberal Social Policy in the US and Britain*. Oxford: Oxford University Press, 1999.
Koselleck, Reinhart. *Futures Past: On the Semantics of Historical Time*. Cambridge, Massachusetts: MIT Press, 1985.
____*Vergangene Zukunft: Zur Semantik Geschichtlicher Zeiten*. Frankfurt: Suhrkamp, 1985.
Koselleck, Reinhart and Todd Samuel Presner. *The Practice of Conceptual History: Timing History, Spacing Concepts*. Stanford: Stanford University Press, 2002.
Leadbeater, Charles. *Living on Thin Air: The New Economy*. London: Penguin, 2000.
____"Welcome to the Knowledge Economy." *Tomorrow's Politics: The Third Way and Beyond*. Ed. Ian Hargreaves and Ian Christie. London: Demos, 1998. 11–24.
Levitas, Ruth. *The Concept of Utopia*. Syracuse: Syracuse University Press, 1990.
____*The Inclusive Society: Social Exclusion and New Labour*. New York: Routledge, 1998.
Meiksins Wood, Ellen. "Modernity, Postmodernity, or Capitalism?" *Capitalism and the Information Age: The Political Economy of the Global Communications Era*. Ed. Robert McChesney, Ellen Meiksins Wood and John Bellamy Foster. New York: Monthly Review, 1998. 27–51.
Miliband, David. *Reinventing the Left*. Cambridge: Polity, 1994.
Mokyr, Joel. *The Gifts of Athena: Historical Origins of the Knowledge Economy*. Princeton: Princeton University Press, 2002.

Mouffe, Chantal. *On the Political*. New York and London: Routledge, 2005.
Mulgan, Geoff. *Connexity*. London: Vintage, 1998.
____Personal interview. 2 March 2005.
Nexus. "The Third Way – Summary of the Nexus Online Discussion. Summary Paper." 17 March 2005 <www.netnexus.org>.
Pierson, Paul. *The New Politics of the Welfare State*. Oxford: Oxford University Press, 2001.
Renewal: Journal of Labour Politics. London: Labour Party, 1993.
Ricoeur, Paul. *Ideologie et l'Utopie*. Paris: Editions du Seuil, 1997.
Rose, Nikolas. *Powers of Freedom: Reframing Political Thought*. Cambridge: Cambridge University Press, 1999.
Sassoon, Donald. *One Hundred Years of Socialism: The West European Left in the Twentieth Century*. London: Tauris, 1996.
Schmidt, Vivienne A. "Values and Discourse in the Politics of Adjustment." *Work and Welfare in the Open Economy: From Vulnerability to Competitiveness*. Ed. Fritz W. Scharpf and Vivien A. Schmidt. Oxford: Oxford University Press, 2000. 228–309.
Stehr, Nico. *Knowledge Societies*. London: Sage, 1994.

Andrew J. Brown

Witchcrafting Selves: Remaking Person and Community in a Neo-Pagan Utopian Scene

A Utopian Experiment

Dorinne Kondo's 1990 ethnography of a Japanese workplace, *Crafting Selves*, was influential in cultural anthropology because it articulated an important change of emphasis for this field of study. This change in emphasis was to treat the individual not just as a product and carrier of culture but as an active agent who was manipulating cultural materials for various ends – including the creation of a socially embedded self. This perspective does not, however, *replace* earlier insights that individuals are intimately constructed within social and cultural environments. In Kondo's ethnography, a stress upon individual agency does not mean that these workers then transcend culture or gain some particular, self-conscious vantage point from which they can view their own efforts at strategic self-construction. Kondo is describing people who are acting with and within culturally- ordered expectations: they are being Japanese, being women, being young women, and being Japanese employees. The point is that their renderings of cultural scripts are by no means static, passive, or predictable.

In this essay, however, I look at people who *are* actively trying to transcend their culture. In so doing, they are seeking to re-create not only a new kind of socially-embedded self but a new kind of culture as well. In some sense, this brings us back to old dilemmas of structure and agency. As we try to conceptualize and explain the actions of human beings, where do we strike the balance between treating people as self-willed, creative actors and treating them as things that simply derive from particular environments and histories? In the case described below, this dilemma itself is a place of self-conscious, dynamic tension.

On the agency side of the spectrum, we have ideologies of individualism and the "cultural supermarket" of the United States, wherein a large part of the population regards religious practice and political ideology as a matter of individual choice and preference. People can seek out religious, spiritual, and political stances that "suit them." They and their orientations are not bound or created by their backgrounds. On the structural side, there is an acknowledgement by many people that external structures have the power to shape the individual – whether these structures be family life, gendered expectations, the social constraints of mainstream society, or the habits of consumer capitalism. For people in the utopian scene described below, we see an attempt to resolve the contradiction between agency and structure by choosing spiritual practices that are meant to replace one structure with another. The very recognition that communities and individuals themselves have been and continue to be constructed and molded in the most fundamental ways by a mainstream society leads to a situation wherein the structuring, de-structuring, and re-structuring powers of cultural practices are purposefully brought into play. Religion, mythology, language, economics, consumption, and daily practices of all sorts are being used to remove the person from one sort of constructedness in order to make possible a reconstruction into the revolutionary.

I describe herein part of an ethnographic study of a radical political and spiritual scene in the U.S. city of Eugene, Oregon. This is not an intentional community characterized by boundaried place or membership or unified by any specific political or social manifesto. It is rather the case that a significant minority in the city occupies a vibrant, but disorderly milieu where political and cultural experimentation is common and vigorous. A major portion of this scene is characterized by witchcraft, politicized neo-paganism, goddess worship, and eco-feminism. People with ties to the scene engage in the systematic rejection of a mainstream society that they universally regard as destructive and unsatisfying; and through their spiritual practice and political activism, they see themselves working toward the creation of a fundamentally better world.

In other words, Eugene plays host to a utopian experiment, although the situation there does not fit neatly into Lyman Tower Sargent's influential typology of utopias or intentional communities (see Sargent). In fact, drawing from American vernacular, I specifically call it a utopian "scene" in order to underline the difference between this and more familiar utopian or intentional communities. One can, I suggest, talk about a "pagan utopian scene" in the same sense that one can talk about the "New Orleans jazz scene." A scene, in my usage, is an observable, and usually self-acknowledged, set of social networks that is not well-defined or well-boundaried. It is one that enables varying degrees of commitment among the people involved; that is symbolically ordered rather than socially or institutionally integrated; that may move from moments of clarity and consensus to ferment and dissension and back again; that may or may not have leaders; that is organized along flexible axes of physical proximity, interlocking roles, and shared understandings; that is characterized by some freedom to enter and exit at will; that favors the sanctioning power of collective regard, more than institutional power of any sort; and that is often characterized by an ongoing process of metamorphosis.

As Ruth Levitas has noted, there is no reigning consensus in utopian studies as to the specific object of study in the field. I will leave it to others ultimately to decide where or whether this particular scene fits into a typology of utopianism. As an anthropologist, however, I take it for granted that people's lives are organized, on the one hand, through playing by the rules of culture and, on the other hand, by creatively and collectively dreaming (and acting) beyond a culture's apparent, delivered limitations. I argue, therefore, that when "social dreaming," as Sargent terms it, becomes a defining characteristic of living, as it is for the people of this Eugene scene, we enter into the realm of creative utopianism.

Neo-Paganism, A History of Adaptation

Neo-paganism is a blanket term often used to refer to a diverse range of new religions (or spiritual practices) that have developed recently in the west as a kind of subset within the so-called New Age movement.[1] There is no formal church organization, and no one voice or collection of voices speaks for all Pagans. Furthermore, creativity and improvisation among individuals and small- groups is typically expected and encouraged, and the variation within Paganism is extensive. In general, Pagans practice a nature-oriented religion that involves some variety of ritual magical practice. In a conspicuously active process of syncretism, they draw upon the practices and pantheons of religious systems from around the world and throughout history. They may see themselves specifically as Pagans, Neo-Pagans, Wiccans, Witches, Druids; although many would not consent to having themselves confined to any such category. They tend to be polytheistic and emphasize the immanence of the divine – especially its potential to be anywhere in the world. They usually view themselves as inheritors or re-discoverers of pre-modern, pre-monotheistic spiritual practices – either narrowly out of European and Mediterranean traditions of witchcraft and paganism or more broadly out of a more general, pan-human, Paleolithic legacy that survives in indigenous traditions to this day.

To the extent that neo-paganism can be "summed up," it has been called a post-modern religion for its rejection of totalizing structures, its hostility toward delivered truths, and its prioritizing of the individual path and perspective (see Eilberg-Schwartz). My analysis, however, is not

---

[1] Analysts use the label Neo-Paganism in order to distinguish these new practices from those covered by the more traditional use of the term Paganism. In this essay, I usually drop the prefix and follow the usage of the Pagans themselves, who (in Eugene, at least) mostly collapse the distinction.

meant to sum up Paganism in general or universal terms. Instead, I offer an ethnographic look at one particular variant, which I have called Politicized Paganism in order to highlight an intersection of radical politics and alternative spirituality that I think deserves to be fully considered as a contemporary utopian experiment.

At its modern inception in the hands of men like Gerald Gardner and Charles Leland, witchcraft, including what would become Neo-Paganism, was not overtly political, although it had its anti-modern overtones. Twentieth-century witchcraft practices were portrayed as a rediscovery and re-emergence of an ancient, pre-Christian, nature religion focused on the worship of pagan gods and goddesses. In 1939, Gardner, an amateur anthropologist, claimed to have been initiated into a witches' coven and subsequently went on to write about, organize, and popularize this kind of witchcraft. Thus, an historical legitimization bolstered by a selective use of popular and scholarly works in anthropology, archaeology, and folklore was constructed. This eventually unraveled under the attack of critics hostile both to the scholarly works and the uses that the Pagans made of these works; although even today Paganism preserves distinct echoes of such works as Johann Jakob Bachofen's (1861) evolutionist work on matriarchy and Margaret Murray's (1921) history of European witchcraft.

Pagan writers eventually shifted their claims to validity away from narratives of antiquity and historical continuity and re-oriented toward claims about the efficacy of Pagan belief and practice for meeting human needs and articulating the truths to be discovered in (and beyond) the human psyche (see Adler). Paganism thus became more concerned with how magic works to effect change both internal and external to the individual. Discussions of validity came increasingly to be put in terms of psychology, para-psychology, and the effectiveness of the magic in enabling a desired change. The new emphasis on the psychological aspects of Pagan witchcraft made it attractive to women with feminist concerns. Indeed, for the particular variety of Paganism that I have labeled Politicized Paganism, the interaction with feminist ideas proved to be transforming.

Feminism has a long and multifaceted history in the U.S. and Europe; and it has been characterized by various goals, ideologies, and strategies, including occasional forays into spirituality and occultism.[2] The post World War Two period saw an especially dramatic redefining of gender gender-related issues. The intellectual, political, and utopian aspects of this redefinition came to the fore in the 1960s and 1970s with the women's liberation movement. The most public and socially contested endeavors of the women's liberation movement concerned issues such as equalizing economic opportunity and expanding the social definition of women's roles. Complementary to this, however, was another current running through feminist thought and political action. There was a growing realization that many dimensions of the liberation of women needed to be accomplished upon an intra-psychic landscape. Psychologically oriented feminists began to argue that what was needed was a change of consciousness and a counterculture. That is, the limitations on women's self-definition and aspiration were to a great extent internalized by women themselves, even as the undoing of these limiting patterns was destined to be a complex and devastatingly difficult task.

At some point, it appears that the feminist "consciousness-raising" group met the Pagan witches' coven and something new was created. Paganism offered a mythology that gave women a central and valued role, along with the tools of a "magic" that was to be turned toward personal transformation, psychological empowerment, and the creation of sisterhood.[3] For the woman struggling to disentangle herself from a

---

[2] Bednarowski examines the histories of three occasions that feminism has incorporated an occult rhetoric: namely, nineteenth-century Spiritualism, theosophy, and feminist witchcraft.

[3] Many feminists in common with Pagans use the word "empowerment" to mean a psychological liberation from the dominating culture – for only when a person is freed from the crippling inhibitions of their enculturated ideas about gender, power,

patriarchal society, which she saw as oppressive to women, Paganism offered a precedent and template for the female exercise of power. It offered spiritual expression to women who were ideologically alienated from Christian and Jewish traditions. And it offered a potentially new, less contaminated language in which to articulate new ideas, whether political, aesthetic, or psychological. While the apolitical nature of many Pagan groups testifies that Paganism is not inevitably political, in the hands of feminists Paganism has shown itself amenable to political uses.

Much of feminist Paganism has been separatist in nature. Zsuzsanna Budapest, one of its foremost witches, has called Pagan witchcraft "Wimmins Religion" and declared that it is closed to men. Among the Politicized Pagans I knew in Eugene, however, Budapest was little known; and it was Starhawk who was much more influential. In her widely read book, *The Spiral Dance*, Starhawk focuses on women's issues and a woman-centered symbolism; but she also indicates an important, complementary role for men and "male energy." She also explicitly addresses issues of oppression not limited to gender; and she enjoins a political responsibility to the earth, which includes such issues as ecological and anti-nuclear activism. It seems that at some point, with Starhawk as a major popularizer, Paganism came to be a form of religious expression within this political, feminist and environmentalist, milieu. As a form of spirituality first adapted to the needs of feminism, it thus proved adaptable to people pursuing various political, social, and psychological goals.

individuality, etc., can they begin to act effectively politically. Thus, empowerment is both an internal experience and a political result. I follow their usage here.

A Pagan Scene

Eugene, Oregon is a place that is widely known for its lively "alternative scene." It is a small American city with a mixed economic base that has traditionally emphasized agriculture and the timber industry. It contains a university and a smaller community college, and there is a vigorous and variegated political culture, both mainstream and alternative. Political demonstrations are well-attended, and there is an array of politically active organizations and cooperatives. In the 1990s when this study was undertaken, there was a tremendous range of political stances available, up to and including an idealistic advocacy of revolution. Political activity was interwoven with a kind of cultural ferment as well. Within the city, there was a vibrant array of alternative lifestyles and related spiritualities. Varieties of New Ageism, Eastern eastern mysticism, Native American ritual systems, yogic regimens, bits and pieces of a "hippie" lifestyle, and anything that could be conjured out of the literatures of religion, mysticism, or anthropology was fair game. The cross-pollination among all of these was extensive. Politicized Paganism was located within this context – where, in an orientation given to experimentation and eclecticism, most people seemed to have a knowledge of, and an interest in, a wide variety of spiritual and cultural systems. Pagans were thus part of the local exploration into a wide range of ritual technologies. Dance, drumming, chanting, meditation, and the manipulation of ritual objects were common, as were visualization, trancing, story-telling, feasting, fasting, singing, sweating, and sex, and psycho-active drug taking.

From this kit of potential ritual tools, and based on the tastes and goals of any given group, Pagans created rituals and practiced their magic. In sum, by the early 1990s in Eugene, there was a Neo-Pagan scene wherein people articulated what I would clearly call a *utopian* vision of a culture that could sustain itself without destroying the environment and that could guarantee that each individual would have a chance at intellectual, spiritual, and emotional self-actualization. Politicized

Paganism offered a worldview that encompassed this utopian vision and reinforced it with corresponding ritual and symbology. It offered habits and rationales for action and evaluation; and it served to lend form, validity, and vitality to a lifestyle that was adapted to life on the cultural, economic, and political periphery. There is, however, nothing inevitable about this admixture of Paganism and politics. The majority of Pagans in the U.S. and elsewhere seem not to be exceptionally political (see Adler; Luhrmann). And certainly political expression even when it does occur within Paganism is neither consistently radical nor utopian (see Kuhling). And, in turn, much of the political fringe seems to operate comfortably without an overtly spiritual emphasis. Thus, the complementarities that I outline between Paganism and radical politics does not determine that a Politicized Paganism must necessarily emerge, it simply makes its appearance comprehensible.

Structural Functionalism, and a New Reading

I would now like to use a somewhat old-fashioned anthropological paradigm to explain something of the contours of this utopian political and cultural scene. Anthropologists spent much of the nineteenth and early twentieth centuries analyzing how people occupied communities and maintained a semblance of organization and consensus without states or bureaucratic institutions and often without official leaders or fixed hierarchies. They noticed that people were knitted together into groups by things like religion, ritual, language, symbols, and myth. They also noticed how material production and consumption, reciprocity, and daily practices of all sorts anchored people into coherent and structured social and cultural lives. Among North American anthropologists, one of the reigning paradigms during much of the twentieth century was structural functionalism. In this model, any given aspect of culture that was not directly explained by the needs of subsistence and survival could be explained by showing that it played a role in integrating and stabilizing a cultural community. Thus, we could understand things like religious beliefs, dietary restrictions, gender roles, residential patterns, or economic practices by looking at how they played a function in maintaining the structure. However, this model, at least as a guiding paradigm, was forced into thorough retreat under a well-deserved barrage of criticisms, including especially those argued that it tended to be blind to the heterogeneity of cultural spaces and to the conflicting projects of the people and groups involved. Too often, it was claimed, did it beg the important political question of who wanted the status quo stabilized and why. It may seem odd at this point in time to (re)propose a paradigm that has been discarded as too politically conservative and blind to diversity in order to examine the heteroglossic and contested terrain of a utopian scene; but that is precisely what I propose, for I believe that this is what the Pagans themselves have done.

A defining characteristic of Paganism is its use of ritual magic and the manipulation of symbols and myths. The Politicized Paganism that I describe has shown a preoccupation with the re-articulation of myths, and their applications in ritual – and these have implications for a revolutionary agenda. I have argued elsewhere that myths and rituals are important, even in our own society (see Brown). Myths are not simply badly researched histories or stories to entertain. Indeed, the most central cultural tenets of a society can be reinforced with these symbolic tools. Clyde Kluckhohn, in a classic evocation of structural functionalism, states that myths "promote social solidarity, enhance the integration of the society by providing a formalized statement of its ultimate value-attitudes, and afford a means for the transmission of much of the culture with little loss of content – thus protecting cultural continuity and stabilizing the society" (62). It is clear that myths and rituals do offer some statement of "ultimate value-attitudes," even in our own society; and Pagans seem to take them seriously for this very reason. Yet, my example of Politicized Paganism shows that these myths are not inevitably the socially conservative force that Kluckhohn describes. In cases where those value-attitudes are being contested, myth can become another forum within which culture is contested and debated. In a further twist, a mythology of revolution can especially work simultaneously to integrate and disintegrate. The Politicized Pagan project of defining a new mythology can therefore be understood as a tripartite attempt: first, to disentangle individuals from the powerful and conservative webwork of standard mythology; second, to develop and occupy a mythology of revolution and utopian transformation; and third, to harness the structure-building powers of myth, ritual, and symbol as an integrative force within their own ranks (and even within their own psyches). [4]

As I mention above, some feminists and others had come to conclude that the crucial work of political and cultural liberation would have to be done within the mind. The failures of past utopian projects were not proof of futility, but rather a warning that the utopian visions of social reformers and revolutionaries can only succeed with individuals who have been freed from all of the subtleties of social control. As an illustration from my study, Jeanine was a young woman in Eugene who identified herself as a Pagan witch. She felt she had trouble asserting herself in relationships, sexually or politically. She could complain articulately about how gender roles are consigned by patriarchal society and how passivity and complaisance is imposed not only on women but on citizens generally. She could evaluate her own behavior and try to change this, but among Pagans there was a supportive willingness to admit the difficulty of this act of will. Paganism thus offered her a language and the symbolic tools with which she could undertake personal change, and by extension cultural change. In order to help herself become more assertive, Jeanine would invoke the Hindu goddess, Kali – who for many Politicized Pagans had come to embody action, assertion, destruction, and inevitably,

---

[4] One could include narratives of social progress or individual success, and "femininity" as developed in boy-meets-girl stories, and so on.

creation. She read about Kali, meditated upon a representation of her, and performed rituals alone, with supportive friends, or in the context of a fully committed coven. She may have been seeking to name and therefore grasp an archetypal aspect of her psyche that has been repressed or was perhaps harnessed to the service of the mainstream culture. She may have been seeking to communicate with a being, "Kali," who could offer her strength and power to transform herself and others. The typically fuzzy nature of language around magic leaves vague just what may have been going on. At the very least, for Jeanine, Kali served as a complex, polysemic symbol onto which she could attach her feelings and conflicts, and with which she and her friends could talk about and re-think female power. Kali, however, was just one symbol among many that were being mobilized in this scene in order to undertake a utopian re-making of individuals and their cultural surroundings.

One of the more dramatic sets of symbols in Paganism was to be found in the conceptualization of change and transformation. In Pagan thought as it was developed in myth and ritual, the concept of death (or its cousin, destruction) contained not just the ending of something but the necessary clearing of the stage for something new. The fifteenth figure in the Tarot deck was not Death, but Death-and-Rebirth. The waning and waxing of the moon, the cycle of the seasons, the cycle of life from animate to inanimate and once again to animate were all discussed in light of the (re)generative nature of death. It is a metaphor that served as a framework to both the Pagan strategies of psychological empowerment and of organized group action. Persephone, from Greek mythology, and Inanna, from the myths of ancient Sumer, were two commonly evoked goddesses and the two that most often represented this process of change. Both descend into the world of the dead, leaving behind all worldly things. Both re-emerge from this death transformed. Although the symbolism of death and rebirth is partly a political parable, it is also a set of symbols by which people could deal with the stressful, disorienting, and painful project of de-coupling themselves from their culture. In fact, the deeply entrenched and psychologically active feedback loops that exist between spiritual practice, individual subjectivities, and social group dynamics are familiar to anthropologists who study religion. Their presence here is one of the reasons why I think it is important to take seriously this utopian scene as a important experiment in crafting a utopian culture.

Politicized Pagans and some others with revolutionary agendas consider it an essential political act for the individual to disentangle her- or him self from the (psychological, spiritual, and material) limitations of a hostile and repressive society. As the revolutionary task that Pagans discuss, it is necessarily a difficult process. To be sure, Émile Durkheim overstates the absolutism of cultural embeddedness, but nevertheless he evokes the entangling nature of culture when he discusses the power that fundamental social and religious categories hold over the minds of individuals:

> [Society] uses all its authority upon its members to forestall such dissidences. Does a mind ostensibly free itself from these forms of thought? It is no longer considered a human mind in the full sense of the word, and is treated accordingly. That is why we feel that we are no longer completely free and something resists, both within and outside ourselves, when we attempt to rid ourselves of these fundamental notions, even in our own conscience. Outside of us there is public opinion which judges us; but more than that, since society is also represented inside of us, it sets itself against these revolutionary fancies, even inside of ourselves; we have the feeling that we cannot abandon them if our whole thought is not to cease being really human (30).

What these narratives about Persephone, Inanna, and Kali encompass is the painful process of change and loss. Clifford Geertz notes that "as a religious problem, the problem of suffering is, paradoxically, not how to avoid suffering but how to suffer" (173). These myths, along with an entire arsenal of other symbols, were being put into play to lend collective meaning and emotional resonance to an ongoing process of breaking old patterns in order to create new patterns. The power that religion, ritual, and social relationships can exert to structure and maintain humanness was being turned toward a project of altering and subsequently re-establishing humanness.

The Politicized Pagan symbolism of transformation is, of course, meant to extend beyond this attempt at individual, psychological renewal. As a group, the Eugene Pagans espoused the goal of a radical transformation and reformulation of society. Their willingness to embrace in idealistic and spiritual terms the notion of destruction-as-creation thus paved the way for a commitment to disruption and revolution that is otherwise more difficult to engage. For a person who wants to revolutionize society and who sees the present society's destruction as a necessary precursor to that, an ideology that emphasizes the positive aspects of destruction must have obvious appeal. I should probably note here – in the midst of this language of revolution and destruction – that the particular Politicized Pagan scene I observed was more or less committed to pacifism. Physical interference (like chaining oneself to logging equipment or pouring sand into the petrol tanks) and the modest violence of scuffling with police or security guards at demonstrations against nuclear power or militarism were incidental rather than central to their political activities. People did not really entertain much interest in overt violence as a means of transforming society. Instead, what was meant to turn things on their head was a combination of effects from their lives and their rituals, their political activism, and a coming, universal realization about the disastrous nature of modern living.[5]

---

[5] From Marx onwards, there is a familiar critique that treats religion as politically enervating, at least in part because its faith in supernaturally enforced justice distracts from the requirements of actually creating worldly justice; and one could certainly hear versions of this criticism in Eugene. For a description of this critique vis-à-vis feminist spirituality, see Puttnick. In any case, social science offers no effective way of evaluating the actual political effectiveness of culturally reinforced radicalism such as I describe.

So far, I have focused on myth, ritual, and religious beliefs and practices, because they are important ways through which human communities organize themselves as cultural beings. And I have sought to show that, within this scene at least, this knowledge has led people to try to craft a more satisfying arrangement of meanings. Structural functional analysis was never limited to these spiritual and psychological dimensions, however. In fact, the paradigm's emphasis on integration implies that most aspects of human living reinforce one another and could be interpreted in such terms. Economic exchange and networks of reciprocity are, therefore, another of the important means through which people build cohesion and order. Social analyses, from Marcel Mauss's study of gift exchange to work by those in the Marxist tradition, have viewed people and groups as fundamentally shaped by the nature of their economic relationships. Among the Politicized Pagans of Eugene, the potentially conservative and integrative force of economic participation was being used to disintegrate and reintegrate people into a coherent place on the margins of the mainstream society. If Paganism in general varies widely in terms of its spiritual and political practices, it varies even more widely in regard to its relationship to wage work, consumerism, and the cash economy (see Kuhling). One of the most striking characteristics of the Politicized Pagan community in Eugene was the way in which the individuals were disentangled from the demands of the mainstream economy and re-organized into an alternative economy through a new set of entanglements.

The degree of participation by Pagans in Eugene's cash economy was variable, but all found some means of minimizing it. The usual commitment ranged from people like Marcus who worked four to ten hours a week in the local tofu factory, to Cathleen who worked at a day-care center as a teacher twenty hours a week, to Gregory who worked in a bakery for thirty hours a week until he moved to an organic farm where he lived rent-free and was paid $100a hundred dollars a month for his labor. Many people had a more or less profitable sideline such as a technical form of healing, like Reiki massage or the concoction of herbal tinctures, or a craft such as hat-making or drum-making. These products or services were traded and sold among networks of friends and acquaintances as well as at the weekly town market and various Pagan or political gatherings. Since work for wages was considered an unpleasant compromise with the mainstream society, there was no shame in not working. People reduced their need for money by living together in more or less dilapidated housing that most could finance with as little as six to ten hours per week of minimum wage work. Other expenses of modern life were simply avoided. Dumpster diving was an acceptable means of getting food; although many people worked in the natural food industry that was burgeoning in the city. Life in a group house might mean that the household had a twenty percent discount at the local grocery store, a thirty percent discount at the juice cooperative, and all the free tofu that they could eat. Since such discounts were often extended to friends, this alternative economic strategy permeated even further. Mistakes, surpluses, and unsalable articles that would otherwise be discarded were distributed through an informal network of acquaintances that served to integrate an alternative moral-political economy.

The relative economic poverty, including the scrounging for food, was far from being considered tiresome or embarrassing; and it was made virtuous through Pagan political philosophy and spirituality. Ideals of success were not articulated through mainstream consumerism, and this rejection was reinforced by a reading of the American capitalist culture as profligate and an engine of social injustice and environmental and spiritual destruction. Consuming little and living off the surplus became these urban-dwellers' method of "living lightly on the Earth." Lust for consumer goods was the awful antithesis. Clearly, the religious and ideological systems of Politicized Paganism constituted a way in which such a dissociation from mainstream society could be made meaningful and attractive. However, I also want to make the point that these practices, as they disentangled people from the mainstream society in very concrete ways, were a necessary condition for direct participation in the activist practices of Politicized Paganism. Many of the most effective threats that the mainstream culture can bring to bear on political and cultural dissent involve economic sanction and exclusion. Concerns about jobs, economic security, and economically dependent ambition contribute to people's willingness to conform to the established rules. The success of Pagans' de-coupling from these contexts and concerns and their re-commitment to an alternative way was clearly illustrated in the context of direct political action.

During the time of my study, for example, Earth First! (the radical environmentalist organization) organized a "tree-sit" in the near-by National Forest. While Earth First! is not a Pagan organization, in Eugene at that time its membership included many Pagans. The tree-sit involved the occupation of a section of old-growth forest slated to be clear-cut by timber companies. A camp was set up by Earth First! at the end of an access road where food was cooked and people gathered, and several of the enormous 500-year-old firs were scaled by experienced climbers who established living platforms sixty feet above the forest floor. An individual tree sitter camped on each. The activists' goal was to be as difficult to dislodge as possible, and thus to slow down the process of deforestation. Even if they could not save this particular grove, some hoped that they could draw media attention and inspire other opposition, thus creating a more favorable environment and more time for the litigation and lobbying efforts that many environmental groups were pursuing. Typically, not everyone agreed with this political calculation. However, I knew one of the tree-sitters, Ted, who was deeply involved in Paganism. He objected to this political rationale for his actions, and he spoke instead about the tree-sit as an act of spiritual sympathy with the pain of the earth – thus, as an act of moral solidarity and support. He was annoyed by the concern that many of the others were showing for what he regarded as more mundane political machinations.

There was an expectation of confrontation between the activists and the police or forestry officials, and a division of labor developed depending on each individual's commitment to this kind of confrontation. First were those most committed who were willing to tree-sit or lock themselves to logging equipment with chains and bike locks. This involved a risk of arrest, internment, and physical injury. A second group maintained the camp and looked after the needs of the tree-sitters. This group also faced possible assault and arrest, although only for lesser charges. The third and largest group of activists comprised those who supplied food or materials for the action or came out to the site to socialize and lend moral support. Their action offered a communal and social context wherein this range of activism could be expressed. To a striking degree, the most committed activists were the least integrated into the mainstream economy. A person simply cannot spend weeks demonstrating in an old old-growth grove, possibly followed by weeks in jail, and expect to hold a normal job. Among the Politicized Pagans, the kind of economic exclusion and marginalization that normally, and disciplinarily, functions as a threat and a punishment had already been embraced, thus freeing them for this political work.

There are many other ways through which people are enmeshed (or un-meshed) with social life and culture, but here I can only highlight a few. In the case of Jeanine, with her icons of Kali and Persephone, the effort to re-make herself and her world was supported by a set of interrelated orientations. As we know, critical social theory has emphasized that people are constituted through their participation in relationships of power; and for Jeanine there were the positive practices of her political activism – not just ritual activity but participation in demonstrations and in consensus building meetings within the progressive community. On the other hand, hierarchies like bureaucracies, corporations, and workplaces played little role in her life. She worked part time in a health food store and supplemented that with soaps that she would make to sell or barter. Her domestic situation – living with three other women in a house that they called the "mama shack," where boyfriends were the interlopers – also served to locate her outside of the mainstream in numerous practical and symbolic ways. Altogether, she lived and socialized and worked in places that had different aesthetics and different rhythms, and different politics.

Finally, consumption is another way through which people constitute themselves in contemporary U.S. society. In the Politicized Pagan scene, consumer temptations like cosmetics, fashionable clothing, and expensive hobbies like boating or downhill skiing, were not only beyond people's financial means but also were also explicitly devalued. Jeanine, like her friends, had withdrawn her attention from popular mass culture. Instead, potlucks, camping, visiting, and music-making at the local community center were inexpensive centers of activity. The efforts to re-constitute self (literally) were especially marked in that unavoidable form of consumption, eating. Food is a quintessential marker of culture. Food preferences, food taboos, habits of sharing, and exclusivity are always weighted with symbolic meanings and embedded in complicated ways into family and social life. For Politicized Pagans, like Jeanine, the decision about what to eat was one of the most intimate expressions of a political, moral, and spiritual stance, and it involved a seemingly arcane calculus of desires and priorities. Jeanine's vegetarianism and other decisions about what to eat and what to consume carried all of this weight—and distinguished her in very distinct ways from non-pagans.

Culture, Politics, and Utopia

In Eugene, the degree of internal coherence that was being put into place in the alternative, utopian Pagan scene was striking. Many aspects of the local culture were turned toward organizing a solid community and the subjectivities appropriate for that community. In my discussion of this scene, I have stressed a functional congruence between Politicized Paganism and certain types of revolutionary politics, one that makes their admixture sensible. And, I have tried to show that these forms of human endeavor resonated with one another so that what emerged was culturally and politically distinctive. However, I do not make the claim that the ensuing precipitate was perfect, stable, or viable in the long run. To be sure, this Political Pagan scene can be understood as successful within the structural functionalist framework I have supplied; but it nevertheless exhibits many internal stresses and inconsistencies, and it continually puts itself in the path of external stresses that could very well overwhelm its ability to offer something meaningful to its adherents. It is unquestionably a cultural system undergoing constant change and modification; and, indeed, even as I have sketched something like an analog to the pre-modern village, this community is thoroughly involved in the global, postmodern imperative requiring the construction of identities and communities in a destabilized and polyglot world of continual and insistent destruction and reinvention. What I am arguing here, however, is that the experience of this community does exhibit a relatively successful cultural transformation toward a more utopian ethos and way of life. Thus, despite the degree of radical change, or indeed because of it, I would not conclude that humanity's cultural toolkit (which *homo sapiens* has been assembling since at least the Paleolithic Age) has simply become irrelevant in this context of dissolution and change. In fact, although culture is not imposed or transferred amongst the Pagan community in the same ways that it may have been in traditional societies, it has not lost its power to organize, and sustain, people's humanness. Indeed, it continues to enable, even if in a radically alternative manner.

Ultimately, I do not have a solid way of measuring the political success of the Eugene Pagans. While they cannot claim to have stopped militarism or environmental despoilment, they may claim that it would have been worse without their cultural and political, utopian, activism. They cannot point to a revolution in the U.S., but they might claim to be leaders of a "re-enchantment" of North American spiritual life. I do not have the cognitive data to know to what extent even personal transformations really happened – although I believe people were changed, dramatically or partially. At the moment, I do not have the longitudinal data to know where these lives went; although I do know that a few of the individuals are still there, and still at it. Most have gone elsewhere: some to the woods, some to the cities, some to work. For many, what I witnessed was youthful experimentation – and for some probably a mistake. However, the scene remains. For Pagans and others alike, Eugene is still a hotbed of utopian experimentation, an island of radical political expression and spiritual ferment. The scene is not anchored by a leadership or a core membership; but is a place that continually beckons to people dissatisfied in particular ways with the modern world and dissatisfied with their participation in it. The scene draws them to this utopian workshop, and makes them part of it. By the time they leave, if they leave – passing on their tattered sleeping bag and bicycle to some new immigrant—they have done their part to perpetuate this experiment in utopian creation.

Works Cited

Adler, Margot. *Drawing Down the Moon*. Boston: Beacon, 1986.
Bachofen, Johann Jakob. *An English Translation of Bachofen's Mutterers*. Lewiston: Melle, 2005.
Bednarowski, Mary Farrell. "Women in Occult America." *The Occult in America: New Historical Perspectives*. Ed. Howard Kerr and Charles L. Crow. Urbana: University of Illinois Press, 1983. 177–95.
Brown, Andrew. "The Righteous Use of Violence: Rhetoric and Myth-Making before the First Gulf War (1990–91)." *Political and Legal Anthropology Review* 27.2 (2005): 20–43.

Budapest, Zsuzsanna. *The Holy Book of Women's Mysteries*. Los Angeles: Susan B. Anthony Coven, 1979.
Crowley, Aleister. *Magick in Theory and Practice*. Secaucus: Castle Books, 1991.
Durkheim, Émile. *The Elementary Forms of the Religious Life*. Trans. Joseph Ward Swain. New York: Free Press, 1915.
Eilberg-Schwartz, Howard. "Witches of the West: Neopaganism and Goddess Worship as Enlightenment Religions." *Journal of Feminist Studies* 5.1 (1989): 77–95.
Gardner, Gerald. *Witchcraft Today*. New York: Citadel, 1955.
Geertz, Clifford. "Religion as a Cultural System." *Reader in Comparative Religion*. Ed. William A. Lessa and Evon Z. Vogt. San Francisco: Harper and Row, 1972. 78–90.
Kluckhohn, Clyde. "Myths and Rituals: A General Theory." *Harvard Theological Review* 35 (1942): 45–79.
Kondo, Dorinne K. *Crafting Selves: Power, Gender, and Discourses of Identity in a Japanese Workplace*. Chicago: University of Chicago Press, 1990.
Kuhling, Carmen. *The New Age Ethic and the Spirit of Postmodernity*. Cresskill: Hampton, 2004.
Leland, Charles. *Aradia: Gospel of the Witches*. New York: Samuel Weiser, 1974.
Levitas, Ruth. *The Concept of Utopia*. Syracuse: Syracuse University Press, 1990.
Luhrmann, Tanya M. *Persuasions of the Witch's Craft*. Cambridge: Harvard University Press, 1989.
Murray, Margaret. *The Witch-Cult in Western Europe*. London: Oxford University Press, 1962.
Puttnick, Elizabeth. *Women in New Religions: In Search of Community, Sexuality and Spiritual Power*. New York: St. Martin's, 1997.
Sargent, Lyman Tower. "The Three Faces of Utopianism Revisited." *Utopian Studies* 5.1 (1994): 1–37.
Starhawk. *The Spiral Dance*. San Francisco: Harper and Row, 1979.

BARRIE WHARTON

From Shukri Mustafa to the *Ashwaiyat*: Utopianism in Egyptian Islamism

The tragic events of 11 September 2001, with the attack on the World Trade Center in New York by *Al-Qaeda* terrorists, catapulted Islam and Islamist political movements onto television screens and the front pages of newspapers worldwide. The events of that momentous day have left an indelible imprint on contemporary society, and subsequent military campaigns and terrorist attacks in Afghanistan and Iraq have kept Islamic activism at the forefront of global attention.[1] However, this concern with the growth of "political" Islam is not new; for over the last forty years the rise of Islam, or more correctly the development of various Islamist movements, as a political phenomenon across the Muslim world has been greeted with fear and trepidation by both western governments and academics (see Sardar). In fact, the singular usage, "Islamist movement" is itself a misnomer, as it tends to suggest that there is *one* movement which, according to western observers, is an expansionist, borderless entity with a highly developed program of societal transformation that threatens the values, mores, and indeed the sheer existence of western civilization (see Roy). On the contrary, the emergence of various, often competing, Islamist movements bespeaks a deeply fragmented situation in which is encountered a myriad of deeply divergent and often radically opposed groups, currents, and trends whose methods,

---

1   Afghanistan and Iraq are but two examples of Islamist insurgency. Insurgency in Asia has led to atrocities in Bali and a continuing conflict in the Philippines, while the Madrid train bombings of 11 March 2004 and the 7 July 2005 bombings in London brought the specter of Islamic extremism to western Europe.

aims, and objectives differ not only from country to country across the Islamic world but indeed within the states themselves.

One could argue that much of this fear stems from the utopian dimension in Islamic movements; thus the commonly accepted western hegemony over the foundation and development of the field of utopian studies could well be disputed (see Sargent 19–21).[2] Although many of the seminal texts in this growing field tend to concentrate on the concept of Utopia as primarily a western phenomenon, ideas of social dreaming and diverse variants on intentional communities have long formed the cornerstone of alternative Islamic societies; and many of these, such as the Sufi brotherhoods, wield significant influence and power throughout the Islamic world (see Levitas). Indeed, the Islamic world may provide a very interesting, albeit hitherto neglected, forum for the analysis of the complex and often fraught relationship between Utopia and mainstream socio-religious practices (see Trousson 115–28).

From the discourse and practice of sheikhs to suicide bombers, rich currents of utopianism run throughout Islamic belief systems; and in this essay I will endeavor to examine the influence and reach of some of these currents within the specific context of contemporary Egyptian society. One could, however, extend many of my findings in this essay on Egypt to a wider Arab or Islamic context in societies that have produced their fair share of utopian visionaries from the Prophet Muhammad to the Mahdi, and in the contemporary era, from the Ayatollah Khomeini to Usama Bin Ladin (see Halliday). However, for now, I will confine myself to Egypt and offer an overview of the role and trajectory of utopianism in contemporary Islamist movements there, concentrating on selected specific figures or phenomena such as Shukri Mustafa and the *ashwaiyat* or urban slums of Cairo and Alexandria.

---

2   Although utopian studies as an academic discipline seems to be almost nonexistent in the Islamic world, centers of futuristic studies such as that of Asyut University in Egypt often fill this role, and the *inshallah* or god-willing culture that is utopian in design and motivation is the quintessential harbinger of contemporary Islamic society.

In Egypt, political Islam was born with the foundation of the Muslim Brotherhood in 1928, an organization that still wields considerable power today (see Mitchell).[3] Indeed, the Brotherhood played a major role in the Free Officer's Revolution of 1952, and in the early days of the revolution, it operated as a virtual government of the people. The support of the Brotherhood had been crucial in the original success of the revolution, but such was the power of the Islamist message in Egypt that its consequent suppression and dissolution would be a fundamental requisite for the consolidation of power in the new Egyptian regime (see al-Hudaybi; Bello). Consequently, a spiral of repression was unleashed by Nasserist forces as the Brotherhood was banned, and the Islamist movements as we know them today were born. The years of repression gave new impetus to the already growing radical wing of these movements, which came to see any cooperation with or recognition of the regime as equivalent to liaising with infidels and apostates. Supporters of the radical elements were encouraged, and saw their stance vindicated, by the brutal torture and inhuman treatment that the Brothers were receiving in Egyptian jails. Thus, the cleavage that already existed between the pacifist Islamism of al-Hudaybi and the militant extremism of new theorists such as Sayyid Qutb began to deepen.

Qutb's seminal *Signposts on the Road* differs greatly from the previous literature of the Muslim Brotherhood in its direct attack on and vilification of contemporary society in Egypt.[4] With an overt denunciation of Nasserist Egypt as a *jahiliyya* society, Qutb departs from the aegis of Koranic exegesis that had characterized much Islamist literature up until then. The accurate translation of this term,

---

3   In the summer of 2005 Egyptian presidential election campaign, the Muslim Brotherhood again emerged as the major threat to the re-election of Mubarak, and is again facing a consequential wave of repression.
4   The epistle for many groups comprising political Islamist movements, it wields powerful influence today. Qutb was hung on 29 August 1966, after being convicted of plotting to overthrow the Nasserist government. The photo of him taken before his death portrays a frail figure weakened by years of torture even as his messianic smile signifies a new and powerful martyr for the Islamist movement.

jahiliyya, is extremely problematic, but in a Koranic context it refers specifically to the "barbaric" pre-Islamic society.[5] This denunciation sent shock waves throughout political Islam with its condemnation of all Egyptian society as un-Islamic, as living in a state of paganism and worshipping the false god of Gamal Abdel Nasser and his totalitarian state. Al-Banna and previous Brotherhood leaders had never gone further in their writings than to level general criticism of Egyptian society and to highlight immoral practices. Qutb thus became the new spokesman of the generation of the detention camps, and his writings preached the end of tolerance and invoked a *hijra* or withdrawal from society akin to Muhammad's retreat to Medina from Mecca. Qutb's position was that this tactical withdrawal would serve to strengthen an Islamist activism that could only be tainted and weakened by its interaction with the forces of *jahiliyya* Nasserist society. The belief was that this withdrawal would eventually lead to a triumphant return and the restoration of a true Islamic society based on the principles of the Prophet Muhammad.

The enormous implications of Qutb's manifesto were clearly apparent. The time for dialogue was now over, and, with their resolve strengthened by years of torture and repression, a section of Islamism was now ready to openly challenge the state apparatus. *Signposts on the Road* would justify their *jihad* or holy war – even as the traditional Brotherhood leadership embodied in the aging al-Hudaybi was profoundly shocked by the scenario that the interpretation of Qutb's writings presented. The Muslim Brotherhood, which had never sought open conflict with the ruling regime, now seemed to be openly intent on overthrowing it. A great paradox was that Qutb himself was not a man of violence, and it is quite plausible that he never envisaged the

---

5   The term *jahilliya* is difficult to translate, as it is open to various interpretations. It denotes the barbarism of pre-Islamic society in Arabia. In a modern context, from a radical Islamist perspective, the closest approximation is a society of decadence and ignorance that is not part of and cannot identify with the Muslim *umma* or community. According to Qutb and radical Islamism, this *jahilliya* is a creeping menace, seen in the onslaught of globalization at work in Islamic societies.

interpretation of his writings in such a manner.[6] Nevertheless, his writings, along with his martyrdom, were instrumental in the relaunch of political Islam in the contemporary era and in its further division into two separate wings.

After Nasser's death, the *jama'at islamiyya*, or Islamist associations, were among the first novel elements in the new generation of Islamism. Having sprung up on university campuses all over Egypt and having developed through aggressive and often violent tactics, these disciples of Qutb attempted to bring the entire Egyptian educational system under Islamist control. This process was seen as a precursor for the eventual Islamist takeover of Egyptian society. Paradoxically, the *jama'at islamiyya* were in many ways a Nasserist creation, in that their ranks were made up of the first generation of the beneficiaries of the Nasserist core policy of education for the masses. Egyptian universities were now no longer the domain of the elite, even though the vast swell in numbers had not been accompanied by a corresponding increase in resources. Therefore, the Egyptian university system at the beginning of the 1970s found itself heavily overpopulated and grossly underresourced. This was a lethal cocktail for political unrest and disorder, and Anwar Sadat feared the extension of support for Nasserist and other left-wing groups. He therefore decided to play the Islamist card and encouraged the establishment of Islamic groups on the campuses in order to combat anti-regime, left-wing tendencies. The *jama'at islamiyya* were thus born, a revolutionary child of Sadat's political folly; yet it was the brother of a *jama'at islamiyya* leader who would force Sadat to pay the ultimate price for this folly when he assassinated him in September 1981 (see Kepel).

The *jama'at islamiyya* multiplied their membership throughout the 1970s by virtue of their dynamism and their ability to identify the

---

6   Qutb was an unlikely radical. A shy intellectual and civil servant whose interests were in literature and poetry, he was converted to the Islamist cause at the age of forty-five after he returned in 1951 from a three-year posting in the U.S. where the materialist society and amorality that he encountered had had a profound negative effect on him.

problems in Egyptian society and to articulate an Islamist response to them. They were especially successful in highlighting the cultural and social dislocation – first, of Egyptian university students, and later of the population at large (see el-Guindi). The burgeoning university sector thus provided the first target for the rhetoric of the *jama'at islamiyya*. Students studied for degrees and diplomas that were based almost exclusively on rote-learning and graduated in western academic disciplines that were inapplicable to the Egyptian labor market. Lecture halls were overcrowded and professors were chronically underpaid. Law graduates dreamed of posts as receptionists in Saudi Arabian hotels, while scholarships abroad for the privileged few remained the only hope of real advancement. Students were hungry and lived in slums surrounding the universities. Books were unattainable, and professors lived off illicit sales of their lecture notes or private classes where matriculation was necessary for success in the university examination. The imported western idea of a university thus clashed with traditional Islamic modes of learning, and examinations consisted of rote-learning and simple regurgitation of texts. There was no *madrasa* for discussion, nor was there any forum for critical thought or questioning as traditionally exists in western academia (see Leiser 29–47). Egyptian universities had become the worst of both worlds; and the campuses were full of bright, dynamic young Egyptians with no channel for their energies or discontent. In this hyper-unreal world of superficial advancement and opportunity, the *jama'at islamiyya* prospered and grew.

The *jama'at islamiyya* addressed the quotidian concerns of this university population. Transport was arranged to take female students to the universities, and books and accommodation were provided to any student who needed them. Tyrannical landlords were brought to justice, and students were offered financial support by Islamist groups. Most importantly, the *jama'at islamiyya* offered students an identity and a secure support framework. Many of the new class of students were from a rural background, and they found themselves isolated and lost in an urban milieu that had very little relevance to their upbringing. The *jama'at islamiyya* provided them with a meaning and a way of life with which they could identify (see Tibi). Akin to the experience of many who have participated in other utopian groups or experiments, therefore, many of the new recruits found, and entered into, an alternative, systemic vision and context within which they could find a new way forward in their own lives as well as in Egyptian society in general. While most were unfamiliar with the intricacies of the writings of Qutb or the precise goals of the *jama'at islamiyya*, they did learn that reading the Koran and donning the white *gallibiya* at least restored to them the semblance of a familiar, traditional identity and filled the chaotic identity vacuum that the onset of modernity and globalism had provoked in their lives (see Arkoun).[7]

If the Muslim Brotherhood claimed to represent the interests of moderate, mainstream Islamism and the *jama'at islamiyya* were seen as the new dynamic and progressive wing of Islamism, there was a further cluster of groups with a more radical utopian vision on the extremes of extremism (Tuveson 3–21). These various groups either insisted on total withdrawal from the perceived pagan society in which they were living or on the waging of a *jihad*, or holy war, to overthrow the regime and create a new society based on Islamist principles. They categorically chose revolution rather than reform, and their activities received wide media coverage, especially in the western press where they were demonized as the vanguard of the new Islamist threat. In fact, the notoriety and column space that many of these groups earned throughout the 1970s in the western media was far out of proportion to their actual size and influence (see Agha). Meanwhile, the exaggerated focus on this extreme Islamist threat, with its terrorist tendency, diverted attention away from the examination of the deep sociopolitical factors behind the rise of political Islam and an accurate analysis of its actual scope and strength in Egyptian society.

The most extreme Islamist groups were offshoots and splinters of both the Muslim Brotherhood and the *jama'at islamiyya*. Many of these groups were numerically small and insignificant, but several formations did come to public prominence and revealed a new strand

---

7   The *gallibiya* or *jallibiya*, as it is referred to in Upper Egypt, is the traditional long unisex dress of Egyptians, akin to the North African *burnous*. It has become associated with Islamist leanings, particularly in its traditional white version.

of Islamism that directly challenged and threatened not only the state's authority but also questioned its very existence while threatening to invade and engulf the entire Egyptian societal landscape (see Ibrahim, "Egypt's Militant Islamic Groups" 423–53). Two of the most significant were Salih Sirriya's group, which launched an attack on the Heliopolis Military Academy in April 1974, and Shukri Mustafa's Society of Muslims. Sirriya was executed after the failure of his Heliopolis coup in 1974; and many of his supporters, such as Talal al-Ansari, flocked to the camp of a rival extremist group, Shukri Mustafa's Society of Muslims. This grouping was even more radical and revolutionary than its predecessors, as it attempted to establish an Islamic counter-society in the image of the Prophet Muhammad's *hijra*, or withdrawal to Medina from Mecca. These extremist groups, although still relatively small in membership, were growing; and they provided an excellent organizing opportunity for Islamists who had received their primary education in the Muslim Brotherhood before progressing to the *jama'at islamiyya*. Formations such as Salih Sirriya's and Shukri Mustafa's were therefore of fundamental importance in their function as siphons for radical and extremist elements. As a result, the energies of deeply alienated and oppositional Islamist subjects were channeled into violent activities on the margins of political Islam. This coalescence, however, minimized the danger of potentially fatal power struggles in the ideological and political core of Egyptian Islamism.

The Society of Muslims, led by Shukri Mustafa, was the most radical incarnation of Islamist extremism. The Society was not at all interested in the reform of the *jahiliyya* or the pagan society of contemporary Egypt; neither were they interested in vying for the reins of political power. On the contrary, they simply withdrew completely from society and set up in effect a microcosmic counter-society, living out a utopian vision totally severed from the Egyptian pagan metropole (see Claeys and Sargent 312–420). The Society of Muslims also bore many of the hallmarks of an intentional community (see Sargent 13–17). Its members lived among each other in the alternative setting of the caves of Upper Egypt; and they based their affiliation and activism on their shared literal interpretation of Qutb and a re-enactment of the *hijra* or withdrawal of the Prophet

Muhammad from Mecca to Medina at the dawn of Islam. Despite their radical standpoint, however, the state regime placed little importance on their activities during their early years of organizing as they were not perceived as a major security threat. Thus, free from immediate repression, the entire political movement grew steadily.

In late 1976, however, during a general government crackdown on political Islam, the Society of Muslims was targeted and many of its members were arrested in their isolated caves in Upper Egypt.[8] This repression finally brought the group into the media spotlight; and, as a direct response that highlighted their demands, the Society orchestrated the much publicized kidnapping of the former Minister of *Waqfs* or Religious Affairs, Muhammad al-Dhahabi. When these demands were not met, al-Dhahabi was killed. Al-Dhahabi was thus the first major political figure to die at the hands of the extremists, but he would not be the last. With his assassination, the extremist wing embarked on a new policy of terror that targeted the leading and most influential figures in Egyptian society. This policy departure would do much to blur and tarnish the real issues and motivations behind the utopianism of Egyptian Islam and the growth of political Islam in Egypt as a whole; it would also propel Islamism onto the front pages of the international press. The hitherto embryonic idea of the "Islamist threat" was now well and truly born.

Shukri Mustafa himself was a typical Islamist by-product of the brutal Nasserist years of repression. A native of Asyut, he was recruited by the Muslim Brotherhood while at university, where he was arrested in 1965 at the age of twenty-three and imprisoned for the crime of having distributed Islamist pamphlets on campus.[9] He spent six years in the Nasserist jails. When he emerged, he never forgot what he had seen inside, and he would articulate his experience in a

---

8   After an article in the Egyptian daily, *Al-Akhbar*, in May 1975 that referred to the Society of Muslims as *ahl al-kahf* (people of the cave), their members were often referred to as such in the media. The usage derives from their custom of living in caves in the Asyut governorate

9   Asyut in Upper Egypt between Cairo and the Sudan is the heartland of political Islamism in Egypt. My research for this essay comes from my time of living and lecturing at the University of Asyut.

call for total withdrawal and separation from what he perceived as an inhumane and pagan contemporary Egyptian society. The radical politicization of Shukri in the detention camps was not, of course, an isolated occurrence. In the late 1960s, the debates that raged in the camps were radicalizing an entire generation.[10] However, on their release, many followed the more mainstream and less radical trends, and the idea of total separation as advocated by Shukri was seen as unworkable and falsely "utopian."

And yet, a concrete utopian option was gradually articulated by Shukri. He himself never identified with the mainstream; as such, it was difficult for al-Hudaybi or other mainstream leaders to attempt to entice him back into the fold. On one level, his newly formed Society of Muslims seemed to be simply an idiosyncratic cult of eccentrics characterized by long beards and black *gallibiyas* and a primitive existence in caves. However, on closer analysis and in a radical and revolutionary manner, I would argue, the Society of Muslims was actually addressing and redressing many of the problems and grievances of contemporary Egyptian society. In essence, they were in fact creating what was for them a working utopia. Shukri's total rejection of the Egyptian educational system had struck a deeply critical chord in a society wherein state education was increasingly perceived as an assembly line churning out irrelevant diplomas and qualifications that were of little use in contemporary life. Furthermore, the Society creatively addressed the problem of marriage in contemporary Egypt, an impossibility for many young men given the chronic lack of housing and the exorbitant prices charged by landlords (see Feiler 295–312). In a utopian negation of these negations, the Society therefore offered a radical, apparently viable, alternative way of learning, living, and serving society. Thus, at the level of everyday life, even as he proffered a larger social vision and commitment, Shukri proposed the arrangement of early marriage for Society members and their temporary accommodation in flats financed by

---

10 It remains to be seen whether detention camps such as Guantanamo Bay will have a similar effect on the Islamist movement as those at Tura and Qanatir in Egypt.

Society members who had emigrated to the oil-rich Gulf states in a further geographical extension of their *hijra* or withdrawal. These innovative and original solutions shocked the regime and conservative elements in Egyptian society, who then accused Shukri of operating a harem and of practicing amoral primitivism. Intentionally or not, Shukri had touched the nerve of a massive and widespread sense of cultural dislocation in Egypt. Far from ridiculing his obscurantism and backwardness, many Egyptians found more in common with his utopian ideas than with the mainstream society in which they were living.

The Society of Muslims was never a mass movement, and it never counted more than two and a half thousand members. However, these members were staunch devotees, and their devotion and loyalty brought them increased public attention throughout the 1970s. A pariah of the mainstream, the Society of Muslims was often accused of collaboration with the state. Meanwhile, the relationship between the regime and the Society of Muslims took a drastic turn with the aforementioned kidnapping and murder of al-Dhahabi in 1977 as a response to what Shukri saw as unfair repression instigated against the Society. Even before al-Dhahabi's murder, the repercussions of the activities of the Society of Muslims had reached far beyond illicit marriages in isolated caves. Shukri's alternative societal experiment had highlighted the social and cultural alienation of contemporary Egyptians, and his activities had pointed the finger at a deficient and subservient al-Azhar, out of touch with their flock and its needs.[11] Islamic establishment figures such as Shaykh Shar'awi and Shaykh Su'ad Jalal felt the heat of Shukri's criticism, and the observations of the backward *Sa'idi* began to reverberate throughout Egyptian society (see Jansen 379–89).[12] The Society of Muslims disappeared after Shukri's death, but new manifestations of extremist Islamism were already appearing. These groups would study carefully the experience

---

11   Cairo-based Al-Azhar is the ultimate authority of official Sunni Islam, with the Sheikh of Al-Azhar being the final arbiter on questions of religious law.
12   *Sa'idi* refers to an inhabitant of the *Sa'id* or Upper Egypt and is often used in Egypt as a mocking term suggesting backwardness or bumpkin status.

of the Society of Muslims, and, in many ways, they would learn from the innocence and incredulity of Shukri as he sought to deal with an experienced and powerful state. Thus, the Society's utopian vision would live on in a cultural surplus that was available to the newer groupings.

After Nasser's death in 1970, the student movement of the *jama'at islamiyya* had come to the forefront of political Islam, but there was a further layer below it; the Muslim Brotherhood was also playing a vital role in the preparation of raw recruits that would now inherit and harness Shukri Mustafa's legacy. The *'usar,* or Koranic study clubs, were the origins and base of the *jama'at islamiyya* on many campuses, but a vital role was also played by the *jam'iyat,* or Islamic societies, that – although ostensibly less radical than the *jama'at islamiyya* – contributed greatly to the Islamization of Egyptian society as a whole. Indeed, the *jam'iyat* and the *jama'at diniyya,* or religious associations, were the real molders of contemporary Islamism in Egypt. It was the increase in their activities and operations after the death of Sadat that began a new, deeper permeation of Egyptian society by Islamist movements. The radical extremists and the *jama'at islamiyya* had scored significant successes in Sadat's Egypt, but it was the *jam'iyat* that would find the weak underbelly of Egyptian secular society and penetrate it in the 1980s. Their activities in everyday society would take radical Islamist politics to a new plane as they provided the education and support network that was essential to the overall growth of the movements.

Throughout the 1970s, the line between the *jam'iyat* and the *jama'at islamiyya* was extremely blurred. Indeed, the terms and the groupings they signified became almost interchangeable. However, in the 1980s, the *jam'iyat* began to assert a separate identity as community-based groups, and they were often gathered around the figure of a charismatic Islamist preacher when the mosque returned to its traditional place at the heart of this new Islamist society.[13] After

---

13 The most celebrated of these preachers include Shaykh Kishk, originally based in the poor area of El-Demerdash in Cairo and Shaykh Salama. Tapes of their

Sadat's death, the *jam'iyat* were thus among the first of the movements to reorganize and accept a leading role in the voyage of Egyptian Islamism towards the next millennium. The *jam'iyat* reveled in the societal conditions of Hosni Mubarak's Egypt, and their radical resocialization program provided a new alternative (see Hanafi 54–74). As older sections of political Islam began to move towards the corridors of power in the 1980s, they had to lose some of their revolutionary rhetoric. Therefore, the emergent role of the *jam'iyat* was fundamental as they continued to provide a steady stream of radical Islamist recruits. Thus, their instrumental interventions in the ongoing Islamization of Egyptian society from below became a major factor in the movements' continued growth and success.

In the 1980s and 1990s, the *jam'iyat* returned to the campuses. Their role was less visible, yet in many ways it was more effective than that of the *jama'at islamiyya* in the heady revolutionary days of Sadat's Egypt. The *jam'iyat* organized student members' transport to and from the university campuses and provided them with subsidized accommodation, course material, and even clothes. Moreover, the *jam'iyat* began to provide a larger sociocultural support network for its adherents. The experience of this alternative Islamist society would prove to be a key rite of passage for the young partisans of the 1990s as they became the recruits in the next millennium. By the beginning of the 1990s, the *jam'iyat* found themselves at the vanguard of the defense against globalism and the resultant destruction of traditional Egyptian society. Since the *jam'iyat* constantly avoided involvement in overt political actions, they were able to draw upon a much larger support base and extend their already wide appeal.

Furthermore, in Mubarak's Egypt, community *jam'iyat* groups began to proliferate and this allowed the *jam'iyat* message to reach hitherto untouched corners of society. Many of these groups were formed by ex-students; and their message spread quickly, particularly in the densely populated slums of Egypt's urban centers, in particular Cairo. These *jam'iyat* community organizations devoted their energies

---

Friday sermons can be found for sale on street corners all over the Arab and Islamic world.

to the provision of health clinics, Islamic schools, and lending clubs – all of which were based around the traditional central focus point of the mosque. Campaigns were launched against alcohol consumption and other "un-Islamic" activities. The *jam'iyat* began to mobilize large sectors of the population, and Islamist purges were carried out in the areas under their control. *Jam'iyat* members thus played a vital role in the Cairo riots of 1986. As their power grew, it became apparent that the regime might yet rue the neglect and ambivalence it had shown towards them in the early 1980s in favor of a concentration on the security threat presented by more recognizably Islamist extremists.[14] By virtue of *jam'iyat* activism, entire neighborhoods of Cairo came under Islamist control. More importantly, Islamist pockets developed in the traditional heartlands of regime support as the government retreated further from society. Ain Shams, only a couple of metro stops from the Presidential Palace, is one of these new Islamist strongholds; Imbaba, adjacent to prosperous Mohandiseen, is another. In this way, the regime's problems continue to be aggravated by the continuing flight of people to Cairo from the provinces and the resultant chronic shortage of housing and resources. The new arrivals in the slums of the Muqattam Hills or the growing population who live below the hills in the macabre setting of the Cairo cemeteries or "Cities of the Dead" are easy targets for the *jam'iyat* discourse; and, although the *jam'iyat* persistently reiterate that they are only interested in reform, there is little doubt that they hold the kind of power and influence that could be used to engineer a revolution.

These "forgotten," peripheral areas on the geographical and economic map of Egyptian society have become the bulwark of *jam'iyat* support in present day Egypt. They are the site for the new custodians of the Islamist utopian vision. Their significance is underlined by conservative estimates that put the population of these *ashwaiyat* or urban slums at twelve million on a national level and

---

14 The riots were ostensibly over bread subsidies, but there was a strong Islamist undercurrent that challenged the power of the Mubarak regime.

growing (see Ibrahim, "Reform and Frustration in Egypt" 125–35).[15] It is clear that, with the present regime's continuing neglect of these areas, many have become microcosmic "Islamic Republics," growing at the regime's peril. One-fifth of the Egyptian population now live in these officially forgotten slums, and their existence on the peripheries or indeed outside Egyptian society is only punctuated by intermittent outbreaks of violence often provoked by what is perceived as illegitimate government interference (see al-Sayyid Marsot 178–97).

A typical example of these *ashwaiyat* is the area of Munira-West in Cairo, less than two kilometers from the leafy embassy belt of Zamalek in Central Cairo. Munira-West covers an area of only one square kilometer, but it is home to over one million people. Up until 1992, Munira-West did not officially exist. It had no police presence, government health services, schools, or sanitation. Neither had it running water nor electricity supplies. Not surprisingly, the Munira-West riots of December 1992 changed all this, as it took almost 18,000 troops nearly two months to quell what was in reality an armed insurrection. Again, not surprisingly, the *jam'iyat* are firmly entrenched in Munira-West, as in the hundreds of other slum areas that dot the Egyptian societal landscape. They have stepped into the shoes of the retreating government that continues to turn its back on these areas. Whether this retreat and rejection finds its rationale in the regime's helplessness or whether it is simple neglect, the consequences are seriously damaging to official Egyptian society as the *jam'iyat* and other strands of political Islam annex these areas for their utopian experiment – providing an alternative societal support structure in the fields of policing, health, education, and cultural life in a direct usurpation of the regime's authority and claim to legitimately govern.

The real danger to the regime in the immediate future lies in the spilling over and expansion of these slum areas into the lower-middle-class and middle-class neighborhoods that they increasingly adjoin and into other Egyptian cities. This expansion will logically involve

---

15 These figures are based on my fieldwork in Egypt and are accurate as of my latest visit in May 2005.

an extension of political Islam's already large sphere of influence and a stretching of the parameters of *jam'iyat* involvement in Egyptian life. Such a development is presently in progress in a Cairo that is bursting apart at the seams, and this tendency spells the death knell to the regime's policy of containment of the *jam'iyat* and the Islamist movements. As such, it can only serve to further isolate and detach the regime from an increasingly large group of its citizens finding new meaning and life in a radical Islamist alternative. However, the *jam'iyat* are far from merely a Cairo phenomenon.[16] In Alexandria, as well, *Jam'iyat Fajr al-Islam* has been at the forefront of *jam'iyat* activities; and its leader, Muhammad al-Maraghi, has become a prominent actor in the political arena. *Jam'iyat* are also numerous throughout Upper Egypt; and in many villages in the Asyut and al-Minya governorates they have begun to form the effective government apparatus. *Jam'iyat* were also instrumental in the rise of Islamist power within the professional syndicates and associations, as it was the *jam'iyat* who supplied the candidates and support for the Islamist takeover of this vital sector. Moreover, after the takeover, the *jam'iyat* continued to provide the new leaders of the syndicates and associations a stable and broad power base that was essential in the consolidation of their positions in the light of the regime's initial attempts to remove them.

The *jam'iyat* have therefore become major players in contemporary political Islam in Egypt, principally through their ability to attract and mobilize large sections of the population who are disenchanted with the political and social system. Their rise has also allowed the Muslim Brotherhood to concentrate much of its energies

---

16 Cairo, with a population of almost twenty million, remains the home of almost one-third of the population; and its dominance of Egyptian social, cultural, political, and religious life remains, albeit undesirable, a reality. In fact, Cairo is popularly referred to as Egypt, *Masr* in Egyptian Arabic, with the two entities rarely distinguished between.

on political activities; while the *jam'iyat* provide the Brotherhood with a steady and prepared stream of recruits out of its alternative enclaves. The nature of this support structure has therefore been fundamental in unifying the Islamist movements at a grassroots level, especially as the *jam'iyat* have been additionally, and increasingly, able to tap into and harness latent political potential from other Islamic sources such as the Sufi Brotherhoods and the various *jama'at diniyya* or religious associations. The *jam'iyat* have also highlighted the increasing irrelevance, and hence delegitimation, of official Islam to the plight of many Egyptians. The older institutions of al-Azhar, closely associated with the regime, have come in for ever increasing scrutiny throughout the Mubarak era. By the mid 1990s many of the leading *'ulema* and prominent figures of official Islam were already gravitating in the direction of the *jam'iyat* and their utopian *ashwaiyat* in a late effort to recover lost legitimacy. Throughout the 1990s, therefore, the scope and influence of the *jam'iyat* continued to grow as they extended their highly complex matrix of influence and control. It is becoming ever more apparent that it is groups such as the *jam'iyat* who are now the emergent powerbrokers in Egyptian society as they increasingly develop the capacity to engender regime change and even social revolution.

The activities of the *jam'iyat* and similar Islamist groups have been on a steady rise over the last twenty-five years in Egypt, while the Muslim Brotherhood, under the guise of the *Tahaluf* or Alliance, has made tentative steps into the mainstream democratic political arena. However, Islamist inroads into society have not spelled an end to Islamist extremism, and, from the mid 1980s onwards, radical groups have launched what has amounted to an almost full-scale offensive against the regime. This offensive has brought Egypt's Islamist movements back onto the front pages of the international press, as the regime has found itself under pressure on all fronts. The economic situation has continued to deteriorate, and the reformist Islamists have made steady advances throughout all spheres of Egyptian society. However, it is the terrorist offensive that has become the regime's obsession, since the security threat that it presents effectively holds the government hostage as potential tourists and foreign investors avoid the evolving scenario. The regime's campaign to eradicate and exterminate Islamist extremism has placed an enormous strain on its resources, and this has entailed the resultant neglect of pressing social issues and needs. Thus, as with many utopian trajectories, the oppositional movements grow: negatively, by virtue of increasing social deprivation and dispossession and by increasing repression; and positively, by a growing utopian alternative that offers people a new life, a new culture and society. Whether the regime will eventually crack under this pressure and whether the official or oppositional utopia will prevail still remains to be seen.

Works Cited

Agha, Olfat. "Islamic Fundamentalism; its Image in the Western Media." *Kurusat Istratijiya (Strategic Papers)-Al-Ahram Centre for Political and Strategic Studies* 5.25 (1995): 5–24.

Arkoun, Mohammed. *Ouvertures sur l'Islam*. Paris: Ed. Maisonneuve et Larose, 1992.

Bello, Iysa Ade. "The Society of the Muslim Brethren – An Ideological Study." *Islamic Studies* 20.2 (1981): 111–27.

Claeys, Gregory and Lyman Tower Sargent (eds). *The Utopia Reader*. New York and London: New York University Press, 1999.

Feiler, Gil. "Housing Policy in Egypt." *Middle Eastern Studies* 28.2 (1992): 295–312.

Halliday, Fred. *Islam and the Myth of Confrontation: Religion and Politics in the Middle East*. London: I.B. Tauris, 1996.

Hanafi, Hasan. "The Relevance of the Islamic Alternative in Egypt." *Arab Studies Quarterly* 4.1–2 (1982): 54–74.

al-Hudaybi, Hasan. *Du'ah la Qudah (Preachers not Judges.)* Cairo: Muslim Brotherhood Publications, 1977.

el-Guindi, Fadwa. "Veiling *Infitah* with Muslim Ethic." *Social Problems* 28.4 (1981): 465–85

Ibrahim, Saad Eddin. "Anatomy of Egypt's Militant Islamic Groups: Methodological Note and Preliminary Findings." *International Journal of Middle East Studies* 12 (1985): 423–53.

___. "Reform and Frustration in Egypt." *Journal of Democracy* 7.4 (1996): 125–35.
Jansen, J.J.G. "A Little-Known Endorsement by Sheikh as-Sha'rawi." *Union Européene d'Arabisants et d'Islamisants-Actas del XII Congreso de la U.E.A.I (Malaga, 1984)* 12 (1986): 379–89.
Kepel, Gilles. *The Prophet and the Pharaoh-Muslim Extremism in Egypt*. London: Al-Saqi Books, 1985.
Leiser, Gary. "The *Madrasa* and the Islamization of the Middle East: The Case of Egypt." *Journal of the American Research Centre in Egypt* 22 (1985): 29–47.
Levitas, Ruth. *The Concept of Utopia*. Syracuse: Syracuse University Press, 1990.
Mitchell, Richard. *The Society of the Muslim Brothers*. London: Oxford University Press, 1969.
Qutb, Sayyid. *Ma'alim fil Tariq (Signposts on the Road)*. Beirut and Cairo: Dar al-Shuruq, 1980.
Roy, Olivier. *Political Islam*. London: I.B. Tauris, 1994.
Sardar, Ziauddin. *Desperately Seeking Paradise: Journeys of a Sceptical Muslim*. London: Granta, 2004.
Sargent, Lyman Tower. "The Three Faces of Utopianism Revisited." *Utopian Studies* 5.1 (1994): 1–37.
al-Sayyid Marsot, Afaf Lutfi. "Revolutionaries, Fundamentalists and Housewives: Alternative Groups in the Arab World." *Journal of Arab Affairs* 6.2 (1987): 178–97.
Tibi, Bassam. *Islam and the Cultural Accommodation of Social Change*. Boulder: Westview Press, 1990.
Trousson, Raymond. *D'Utopie et d'Utopistes*. Paris: L'Harmattan, 1998.
Tuveson, Ernest Lee. *Millennium and Utopia: A Study in the Background of the Idea of Progress*. Gloucester: Peter Smith, 1972.

Notes on Contributors

JENNY ANDERSSON is an economic historian and assistant professor at the institute for contemporary history at Södertörn University College, Stockholm. She is the author of *Between Growth and Security: Swedish Social Democracy from a Strong Society to a Third Way* and is currently working on a project called *The People's Library and the Electronic Workshop – British and Swedish Social Democracy interpret the Knowledge Society*.

LUCIAN M. ASHWORTH is Head of the Department of Politics and Public Administration at the University of Limerick. He is the author of two books on interwar writers in International Relations, and his latest book, *International Relations and the Labour Party*, will be published in 2007.

ANTONIS BALASOPOULOS is assistant professor in the Department of English Studies at the University of Cyprus. His essays on the literary, theoretical, and political dimensions of utopianism have appeared in *Gramma*, *Utopian Studies*, *Cultural Critique*, and *Transtext(e)s-Transcultures*. He is currently working on completing *Groundless Dominions: Utopia, Science Fiction and the Cultural Politics of US Expansionism*, and *Figures of Utopia: Literature, Politics, Philosophy*.

MATTHEW BEAUMONT is a Lecturer in the Department of English at University College London. He is the author of *Utopia Ltd.: Ideologies of Social Dreaming in England 1870–1900* and the editor of the Oxford World's Classics edition of Edward Bellamy's *Looking Backward*.

ANDREW J BROWN, Research Director for Cultural Logic, LLC, is an anthropologist whose primary work explores the conceptual and cultural models that citizens in North America and Europe use to think about public policy issues. These researches, commissioned by non-profit foundations, have been applied to advocates' efforts to improve public understandings on topics as diverse as racism, health, poverty, labour, sustainable food systems, and climate change. He has been a visiting professor of anthropology at University College Cork, Kazakhstan National University, and Colby College in Maine, and has taught extensively on utopianism, cultural anthropology, and globalization.

VINCENT GEOGHEGAN is Professor of Political Theory and Director of Research in Political Theory at Queen's University Belfast. He is the author of *Reason and Eros: The Social Theory of Herbert Marcuse*; *Utopianism and Marxism*, and *Ernst Bloch*. He has published a number of articles on topics such as Irish political thought, early Irish socialism, and writers such as Edward Carpenter and Olaf Stapledon. He is currently exploring the utopian dimensions of religious narrative, attempting to relate this to the development of post-secularism.

MICHAEL J. GRIFFIN lectures in English Studies at the University of Limerick. He has published widely in eighteenth-century, utopian, and Irish studies, in journals such as the *Review of English Studies*, *Eighteenth-Century Ireland*, the *Field Day Review*, and *Utopian Studies*.

TIMOTHY KEANE teaches in the Department of English at the National University of Ireland, Galway, where he is a researcher in the Moore Institute for Research in the Humanities and Social Studies. His research examines the links between English radicalism and Irish nationalism in the nineteenth century. He has previously published on William Cobbett and Ireland.

MICHAEL G. KELLY is Junior Lecturer in French at the University of Limerick, Ireland. His doctoral work related theories of utopia to models of poetic language in Segalen, Daumal, and Bonnefoy. A revised version of this work is forthcoming. In addition to further articles on those poets, he has written on a number of other twentieth-century French poets including Pierre Jean Jouve, Paul Claudel, and

Robert Desnos, as well as on authors as diverse as Marcel Schwob and Jean Rolin. His translations into Irish include works by Michaux, Larbaud, and García Lorca as well as Alfred Jarry's *Ubu Roi*, performed in 1997.

RUTH LEVITAS, Professor of Sociology at the University of Bristol, is the author of *The Concept of Utopia* and *The Inclusive Society? Social Exclusion and New Labour*, and editor of *The Ideology of the New Right*. She has published numerous articles on aspects of utopianism and political thought. She is co-founder and chair of the Utopian Studies Society (Europe), and vice-chair of the William Morris Society. Thinking about space, time, and Utopia, she is currently working on two books: *The River Runs Through It*, on William Morris, *News from Nowhere*, and Hammersmith, and *The Imaginary Reconstitution of Society: Utopia as Method*, on Utopia and social science.

SUSAN MCMANUS is Lecturer in Political Theory in the School of Politics, International Studies and Philosophy at Queen's University, Belfast. She is author of *Fictive Theories: Toward a Deconstructive and Utopian Political Imagination*. She does research in radical political theory and cultures of resistance. She is currently working on a book-length project titled *Theorizing Affect: Subjectivity, Agency, Politics*.

TOM MOYLAN is Glucksman Professor of Contemporary Writing and Director of the Ralahine Centre for Utopian Studies at the University of Limerick. He is the author of *Demand the Impossible: Science Fiction and the Utopian Imagination*; *Scraps of the Untainted Sky: Science Fiction, Utopia, Dystopia*; and essays on sf, utopia, cultural studies, and theology. He co-edited *Not Yet: Reconsidering Ernst Bloch* (with Jamie Owen Daniel), and *Dark Horizons: Science Fiction and the Dystopian Imagination* and *Utopia Method Vision: The Use Value of Social Dreaming* (Ralahine Utopian Studies, volume one) (with Raffaella Baccolini). He is currently working on Irish utopianism and Irish sf.

PAULA MURPHY is a lecturer in the Department of English Language and Literature in MIC, Limerick. Her research interests are literary theory, especially psychoanalysis, deconstruction and postmodernism, and contemporary Irish studies. She is the editor of the forthcoming *New Voices in Irish Criticism*, and is currently writing a book on Irish drama. She is an associate editor of *The Irish Book Review* and *Kritikos: Journal of Postmodern Cultural Sound, Text and Image.*

CAITRÍONA NÍ DHÚILL is a researcher at the Ludwig Boltzmann Institute for the History and Theory of Biography, Vienna, where her research areas include the history of biography in the nineteenth and twentieth centuries and the Austrian writer Hugo von Hofmannsthal. She has held lectureships at the universities of Durham and St. Andrews.

EUGENE O'BRIEN is Senior lecturer, Head of the English Department and director of the Mary Immaculate College Irish Studies Centre in Mary Immaculate College, Limerick. He has published five books to date on critical theory and Irish Studies. He is editor of the *Contemporary Irish Writers and Filmmakers* series, of *Studies in Irish Literature* and *Irish Studies* series, and of the *Irish Book Review*.

AIDAN O'MALLEY graduated from the European University Institute, Florence in 2004 with a PhD on the Field Day Theatre Company. Since then, he has worked at the Humanities Institute of Ireland at University College Dublin, where he has been preparing a monograph on the Field Day enterprise.

PHILIPP SCHWEIGHAUSER is currently teaching at the University of Berne. He is the author of *The Noises of American Literature, 1890–1985: Toward a History of Literary Acoustics*. He has also published articles on Nabokov, DeLillo, American realism, French philosopher Michel Serres, literary soundscapes from realism to postmodernism, the poetry of Ruth Benedict, and masculinities. He co-edited (with Paula Bernat Bennett and Karen Kilcup) *Options for Teaching Nineteenth-Century American Poetry.*

GERALDINE SHERIDAN is Associate Professor of French at the University of Limerick. She has published widely on aspects of eighteenth-century culture and the history of ideas, including a monograph on *Nicolas Lenglet Dufresnoy and the Literary Underworld of the Ancien Régime*. She developed an interest in the history of women in the trades when researching an article on "Women in the book trade in eighteenth-century France" for *Eighteenth-Century Studies*, and is currently completing the manuscript of a book on visual images of women and work in the eighteenth century.

DAN SMITH is a Senior Lecturer in Fine Art Theory at Chelsea College of Art and Design, University of the Arts London. He is a regular contributor to Art Monthly magazine, and has published critical and historical writing on art and material culture in *New Statesman*, *Parachute* and *Things*. At the time of writing, he is engaged in the final stages of a PhD thesis on H.G. Wells and Material Culture at the Slade School of Art, University College London.

DARA WALDRON is Assistant Lecturer in the Department of Critical and Contextual Studies at the Limerick School of Fine Art and Design. His doctoral research concerned the problem of evil in different yet related genres of international film and his published work has dealt with ethical and aesthetic concerns in the films of Pier Paolo Pasolini, Liliana Cavani and Andrei Tarkovsky.

BARRIE WHARTON was awarded his PhD at the University of Limerick in 1997 for work on Islam and Europe. He has lectured and published throughout Europe, North America, and the Islamic World. He lectures at the University of Limerick and he is currently on leave as a Senior Research Fellow at New Zealand's National Centre for Research on Europe at the University of Canterbury.

CHRISTOPHER YORKE is currently based in the Department of Philosophy at the University of Tokyo as a visiting research student, and is a PhD candidate at the University of Glasgow. Previous areas in which he has published include ethical and political philosophy.

Index

8½ 301
Abbé de Saint-Pierre 336
Abbott, Edwin 173–4
   Flatland 173
Abensour, Miguel 179, 280
Accursed Share, The (George Bataille) 266
Acts and Monuments (John Foxe) 109
Adams, Gerry 294, 296
   Hope and History 294
Adorno, Theodor 13, 74, 231, 261, 263
   Aesthetic Theory 13
   "Music and Language: A Fragment" 13, 261
Æ 15, 207, 211, 213
   A partir du rêve de Musil 211
   The Candle of Vision 211, 214–16, 220–221
Aesthetic Theory (Theodor Adorno) 13
Agamben, Giorgio 70
Al-Ansari, Talal 404
Al-Banna, Hassan 400
Al-Dhahabi, Muhammad 405, 407
Al-Hudaybi, Hasan 399, 400, 406
Alighieri, Dante 84
   Paradiso 84
Al-Maraghi, Muhammad 413
Althusser, Louis 165, 173, 165
   "Ideology and Ideological State Apparatuses" 165
Amsterdam (Ian McEwan) 260
Andersson Jenny 17
Angell, Norman 337, 345–6
A partir du rêve de Musil (Æ) 211
Archaeologies of the Future (Fredric Jameson) 163, 229
Arendt, Hannah 122–123, 269, 306
Aristotle 119, 133
   Constitution of Athens 119
   Metaphysics 119
Arnold-Foster, William 337, 343, 345, 347
Ashworth, Lucian 17, 37
"A Social Sketch" 315, 317, 330
Atwood, Margaret 62, 64
   Cat's Eyes 62, 64
Augustine 43, 103–104, 268
   City of God 43
Aware of Utopia (David Plath) 89

Baccolini, Raffaella 236
   and Tom Moylan: *Dark Horizons* 237-7
Bachofen, Johann Jakob 282, 379
Bacon, Francis 43, 108, 275, 277
   The New Atlantis 43, 108, 277
Badiou, Alain 58, 67, 76–8
Balagangadhara, S.N. 102
Balasopolous, Antonis 14
Bammer, Angelika 278–80, 284, 290
Barthes, Roland 141–2, 144–6, 154, 158
Bataille, George 266
   The Accursed Share 266
Baudelaire, Charles 23
Baudrillard, Jean 195, 203, 209–10
   "The Ecstasy of Communication" 195, 203
   Le miroir de la production 209
   The System of Objects 203
Bauman, Zigmunt 362
Beach, The (Alex Garland/Danny Boyle) 15, 245–50, 252–4
Beaumont, Matthew 14
Beckett, Samuel 64
Beckmann, Johann 140
Bednarowski, Mary Farrell 380

Beerbohm, Max 158
Beethoven, Ludwig van 261, 263–4, 269, 283
   Ninth Symphony ("Ode to Joy") 263–4, 269
Belfiore, Elizabeth 303
Belfort Bax, Ernest 178
Bell, Daniel 227
Bellamy, Edward 14, 26, 44, 169–71, 173–4, 177
   Looking Backward 14, 26, 44, 169–71, 173, 175–6, 177
Benjamin, Walter 25, 39, 52, 60, 67, 70–6
Bennett, Jane 58
Bergonzi, Bernard 184
Bergson, Henri 64, 258
Bertens, Hans
Between Hope and History (Bill Clinton) 294
Bignon, Jean-Paul 140, 144
Bin Ladin, Usama 398
Bird, Robert 258
Blair, Tony 366
Blanchot, Maurice 45
Blatchford, Robert 172
   The Sorcery Shop 172
Bléchet, Françoise 140
Bloch, Ernst 11, 16, 20, 50–1, 59–61, 64, 72–3, 76, 101, 103–5, 107, 180, 183, 207–9, 219, 243, 254, 260–2, 268, 273–4, 276, 278, 280–90, 322
   Das Prinzip Hoffnung/Principle 16, 207, 243, 273–4, 281, 284–5, 290
Bonaparte, Napoleon 154
Bonnefoy, Yves 222
Booker, Keith M. 184
Borges, Jorge Luis 193–4
   Things 193
Böss, Michael 298
Bourne, Hilary 38

Boyle, Danny 246–7
   The Beach 15, 245–50, 252–4
Braidotti, Rosi 59, 61
Brailsford, H.N. 337
Brande, David 238–9
Brave New World (Aldous Huxley) 275
Brinton, Crane 145
Bronfen, Elisabeth 288
Brooker, Peter 232
Brown, Andrew 17
Brown, Gordon 365–6
Brown, Wendy 75
Buch, Estaban 264
Budapest, Z. 381
Burke, Edmund 108, 228
Butler, Samuel 44
   Erewhon 44
Buxton, C.R. 344

Cabet, Étienne 43
Calvino, Italo 24
Campanella, Tommaso 43
   The City of the Sun 43
Candle of Vision, The (Æ) 211, 214–16, 220–221

Caputo, John D. 52, 54, 306
Carey, John 189, 274
Carlyle, Thomas 198–9
   Past and Present 198
   Sartor Resartus 198–9
Carr, E.H. 338
Castells, Manuel 227
Castoriadis, Cornelius 120–2, 208
   "The Greek Polis and the Creation of Democracy" 120–1
Cat's Eyes (Margaret Atwood) 62, 64
Caudwell, Christopher 172
Chancellor Pontchrtrain 140
Chase, Malcolm 318, 322, 326
Chavez, Hugo 72
Chiswik (Warwick Draper) 37
Churchill, Winston 172

Cicero 102
   The Nature of the Gods 102
City of God (Augustine) 43
City of the Sun (Tommaso Campanella) 43
Claeys, Gregory 108, 318
Clinton, Bill 294
   Between Hope and History 294
Cobbett, William 314, 320, 328
   Cottage Economy 320
   Rural Rides 320, 328
Cohen, David 119
Colbert, Jean-Baptiste 140
Cole, Arthur 139
Colebrook, Claire 62
Comenius (John Amos) 336
Communist Manifesto (Karl Marx) 49
Comte, Auguste 22
Connerton, Paul 22–3, 25
Connolly, James 319
Connolly, William 58
Conrad, Joseph 189
   Heart of Darkness 189
   Youth 189
Constitution of Athens (Aristotle) 119
Copjec, Joan 265–6
Corbett, Elizabeth 168–9
   New Amazonia 168
Cottage Economy (William Cobbett) 320
Craig, Edward Thomas 33, 35
Critias (Plato) 24–5, 127–9, 131, 133
Crucé, Eméric 336
Crying of Lot 49, The (Thomas Pynchon) 239
Culpin, Ewart G. 35
Cure at Troy, The (Seamus Heaney) 16, 293, 302–3

d'Eaubonne, Françoise 276
   La féminisme ou la mort 276
Dahrendorf, Ralf 95–6
Dalton, Hugh 337, 343–4
Daly, Mary 277

Gyn/Ecology 277
Dark Horizons (Raffaella Baccolini) 237–7
Darnton, Robert 154
   "The Great Cat Massacre" 154
Dauenhauer, Bernard 300
Davis, J.C 86–8, 91
Dawson, Doyne 125–6
de Beauvoir, Simone 276
de Saussure, Ferdinand 249
Debord, Guy 68–70
Delaire, Alexis 152
Deleuze, Gilles 58, 63, 67, 258–9
   The Time Image 258
   The Movement Image 258
DeLillo, Don 237
   White Noise 237
Denard, Hugh 293–4
Derrida, Jacques 13, 43–54, 57–8, 62, 73–6, 118, 125, 127, 132, 164, 180, 243, 249–50, 254–5, 306, 308
   "The Force of Law" 47–8
   "Letter to a Japanese Friend" 50
   On the Name 52
   The Other Heading 52, 54
   Points 52
   Specters of Marx 48–9, 53 57, 62, 74, 243
des Billettes, Filleau 140
Descriptions des arts et métiers 152
Devett, Grace 37
Dewey, John 170
Dichtung und Wahrheit (Johann Wolfgang von Goethe) 283
Dictionary (Edward Phillips) 140
Diderot, Denis 139, 141, 145–8, 153–5, 158
   Encyclopédie 14, 139, 141, 144–7, 150, 152, 155–6, 158
Dombrowski, Daniel A. 125
Donne, John 16, 274–5

"Elegy 19: To His Mistress Going to Bed" 16, 274
Dostoevskij, Fëdor Mikhajlovič 233
Double Indemnity (Billy Wilder) 265–6
Draper, Warwick 19, 35, 37–8
   Chiswick 37
   Hammersmith: A Study in Town History 37
   The New Britain 37
   The Tower 37
Duc de Sully 336
Duke of Orléans 148
Durkheim, Émile 106, 387

Early Irish History and Mythology (T.F. O'Rahilly) 295
Eighteenth Brumaire of Louis Bonaparte, The (Karl Marx) 108–9
Eisler, Hanns 263
Eliot, T.S. 267
Emperor Julian 102
Encyclopédie (Denis Diderot) 14, 139, 141, 144–7, 150, 152, 155–6, 158
Engels, Friedrich 44, 49
Erewhon (Samuel Butler) 44
Ethics of Memory, The (Avishai Margalit) 111
Etzioni, Amitai 365
Euripides 285

Fabian, Johannes 70
Farge, Arlette 155, 156, 157
Ferns, Chris 184
Feuerbach, Ludwig 103
Fifth Province, The (2 films) 301
Fight Club (David Fincher) 233, 236–7
First Men in the Moon, The (H.G. Wells) 186
Flatland (Edwin Abbott) 173
Fincher, David 233
   Fight Club 233, 236–7

Fitting, Peter 163, 237
Focillon, Henri 188
   The Life of Forms 188
Foote, G.W. 166
Fortunati, Vita 19
Foucault, Michel 58–9, 251, 299–300
   Madness and Civilization 251
Fourier, Charles 43
Foxe, John 109, 111
   Acts and Monuments 109
   "Book of Martyrs" 109
Freud, Sigmund 244
Friel, Brian 302, 308–9
   Translations 308
Fromm, Erich 282
Frye, Northrop 280
Fukuyama, Francis 75
Fyson, Robert 317

Galilei, Galileo 78
Gardner, Gerald 379
Gargantua (François Rabelais) 43
Garland, Alex 15, 245–6
   The Beach 15, 245–50, 252–4
Gay Science, The (Friedrich Nietzsche) 66
Geertz, Clifford 387
Geoghegan, Vincent 14, 21 26, 64, 282, 319
Ghost Dog 236–7
Gibbons, Luke 12
Gibson, William 15, 225–28, 230, 233, 235–9
   Neuromancer 15, 225–7, 230, 233, 235, 239–41
Gill, Eric 33, 35
Gilman, Charlotte Perkins 31
Goethe, Johann Wolfgang von 283
   Dichtung und Wahrheit 283
Golffing, Barbara 95–6
Golffing, Francis 95–6
Gordimer, Nadine 294
   Living in Hope and History 294

Index 427

Gould, John 303
Grella, George 238
Griffin, Michael J. 15
Grosz, Elizabeth 63–4, 73
Guattari, Félix 67
Guillerme, Jacques 140, 144
Gulliver's Travels (Jonathan Swift) 193
Gyn/Ecology (Mary Daly) 277

Halbwachs, Maurice 21–2, 108
Hamlet 49
Hammersmith: A Study in Town History (Warwick Draper) 37
Haraway, Donna 58
Harrington, James 43
    Oceana 43
Harvey, David 23, 299–300
Haussman, Georges Eugène 23
Häutungen (Verena Stefan) 278
Hay, Colin 360
Heaney, Seamus 16, 274, 293–4, 302, 304, 306
    "Act of Union" 274
    The Cure at Troy 16, 293, 302–3
Heart of Darkness (Joseph Conrad) 189
Hederman, Mark Patrick 295–9
Heidegger, Martin 51, 208, 297
    Poetry, Language, Thought 297
    Sein und Zeit 208, 297
Heller, Agnes
Hemling, Steven 229
Hermand, Jost 280
Hervieu-Léger, Danièl 110
    La Religion pour Mémoire 110
Hillegas, Mark R. 184
Hills, Richard L. 156
Hitler, Adolf 340, 351
Hobson, John A. 173, 175–6, 337, 347
Hölderlin, Friedrich 212
Holloway, Mark 252
Hope and History (Gerry Adams) 296
Huard, Georges 141
Hulse, Matt 38

Hunter, Robert 19
Hutcheon, Linda 227, 231–2
Huxley, Aldous 275
    Brave New World 275
Huyssen, Andreas 23–5, 39

Ingram, James 78
International Government (Leonard Woolf) 342
Invisible Man, The (H.G. Wells) 186
Island of Doctor Moreau, The (H.G. Wells) 186
Island of Pines (Henry Neveille) 97

Jaccottet, Philippe 15, 207, 211–21
    La Vision et la vue 211
James, William 105–6
    The Varieties of Religious Experience 105
Jameson, Fredric 11–12, 15, 20, 59, 61, 76, 132–3, 163–4, 168, 176, 180, 225, 228–39, 257, 270, 281, 296, 309
    Archaeologies of the Future 163, 229
    "The Desire Called Utopia", 229, 234–5
    "The Politics of Utopia" 232
    Postmodernism 163, 229, 231
    "Progress Versus Utopia" 231, 233
    "Reification and Utopia in Mass Culture" 176
    The Seeds of Time 231–2, 234, 236, 238
Jaugeon, Jacques 141
Johnson, Vita 264
Jones, Ernest 327
Jung, Karl 102, 244

Kant, Immanuel 228, 283, 336
Kateb, George 90, 96–7
Kay, Sarah 254

Keane, Timothy 16
Kearney, Richard 47, 296–302, 310–1
Kellner, Douglas 322
Kelly, Michael G. 15
Kelvin, Norman 30
Khomeini, Ruhollah Mustafavi 398
Kierkegaard, Søren 287
King James 109
King Richard 102
Kirk, Neville 172
Klinger, Maximilian 283
Kluckhohn, Clyde 384–5
Koepp, Cynthia 147, 154, 154
Kondo, Dorinne 375
  Crafting Selves 375
Koselleck, Reinhart 307–8, 358
Kraus, Karl 282
Kumar, Krishan 170, 280

La féminisme ou la mort (Françoise d'Eaubonne) 276
La Religion pour Mémoire (Danièl Hervieu-Léger) 110
La Vision et la vue (Philippe Jaccottet) 211
Lacan, Jacques 243–6, 248–9, 253–5
Lacaux, André 220
Lactantius 102
Laws, The (Plato) 125, 127
Lectures on Ideology and Utopia (Paul Ricoeur) 300
Le Guin, Ursula K. 129, 233
  The Dispossessed 129
Leech, John 315–6, 330
Leibniz, Gottfried 140
Leland, Charles 379
Lenin, Vladimir I. 185
Lessing, Doris 20, 26
  Shikasta 20, 26
Lévi-Strauss, Claude 246
Levitas, Ruth 13–14, 60, 84–5, 92, 244, 252, 337, 371, 377

Morris, Hammersmith and Utopia 30
Libeskind, Daniel 24
Life of Forms, The (Henri Focillon) 188
Lissarrague, François 119
Little Wars (H.G. Wells) 184
Living in Hope and History (Nadine Gordimer) 294
Looking Ahead! (Alfred Morris) 171
Looking Backward (Edward Bellamy) 14, 26, 44, 169–71, 173, 175–6, 177
Longley, Edna 298
Loraux, Nicole 117,119–20, 124
Lord Lytton 349
Lough, John 139
Louis XIV 140
Lovett, William 313
Lowe, Lisa 299
Luft, David S. 219
Luther 108

MacDonald, James Ramsay 347
Madness and Civilization (Michel Foucault) 251
Mahon, Derek 222
Malcolm X 70
Maley, Willy 48
Malmgren, Carl D. 237
Man without Qualities, The (Robert Musil) 211, 216
Management of Small Farms, The (Feargus O'Connor) 320–2
Manifesto of the Socialist League (William Morris) 178
Mannheim, Karl 279
Manuel, Frank 244
  Utopian Thought in the Western World 244
Marcuse, Herbert 252
Margalit, Avishai 106, 111–12
  The Ethics of Memory 111
Marin, Louis 129, 250

Index

"The Frontiers of Utopia" 250
Marquis de Sade 97
   Philosophie dans le Boudoir 97
Marx, Karl 44, 48–49, 68–69, 74–75, 107–8, 360, 365, 388
   The Eighteenth Brumaire of Louis Bonaparte 108–9
   On the Jewish Question 107
   The Poverty of Philosophy 69
Mauss, Marcel 389
Mauzi, Robert 158
McCarthy, Imelda Colgan 301
McClintock, Anne 274
McClure, Kirstie 134
McEwan, Ian 260
   Amsterdam 260
McGowan, Todd 245–6, 252
McGuinness, Catherine 294
McHale, Brian 237
McManus, Susan 13, 45, 48–9
McWilliam, Donad 301
   The Fifth Province 301
Mémoires (Pajot des Charmes) 155
Memoirs of Captain Rock (Thomas Moore) 328
Memory, History, Forgetting (Paul Ricoeur) 104
Menexenus (Plato) 127
Metaphysics (Aristotle) 119
Miller, David 111
Miller, Mervyn 19
Milliot, Vincent 143
Milton, John 243, 247
   Paradise Lost 243, 247
Miroir de la production, Le (Jean Baudrillard) 209
Mitrany, David 344–5
Modern Utopia, A (H.G. Wells) 26, 44, 189
Morales, Evo 72
Moore, Thomas 328
   Memoirs of Captain Rock 328
More, Thomas 43–4, 46–7, 91, 187, 328

   Utopia 44, 46, 91, 187, 279, 296
Morris, Alfred 171–2, 178
   Looking Ahead! 171
Morris, May 34–5
Morris, William 14, 25–31, 33, 37, 44, 60–61, 177, 179, 191, 201–2, 280
   "Art under Plutocracy" 178
   Manifesto of the Socialist League 178
   News from Nowhere 14, 25–31, 33, 44, 177, 179, 191, 201
Morris, Hammersmith and Utopia (Ruth Levitas) 30
Morrison, Herbert 351
Mouffe, Chantal 368
Movement Image, The (Gilles Deleuze) 258
Moylan, Tom 187–190, 235–6, 266, 327
   Scraps of the Untainted Sky 236
Mubarak, Hosni 409–10, 413
Muhammad, 398, 400, 404
Mulgan, Geoff 357
Mumbo Jumbo (Ishmael Reed) 238
Murphy, Paula 15
Murray, Margaret 379
Musil, Robert 15, 207, 211, 216–21
   The Man without Qualities 211, 216
Myers, Tom 239

Nasser, Gamal Abdel 400–1
Nature of the Gods, The (Cicero) 102
Negri, Antonio 58, 63, 67–8, 78
Neuromancer (William Gibson) 15, 225–7, 230, 233, 235, 239–41
Neveille, Henry 97
   Island of Pines 97
Neville, Ralph
New Atlantis, The (Francis Bacon) 43, 108, 277
New Amazonia (Elizabeth Corbett) 168
New Britain, The (Warwick Draper) 37

News from Nowhere (William Morris) 14, 25–31, 33, 44, 177, 179, 191, 201
Ní Dhúill, Catríona 16
Nietzsche, Friedrich 58, 66–9, 282, 306
   The Gay Science 66
   Thus Spake Zarathustra 66
Nineteen Eighty-Four (George Orwell) 20, 233
Ninth Symphony ("Ode to Joy") (Ludwig van Beethoven) 263–4, 269
Noel-Baker, Philip 337, 240, 245, 247
Novalis 214

O'Brien, Eugene 13
Oceana (James Harrington) 43
O'Connor, Arthur 318–9
   The State of Ireland 318–9
O'Connor, Feargus 313–4, 317–27
   The Management of Small Farms 320–2
O'Grady, Standish James 261–2
   Sun and Wind 261
O'Hara, Harry 322
O'Malley, Aidan 16
On the Jewish Question (Karl Marx) 107
O'Rahilly, T. F. 295
   Early Irish History and Mythology 295
Olsen, Regine 287
On Belief (Slavoj Žižek) 220
On the Name (Jacques Derrida) 52

Orwell, George 20, 233
   Nineteen Eighty-Four 20, 233
Other Heading, The (Jacques Derrida) 52, 54
Our World Is Our Weapon (Subcomandante Marcos) 57
Owen, Robert 43, 319

Pajot des Charmes 155, 157

Mémoires 155
Paradise Lost (John Milton) 243, 247
Paradiso (Dante Alighieri) 84
Parrinder, Patrick 184, 185–6
Past and Present (Thomas Carlyle) 198
Pater, Walter 264
Pearce, Susan 194
Penn, William 336
Pepler, Douglas (Hilary) 33, 35, 37, 38
Petrie, Graham 264
Pevsner, Nikolaus 29
Phillips, Edward 140
   Dictionary 140
   Philosophia rationalis sive logica 140
Philoctetes (Sophocles) 16, 302–3
Philosophia rationalis sive logica (Edward Phillips) 140
Philosophie dans le Boudoir (Marquis de Sade) 97
Philosophy of Money (Georg Simmel) 288
Piercy, Marge 276
   Woman on the Edge of Time 276
Pinault, Madeleine 141
Plath, David 89–91
   Aware of Utopia 89
Plato 43, 90, 104, 117, 121–3, 127–9, 132, 134–5, 260–2
   Critias 24–5, 127–9, 131, 133
   The Laws 125, 127
   Menexenus 127
   The Republic 43, 122–3, 126–9, 133, 261
   Statesman 127
   Timaeus 123–7, 131, 133
Poetry, Language, Thought (Martin Heidegger) 297
Points (Jacques Derrida) 52
Ponsonby, Arthur 343
Popper, Karl 91, 280
Postmodernism (Fredric Jameson) 163, 229, 231

Poverty of Philosophy, The (Karl Marx) 69
Pradeau, Jean-François 126–7
Prinzip Hoffnung, Das/Principle (Ernst Bloch) 16, 207, 243, 273–4, 281, 284–5, 290
Proudhon, Pierre Joseph 43
Proust, Jacques 139, 146
Psycho 301
Punch 315–6
Puttnick Elizabeth, 388
Pynchon, Thomas 237–9
    The Crying of Lot 49 239

Queen Mary 109
Queen Victoria 168–9
Qutb, Sayyid 399–404
    Signposts on the Road 399–400

Rabelais, François 43
    Gargantua 43
Ramazzini, Bernardino 155
Essai sur les maladies des artisan 155
Rancière, Jacques 120, 123
Rea, Stephen 302
Réaumur, René-Antoine Ferchault, de 140, 152
Reed, Ishmael 238
    Mumbo Jumbo 238
Rees, Alwyn 295
Rees, Brinley 295
Regarding the Pain of Others (Susan Sontag) 21
Republic, The (Plato) 43, 122–3, 126–9, 133, 261
Revolution (Raoul Vanegeim) 67, 71
Richmond, William
Ricoeur, Paul 25, 104, 106, 299–300
    Lectures on Ideology and Utopia 300
    Memory, History, Forgetting 104
Riedel, Wolfgang 277

Roadside Picnic (Arkady and Boris Strugatsky) 257
Robinson, Kim Stanley 163, 233–4
Robinson, Mary 236, 294, 301
Roemer, Kenneth 26, 166
Ronalds, Francis 33
Roosevelt, Franklin D. 185
Roosevelt, Theodore 185
Rorty, Richard 112
Rose, Steven 104
Ross, Andrew 238
Rousseau, Jean-Jacques 43, 46, 48
Rowntree, Fred 35
Rural Rides (William Cobbett) 320, 328
Ruskin, John 201

Sadat, Anwar 401, 408–19
Safiullin, Rashit 269
Saint Paul 108
Saint-Simon, Henri de 43
Salih Sirriya
Salomon-Bayet, Claire 140, 144
Santer, Jacques 294
Sargent, Lyman Tower 47, 84, 298, 320, 322, 324, 335, 339, 377
Sartor Resartus (Thomas Carlyle) 198–9
Sartre, Jean Paul 176
Saville, John 318
Schama, Simon 25
Schiller, Friedrich 277
    "Dignity of Women" 277
Schnapp, Alain 119
Schwab, Richard N. 139
Schweighauser, Philipp 15, 232
Scraps of the Untainted Sky (Tom Moylan) 236
Sebald, W.S. 23
Sebestik, Jan 140, 144
Seeds of Time, The (Fredric Jameson) 231–2, 234, 236, 238
Seguin, Jean-Pierre 141
Sein und Zeit (Martin Heidegger) 208, 297

Sewell, William 153–4
Sex and Character (Otto Weininger) 288
Shaw, George Bernard 31
Shaykh Kishk 408
Shaykh Salama 408
Shaykh Shar'awi 407
Shaykh Su'ad Jalal 407
Sheikh of Al-Azhar 407, 413
Sheridan, Geraldine 14
Shklar, Judith 94
Shukri Mustafa 17, 398, 404–8
Shyamalan, M. Night 245
  The Village 245
Signposts on the Road (Sayyid Qutb) 399–400
Silvani, Giovanna 286
Simmel, Georg 288
  Philosophy of Money 288
Singer, Bryan 265
  The Usual Suspects 265
Sirriya, Salih 404
Smith, Adam 152
  The Wealth of Nations 152
Smith, Dan 14–15
Smith, Paul 70
Socrates 104, 123–6, 133
Solaris (Andrei Tarkovsky) 265
Sontag, Susan 21, 23, 25
  Regarding the Pain of Others 21
Sophocles 16, 302–4
  Philoctetes 16, 302–3
Sorcery Shop, The (Blatchford Robert) 172
Specters of Marx (Jacques Derrida) 48–9, 53 57, 62, 74, 243
Spenser, Edmund 316
Spinoza, Benedict 58, 68
Spiral Dance, The (Starhawk) 381
Stalin, Josef 185
Stalker (Tarkovsky Andrei) 15, 257–60, 262–5, 267–71
Stapleton, Frank 301
Starhawk 381

The Spiral Dance 381
State of Ireland, The (Arthur O'Connor) 318–9
Statesman (Plato) 127
Stefan, Verena 278
  Häutungen 278
Stendhal (Henri Beyle) 286–7
Stephenson, Helena 35
Stirner, Max 68
Stover, Leon 184, 198, 201
Störfall. Nachrichten eines Tages (Christa Wolf) 277
Strugatsky, Arkady 257
  and Boris Strugatsky: *Roadside Picnic* 257
Strugatsky, Boris 257
  and Arkady Strugatsky: *Roadside Picnic* 257
Sturdy, David 140
Subcommandante, Marcos 57
  Our World Is Our Weapon 57
Sun and Wind (James O'Grady) 261
Suvin, Darko 163, 186–7, 192, 200, 231
Swift, Jonathan 193
  Gulliver's Travels 193
System of Objects, The (Jean Baudrillard) 203

Tarkovsky, Andrei 15, 257–9, 260, 262–5, 267–8, 270
  Stalker 15, 257–60, 262–5, 267–71
  Solaris 265
Tarr, Bela 265
  Damnation 265
Taylor, A. E. 125
Taylor, Charles 105–6, 112
  "A Catholic Modernity" 112
The Crane Bag 293–6, 301
The Labourer 318, 326–7
The Northern Star 313, 319, 323–4, 326–328

Index 433

"The Narrative of Malcolm McGregor" 327–9, 332
"The People's Charter" 313, 315, 318, 322–4, 334
The Simpsons 253
Thompson, Dorothy 317, 319–21
Thus Spake Zarathustra (Friedrich Nietzsche) 66
Timaeus (Plato) 123–7, 131, 133
Time Image, The (Gilles Deleuze) 258
Time Machine, The (H.G. Wells) 15, 186–90, 194–5, 197, 199–201
Tower, The (Warwick Draper) 37
Translations (Brian Friel) 308
Turner, Paul 91

Uncle Tom's Cabin 170
Usual Suspects, The (Bryan Singer) 265
Utopia (Thomas More) 44, 46, 91, 187, 279, 296
Utopian Thought in the Western World (Frank Manuel) 244

Van der Straat, Hans 153
Vandeleur, John Scott 319–20
Vanegeim, Raoul 65, 67–9, 71–2, 76
Revolution 67, 71
Varieties of Religious Experience, The (William James) 105
Varsam, Maria 327
Vedder-Shults, Nancy 276
Vernant, Jean-Pierre 134
Verne, Jules 191, 193
Vidal-Naquet, Pierre 119–20
Village, The (M. Night Shyamalan) 245
von Hofmannsthal, Hugo 285

Wagner, Richard 263, 283
Waldron, Dara 15
Walsh, Chad 96–7
War of the Worlds, The (H.G. Wells) 186
Watts, George B. 139

Wealth of Nations, The (Adam Smith) 152
Webster, Frank 227
Wedekind, Frank 282
Wegner, Phillip 236, 327
Weininger, Otto 288
Sex and Character 288
Weinrich, Harald 104, 107
Wells, H.G. 14–15, 26, 44, 90, 172, 183–8, 190–193, 195, 198, 202
The First Men in the Moon 186
The Invisible Man 186
The Island of Dr Moreau 186
Little Wars 184
A Modern Utopia 26, 44 186, 189
The Time Machine 15, 186–90, 194–5, 197, 199–201
The War of the Worlds 186
Wharton, Barrie 17
Wheen, Francis 189
White Noise (Don DeLillo) 237
Whitman, Walt 91
Widdicombe, Toby 109
Wilde, Oscar 94
Wilder, Billy 265
Double Indemnity 265–6
Wilkins, Sophie 218
Williams, Raymond 166
Willis, Susan 163
Winstanley, Gerrard 109
Wittgenstein, Ludwig 88, 98
Wolf, Christa 277
Störfall. Nachrichten eines Tages 277
Wolff, Christian 140
Woman on the Edge of Time (Marge Piercy) 276
Wood, David 62
Woolf, Leonard 337, 342, 350–1
International Government 342

Yeats, Lily 34

Yeats, Lolly 34
Yeats, William Butler 34–5
Yorke, Christopher 13
Youth (Joseph Conrad) 189

Zamyatin, Yevgeny 275: *We* 275
Žižek, Slavoj 220, 249, 254
   On Belief 220

Ralahine Utopian Studies

Ralahine Utopian Studies is the publishing project of the Ralahine Centre for Utopian Studies, University of Limerick, and the Department of Intercultural Studies in Translation, Languages and Culture, University of Bologna at Forlì.

The series editors aim to publish scholarship that addresses the theory and practice of utopianism (including Anglophone, continental European, and indigenous and postcolonial traditions, and contemporary and historical periods). Publications (in English and other European languages) will include original monographs and essay collections (including theoretical, textual, and ethnographic/institutional research), English language translations of utopian scholarship in other national languages, reprints of classic scholarly works that are out of print, and annotated editions of original utopian literary and other texts (including translations).

While the editors seek work that engages with the current scholarship and debates in the field of utopian studies, they will not privilege any particular critical or theoretical orientation. They welcome submissions by established or emerging scholars working within or outside the academy. Given the multi-lingual and inter-disciplinary remit of the University of Limerick and the University of Bologna at Forlì, they especially welcome comparative studies in any disciplinary or trans-disciplinary framework.

Those interested in contributing to the series are invited to submit a detailed project outline to Professor Raffaella Baccolini at Department of Intercultural Studies in Translation, Languages and Culture, University of Bologna at Forlì, Forlì, Italy or to Professor Tom Moylan or Dr. Joachim Fischer at the Department of Languages and Cultural Studies, University of Limerick, Republic of Ireland.

E-mail queries can be sent to a.kirschbaum@peterlang.com.

Series editors:
Raffaella Baccolini (University of Bologna, at Forlì)
Joachim Fischer (University of Limerick)
Tom Moylan (University of Limerick)
Managing editor:
Michael J. Griffin (University of Limerick)

Ralahine Centre for Utopian Studies, University of Limerick.
See: http://www.ul.ie/ralahinecentre/

Volume 1	Tom Moylan and Raffaella Baccolini (eds.) Utopia-Method-Vision. The Use Value of Social Dreaming. 345 pages. 2007. ISBN 978-3-03910-912-8

Volume 2	Michael J. Griffin and Tom Moylan (eds.): Exploring the Utopian Impulse. Essays on Utopian Thought and Practice 434 pages. 2007. ISBN 978-3-03910-913-5
Volume 3	Vincent Geoghegan: Utopianism and Marxism. Forthcoming
Volume 4	Barbara Goodwin and Keith Taylor: The Politics of Utopia. A Study in Theory and Practice. Forthcoming
Volume 5	Ruth Levitas: The Concept of Utopia. Forthcoming